Jesus and Politics

Jesus and Politics

Confronting the Powers

Alan Storkey

Baker Academic
Grand Rapids, Michigan

Published by Baker Academic
a division of Baker Publishing Group
P.O. Box 6287, Grand Rapids, MI 49516–6287
www.bakeracademic.com

Printed in the United States of America

Library of Congress Cataloging-in-Publication Data
Storkey, Alan.
    Jesus and politics : confronting the powers / Alan Storkey.
        p.   cm.
    Includes bibliographical references and index.
    ISBN 0-8010-2784-5
    1. Christianity and politics. 2. Jesus Christ—Influence. 3. Bible. N.T. Gospels—Criticism, interpretation, etc. I. Title.
    BR115.P7S754 2005
    261.7—dc22   2004028170

Contents

Jesus' Politics?

The Odd Story

Christianity has had political influence throughout much of the world and has especially touched over a quarter of the world's population. Yet the history of Christianity in relation to politics is odd. On the one hand, it seems subversive. In the Magnificat we read, "[God] has brought down rulers from their thrones" (Luke 1:52), and he has so done. Within a relatively short time, the Roman Emperor Constantine moved from his throne to his knees before God. For centuries, other kings and emperors kneeled before God as popes and archbishops crowned them. Sometimes the dethroning became violent; God-fearing men in the seventeenth century chopped off the head of an English king in the first revolution of modern times. In another move, the Pilgrim fathers left Britain with a Christian vision, seeking a better "kingdom" but definitely without a king, and were the precursors of American government. More recently, the great Communist system of the USSR was confronted by a Christian irritant in the form of Alexander Solzhenitsyn, who bit like a mosquito on the hide of an elephant.[1] After a while the elephant rolled over. There is something about the Christian faith that has unsettled political systems, whether they are empires or dictatorships, Communist or pagan regimes, and it is not clear what it is.

At the same time, Christianity seems acquiescent. The Roman Empire became the "Holy" Roman Empire. Christians pray for rulers. Archbishops become part of the apparatus of the political establishment. Cathedrals or abbeys sit alongside parliaments, or in the case of Russia, four cathedrals sit inside the Kremlin. Most Christians act as model citizens—voting, paying their taxes, and being strongly in favor of law and order. What is going on here? What does this mixture mean? Is the acquiescent model or the subversive model right, or is neither?

How Christians relate to these models is also confusing. Church services make reference to Jesus as King of kings and with obvious concern about world events pray to God, who is sovereign over the whole creation. In some sense Christians seem to have a perspective that addresses the broad sweep of politics. Indeed, in some countries Christian political parties have been normal and influential. Yet in other countries this perspective largely stops within churches. Christian engagement with politics often seems limited to concerns about family life, abortion, and sexual matters. This Christian political vacuum has become more obvious in the twenty-first century in contrast to Islam, which has presented a visible political face, albeit a confused one. So, where do Christians stand on politics? The question hangs in the culture, and it is deeper than party politics. It goes to the roots of the meaning of both politics and the Christian faith.

The answers must have something to do with the person of Jesus Christ. Christians relate strongly to his life and teaching. Each week in a million or more churches his thoughts are taught and pondered, and hundreds of millions, from presidents to peasants, have been in some sense guided by him. There must be something substantial from Jesus Christ in political history, though his followers may well have twisted it. To investigate what this might be, we try to look as directly as we can at the political content of Jesus' life and teaching.

Approaching Jesus' Politics

This is not as easy as it might seem. From the vantage of twenty-first-century scholarship, we can see distortions from the past claiming our attention. Perhaps the most common is the fact that for two thousand years political rulers have tried to control Christianity, often quite successfully. Christians have often been told how their faith should be lived in relation to politics. Usually these outsiders want Christians to do what they are told. Sometimes, using Paul's statements in Romans 13, they have conveyed that Christians are supposed to obey and support their government, and that should settle the question. Often Christians were far from compliant, but generally this has been a remarkably successful policy.

The underlying message of many politicians is that Jesus' life and teaching are not about politics; he is portrayed as otherworldly or as simply the friend of little children. The latter may be true, but this apolitical Jesus is often fabricated by the attitudes of those who want to tame Christianity in order to leave the political scene free for their own views. Biblical texts have been used to support monarchy, empires, and Christian withdrawal into "sacred" or monastic activity. As a result, many Christians have automatically conformed to whatever regimes they live in and see a study of Jesus' politics as flawed in conception. "Render to Caesar the things that are Caesar's" (Mark 12:17 KJV), they might say to finally settle the issue.

More recently we observe the developing assumption that religion and politics do not mix. This attitude seems to have arrived in Britain in about 1660, when the authorities were worried at the radicalism of Christian groups and decided to keep them out of politics as nonconformists.[2] Political thought and ideology were gradually divorced from theology. Hobbes's *Leviathan,* a key political text, puts most of its Christian thought in a separate section at the end. Later political philosophy often saw itself as secular in nature, excluding Christianity a priori. Thinkers like Montesquieu, Rousseau, Hegel, Comte, Marx, and Mill operated in what they saw as a secular way, and many people learned the separation of religion from politics. If Christians made contributions to political debate, they were expected to exclude their Christian understanding from the discussion. A similar tradition in the United States saw the disestablishment of religion in the First Amendment (perhaps a good principle) as excluding religious considerations from politics; this was poor logic but nonetheless influential. The two are seen as oil and water, best kept in different containers. As a result, thinking about Jesus' politics was unnecessary; *of course* it was irrelevant to contemporary affairs of state. Many Christians also learned to think this way; their political thought would automatically be secular.

Alternatively, others have found in Jesus some reflection of their own ideological position. Jesus has been portrayed as a revolutionary, an independence fighter, a socialist, or a conservative. These perspectives read modern ideologies back into the Gospels, often in quite a selective way. In the nineteenth century God was often presented as the one who kept workers in their place. Later, the Nazis asserted that Jesus was Aryan rather than Jew. Or else he was identified as a Marxist, a Hippie, or a Thatcherite.[3] From our vantage it is sobering to see the way in which ideological contamination of the understanding of Jesus takes place.

The danger is no less for us now. We tend to read, talk, and write about the Gospels in ways that reflect our culture and views.

Yet there have been many Bible readers and scholars who have sought to do more, to study the life and teaching of Jesus without this self-centeredness and to submit to the Gospel texts. What have they found? Many earlier studies focus on the text, are aware of the Jewish background, and cover much of what we will consider here. One great example is Edersheim's *The Life and Times of Jesus the Messiah*.[4] Without being politically centered, it nevertheless clearly shows the political content of the Gospels. A later study is Yoder's *The Politics of Jesus*,[5] now thirty years old. It examines what its title suggests. More recently, Wright's study *Jesus and the Victory of God*,[6] while theologically focused, also opens up the political content of Jesus' way, as do other texts.[7] In the last few years, quite a few studies have concentrated strongly on the political and socioeconomic backgrounds of the Gospels, and all kinds of political issues have come to the fore. This book continues this kind of work. Its focus is Jesus' politics. Yet those who do study this aspect of the Gospels will be aware that many other scholars are oblivious of it.

At this stage it is important to clarify what is meant by "politics." Many people say, "I am not political," meaning that they do not engage in party politics or even vote. Here we do not mean "narrow party politics," although party activity is not necessarily narrow and the Gospels are full of party strife. Rather, we mean all the business of the state—rule, law, nationhood, power, justice, taxation, statehood, international relations, war, and government economic policy—all of which have been part of human life down through the centuries. At first, it seems, Jesus falls outside even this definition; he did not have an army, collect taxes, or wear royal robes, except in his final trial. In this sense, he does not seem political. But when we look at the events of the Gospels in more detail, a different view emerges. Jesus is feared by the major political parties and makes comments on all kinds of political issues. We realize that the important politicians are not always the ones in power. The influence of Gandhi or Marx is indisputable, yet they only weakly reflect the impact of the Galilean. In this wider sense—legitimate rule, law, power, justice, parties, conflict, popularity, welfare, and taxation—we will see that there is more than enough material on Jesus' politics to fill a substantial book.

Another point is significant here. We often assume we know what "politics" is. Presidents, palaces, taxes, elections, and political parties confront us every day. Political science studies legislatures, foreign policy, administration, and other subjects in ways that are quite tightly defined in life today. But these conceptions have changed and will change again. Important variations are studied in the history of political thought.

Here we look at a different period from our own, when crowds did not vote but shouted, and prime ministers did not appear on television. We have to read these cultural changes, and it is not too difficult to do so. The bigger challenge is to face a person who overturns many conceptions about politics itself. We may think of politics in terms of getting to, or remaining in, power. They also thought that way in the first century. Jesus did not teach or act thus in our terms; he had a different view of power. Clearly, he may shake our views of politics, as he did those of most of his contemporaries. Thus, we may have to face quite fundamental questions about our political views.

In this wider sense, therefore, politics was an important part of Jesus' life. The political leaders perceived his teaching as attacking their government. The confrontation and trial in Jerusalem were dominantly political. Crucifixion was a Roman political death. Jesus' teaching and parables on law, taxation, party attitudes, the judicial process, and foreigners challenged the political leaders of his day. His position as "King of the Jews" is considered right through the Gospels. These aspects are the focus of our study. We draw back from other areas of Christ's teaching. This book is partial in the sense of being limited to a political study of the Gospels. Hopefully, it is not partial in the sense of being politically biased and overemphasizing or importing political meaning. That has to be a matter of detailed judgment of the Gospel texts. So, Jesus sends out the twelve disciples and says to them, "On my account you will be brought before governors and kings as witnesses to them and to the Gentiles" (Matt. 10:18). Here we see that something political is going on, though it is not quite clear what it is. Politics is thus only part of the Gospels, not even the dominant part. The guiding principle here is that subject matter should only be treated as political when it clearly is so. This is hardly a profound principle, but it is one by which interpretation can be clearly judged. Even then we find that the focus on Jesus' politics alone is one of the greatest stories ever told, and it is ample for this one book.

God's Ruler?

Religion and politics are dangerous topics. They ruin polite conversation, and yet this study focuses on both. Countless people look to the teachings of Jesus, and politics frames the lives and deaths of millions. In large measure, this study merely retells parts of the Gospels, opening up the political content of events and teaching, but the implications are far-reaching. The events, in their setting, are strange and full of joy. This person, by action and teaching, departs from the hard and vicious policies that have dominated world political history and opens up new ways of doing and seeing things. It is like observing a great door swinging open on rusty hinges, revealing the way God's gentle rule runs, and changing the very nature of politics. Some have opposed it, as others did at the time of Jesus, but it is perhaps the greatest transformation in political history there has ever been. Hence, it is worth our while to examine it as fully as possible. This we try to do. First, we locate ourselves in the politics of Jesus' time by looking at a dominant figure, Herod the Great.

King Herod the Great

The King

No modern kings have effective power. The United Kingdom has had Elizabeth as ceremonial queen for half a century, and the odd prince or two, but real political power lies elsewhere. In the United States, kings and queens seem to be regarded as fashionable clotheshorses from overseas. The last direct American experience of monarchy was of mad King George, and he does not invite a repeat experience. In areas where dynasties still survive, technical experts often act more effectively. Kingship has become quaint and ceremonial. Yet for most of history it was different. Kings were rulers, generals, chancellors, city planners, judges, and lawmakers. We are going back to a culture where kingship was real. Herod the Great was king of the Jews (Judea—plus Galilee, Samaria, Idumea). He fought for the title. It confirmed his status in relation to Rome. He had three of his sons killed in order to retain his position, so he obviously felt seriously about it. On his death, other sons succeeded to bits of his kingdom, but a greater political power, Augustus Caesar, denied them the title "king of the Jews." They were mere tetrarchs (subordinate princes). To be king was to be an effective ruler, but these tetrarchs were permitted only a little authority under Roman rule, and one of them was quickly sacked.

Kings ruled by conquest and military control. That was true of Herod and has been for most of the world's political history. The old accounts of 1066 and all that—of history as battles, wars, and conquest—were substantially right. British history was shaped by William the Conqueror, the Wars of the Roses, Napoleon, and World Wars I and II. In the United States the War of Independence, the Civil War, Pearl Harbor, the Cold War, Gulf Wars I and II, and September 11 (2001) chart a different history. Fights for rule and territory have usually been the name of the game. The same story can be repeated in China and Japan, in the Indian subcontinent, in South America, Africa, and the great plains of Northern Eurasia. Genghis Khan is still the most important person in Mongolia. Czars, moguls, warlords, overlords, chiefs, dynasties, and emperors rule and are defeated. Herod merely replicated a worldwide culture; he was a powerful king.

Herod the Great and the Roman Empire

We go through the story of Herod's relationship with the infant Jesus every Christmas, but Herod the Great deserves fuller treatment. He was the king of the Jews from 40 to 4 BC. Conquest, building, prosperity, internal conflict, and centralized power marked this thirty-six-year reign. Herod the Great, no less, shaped the nation in ways physical, spiritual, social, and political. If we understand him, we begin to see the world in which Jesus lived. So, what was this king's life like?

The Jews had long fought for their independence but had been steadily losing ground. They had been conquered by Alexander the Great and, later, by rulers of the Seleucid Empire. One of these was Antiochus Epiphanes, who was a vicious persecutor of the Jews and of their faith. Then a family, the Maccabees (a nickname meaning hammer, warrior, quick to strike), emerged as deliverers of the Jewish nation. By courageous fighting they succeeded in gaining some measure of independence for the Jewish people. They founded a royal family, the Hasmoneans, who acted as both kings and high priests, and their vision was for a nation united under God. The history of the Israelites was one of deliverance from Egypt, and later from Babylon, and this theme of national deliverance by God was central to their hopes. There was a strong awareness that this required obedience to God, as the prophets had taught. Indeed, one of the biggest issues of the era was whether the army should fight on the Sabbath. The law seemed to say it is wrong. Yet when the enemy knows you are going to put down your weapons and do no work for twenty-four hours, that puts you at a disadvantage. Eventually, they decided that it was right to fight on the Sabbath, and their defenses improved (1 Macc.

2:29–41). However, even this compromise over the Sabbath did not save them, and they gradually succumbed to the Romans. Some sixty years before the birth of Christ, Rome effectively controlled the Hasmonean ruler Hyrcanus II. During this time Hyrcanus came to depend on Antipater, his chief minister, who had two sons, Pharsael and Herod, and so our subject comes onto the scene. Herod moved from being son of the king's minister to becoming king of the Jews in a dramatic series of events.

Hyrcanus had a brother Aristobulus, who wanted to be king and was quickly able to dominate him and then take over the throne as Aristobulus II, seemingly ending Herod's career. But in 63 BC Aristobulus backed away from helping Pompey in a military campaign and incurred the displeasure of the Roman leader. Pompey attacked, took him prisoner, and then set siege to Jerusalem, where many of the people were still in rebellion against Rome. There was a three-month confrontation with Roman engines, missiles, and ramparts, and then a bloodbath followed. Priests were cut down at the altar, and some twelve thousand Jews were slaughtered. Pompey even went into the Holy of Holies. This defeat saw Aristobulus and his family pushed to the side, but it was no victory for Hyrcanus. It left him stripped of the title of king and emptied of most of his political power, as Rome asserted its direct control. In 54 BC Crassus, the new Roman governor of Syria, removed all the gold and precious objects from the Temple, worth some eight thousand talents, the equivalent value of about fifty million sheep. This fixed relentless Jewish anger against Rome and gave them a firm sense of what it was to be a vassal state, but the Roman might under Julius Caesar was unassailable.

Hyrcanus and Antipater were not finished. They courted the support first of Pompey, and then after 49 BC of Julius Caesar. They helped Caesar in battle in Egypt. Two years later, another event shows the drama that was being played out. Antigonus was the son of Aristobulus, and though his father was out of favor, he appealed directly to Julius Caesar, professing his loyalty and trying to damn Hyrcanus and Antipater. Herod's father, Antipater, would not allow this outrage and threw off his clothes before Caesar, showing the scars he had received in fighting for Rome. He also pointed out that Antigonus was, like his father, an enemy of Rome, stirring sedition and seeking his own power. Julius Caesar was duly impressed and decided to rely on Hyrcanus and Antipater. He appointed Hyrcanus as ethnarch and high priest, and Antipater as commissioner for all Judea.[1] In this way Antipater established his loyalty and credence with the great Caesar himself, and henceforth he was the power behind the throne, the strategist who would shape the development of Israel. Antipater effectively began to control the area, subject to the Romans, and nominated his two sons, Pharsael and Herod, as governors in Jerusalem and Galilee.

One event illustrates the character and strategies of the twenty-five-year-old Herod when he was governor of Galilee and helps us understand much of his subsequent history. In Galilee Herod set about attacking some groups whom Josephus calls "bandits." They probably were not just bandits, but nationalists, wanting the removal of the Roman yoke.[2] Herod defeated them and had the leader, Hezekiah, and many of his followers summarily killed. This gained him the gratitude of Sextus Caesar, kinsman of Julius and governor of Syria. The Sanhedrin in Jerusalem was angry and summoned Herod to appear before them, an eerie precursor of what was to happen seventy-seven years later to Jesus. At this time the Pharisees controlled the Sanhedrin. Herod went, but dressed in kingly purple and with soldiers backing him up. He knew he had Roman support and eyeballed his Pharisee judges. Hyrcanus, still acting as high priest, made sure the court did not come to a verdict that would fly in the face of the Roman overlords; so Herod won. He strutted out and came back to Jerusalem shortly afterward with an army, threatening revenge on his accusers, which he did not actually exact.[3] The incident passed, but the lesson Herod learned was never to trust the Pharisees. Throughout the time he ruled, they were effectively out of power. Instead, the group we loosely identify as the Sadducees dominated the high priesthood. This was when the political loyalties of the next few decades were set.

While Julius Caesar ruled, there was a stable situation in Israel. But when the great Caesar was murdered in March 44 BC by Brutus and Anthony, various Jewish groups believed that the disorder in the Roman Republic would allow a successful rebellion to take place. It was also when Herod's political strategy became clear—simply a continuation of his father's pattern.[4] He recognized the might of the Romans and concluded that he should always be loyal to Rome, even when times were unstable. After the death of Julius Caesar, he transferred his loyalty to Mark Anthony. Nevertheless, there was chaos. Rebellions sprang up in Jerusalem, and Herod's father, Antipater, was poisoned to death. Herod assassinated the murderers. Then a great Parthian invasion swept in from the East. At this stage Antigonus, the son of the defeated Aristobulus II, swung back into Jerusalem, hoping to regain power. This he temporarily did. Herod's brother, Pharsael, took his own life to avoid being killed by Antigonus, who forced Herod to flee south with his family, fighting rearguard actions, completely defeated. Antigonus became king. He had the dubious backing of the Parthians, who also looted Jerusalem while they were there. The character of Antigonus can be judged by the fact that he mutilated the ear of Hyrcanus with his own teeth[5] so that the ethnarch could never again be high priest, for a high priest must be physically perfect. He was not a nice man.

Herod's response was amazing. He left his family with troops and provisions in the great fortress of Masada and retreated into Arabia, looking for allies but finding none. Alone he set off through the desert and swung round to the Egyptian coast, met Cleopatra, and then made a long sea voyage via Rhodes to Rome. There he won the support of both Anthony and Octavius, the two great figures vying for the position of Caesar. The Roman Senate declared him king of the Jews. He only had the title, but as King Herod he set off, gathering the help of Romans, Samaritans, and Galileans to undertake the reconquest of his own country in a steady and brilliant military campaign between 39 and 37 BC. At this point we recognize the violence that was part of Herod's life. Earlier, Antigonus had captured Pharsael, his brother. In order to prevent death by torture, he dashed his own head against a rock until he died. On hearing that Herod had escaped, Pharsael's final words were, "Now I shall die happy, as I'm leaving behind me a living man to avenge me."[6] Herod *did* kill thousands in his battles, but reluctantly and not indiscriminately. In his reconquest of Galilee, he finally trapped some rebels in the caves of Arbela, in a sharp, rocky cleft a couple of miles west of the lake, a spot Jesus must later have known well. Herod stood across the ravine, trying to persuade the rebels to give themselves up, and faced a horrific incident, which you may not want to read:

> One old man, father of seven children, was begged by the children and their mother to let them come out as their lives were guaranteed [by Herod]. His response was terrible. One by one, he ordered them to come out, while he stood at the cave-mouth and killed each son as he emerged. Herod, in a good position to watch, was cut to the heart, and stretched out his hand to the old man, begging him to spare his children; but he, treating the suggestion with contempt, went so far as to sneer at Herod for his lack of guts, and after disposing of the last of his sons and killing his wife too, flung their bodies down the precipice and finally leapt over the edge himself.[7]

A scene like that would damage anyone. Herod hoped for a peaceful reconquest of Jerusalem, but thousands died in four months of bloody carnage. Antigonus was captured, carted off to Anthony, and killed with an axe. Herod nevertheless managed to stop Roman looting and occupation of the temple by spending his own money and gradually established control. So he was a ruler seeped in the blood of his own citizens and hated with blood hate. Appointed king in 40 BC, he was fully in control by 37 BC as king of the Jews. Such a long reign until 4

BC, the equivalent of nine presidencies, allowed him to shape national development quite decisively.

As king of the Jews, Herod was involved in relationships with neighboring monarchs. One of them was Queen Cleopatra. By this stage the Romans had subdued Egypt, but Anthony was infatuated with Cleopatra and living largely at her whim. Herod visited her when he was on the run from Antigonus and journeying to Rome. According to rumor, she made sexual advances to him, seemingly a habit of hers, and was repudiated. She was not used to being turned down, felt affronted, and took quite a dislike to Herod. Later, she wanted him killed and demanded of the powerful Anthony the territory of Judea in return for her sexual services. Anthony, though besotted, still had enough political sense at this stage to deny her this request. But in 34 BC he did give her the rich balsam plantations near Jericho and territory further south, much to Herod's annoyance. Shortly afterward she came up to Jerusalem to have tea with Herod, gloat over him, and look over her new possessions, which he would lease back at considerable cost. It was probably quite a frosty meeting. Josephus even suggests that Herod thought seriously about murdering her, arguing it would be good for Anthony if she went. He was dissuaded.[8] As his advisers pointed out, Anthony might not see the loss of Cleopatra that way. They were probably right.

The next threat to Herod's crown came when Octavius defeated Anthony at Actium in 31 BC. The rivalry between the two led to the inevitable confrontation, and Anthony's weaknesses were exposed. Octavius became emperor as the great Augustus Caesar. Immediately, Herod's position became shaky. As Anthony's underlord, he was on the losing side, risking what this normally entailed. As he came before Augustus, Herod laid aside his crown, aware of his precarious position, but Caesar put it once more on his head, recognizing Herod's loyalty to Rome and potential loyalty to himself. And so it turned out Herod and Augustus remained unequivocal allies for a quarter of a century. Despite his earlier support of Anthony, Herod was restored and rewarded with the return of the balsam plantations near Jericho and other territory. Later, the Roman emperor was personally sensitive to him in incidents involving his sons. Finally, he was securely king of the Jews, with full Roman backing.

Herod's relationship with Rome established the underlying structure of Jewish society. It was overlaid with the Roman Empire. Throughout the area Herod set up fortresses against internal rebellion and external attack. These were the power bases from which the Jews had been and could be subdued. Herod's troops were constantly moved around to suppress even the hint of an uprising. The Roman overlords required taxation both to sustain their troops and to send back to Rome. Herod provided it assiduously, and also taxed heavily for his own expenditures and projects.

Map of Herod the
Great's Kingdom

Strong economic development and the absence of war politically offset these heavy taxes of around a quarter of people's earnings. It was a strategy that made the period one of relative economic stability. Under Herod, there was probably a general improvement in the standard of living.

The culture that Herod fostered was a mixture of Roman, Hellenistic, and Jewish. Herod built amphitheaters and stadiums, but the Jews seem not to have warmed to Greco-Roman culture. Thus, it does not feature directly in the Gospels. Devout and even normal Jews did not go to the races. Herod had a great reputation within the Roman Empire for benefactions. He funded and built temples to Apollo and other deities, theaters, gymnasiums, stoas, colonnades, markets, and aqueducts in Greece, Asia Minor, and especially Syria, the Roman province north of his kingdom. He was seen as an influential, loyal, and rich client king of Rome. He also sponsored the Olympic Games every five years and was the first to introduce prizes for those coming in second and third. Silver and bronze Olympic medal winners have Herod to thank for their medals. This culture uneasily overlay the intense Jewish one, and his relationship with the Jews is a complex and intricate story.

Herod the Great and the Jews

At one level Herod was a Roman appointee and was hated by a Jewish nation seeking independence. That he was also a military invader and conqueror of the land did not go down well either. But the actual relationships were more complex and longer-lasting than that. Although his father had entered into an alliance with the Pharisees, he did not do so. He had learned from his experience as a young man. Instead, Herod worked with the Sadducees, a more worldly and less religiously intense group, who were prepared to accommodate somewhat to Roman and Herodian rule. He also favored the Essenes because they were no threat and had withdrawn from the political scene, and because of an incident with an Essene called Manaemus, who prophesied Herod's kingship.[9] Throughout his reign, the Pharisees functioned as a behind-the-scenes opposition to him, cultivating popular support for their cause. This orientation shaped much of the ethos of Pharisaism as it continued into Jesus' adulthood, and later we will address it more fully.

At another level, Herod, although crowned king of the Jews, had to work for his dynastic acceptance. Because his father was Idumean, from the area south of Judea, he was only half Jewish. Consequently, much of his energy went into trying to meet the strong racial loyalties of his subjects. His first wife, Doris, produced a son, Antipater, but she was not Jewish. He then married Mariamme, a Jewish woman from the Hasmonean royal family, and he loved her deeply, as did the Jewish people. She produced two sons, Alexander and Aristobulus, again loved by the Jewish people and educated in Rome for leadership. For a while this seemed idyllic. A Jewish royal family was being established that Rome would easily accept. Then things began to go wrong. Mariamme learned that Herod, when he was required to meet Anthony at Laodicea and clear his name of some charges that Cleopatra was leveling, had ordered that she (Mariamme) should be killed if Herod died. His motive was jealous love and perhaps to avoid her being attacked by the mob. But knowing that her husband was prepared for her to be killed in certain circumstances scarcely pleased her, partly because she was aware that the Jewish mob actually liked her better than Herod. Their marital trust was damaged. Yet worse was to come.

Herod's sister, Salome, was locked in a vicious war with Mariamme. His first wife, Doris, and her son, Antipater, started spreading rumors of the disloyalty of Mariamme and the two sons, Alexander and Aristobulus. These two sons were the ones the Jews looked to as the future truly Jewish leaders. They were trained in Rome and innocent of the charges of trying to poison Herod. Nevertheless, the charges eventually carried weight with Herod as a result of false evidence and bogus witnesses, as more astonishingly did the claim that Mariamme had been unfaithful. Despite a trial in Rome under Augustus's careful supervision that acquitted the two sons, the confused and suspicious Herod eventually ordered their deaths. He also required the death of Mariamme, his beloved, finding out too late that she was innocent. Thus he wrongly killed the three most precious people in his life and was racked with remorse for Mariamme to the point of suffering periods of madness. The whole episode was an appalling tragedy, not unlike *Othello*, except that it was real and shed horror in people's lives. It also killed Jewish hopes of a continuation of the Hasmonean line, which would have restored their belief in a Jewish royal family. Thereafter, Herod's life was shrouded in insufferable grief. He married three further times, to another Mariamme, and to Malthace and Cleopatra of Jerusalem, but at the end of his life he also finished by killing his firstborn son, Antipater, who with Doris had done a lot of the scheming and probably *was* planning to poison him. The calamity in this family was beyond telling. Behind all the mistakes, bloodshed, and guilt lay Herod's dominating fear that one or another son would try to do away with him and assume the kingship. Around the title of king lay a web of evil caused by Herod and those who were close to him. It was a court riddled with intrigue and terror. The fortresses at Masada, Herodium, and elsewhere, so unassailable, attest to Herod's fear. In this context, the Magi (wise men) coming into Jerusalem and asking about a new potential king of the Jews must have seemed bizarre. It would be slightly less safe than putting your head into the mouth of a lion and asking what was for lunch.

After the murder of Mariamme, Herod tried another way to gain Jewish acceptance. The solution was magnificent. He decided to rebuild the Temple at Jerusalem. This was to be an outstanding national shrine, constructed on the scale found in Greek and Roman cultures, but with its own Jewish focus. Like the temples in Athens or Delphi, it would pull in substantial amounts of money to its treasury and therefore create for the high-priestly party a huge source of income. Later, we shall look at the Temple tax and the economic system the Temple generated. The high-priestly group, mainly Sadducees, was very impressed with the offer and as a result entered into an uneasy alliance with Herod. Since he insisted on appointing the high priest, it was not entirely a free choice. But the Temple was built—a glorious, high, white-stone structure, bedecked with gold. A thousand priests were trained as masons so that purity would be maintained during its construction, because only priests should enter the Temple. The size of the Temple area was expanded, and it became the focus of the nation. The main construction occurred in the years 19–10 BC, but other work continued until the time of Jesus (John 2:20) and was not finished until AD 64, if then. It was a great success, though heavy Jewish taxes were the source of the funds. Yet, in spite of this massive undertaking, the people's gratitude to Herod was measured rather than overwhelming.

When the Temple and the surrounding buildings were built, they became the dominant national religious focus in Jerusalem and beyond. We, used to mere cathedrals, could underestimate the Temple's significance. It was the center of the tourist trade as well as of religion and Jewish government. As the system of gifts and taxes expanded, supporting a great religious system, Herod's relationship with the new Jewish elite grew more complex. They owed the Temple to him, but it gave them power independent of him, because it was based on Israel's God rather than Roman rule. This political relationship is summed up in an event occurring very late in Herod's life, probably even after the visit of the Magi (Matt. 2). Herod, always concerned to honor Rome, allowed a golden Roman eagle to be placed at the top of the Temple. This act so incensed the Jews that two rabbis persuaded their students to climb up on the Temple and remove the eagle. When Herod found out, he was angry, addressed the people about his displeasure, and had the rabbis and students burnt alive and others killed.[10] The Temple had not led to stability but had focused the difference between Jewish and Herodian politics.

The suppressed opposition to Herod had a number of different focal points. One was the Pharisees, who gradually organized themselves into a national movement largely independent of Temple religion. They formed a body of teachers of the law who moved through Judea and Galilee, using the growing number of synagogues, or halls, for teaching the Torah of Moses as the basis for national life and righteousness. The Temple system of the Sadducees, though it was not overtly hostile to the Pharisees, was aware of its different power base, and there was some rivalry between the two groups. Another group were precursors of the Zealots, avid nationalists who believed that paying tribute to Caesar was treason toward God. Some of them gathered in more remote areas, aiming to swoop on the Herodians whenever they perceived weakness. More generally, the ordinary rural peasants, poor and heavily taxed, would be hostile, looking for a change or leader from somewhere. Thus, there was a mixture of hatred for Rome and Herod, a highly nationalistic faith, the Torah movement, a new focus in the Temple, and a weariness of taxation. On Herod's death this mixture would once more explode.

Jesus and Herod

As Herod entered his final years, suffering from bowel cancer, the birth of Jesus must have been like a red rag to a bull. After the string of earlier conspiracies, he was now worried that his first son was poisoning him. Suddenly three nobles/astrologers turn up from Eastern territory that is basically Parthian. The Parthians not only were potentially hostile to Rome and to him but had also been instrumental in the deaths of his father and brother. The wise men ask, "Where is the one who has been born king of the Jews?" (Matt. 2:1). Herod must have gone ballistic. Matthew's words are an understatement: "When Herod heard this he was disturbed, and all Jerusalem with him" (2:3). Herod is furious at this direct challenge to himself. He has either just killed, or is contemplating killing, his own son for aspiring to be king of the Jews, and suddenly there is another pretender. Jerusalem is probably more disturbed at what he in his uncontrolled madness might do. But it soon becomes obvious that the visitors are naive and have no local knowledge. Herod probably establishes that they are not Parthian, but Magi from further east, maybe with Zoroastrian beliefs, and outside the politics of Herod's domain. Rather than being hostile to them, Herod focuses fully on the child who might claim the throne. While the rest of Jerusalem buzzes with the possibility of a rival for the hated Herod, he sets up a stratagem to kill the infant. Because he is distant from the Jewish Scriptures, Herod has to consult the scribes. Matthew implies that the process is quite public. Calling together "all the people's chief priests and teachers of the law" (2:4) makes it an event, but not a formal meeting of the Sanhedrin.[11] Micah's (5:2) prophecy about Bethlehem is well known, and the leaders tell Herod of it.[12] The three Magi go off with travel instructions to Bethlehem, about five miles south of Jerusalem, and a strict order to return to Herod with information. They leave, find Jesus, and evade Herod on their way home. Matthew's "by another route" (2:12) probably means they went into the Idumean desert, south of the Dead Sea, and eastward. So Herod's troops move in and wipe out the children in Bethlehem of the relevant age, perhaps twenty or forty infants (2:16). This was entirely in character for this stage of his life. Josephus tells the story that shortly afterward, as he faced his own death, the king ordered hundreds of distinguished men to be locked in the hippodrome at Jericho. He gave orders that when he died, they were to be murdered, too, so that there should be mourning at his death and not rejoicing.[13] He died in 4 BC, mercifully without these people actually being killed.[14] Paranoia thus surrounded these years. Five days before he died, he sent his bodyguard to put his scheming son Antipater to death. Thus this great king of the Jews fought for his throne.

The contrast between Herod and Jesus could scarcely be starker. Herod the Great died after decades of rule as king of the Jews. Jesus was born, as some thought, King of the Jews. Whatever the title applied to Jesus means, it is of the same genre as Herod's title, not a ceremonial pattern practiced in the United Kingdom or elsewhere. The genealogies in Matthew and Luke point to Jesus as Son of David, in the royal line. He is announced King of the Jews by the Magi and identified by the quotation from Micah. The Gospel writers seem intent to acknowledge Jesus as the King of the Jews. How this should be interpreted is one of the central questions of this book. For kingship inevitably has political implications and is clearly intended as more than a "spiritual" title.

In the Gospel accounts the news of the kingly birth is given to a few; clearly, it could not be otherwise. Mary receives from God the unequivocal words, "The Lord God will give [your Son] the throne of his father David, and he will reign over the house of Jacob forever; his kingdom will never end" (Luke 1:32–33). Mary passes these words to Luke after Jesus' death and resurrection, and she and Luke believe them to be fulfilled. The aged pair, Elizabeth and Zechariah, buzzing with the coming birth of their own John the Baptist, learn something of John's relation to the kingly line. "The God of Israel . . . has raised up a horn of salvation for us in the house of his servant David" (1:68–69). In some profound way, they have the deliverer king's trumpeter (John) gurgling here in their living room. Lowly shepherds are told to visit the Lord Messiah as a baby, in the town of David (2:11–12). The baby is born in a stable, it seems by God's design. The status of kingship is laid down, but among the underlings trying to cope with the census and taxation. What was of note to Luke was the counterstatement: born in a manger, not a palace. The idea that God might not need the trappings of importance nagged at Luke, as it does us. When you own the whole show, a palace is as much infra dig as a stable. This is where we first face the uniqueness of Jesus. Could there be a different king? By the time Mark wrote, he was convinced of the answer. At the beginning of his Gospel, he quotes from Isaiah 40 to locate John the Baptist as Jesus' herald. But a few verses further, Isaiah 40:10–11 says:

See, the Sovereign LORD comes with power, and his arm rules for him.
See, his reward is with him, and his recompense accompanies him.

He tends his flock like a shepherd:

He gathers the lambs in his arms and carries them close to his heart;

He gently leads those that have young.

These are strange words. Is God a ruler like this? Rulers demand taxes, slaves, soldiers, but here is a ruler who *rewards*. Rulers govern by fear and conquest, but here is a ruler who is gentle to the young and those who are pregnant. You cannot cradle a lamb and be harsh. Rulers rely on armies, but here is one whose arms hold his subjects close to his *heart*. Is it possible that all this conquest, domination, rape, and pillage are not necessary when we live on God's terms? It is unthinkable in terms of usual world history, but here it actually begins to unfold. There could be another king.

So the birth of Jesus reflects a basic political dilemma: the powerful, vindictive ruler out to kill, in contrast to Jesus, guarded by Joseph and Mary, escaping to Egypt. They leave at night, slipping out on a difficult journey (Matt. 2:14). Bethlehem is not their home, though they might have intended to settle there in the long run. Now they will be moving off anyway, to Nazareth or elsewhere. They pack for journeying, but instead of the eighty or hundred miles back to Nazareth, they face some two hundred miles into Egypt as refugees. No one misses their going, except perhaps Joseph's relatives, and none of Mary's family up north will know where they have gone for a while. It is a lonely journey as refugees, but the infant is safe outside Herod's savage domain. Large Diaspora communities are found in Egypt, a million Jews or so, the largest in the Roman Empire, and integration into them would be relatively easy, mingling with others hiding from Herod. There are big concentrations of Jews in Alexandria, Heliopolis, and other towns and villages. It is like an Irishman coming to London. The Jews do not live in ghettos but are an active minority in this Roman colony. Synagogues abound, and the Romans give the Jews religious privileges. The family can therefore fit in. Joseph can get work and preserve a suitable anonymity. Perhaps messages can be sent back to the family with merchant Jews regularly making journeys north. After a while, news of the death of Herod comes (2:19–20). The family can begin the journey back home, as the incident of the Magi and Herod the Great slides into history.

But where was home? Jewish families are largely patrilocal. Though Joseph has probably been living and working in Galilee, the fact that he is registered to be taxed in Judea suggests that he thinks of returning there (2:22). He likely intends Bethlehem to become the family home. Yet the incident of Herod massacring Bethlehem infants is too recent, and Joseph is warned in a dream to do something different. On Herod's death the sons who have survived are competing for the kingdom. Archelaus is effectively in control in Jerusalem and has the strongest claim. Antipas and Philip also push their cause. In the capital Archelaus starts out with magnanimity, appealing to the crowds vastly swelled for the Passover of 4 BC. But his popularity leads him into a problem. Soon the Jews begin asking for lower taxes and also want vengeance for those who participated in killing the scholars who had torn down the Roman eagle from the Temple. In other words, he is being pushed by the nationalists to support the Jews against the Romans. He prevaricates; the Jews, sensing his weakness, riot. Immediately, the old Herodian style has to be re-established. Soldiers go in, mowing people down and even fighting on the Temple Mount. Thousands are killed, and Archelaus, like his father, has hands red with blood.[15] More than this, Sabinus, the Roman procurator, is also fighting independently to establish his position, seeing rich pickings in Jerusalem. He even plunders the Temple. These bits of news shoot into Egypt like wildfire to Joseph and Mary. Archelaus is just like his father and very dangerous. Even after Herod's death, it is not safe to go to Bethlehem, only five miles down the road from Jerusalem.

The three sons of Herod—Archelaus, Antipas, and Philip—journey to Rome to see what the decision of Caesar Augustus is on the succession. While they are away, a rebellion breaks out through the territories. In Galilee, Judas (son of Hezekiah, earlier killed by Herod the Great, then the young governor of Galilee) raids the royal arsenal at Sepphoris, just down the hill from Nazareth. Judas distributes the weapons to his followers, mounting a heady insurrection of vindication for his father. In Perea, east of Jordan, one of Herod's slaves named Simon mounts an uprising and burns the royal palace at Jericho. For a while it seems that the uprisings are successful. But the hopes are dashed. Varus, the Roman commander, comes through with clinical military dominance and defeats Judas. He burns Sepphoris to teach the locals a lesson and enslaves its inhabitants, selling them off throughout the empire and depopulating the area. He also subdues Judea in a classic Roman reprisal, establishing again Roman invincibility. Then he has two thousand rebels crucified along the road at Sepphoris, and the Romans have indubitably established their control. This news from home is not good.

After their journey to Rome, the three brothers are given their territories, two as tetrarchs and one as an ethnarch, rather than as kings. Archelaus as ethnarch is in control of Judea, ruling out Jesus' family returning to that territory. Even then, the issue is complicated. Bringing a putative Messiah to the matrilocal home at Nazareth, just down the road from Sepphoris, will not be easy. Yet the family does settle there.

More children are born. Joseph may have rebuilding work in Sepphoris, and he visits Jerusalem for festivals. Locals learn to evade Roman cruelty, which slowly recedes in memory. Herod Antipas is enough in control in Galilee that he does not need to murder vast numbers of people. For a while the nationalists are quiet, stunned by the death of Judas (son of Hezekiah) and his followers. The child Jesus grows to manhood.

Bibliography

Boardman, John, Jasper Griffin, and Oswyn Murray. *The Oxford History of the Classical World.* Oxford: Oxford University Press, 1986.

Grant, Michael. *Herod the Great.* New York: American Heritage, 1971.

Gross, William. *Herod the Great.* Baltimore: Helicon, 1962.

Jones, A. H. M. *The Herods of Judaea.* Oxford: Clarendon, 1938.

Josephus, Flavius. *The Jewish War.* AD 80s. Translated by G. A. Williamson. New York: Dorset, 1981.

Lien, Judith, John North, and Tessa Rajak, eds. *The Jews among Pagans and Christians in the Roman Empire.* New York: Routledge, 1992.

Neusner, Jacob. *An Introduction to Judaism.* Louisville: Westminster/John Knox, 1991.

———. *From Politics to Piety: The Emergence of Pharisaic Judaism.* Englewood Cliffs, NJ: Prentice Hall, 1973.

Perone, Stewart G. *The Life and Times of Herod the Great.* London: Hodder & Stoughton, 1956.

Richardson, Peter. *Herod: King of the Jews and Friend of the Romans.* Edinburgh: T&T Clark, 1999.

Roller, Duane. *The Building Program of Herod the Great.* Berkeley: University of California Press, 1998.

Safrai, Shemuel, and Moritz Stern. *The Jewish People in the First Century: Geography, Political History, Social, Cultural and Religious Life and Institutions.* 2 vols. Philadelphia: Fortress, 1974–76.

Schürer, Emil. *The History of the Jewish People in the Age of Christ (175 B.C.–A.D. 135).* 1885–1924. Revised and edited by Geza Vermes and Fergus Millar. Translated by T. A. Burkill et al. 3 vols. in 4. Edinburgh: T&T Clark, 1973–87.

Stambaugh, John, and David Balch. *The New Testament in Its Social Environment.* Philadelphia: Westminster, 1986.

2

Jesus' Political Arena

Introduction

We tend to take for granted how much we know about our own political scene. Actually, the Gospels themselves include a lot of the necessary awareness of Jesus' political interactions. Those who want to get to these events might be impatient with this background chapter. Yet the events of the Gospels move quickly and are complex. Hence, we need to spend some time absorbing this background, meeting the actors before they appear onstage.

After the death of Herod the Great in 4 BC, three political zones emerged, governed by three of his sons. In the south Archelaus governed as ethnarch in Judea, Samaria, and Idumea. In the north as tetrarchs, Herod Antipas controlled Galilee and Perea, and Philip Herod had the area east of Galilee. Archelaus only lasted until AD 6, and then his regions were taken over by Roman procurators, who later included Pontius Pilate. The events in the Gospels are largely played out in these three political territories. They are important as political domains, and we must note their characteristics and significance.

But another change also takes place. Herod the Great was so dominant that the parties with which he dealt were relatively subdued. After his death these factions or parties emerged more strongly. They were not unlike our own political parties in their concerns about power and government. We think of democracies as decidedly different

Map of the Territories of Herod the Great's Sons

from ancient political systems, but actually the process of gathering popular support is quite clearly an important part of what is going on in the Gospels, although less formalized. Because Jewish society was not slave-based, people mattered politically more than in other cultures.

Further, we may interpret groups like the Pharisees or high priests as religious rather than political, using a more recent understanding of the separation of the two. For some of them, such as the Essenes and strict Pharisees, this was true, but the other groups we examine were religious *and* political. They focus round the points of power in Galilee and Jerusalem the way any parties do in a modern state. Their views are inseparably religiopolitical because for Jews since the time of Moses the two were inseparable. Throughout the Gospels, these groups turn up and react to Jesus. His actions force the leaders to form strategies for defeating him. They sit around, developing lines of debate that will, they hope, put him down. They like power and establishing their political position. Their priorities differ, and they have their own political heroes.

This chapter provides the background of these political parties and the main groups operating in them.

When the drama is played out, it moves fast. Jesus attacks the Pharisees as political leaders, sitting in Moses' seat (Matt. 23:2). He sees John the Baptist as the greatest prophet, challenging rulers to answer to God's ways. Because Jesus is a political threat, his life is sought by Herod Antipas in the north and the Temple party in the south. Jesus is finally tried by the Sanhedrin, Pilate, Herod Antipas, and the crowds in Jerusalem in a crucial political event, based on clear political strategies. There are the crucifixion and resurrection.

The Political Regions

The Territories of Herod Antipas

Much of Jesus' life is set in Galilee. The region west of the Sea of Galilee was ruled by Herod Antipas from 3 BC to AD 39. He was the dominant political figure in Galilee throughout Jesus' life until the crucifixion. The region was about 25 by 40 miles, the size of a medium English county, two-thirds the size of Rhode Island. It was mainly occupied by Jews, with some Greek and Roman settlers. Roads, developed by the Romans, were the main instrument of Herodian control, carrying wagons, horses, and troops. They crisscrossed southern Galilee, but the north was hilly and wilder. A major Roman road went from Ptolemais (in Syria) on the Mediterranean coast, swung north of Sepphoris and Nazareth, then went down to the Galilee shore, where it circled north and south round the lake. This left a large area of Galilee farther to the north and out toward the Phoenician coast with fewer Roman roads.[1] Jews normally traveled by foot on paths and other customary routes largely independent of the Roman roads, and wheels had limited uses. Richer and more fertile plains and valleys stretched from the lake out to the coast in the west, studded with the main cities and towns of the area. It was more hilly again to the south. Nazareth was perched on one of the hills, and the region southward opened into the valley (or plain) of Esdraelon before merging into the hills of Samaria. Galilee was rich and fertile, with fish aplenty, and an expanding population.

Herod Antipas controlled the territory as an established tyrant like his father Herod the Great. Unlike his father, he was tetrarch, not king, implying less autonomy from Rome. Galilee's boundary in the east was the region of his brother Philip, with whom Antipas had a hostile relationship. Several times, probably, Jesus and the disciples deliberately went by boat and on foot out of Antipas's territory, escaping the tyrant's

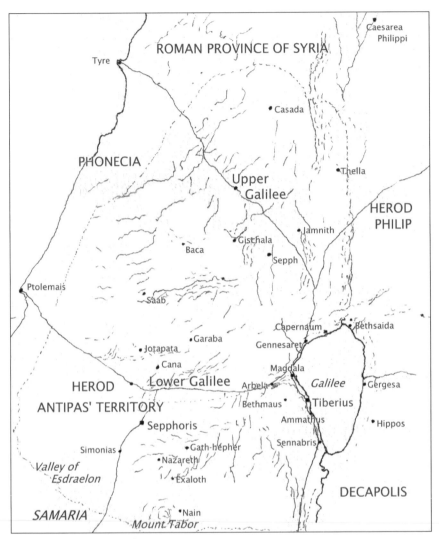

Map of the Region of Galilee

autocracy. To the north and west the Galilee boundary straggled through the hills to the regions of Tyre and Sidon, or Phoenicia (in the province of Syria), also controlled by the Romans. To the south was Samaria, slightly hostile, but one route to Jerusalem. In Jewish thinking, the holy city remained the beloved capital of Galilee, although it was nearly a hundred miles south and outside their territory. By contrast, Herod's capitals were quite strongly repudiated by most of the Jews and are scarcely mentioned in the Gospels. They were, however, important cities.

Sepphoris, four miles north of Nazareth, was Herod Antipas's first capital. It was the focus of a rebellion against the Romans in 4 BC, probably while Jesus was in Egypt, when the Roman arsenal was seized. It was recaptured and the whole city burned down. Then the city's inhabitants were taken off and enslaved, and probably quite a few were seen among the two thousand crucified rebels. Herod Antipas rebuilt Sepphoris during the period AD 1–20, when Jesus was a lad. It is conceivable that Joseph worked there as builder/carpenter. Herod Antipas initially made it his capital. Josephus reflects on the process: "Herod fortified Sepphoris to be the ornament of all Galilee, and called it 'Autocratoris.'"[2] The name is one to conjure with. It means "self-power" and may convey the idea of the ruling city, the capital of the area. On the other hand, it may be linked to one of Augustus's titles. But it signals all we understand by the word *autocrat* and the arrogance of self-rule. "Autocratoris" could be easily seen down the hill from the rocky Nazareth bluffs. It is not mentioned in the Gospels. The population was mainly Jewish, but it was a city of bad memories. Those who were now ready to live there were largely serving the Herodian overlord. The tension of living close to Herodian military control meant that many Jews would normally avoid living there and circle it in their travels.

Tiberias was built rather later, around AD 15–23, and succeeded Sepphoris as the capital of the area. It nestled under hills on the southwest bank of the Sea of Galilee. It had a Greek-style council of some six hundred men but was really under the fairly direct control of Antipas. Its expansion to a very large city of twenty thousand or more in the 20s was partly through the influx of taxation wealth and Herod's building and lifestyle. The city was located on the site of an earlier cemetery and judged unclean by many Jews, a further reason for avoiding it as a Gentile city.[3] It was more Greco-Roman in culture, with slaves drafted to build and work, freed on condition they stayed there. Josephus calls them a "promiscuous rabble."[4] Both cities contained a few Roman and many more Herodian soldiers and tax collectors and reflect the taxation wealth gathered from the territory. Neither city is mentioned in the Gospels (except in John 6:23), likely because ordinary Galileans steered clear of Roman- and Herodian-dominated areas and roads. They distrusted people who worked in these cities. For most Jews, these were not their cities. As a result, the region was strangely without its own civic focus, other than Jerusalem. Villagers and townspeople largely operated under Herodian control with as little contact as possible with the military power.

Further south of Galilee and on the east side of the Jordan was *Perea,* also controlled by Herod Antipas. Perea was detached from Galilee by about fifteen miles of another territory called the Decapolis, but overall Roman control meant that this was not a point of tension. Antipas and many others regularly journeyed from one territory to the other. Perea stretched down the east side of the Jordan and the Dead Sea some sixty miles or so. It was guarded by five fortresses: from north to south they were Amathus, Gadara, Abila, Livias (a city built by Antipas honoring the emperor's wife), and Machaerus, where John the Baptist was killed. Perea marked the eastern border of Roman control, and it was Antipas's duty to defend this border for the Romans. Failure so to do was a very black mark. On the east was the Nabataean Kingdom, ruled by Aretas IV, a powerful independent ruler (2 Cor. 11:32). The Nabataean Kingdom was Arab, with a hot, harsh, and substantially desert climate and a valuable camel trade east to west, and north to south. It stretched from Damascus (sometimes) to Petra and into the Sinai Peninsula. The remains of Petra, the carved, rose-colored, rock capital city to the southeast of the Dead Sea, attest the wealth of the kingdom. The Nabataeans worshipped pagan gods. The Romans had tried to dominate the kingdom but would not succeed until the second century AD. Throughout the period of Jesus' ministry, Aretas was hostile to Herod Antipas and would defeat him in a battle that will concern us later. Perea is the New Testament "land beyond Jordan" (e.g., Matt. 4:25), some twenty or thirty miles away from Jerusalem. John the Baptist speaks from there, supposedly out of reach of his enemies. News travels quickly as to whether Herod and his court were in Galilee or Perea. Pharisees later come to Jesus in Perea to warn him that Herod is in the area, perhaps with the intention to capture and kill him, as he had the Baptist. In this situation the Pharisees are on Jesus' side rather than Herod's (Luke 13:31). The Gospels thus often feature Perea.

The Territory of Herod Philip

Northeast of Galilee were several territories ruled by Philip, the older brother of Herod Antipas. He ruled the area from 4 BC to AD 34, beyond the resurrection. It was a less well-defined region, and after his death it was incorporated into the Roman province of Syria. Its territories were Paneas, Ulatha, Gaulanitis, Batanaea, Auranitis, and Trachonitis. As one moved away from Galilee, the area became an unexciting semiarid plain dissected by an odd wadi (sharp valley) or two, with more rain for higher elevations. In the north it eventually merged into the foothills and heights of Hermon, and in the east into desert. Philip traveled round the area, governing paternally and exciting no real tensions. The area generated a substantial but smaller taxation income than Galilee, and the feeling was that Philip had received the worst deal from his father's will. It was a bit of a backwater with no obvious focus other than Caesarea Philippi in the north (near Mount Hermon) and Bethsaida-Julias near the northeastern curve of the Sea of Galilee, both quite beautiful cities, joined by a valley and road. Philip's quarrels with Antipas meant that there was little political co-operation between the two brothers. There were fewer Jews in the area, and Roman and Greek patterns of religion were more normal, instituted by Philip.

South of Philip's territory and across the lake (eastward) from Galilee was the area of the *Decapolis* panning out into the desert. It was not under the control of either Antipas or Philip. The area resented the rule of Herod the Great and opted for direct control by the Syrian legate. The towns in the area were not likely to cause trouble and were given a fair bit of autonomy by the Romans, as long as they paid their taxes. By origin, they were formed mainly through Alexander the Great's invasion and occupied by Greeks. They retained this Greek flavor and under later Roman influence formed a league. The ten towns (the Decapolis) were Scythopolis, Hippos, Gadara, Pella, Dion, Gerasa, Philadelphia, Damascus, Raphana, and Abila. Gadara, southeast of Galilee, was the cultural center of the area (cf. Mark 5:1–20). These towns were thus largely self-governing under benign Roman supervision and seen as somewhat pagan by the Jews.

Territories of Archelaus, Pilate, and Other Roman Procurators

When Herod the Great's territories were disbanded, Archelaus received the biggest bloc, including Samaria, Judea, and Idumea in the south toward the Sinai desert. On the whole, Judea was at loggerheads with both Samaria and Idumea, which it saw as not properly Jewish, so there were tensions within the area. After the death of his father, Archelaus killed three thousand Jews in Jerusalem at the Passover in reprisal for the killing of some of his soldiers. Hence, the people hated him. Jews and Samaritans complained to Caesar Augustus, and Archelaus was exiled in AD 6, when Jesus was about ten years old. It is interesting that the powerful Jerusalem Jews asked and campaigned for direct Roman control rather than a Herodian replacement, perhaps believing this would offer them more independence. There was a key political battle between Herodian control and "direct" Roman rule, for the latter meant substantial internal control by the high priests and Sanhedrin. A series of Roman procurators took over before Pontius Pilate arrived in AD 26. They tended to make Samaria their power base, especially Caesarea and Sebaste, rather than Jerusalem.

Samaria was south of Galilee between the Mediterranean Sea and the Jordan River. It was a hilly country, with the plains of Esdraelon in the north and Judea in the south. Samaria was in tension with Judea and Galilee because during several centuries colonial powers had killed or deported many of its inhabitants and repopulated the area with Assyrians and Macedonians, who had intermarried with the locals. So, these people were not "pure" Jews (2 Kings 17). Herod had ruled them, trusting them more than the Jews. But when the Temple was rebuilt in Jerusalem, the Samaritans did not support it, for they had established their own place of worship on *Mount Gerazim,* near Sychar, where Jesus chatted with the Samaritan woman. Obviously, this site seemed inferior to the great Jerusalem Temple, and the Samaritan woman at the well brought it up in discussion with Jesus (John 4:20). Samaritans seem to have worked more co-operatively with the Romans than the Jews did, but they had their problems too. About six years after Jesus' crucifixion, a religious fanatic led a crowd of Samaritans up Mount Gerazim, looking for some kind of deliverance. Pilate intervened with his soldiers, and a vicious massacre followed. The Samaritans in turn complained over Pilate's head to the Romans and succeeded in getting him sacked—no mean achievement.

As sacred writings the Samaritans accepted only the five books of Moses and not the later constructions of the scribes and Pharisees, but they shared the main religious precepts of the Jews. There were also strong pagan influences. Herod the Great had built the capital, *Sebaste,* in the style of a Roman and Greek city, with temples, colonnades, a theater, and a hippodrome. It was anti-Jewish in conception, with a great temple dedicated to Augustus. The Roman capital of the whole region, *Caesarea,* was a magnificent city built by Herod the Great on the Mediterranean (in Samaria). A great aqueduct brought Caesarea sparkling fresh water from the hills. It became the Roman capital from which Judea was governed—rich, relaxed, cut off from the troublesome Jews, and some seventy miles northwest of Jerusalem. This distance is important, for it signals some of the disengagement of Roman procurators. They were happy to be at Caesarea and leave the Jews to run things as long as there were no disturbances. Jewish taxation money went to Caesarea. There people practiced pagan worship of Caesar and the local deities. Roman auxiliary or mercenary troops, collected mainly from Samaria and immediately round Caesarea, were called the Sebastenes. The Judean people were thus largely controlled by Samaritan soldiers, which probably explains a lot of the Jewish hostility to Samaritans.[5]

Judea was the heartland of the Jewish people, covering five tribal areas and loosely representing the old kingdom of Judah. Since the fall of Archelaus, the layer of Herodian rule was removed, and it was governed "directly" by Rome. In AD 26 Pilate came as procurator/prefect. He was not liked, quite contemptuous of the Jewish authorities in Jerusalem, and spoiling to exert Roman military power over the locals. But soon he was aware that he was dealing with a sharp race. Judea shared Roman rule with Samaria to the north and Idumea to the south, stretching out into the desert. But with its Jewish identity Judah distinguished itself firmly from the outlying areas and was dominant over them, despising them both. Since Herod the Great built the new Temple at *Jerusalem,* the city became a great national focus, operating as the effective Jewish capital not just of Judea, but of all Jewish territories and dispersed Jews. Jerusalem was a mixture of capital, business center, tourist resort, and wonder of the world, drawing people to the Jewish cultic worship of God. The Temple was like the ones at Delphi, Athens, Hieropolis, and Thebes, with its own religiopolitical power. Moreover, it was gradually stamping its political authority over the region, through the Temple tax, its traveling representatives, and its wealth. It rivaled Roman control from Caesarea, seventy or so miles away, even though Roman rule technically dominated it. The Jerusalem elites believed they were running the show. But there were reminders that they were not—fortresses at Herodium (ten miles south of Jerusalem), Hycania (ten miles southeast of Jerusalem), Cyprus (near Jericho), the great Herodian fortress of Masada (thirty-eight miles south of Jericho, just west of the Dead Sea), and Malatha in Idumea (between Beersheba and Masada). These fortresses declared Roman control but had little impact on the lives of ordinary people. Colonial control was a lonely business: people mostly did not like the Roman officials and preferred to ignore them and spit when they were out of sight.

These three major domains were separate political entities, loosely under Roman rule. They did not have the boundary definition of modern nation-states, and ordinary people could move among them, traveling off or on road. Yet it made a difference who was your overlord—Antipas, Pilate, or Philip. Each avidly guarded his territorial power of taxation and enforcement. But far more was going on in each of these territories as different parties vied for influence and power within this structure.

The Political Parties of the Jews

The politics of first-century Jews were different from our own, and we must avoid some of our own Western cultural assumptions. First, we tend to separate politics and religion and therefore think of groups like the Pharisees and chief priests as religious and not political. They were both, as the textual evidence fully shows. Nor, as we might think, were they "mistaken" in this view. Their worldviews saw religion and politics as integral because God's purposes relate to the nation. We sometimes see the Mosaic law as relating only to personal and ethical codes of living, and not as political. Yet the Jews clearly considered the Torah as their founding political document. God's law, given at Sinai, made them who they were as a nation. Moses was a political leader, and the priests and Pharisees sat on Moses' seat.[6]

In one sense there were competing groups with different views. They included the Herodians, Pharisees, Sadducees, Temple Party, Essenes, and nationalists/Zealots, with the popular masses assuming significance and power at certain times. We will examine each of these groups. Yet competing groups often share a great deal, and this was no less the case in Israel. The sense we gather from the Gospels is of an interplay between groups who acknowledge their relationship with God and give credence to the Mosaic law. The backdrop to the whole of this drama, accepted by most of the Jewish groups, is the relationship God has with the nation and with the political events of the day. In the rest of this chapter, we try to obtain a firmer picture of each of these groups and the relationships between them. The tensions between them and Jesus had an extraordinary character. He deliberately stepped outside the normal political assumptions of the day and centrally reinterpreted the kind of relationship God had with the nation. Jesus predicted the destruction of the Temple at a time when people could see the great blocks of stone as big as their houses and seemingly immovable. He criticized the national leaders and seemed benignly to view the nation's enemies. But the opposition was not total. Friendships crossed the divide. Debate was continuous. There was shared affirmation of Jewish history and revelation. The most fundamental political revolution ever was formed in relation to these political groups, and we need to see them accurately. We begin our review with the colonial power: Rome.

Roman Imperial Rule

Roman imperial rule shaped much of Western history. Never has an empire been so dominant and permanent in world history, lasting nearly half a millennium. Its self-conception was to bring *civilization* to the known world through its roads, rule, religion, cities, infrastructure, law, and culture. The Jewish lands were part of the empire, but not an insignificant part. Some talk of Israel as a minor kingdom in the Roman Empire, but that is not really true. Herod the Great had raised its reputation; he provided patronage to Sparta, Athens, Rhodes, Chios, Pergamum, Laodicea, Tripolis, Byblus, Berytus (Beirut), Tyre, Sidon,

Ptolemais (in Egypt), Ascalon, Damascus, and Antioch—an incredible contribution to the empire.[7] Jerusalem was a world-class city, and Jewish religion was significant throughout the eastern Mediterranean. The Jews were important to Roman foreign policy, and the way they were governed was carefully thought through. The nature of Roman rule at the time of Jesus is an intriguing issue. After all, Jesus died a Roman death, decided by the procurator/prefect.

One view is that the Romans were powerful occupiers, dominating, creating fear, and avoided by the natives, who carried on their lives under oppression, never referring to the overlords and seeking to avoid contact as much as possible. Like Big Brother, they are always there. Though in a background sense this was true, it does not seem to have been the whole picture. Rather, the control Rome exercised at this time was withdrawn and quite muted. The Romans had repeatedly shown that when rebellion occurred, they had the military might and discipline to suppress it. On Herod the Great's death, rebellions were ruthlessly put down by Varus, the Roman commander. In 3 BC he systematically moved through the territory with a band of allies, destroying opposition. In AD 70 the efficiency of this military machine was again evident, and the Romans imposed control through death and terrible destruction (of Jerusalem and the Temple). During the period covered by the Gospels, a long generation away from both these events, Roman rule seemed quiet and rather relaxed.

The general ethos came from Tiberius Caesar. In AD 26 he retired to Capri and intimated that he wanted an empire without disturbances. We have noted the relative passivity of Roman rule. The legate of Syria would only intervene if there was a serious disturbance, and it would take some months for the reprisal to take place. The legate could call on four Roman legions and a formidable number of allies for troops, but he was a withdrawn and ultimate threat. The ruthless Roman military machine was there in Syria, and it was effective, but both Jew and Roman wanted to make sure that it did not come to that. The Roman presence in Galilee and Perea was quite limited and eclipsed by the Herodian system of military control. In Samaria and Judea the Roman military and political presence was light. They had, for example, only one cohort of five hundred in Jerusalem; with a million or so at the feasts, this was a token presence. At Caesarea, the best guess is that there were some three thousand troops, but these were mainly auxiliaries recruited from among the Sebastenes rather than Romans. So the Roman army was a few hundred soldiers making the Roman presence felt, with the ultimate threat from Syria, and with effective control delegated to Herodian and Jewish rule. The legions would march in only to handle serious trouble.[8]

This fits with the broader historical perspective. On Herod's death Rome had faced rebellion and put it down, reimposing its control on this troubled area without its previous loyal ruler. Rebellion had been followed by awesome military reprisal by the superpower, and the natives now knew the score. In AD 66 the mother of all rebellions would occur in Galilee and later in Judea. It, too, would be put down, with more than a million hacked by the sword. Between these two great rebellions, Roman military control was accepted as inevitable and in the background rather than dominating politics.[9] Jews knew enough Roman politics—the murder of Julius Caesar, the war between Octavius and Anthony, and the checkered career of Tiberius—to know that the Roman Empire could fragment and lose its ability to exercise this control. But normally it was unassailable. The Jews were waiting, but the time was not yet.

Meanwhile, as long as the Jews accepted Roman rule, their internal government could be largely their own business. Caesarea was remote, on the coast; the governor's main location suggested distance and withdrawal. He wanted to keep the territory quiet, but beyond that he had no ambitions. There were, of course, disturbances with which the procurator had to deal, but in reality the Jews were free to grow their own political institutions and could have quite a strong sense of autonomy and power to bargain with their Roman rulers. The relationship was complex. Rome wanted its colonies to be effectively governed and knew that uprisings were dangerous. If its crack legions were away, putting down a rebellion in Judea, other insurrections could start elsewhere. Tiberius governed to maintain the Pax Romana, and the procurators did not want to create trouble, but the same was also true of the Jewish leaders. They knew that if there was an uprising, Roman control would instantly become total and destroy their power. A colonial peace gave them considerable scope.

Before and after Archelaus's short rule, the Jews avidly asked for direct rule from Rome. This seems strange, but it was not. It was smart politics. For if the Romans only exercised background control, the practicalities of government moved to the Sanhedrin, to a Jewish rather than a Herodian government. Rule from Rome removed the layer of Herodian rule and gave the Sanhedrin more scope for expanding its power. Josephus records the way Pilate had to back down from displaying Caesar's standards in Jerusalem; the crowd refused to be intimidated by Pilate's threat to cut them to pieces. In a later incident, some of the crowd were cudgeled to death by Pilate's disguised soldiers. There was a continual battle for power between the obstreperous Jews and the vindictive Pilate. Jesus' death was another defeat for Pilate in the face of the crowd and the Sanhedrin. As we have seen, Pilate later faced the

Samaritans' protest to Vitellius, the Syrian legate, and was required to go to Rome, where he may have been forced to commit suicide.[10] The relative light-handedness of Roman rule during this period is evident. As Schürer says, "Josephus . . . considers, not incorrectly, the Roman governor only as an overseer, while the aristocratic Sanhedrin acted as the real governing body."[11] Thus, the Romans do not feature much in the Gospels because they exercised little direct control.

The Romans also refrained from interfering with Jewish law and jurisdiction, except when passing the death sentence, a control of last resort. Temple worship was protected and even supported. The procurator's right to choose the high priest was used passively. No wonder the Jewish parties had a growing sense of confidence in their role. Nevertheless, the Romans were there. The empire, although troubled, was firm under Tiberius. The underlying system of legitimation was military victory and dominance, and the cruelty and viciousness of conquest and reconquest had shaped Jewish culture. Most knew, like Herod, that they could not argue with Roman might. Older people had memories of seeing horrible slaughter. And everyone at some time or another saw a Roman soldier and hated or tolerated their presence. Over the years many Jews had learned to work with and for them, for Rome depended on indigenous groups to run the system. The Herodians and Sanhedrin gained from Roman rule in different ways and kept it running on track. In turn, they, with the Romans, established a pattern of employment, requiring builders, servants, cooks, stewards, and tax collectors. These were people working within the Roman system. They constituted a dependent class of perhaps a fifth of the population, employed directly or indirectly within the Roman-Herodian system.

The Herods and the Herodians

In the north the "Herodians," or more accurately the tetrarchs Antipas and Philip and the groups who served them, were in power, the representatives of Roman government. There was the external Roman military threat from Syria, but Antipas and Philip were the military presence in the area. Later in Antipas's life, he was accused of having the equipment for seventy thousand heavily armed foot soldiers in his armories. He accepted the truth of the statement, even though his brother-in-law, Agrippa, falsely used it to damn him before Caligula. He certainly had thousands of soldiers garrisoned throughout his territory, guaranteeing his uncontested rule and backing the Roman military.[12] Herod the Great's sons also had their own needs for self-glorification and reflected the Roman idiom of dominance, taxation, and extravagant expenditure.

They aimed to keep the Romans happy with tribute and to have a stable state. These Herods were religiously distant from the Jews and more linked to the Greek and Roman culture of their overlords. As much as the Romans themselves, they were the colonial presence, though with attitudes based more on expedience than love of Rome.

For thirty or so years, Herod Antipas kept a system of firm control in Galilee and Perea. It was a relatively simple system of military control, without the complexities of Jerusalem politics except that Herod also used various groups to run the system. He governed through a series of toparchies, with local governors who related to him as administrators, reporting back and receiving orders. Crucial were his cities, especially Sepphoris, Tiberias, and Livias, and he moved around his domain from one city or fortress to another. Antipas had a system of administrators subject to his personal will, and soldiers went out into the area to enforce tax collection. The *publicani*, his tax collectors, were a Herodian group. Jesus and the disciples, with one or two exceptions, were outside this Herodian system, living away from Herodian strongholds. But this informal apartheid was far from complete. The Herodians were around (Mark 3:6; 12:13). Some of them, as well as Herod himself, were influenced by Jesus. Chuza, the manager of Herod's household, was based at Tiberias or Sepphoris, and Joanna, his wife, followed Jesus and traveled with him, an extraordinary act for the wife of one of Herod's chief officials (Luke 8:3).

Although the evidence is inconclusive, it seems likely that Antipas and Philip paid tribute to Rome and collected the necessary taxes so to do. We will consider taxes in detail in chapter 10. In Judea people paid taxes "to Caesar"; in Galilee the taxes went first to Antipas, who funded his city building, lifestyle, and soldiers from the difference between his income and the tribute he passed on to Rome. Thus, he followed his father's pattern. Matthew and his friends were tax collectors for Herod rather than directly for Rome (Matt. 9:9). With his Herodian background and base in Capernaum, Matthew was especially aware of John the Baptist's significance, the Pharisees' usual (but see Mark 3:6) hostility to the Herodians, the local centurion, and Jesus' Galilean ministry.

In the north the Herodians as a party were obviously allied to Herod. Many of them were in the ambit of Herod's cities, drawn by the money that his court, building, administration, and government required. Antipas probably taxed heavily, at about 25 percent per annum. Many Jews resented this, but others fastened on to his considerable expenditure, after he had paid tribute to Rome, as their livelihood. Since it was perhaps 15 percent or more of the overall economy, it had great weight as it was spent in and around Sepphoris, Tiberias, and elsewhere. This group of traders, workers, merchants, and tax collectors would be seen as "on Herod's side." As an affluent group, they would be happy with the status quo and want nothing to disturb it. They would be relatively indifferent to the Jewish faith, focusing more on the realities of politics and accepting Herodian domination. Those outside this economy only felt the weight of the taxes and hostility toward the Herodians.

There are suggestions that the Sadducees were linked with the Herodians. These were politic but hardly cuddly relationships. The Herodians were not "religious" (in our usual terms) and were willing to form any alliances that supported their interests. The Sadducees were probably long-term allies, wanting to be near the seat of power for political advantage, land, and contracts, while coming to terms with Herodian rule. They are the establishment—conservative, rich, leisured, and not popular. They tend to be in favor of the status quo and therefore are naturally Herodian. While on the Sea of Galilee, Jesus warns his disciples, "Be on your guard against the yeast [teaching] of the Pharisees and Sadducees" (Matt. 16:6–12). The parallel passage in Mark refers to the Pharisees and Herodians (Mark 8:15n NRSV). This may mean that the Sadducees had a political modus vivendi somewhat similar to the Herodians—the land-owning establishment that was willing to work with Pilate or Antipas, as the case may be.[13]

The Pharisees are much more antagonistic to the Herodians, hating their lack of religiosity. Through the synagogue system the Pharisees work to maintain popular support for God-fearing religious practices. Yet in Galilee the Pharisees go out, quite early in Jesus' ministry, and begin to plot with the Herodians how to kill him (Mark 3:6). This is a reaction to Jesus' defeat of their Sabbatarianism and a link made by mutual antipathy to Jesus. Nor is it completely consistent, for the Pharisees later warn Jesus to avoid Herod in Perea (Luke 13:31).

The position in the south is different. Here Archelaus has been deposed and replaced by direct Roman rule. The Herodians have been removed from power, and the Temple party and the Sanhedrin are at the center of things. This rankles the Herodians, and they seek to get back in power, as they will in AD 41 with Herod Agrippa I. Throughout Jesus' ministry the Herodians in Judea are more like a party seeking power. Philo reports how they operate, demonstrating a rather exaggerated reaction to some votive shields that Pilate placed in the palace of Herod, his own abode in Jerusalem. The "multitude pushed forward four sons of the king [Herod the Great], who were in no respect inferior to the kings themselves, in fortune or rank, and his other descendants, and magistrates."[14] This shows the Herodians operating in Jerusalem as a coherent party, probably stirring up the incident because "their" palace is involved, possibly during Jesus' ministry in AD 32.[15] Again we note Pharisees and Herodians cooperating to try to trap Jesus in his words at

Jerusalem. They are possibly drawn together by their shared antagonism to the Temple party and the Romans (Matt. 22:15; Mark 12:13).

Thus, the Herodians defend the Roman status quo in the north, including the taxes and tax collecting. They gain from lucrative deals surrounding Herodian patronage, including land deals. They participate more in Greek and Roman culture, in Herodian court life, and are socially and culturally segregated from ordinary Jewish people. For this group, the Jewish nationalist traditions of fighting for independence, linked with a deep religious commitment, is a danger that needs suppressing. At the same time, if Antipas has enough influential Jews who are happy with the status quo, he has a stable regime. In Galilee many have accommodated in this way. However, Herodians in Judea want the procurator removed and a Herod reinstated. In both Galilee and Judea, the Herodians come to be convinced that Jesus must die. They fear an attack on their oppressive system of control and taxation. Both John the Baptist and Jesus could mobilize the righteous indignation of the crowds against Herodian rule and generate a popular uprising.

Personally, Herod Antipas faces the particular fact that Jesus' position on divorce and adultery is even stronger than John's. Herodias would feel even more insecure with Jesus around than she did with John (Matt. 14:1–12; 19:1–9, esp. v. 9, directly addressing Antipas and Herodias). In some strange way, Jesus threatens Herodian rule, but they cannot establish what the threat is. Herodians are unprincipled, do not care about God, and are outside the content and significance of Pharisaic teaching. The local populations have established procedures for keeping out of their way and despise them on practical grounds for extracting grinding taxes and inflicting other forms of suffering.

The Scribes and the Pharisees

In Galilee, the Scribes and Pharisees were probably the next most powerful party. The Scribes represented a tradition in which God-fearing observance and teaching of the law is seen as central to Jewish faith and national life. The Hasidim (Hasideans), or Righteous Ones, were a long-standing group going back two hundred years, who read the Mosaic law and taught it to the people as Scribes (writers of the law), teachers, or rabbis (cf. 1 Macc. 2:42). It is important not to see them as only religious. They were part lawyers, educators, political party, and religious leaders, and it is difficult for us to grasp their full significance. Teaching the Torah is training people how to live; it is education that explains the central meaning of human life and is based on authority from God. They were the educated group in an otherwise relatively uneducated culture and on these grounds felt themselves to be an elite. This group, partly in contradistinction to the priesthood, thus claimed to be central to the culture of the Jews, though as Sanders points out, the priests also taught.[16] That was why it was a surprise when Jesus came from nowhere and started scything through their arguments.

As well as being an educated elite, they also contended for the religio-political direction of Jewish life. Does the nation focus on the Temple or the Mosaic law? Broadly speaking, the priests focused on the Temple, and the Pharisees and rabbis on the law. The Torah was to direct Jewish national life. The polarity can be seen incidentally in one of Jesus' late conversations. A teacher of the law has an open discussion of mutual respect with Jesus, asking him to name the most important commandment. The fuller account is in Mark. Jesus answers, "'Hear, O Israel, the Lord our God, the Lord is one. Love the Lord your God with all your heart and with all your soul and with all your mind and with all your strength.' The second is this, 'Love your neighbor as yourself.' There is no commandment greater than these" (Mark 12:28–31). Jesus is careful to present them as commands for the nation and gives this central awesome summary. It is a glorious statement of what life is about. The teacher, obviously impressed, praises Jesus as a rabbi and affirms all he is saying by repeating it, a common response of student to rabbi. He then adds that these commandments are more important than all burnt offerings and sacrifices—the practices involved in the Temple system (v. 33). Without overstating the opposition, law *or* Temple is clearly an issue between the two groups. After this interchange, no one dares to ask Jesus questions. He is in neither camp. The last word on the law has been spoken in the Temple courts. In Jesus, the God of Torah and Temple is more directly focused than could be conceived in the procedural debates of these two groups.

The Pharisees had also become a *party*. They had been powerful under the Maccabees and Antipater, but Herod the Great distrusted and marginalized them. More than that, he also crushed them. After he came to power, he killed forty-five of the seventy-one members of the Sanhedrin and filled up the numbers with more docile people.[17] A lot of those killed would have been Pharisees. Later in his reign he killed others. As a result, they had organized themselves much more as a grassroots organization, with direct appeal to the people. As teachers, rabbis, they had moved out and begun a town-by-town teaching of Torah. They helped found synagogues, or teaching halls, where their scribes could expound the Torah, and the synagogues became the focus of many villages and towns. Perhaps the Pharisees lost some of the simplicity of the earlier scribes and became partisan, an exclusive group one might join after a period of probation. They built up a movement, numbering some six thousand nationwide at the time of Herod the Great and perhaps more later. Pharisees taught and were taught in schools gathered round the temple and also had influence there. The schools consisted of a senior rabbi and students, who undertook to learn from their master until they too became rabbis as inducted by established teachers. Jesus, though not one of their number, had the status of a senior rabbi just by the power of his teaching (e.g., John 1:38; 3:2). Graduating Pharisees then went out, established synagogues, and arranged for their own income through tithes and gifts "devoted to God" that were channeled in their direction.[18] They were partly dependent on ordinary work and were also in the business of establishing their own economic support. In modern parlance, they charged fees for their professional services. They had differing views and were in constant debate, caught up in their interpretations of the law on the understanding that their words were authoritative. The Talmud mentions seven schools of Pharisees with different emphases on law, purity, and observance; presumably these divisions were developing earlier. Thus, at the time of Jesus they were a powerful group, perhaps the best organized in the land. They had established a widespread synagogue movement and the presumed validity of their teaching at village level and in Jerusalem. All this made them a strong and successful political movement.

There is archaeological discussion as to when and where these synagogues were built. One in Jericho seems to be dated about 50 BC, and synagogues seem to reflect a relatively new movement, expanding especially strongly in Galilee and overseas before and during the time of Jesus.[19] Synagogues had benches along the sides and were more places of teaching than of worship and sacrifice.[20] They tended to be built on high ground. Although there are obscure earlier references to them, it is likely that they really began to expand under Herod the Great and became even more common under Antipas. It is interesting that the centurion whose servant is healed by Jesus has built, or provided the money for, the synagogue in his hometown, likely Capernaum (Luke 7:5). Similarly, we know that Jesus taught in Nazareth, a village of only one or two hundred. If synagogues had reached villages the size of Nazareth, they must have been widespread. It would be a good guess that although Jewish religion remained more Temple centered in Judea, in Galilee Pharisaic synagogue religion was more dominant, although still in competition with Temple worship.[21]

The teaching of the rabbis was religiopolitical. They worked to gain the people's support in order to become the dominant party in Judaism. The law defined the Jewish way of life and politics, and the rabbis were authoritative teachers of the law. They were not magicians, mystics, prophets, philosophers, or gnostics, but, as they saw it, carriers of God's law.[22] In the past, they had strong sympathy with the Zealots, because obeying God's law allowed no truck with Herod, Rome, and their heathen ways. They had been cold toward the Herodians. But as they became more powerful, their political stance changed slightly. Now they were going to negotiate from strength and their hold over the people. Rome did not appear to be going away, but the rabbis would gradually bargain and extend their power over the nation. Because they espoused a strong behavioral view of the way the law was to be fulfilled, and this was the focus of their energy, they tended not to make decisive political interventions. They also did not control the Temple system. But in every town, Torah interpreted in terms of their teaching was the orthodox understanding of the will of God. They debated its interpretation. Differences were partly framed as disputes between the schools of Hillel and Shammai. Hillel's focus was on developing wisdom, moving from textual example to principle or to a family of passages. Shammai's focus was more on behavioral rules. But really, there are a number of schools, local variations, and emerging traditions of commentary on Torah that are intrafamily debates establishing the *halakah*—the procedure and practice of the law. The Gospels are full of examples—Sabbath observance, hand washing, divorce law, tithing, prayer—a vast edifice that told people how to live. The rabbis were used to a certain kind of debate, but Jesus' scything critiques were more difficult to handle. There were political emphases—those who leaned to the Zealot-type of freedom group and those who supported the status quo. But, overwhelmingly, the law was the source of Jewish identity, and the Pharisees saw themselves as its actual and scribal custodians. The Scribe of Mark 12:28, the teacher of the law, is also described as a Pharisee in Matthew 22:34–35. How to observe the law was seen as the dominant issue in Jewish society, and the Pharisees carried and enhanced its authority.

Their main focus was on power within the Jewish nation. Often the Pharisees hankered after the national rebellion model. From the time of Herod the Great onward, there were links between Pharisees and Zealot leaders. Josephus, himself a Pharisee, later fought against the Romans before he changed sides. By the time of Jesus, the Pharisees may well have reached an accommodation with Herod Antipas, a kind of unwritten truce. The Pharisees would not be too awkward if in turn Herod would not impede their religious advance. But there was some animosity toward the Herodians simply because of their lack of respect for Torah. When Jesus goes to eat with Matthew and the other Herodian tax collectors in Capernaum, the Pharisees pour scorn on him for associating with such a group of people (Matt. 9:10–13). Much of their power over people consisted of such judgmental criticism. But generally in Jesus' day, the Pharisees do not quite hold central political power, though they have become strong in the Sanhedrin.

Nicodemus, a Pharisee, is one of the ruling Sanhedrin, and he comes to Jesus the night after Jesus has cleared the Temple of traders in an audacious move against the Temple system (John 2:13–3:21). Nicodemus seems unperturbed by Jesus' action. The Pharisees are close to power. Only a few years later, ambitious Saul, before conversion "a Pharisee, the son of a Pharisee" (Acts 23:6), may have been a member of the Sanhedrin approving the killing of Stephen (6:12–8:1, esp. 8:1). Later, with the obvious backing of the Sanhedrin, he goes from house to house, imprisoning Christians (9:1–2). Gamaliel, also a Pharisee, is Paul's teacher, probably the greatest in rabbinic tradition (22:3). In contrast to Saul, he intervenes in the Sanhedrin's trial of the apostles on their behalf (5:33–40). He presents the clinching argument in an early trial of Jesus' followers: "If their purpose or activity is of human origin, it will fail. But if it is from God, you will not be able to stop these men; you will only find yourselves fighting against God." This all suggests considerable Pharisaic influence within the Sanhedrin.

The Pharisees' position hung on the law: "Obey the law as we teach it, and God will bless you." God's law is close to the center of three religions. Judaism, as it emerged later, centers on observance of the interpreted Torah. Islam focuses on observance of Shariah law, which is deeply Jewish-dependent. Later we consider Jesus' shaping of the law's meaning. Pharisaic law was taught by rabbis and learned by the people. One part is *halakah*, telling people how to walk with God, prescriptive, presenting a binding ethic. Another part is *haggadah*, narrative that requires reflection. It is *midrash*, verse-by-verse interpretation, exegesis, and commentary, or *Mishnah*, topic-by-topic systematization. The full rabbinic method emerged in the Tannaitic period (c. 70–200), but it has its origins in the Pharisaic movements of Jesus' time. Teaching about purity, holy things, marriage and divorce, the Sabbath, and the festivals, clearly Pharisaic concerns, later emerged as orders in the *Mishnah*. In the Gospels, Jesus' critique is therefore crucial, as is the alternative view of God's law that he presents. The standard of Torah teaching, especially in outlying areas, was probably not very high, focusing on rules and prohibition. In Jerusalem it was sharper, with a pedagogic, legal, and religious concentration of thought equivalent to a substantial, elite university. Later rabbis—such as Johanan ben Zakkai, Nahum of Ginzo, and Akiba ben Joseph—continued the tradition up to and beyond the Jewish War, when it became definitive for the formation of Judaism.[23] But Pharisaism was probably at its height at the time of Jesus and the early church.[24] At this stage, the Pharisees were pressing for their views to be orthodoxy for the nation.

They faced opposition from Jesus, who repeatedly taught aga[...] them, as in the Sermon on the Mount: "Unless your righteousness s[...] passes that of the Pharisees and teachers of the law, you will certain[...] not enter the kingdom of heaven" (Matt. 5:20). This is deeply wounding. When you are sure of your relationship with God, to have it made this precarious excites fury. We can imagine the reaction among those who feel themselves to be more righteous than the common masses. "We give the people the law. He cannot dethrone our system and replace it with his own." After other woundings, they decide he has to go. So in Galilee they plot to kill him (Matt. 12:14). Later the Jerusalem Pharisees are pushed to the same conclusion.

The Sadducees and the Temple Party

It is quite difficult to establish who the Sadducees were.[25] Later Christian and rabbinic material does not have a strong grasp on them. Attempts through their name (some link them to Zadok, David's priest, or another Zadok) do not yield much fruit. They differed from the Pharisees on some beliefs, but these do not seem decisive, as though they were only ideologically opposed. The Sadducees apparently developed around the Hasmonean high priests. From the time of Herod the Great, the rulers relied on the Sadducees as the aristocratic group to provide the high priesthood and dominate the Sanhedrin. They were an established group of priests and aristocrats who were used to running Jewish society. They had access to power and wealth as the Temple taxes and gifts grew in scale. As such, they can properly be described as a *class* rather than a party—a political and religious establishment with less of a popular following than the Pharisees. Many Sadducees were priests, often in families continuing the tradition from one generation to the next. Although their focus was Jerusalem, many priests lived out of Jerusalem, coming in for their week of Temple services like Zechariah, John the Baptist's father (Luke 1:5). Again, the priests and the Sadducees were not the same group, but there was a strong overlap. At this time they tended to control the Jerusalem high priesthood and the Sanhedrin, perhaps because the Pharisees could be less trusted to go along with Roman requirements. The Sadducees appeared as Paul faced the Sanhedrin some thirty years later, shortly before his journey to Rome, although now rivaled in power by the Pharisees (Acts 23). So, although the Pharisees were dominant in town and village life, it was still the Sadducees who ran things. They are well-off, dismissive of the masses, aristocratic, and probably less strong in Galilee than in Judea. In Galilee they worked with and merged into the Herodians, but in Judea and Jerusalem they were the power brokers, leading the Sanhedrin, especially in the person of Annas, the deposed but still-powerful high priest. They were less intense than the Pharisees over legal observances and were critical of some Pharisaic inconsistencies. They had been close to the center of power for sixty or so years in some kind of collaboration with Rome, and they knew how things were done.

The Sadducees, however, were more than just a political establishment. The question they asked Jesus about resurrection and marriage was posed in a particularly convoluted style showing their effort to be clever. It presumed to discredit belief in resurrection by showing the impossibility of one woman being married to seven men at the same time. Their "learning" was a mode of inveterate arguing, for they inhabited the Temple area as their own and were often seen as rude. The Sadducees believed in the law of Moses but were prepared to question later rabbinic traditions, not seeing them as sacred in the way the Pharisees did. They denied fate, immortal souls (spirits), angels, and resurrection, and emphasized human choices between good and evil, prosperity and adversity (Acts 23:8).[26] One suspects that Temple observance, doing right by God, was seen as the normal route to God doing right by you. Not surprisingly, the Sadducees did well from the Temple system.

Some of them formed the Temple party. The Sadducees were a social group, held together by family ties, property, and educational loyalties, with natural links into the Temple. Yet the Temple system was so strong that it had its own dynamic and was run by a smaller elite, centered on the high priests. Since Herod's Temple had been built and in use, hundreds of thousands would flock to it with sacrifices and offerings several times a year. It was the only tourist trade that the ancient world knew, and at Passover a million or so would pour into the city, bringing a vast weight of gifts to the Temple. Add in the two-drachma (half-shekel) tax collected internationally from the Jews, and we see the immense wealth pouring into the coffers of this controlling group. It was a powerful economic force, more significant than the temple to Artemis (Diana) at Ephesus, which Paul encountered (Acts 19). The Temple was a great economic success story, and the Temple party, led by the high-priestly families, made it run efficiently, guarding against Roman interference and protecting their own revenue. The Temple party pushed for higher levels of attendance at the great religious festivals and more systematic payment of the Temple tax. It partly competed with the synagogue system and Pharisaic loyalties. Because of their wealth and accumulation, the Temple party was strongly hated by some and not at all popular.

The Temple party and Sadducees were the major group in the Sanhedrin. This body was deeply political and effectively the Jewish government. It was the court deciding all noncapital matters of justice and executive decision and maintaining its moral authority over the people. The Sanhedrin were the elders of the people, what Africans would call "tribal chiefs." They were required to meet in the Temple courts, a procedural rule broken in Jesus' trial (Mark 14:53). The Sanhedrin was constantly pushing for its agenda and used the authority the Romans gave it to pursue its own ends. In Galilee, by contrast, Antipas had effective oversight of the Greek-style Council in Tiberias and did not face this kind of opposition. As Roman control appeared to weaken somewhat in the south, the leaders of the Sanhedrin became used to having their own way. But within the Sanhedrin, power was concentrated in the Temple party and especially in one family of the Sadducees. Annas ben Sethi was high priest between AD 6 and 15, and five of his sons served as high priest. This family dynasty ran the system in a distinct way. Feldman's evaluation emerges from the later literature: "The family of Annas was well known for its large size, wealth and power. Their greed in particular is bitterly attacked by the Rabbis, and the family's wealth appears to have been destroyed by the Zealots."[27] Joseph Caiaphas, son-in-law of Annas, was high priest between AD 18 and 36 (John 18:13). Annas and Caiaphas were two dominant figures in the Sanhedrin of seventy-one men.[28] The high priesthood and the Sanhedrin were the Jewish government in waiting. Previously high priest and king had been the same, and they could be so again, if the Roman rule were removed by a breakdown in the empire.

At the beginning of his ministry, Jesus attacks the Temple system (John 2). He rebukes the commercialism in the Temple courts and drives traders out, to reestablish the centrality of worshipping God. His attack frightens the high priesthood. They too know that the Temple is meant to be God's house, not theirs. Jesus' critique of the Sadducees continues. In the style of the prophets, he calls them a "wicked and adulterous generation" (breaking faith with God; Matt. 16:1–4). In a parable, the Samaritan cares when the priest does not—a smarting exposure (Luke 10:30–37). Long before the final confrontation, they too have decided that Jesus must go, and the Temple party, led by Annas and Caiaphas, calls for crucifixion. They have the power to bring about judicial murder if they can pressure Pilate into it. How does this one person attract so many enemies?

The Nationalists and the Zealots

At first sight, the "Zealots" do not appear as explicitly in the Gospels as other groups, but actually, as we shall see, they are fully present and important, in both Galilee and Jerusalem. There are a number of names in the literature for this group; they are Zealots, Sicarii (the dagger men or assassins at the time of the 66–70 Jewish uprising, perhaps emerging from the Essenes), Josephus's "Fourth Philosophy," bandits, and ordinary nationalists. Some see proper "Zealots" emerging later than Jesus, though Simon the Zealot was Jesus' disciple (Mark 3:18). The view taken here is fairly uncomplicated.[29] Whatever the name, *nationalists* were around throughout the hundred years from the time of Herod the Great's accession until the sack of Jerusalem. Whenever there was potential Roman or Herodian weakness, it would surge into the political arena. People generally looked to God for the Messiah as national deliverer, as Jesus' birth narratives testify. A smaller organized group saw Rome as a heathen insult to God and were prepared to fight to the death to remove the Romans. This group had a long history and earlier links to the Pharisees. Whatever they were called, they later became known as Zealots. Part of this group were terrorists or bandits, sniping from remote regions on the Herodians and Romans whenever they had the chance. Of course, whether they are seen as heroes or villains depends on one's viewpoint. This overall nationalist conviction was widespread at the time of Jesus and is evident throughout the Gospels, as we shall see.

Although our focus is on Jesus' era, we need to take some time looking at the history of the Zealots in Galilee and Judea. We know that thirty years after the resurrection the whole of Galilee was engulfed in a messianic uprising led by John of Gischala, connected with a place in the hills twelve miles north of Capernaum. It is not surprising that Gischala was the last place the Romans retook in Galilee.[30] The revolt spread to Judea and Jerusalem and was bloodily suppressed by the Romans in the great Jewish War of 66–70, the cataclysmic event that effectively destroyed the Jewish homeland.

Zealot dominance of policy at this stage is clear and detailed by Josephus. Here we face a problem with Josephus as historian. He was governor of Galilee, fighting against the Romans during the period preceding the final confrontation between the Jews and Romans in Jerusalem. When the Jews were obviously defeated, he defected to the Romans, survived, flourished, and wrote his history of the period. But because he was leaning toward the Zealot wing of the Pharisees, he had the problem of being an archenemy of Rome before his defection. In order to write this out of the plot, he obscured the history by making John of Gischala and the Zealots into cheating gangsters and troublemakers. He then cast himself and others as merely defending their home area as they best could. In order to wash his hands of fighting against the Romans, he interprets John of Gischala as "the most unprincipled trickster that ever won such ill fame by such vicious habits."[31] He also counts the Zealots as robbers or brigands.[32] This seems to deny what was actually the case: from the time of the Maccabees to the great Jewish War, there was a strong principled tradition of belief in a messianic national deliverer. If this tradition did exist in Galilee, it needs investigating because of its possible relationship to Jesus.

Bits of the historical jigsaw fit together. The first clear example in about 46 BC was the uprising of Hezekiah, whom Herod defeated when he was a young man. Although Josephus called him a bandit chief, the fact that Herod was brought before the Sanhedrin for killing Hezekiah and the other rebels suggests that they had strong legitimation in Jewish eyes and in the Pharisee-dominated Sanhedrin. This was no marginal group; they were the inheritors of the Maccabean tradition, with a lot of support in Galilee and Jerusalem. The Zealots and Pharisees had a similar distaste for Herod's dethroning of God as national ruler. Although the Zealots were not called such at this stage, the idea of a "zeal" for God's covenant that stood against Roman and Herodian oppression was firmly in place (cf. 1 Macc. 2:26–27; Num. 25:6–15).

The second incident occurs around the horrific scene Herod faced in the caves of Arbela (see ch. 1). Again Josephus describes the Zealots as bandits, but the label does not fit. He tells how "they went out to meet Herod with all the skill of warriors as well as the fearlessness of bandits, and joining battle routed Herod's left wing with their right."[33] These are freedom fighters, not robbers and looters. Their willingness to die in the caves later has all the hallmarks of principled nationalism. The Zealots were famous for their ability to bear pain and suffering in their cause. Their central conviction was that God is the only Lord of Israel and that it was wrong for Jews to submit to Rome, to taxation, or to any symbol of deity or absolute rule on Jewish soil. To rebel against Rome became a moral imperative, an expression of their righteousness before God.

Some thirty-three years later, Hezekiah's son Judas—a teacher of the law and no mere bandit, from Gamala (with its synagogue) in Gaulanitis—and Saddock (Sadduc), a Pharisee, mounted a further rebellion in 4 BC, after Herod's death. As we already noted, they overran Sepphoris, looted weapons from the royal arsenal, and staged a major coup. When it was quelled, many of the Jewish population in Sepphoris and the surrounding villages were enslaved or wiped out by the Romans as punishment for the uprising. When the holy family came back from Egypt two or three years after Jesus' birth, the area was devastated. Perhaps some of Mary's relatives were killed by the Roman wrath. Joseph and Mary would come back to decimated villages and grieving people. At the time of Jesus' teaching, nearly half the population would still remember the two thousand crucified bodies that lined the road. Indeed, this throws light on one of the incidents in the Gospels, the demon-possessed men of Gadara (Matt. 8:28–34; Mark 5:1–20; Luke 8:26–39). People who have seen death and mutilation suffer horror and trauma that drives them to madness or deep depression. It often involves suicidal depression and manic states. A World War I journalist describes shell shock, or what we now call traumatic stress disorder:

> I saw a sergeant-major convulsed like someone suffering from epilepsy. He was moaning horribly with blind terror in his eyes. He had to be strapped to a stretcher before he could be carried away. Soon afterwards I saw a soldier shaking in every limb, his mouth slobbering, and two comrades could not hold him still. These badly shell-shocked boys clawed their mouths ceaselessly.[34]

It is possible that many of the healings and exorcising of demons Jesus undertook in Galilee had this origin. "Legion," living among the tombs, mutilating himself, and uncontrollable, may have been deranged by the vast influx of Roman soldiers with their cruelty. "Swear to God that you won't torture me!" he cries (Mark 5:7). Jesus asks him to name the demon, and he gives a Roman name: "Legion, for we are many." Then Jesus casts the evil spirits into the pigs and leaves the man clothed and in his right mind. He sends him back to his family to tell them what God has done for him and his experience of God's mercy. So, patiently, Jesus is healing the wounds of war.

The nationalist convictions continued through the period of Jesus' ministry, but they were contained by the efficiency of Antipas's rule. The people who stayed committed to the cause were pushed back into the hills and became terrorists, mounting occasional raids on the Herodians and even the Romans. Further south the Jerusalem–Jericho road was a notorious place for this kind of attack, with robbers quickly escaping into the hills. Jesus' disciple Simon the Zealot was from Galilee. The Zealot messianic hope grew like pressure in a vessel until it finally exploded in the great destructive revolt and Jewish War of 66–70. Then the apocalyptic hope of the Zealots for national freedom was carried in a frenzy from northern Galilee down into Judea and Jerusalem, right through to its horrific final defeat at Masada (73).

It is this tragic history that Jesus addresses. Later we shall see that drama unfold. At the time of Jesus, the Galileans look avidly for a Zealot leader, but Jesus of Nazareth is not that man. He stands independent of the political culture of his day, proclaiming another way. Nor is the Zealot mood just in Galilee. In the end Barabbas, "a man . . . in prison with the insurrectionists who had committed murder in the uprising" (Mark 15:7)—in other words, a Zealot—is released to the seething crowd, and Jesus is crucified. As Hengel notes, Barabbas was well known in

Jerusalem, and the crowds bayed their support for him.[35] Jesus stands uncompromisingly outside this position.

Yet in Jesus' time the nationalist perspective was strong and burned in the hatreds and hopes of ordinary people. The tax burden, Roman and Herodian soldiers, Herod's viciousness, and the disrespect of Roman culture for the Jewish God—all these rankled the Jews. The Pharisees had not fully lost their links to Zealot hope, even though they largely accommodated to Herod. But in one sense, political nationalism threatened their carefully constructed ideology of Torah, offering more immediate popular appeal. For many it was just a question of *when* and *where* the uprising could occur to destroy the Romans and Herodians. It did not seem to be yet.

The Essenes

The profile of the Essene communities has been raised by work on the Dead Sea Scrolls, and some commentators have become excited about their relationship with Jesus and the Gospels. We can locate them fairly well geographically, religiously, and politically. Their main locus was near the Dead Sea at Qumran and in the southwest corner of Jerusalem. They had some communities elsewhere, probably a few in the north. The Essenes were linked to, but more extreme than, the Pharisees. They were what sociologists would describe as an ascetic sect, partly against marriage, with tight rules, mainly living in community so as not to be corrupted by the rest of society. They had a history of some two hundred years, possibly back even to exiles returning from Babylon, and were formed under "The Teacher of Righteousness," the high priest deposed by Jonathan Maccabee in 152 BC.[36] With him they moved into a marginal, withdrawn religious position. They were also introspective and apocalyptic, believing their way would finally be vindicated by God. The community had a heavy internal discipline, like a closed monastic order. Their teaching generated certain kinds of knowledge, and they became absorbed in texts and special meanings. They sought perfection in relation to God by isolation from the wider community. The Dead Sea Scrolls show a focus on community rules, hymns, calendars, liturgies, apocalyptic, wisdom literature, and Old Testament (OT) and apocryphal interpretation. Their dominant concern was to maintain ritual purity before God.

Their fundamental political stance was shaped by their founder's withdrawal from political power and the high priesthood. As a result, they were more intensely religious and related to politics with distaste or through apocalyptic. They tended to eschew marriage, and they shared property, observed ritual purity, developed their own sacred literature, and did not spit to the right.[37] They also looked to God's Messiah, but as a cultic hope. There was a contrast between these withdrawn, apolitical communities and Jesus' and the early Christians' everyday engagement with life and politics. The Essenes do not feature in the Gospels because they were so withdrawn. Although some like to paint Christianity as otherworldly, its cultural distance from this kind of sect shows it to be different. Rather than withdraw, Jesus headed for the eye of the political storm. The Essenes shed little light on this process, nor were they involved in its dynamics. Far more important were the ordinary people.

The People

The previous groups were parties in a definable sense. They had a position and orientation to the politics of the day. With the exception of the Essenes, they were political parties and not just or mainly religious ones. And as parties they related to the people, not precisely in the modern democratic sense, but with strong persuasive patterns of engagement. Jesus notes that the Pharisees travel about trying to win converts (Matt. 23:15). The Gospels are full of crowds, and whose side they are on matters. We identify "democratic" politics with obtaining the vote, ignoring how important the demos (common people) have been through much of history. Crowds frequently appear in the Gospels and clearly know their own potential power. They are dangerous to rulers suppressing people, because they can and do lead to revolutions, uprisings, and rebellion.

Yet people who are poor, overworked, and unorganized can also be subdued out of politics. This was partly true of the Galilean people, but they had some of the independence of peasants. Armies can come in and sort them out for a while, but the natives can melt into the hills and arm themselves, and this is really their land. They have stamina and can survive. It is a lesson both Russia and the West have learned more recently in Afghanistan and Iraq. The people can even take matters into their own hands. So the power of the people is negotiated, unpredictable, partly controlled, used, and flows through the events of ancient and modern politics.

Crowds feature in Galilee, as we shall see, but it is in Jerusalem that awe-inspiring crowd dynamics take place. When something like a million people gather there for the festival, trooping in from Judea, Galilee, and overseas into a great throbbing throng, the drama is palpable, and the crowd becomes a political force. A near equivalent is the Notting Hill Carnival or Millennium night in central London, or a New Year's celebration in New York's Times Square. The worry is about being crushed to death. Here is a potential like that of revolutionary Paris or Moscow. Policing must be heavy. The authorities have spies out reporting on the crowds. The Romans especially know this is the danger time, and what the people think becomes of paramount importance. These dynamics we encounter later in the Gospels. Of course, the people are not usually a coherent bloc. They mostly consist of groups, with ebbs and flows of interest. Crowds are also discrete persons, each with lives, attitudes, and relationships. Jesus relates to the crowds, but also insists on addressing persons. He seems to discourage massification and whipping crowds into fervor. His early reflection on a crowd is recorded by Matthew: "When he saw the crowds, he had compassion on them, because they were harassed and helpless, like sheep without a shepherd" (Matt. 9:36). Led by the wrong people, they could suffer intensely, as indeed they did.

The Rulers and Parties

This review of the different groups gives us a perception of the political dynamics of the Jewish people, albeit a limited one. We can see something of the viciousness of the Romans and Herodians as rulers. We can also see the weaknesses of the parties pushing for power. Nationalism leads to calamity. The Temple system is exploitative. The Pharisees demand their own conformity. Sadducees are predictably status quo. These groups are no different in kind from later parties. They consist of people who believe they are largely right and understand the way for the nation. They work for a political vision. There are sometimes brave and God-fearing people, but also people operating with compromised motives. As the interaction of these parties with the events of the Gospels unfolds, we see a process that could occur in the national or international sections of our newspapers today. It is a normal set of political dynamics. The enigma is the one who interacts with all of them, but stands outside them, who has a different perspective on politics.

We have to be careful how we read these events. All of us, whether Christian or non-Christian, live in the years of our Lord (AD) and have probably absorbed some of Jesus' understanding and perspective. We need to reflect on how unprecented these teachings and actions were. In the past some people have tried to show that Jesus was a product of the culture of his day. My perception as a cultural sociologist is that he taught and operated in ways completely different from these groups. This is a way of politics that cuts across all these groups. For the most part, they cannot understand what Jesus is about. It is so different from anything that has gone before. Even today, with long historical exposure to the tradition, the views will probably still seem joltingly different. Contemporary rule is often constructed on calculations similar to the Herodians or Sadducees. Western economic, political, and military imperialism, sired by the Roman Empire, has marked the last two hundred years. There is continual popular management through media and political bribes. Parties vie for power and are convinced their ideologies are right. Established groups want to maintain their position. Awkward or dangerous groups have to be done away with. In all of these ways, the politics of Galilee and Judea are similar to our own.

Our focus will now be on Jesus' relationships with these groups and his own political contributions. Then, as now, politics was a life-and-death issue, touching life, justice, nation, war, law, and God. The Nazarene may help us to see beyond our present comprehending, and of that we have a desperate need.

Bibliography

Andrews, C. F. *Mahatma Gandhi's Ideas*. London: George Allen & Unwin, 1921.

Avery-Peck, Alan J., Jacob Neusner, and Bruce D. Chilton. *The Judaism of Qumran: A Systematic Reading of the Dead Sea Scrolls*. Part 5 of *Judaism in Late Antiquity*. 2 vols. Leiden: Brill, 2001.

Binder, Donald D. *Into the Temple Courts: The Place of Synagogues in the Second Temple Period*. Atlanta: Society of Biblical Literature, 1999.

Bowker, John. *Jesus and the Pharisees*. Cambridge: Cambridge University Press, 1973.

Cook, Michael J. *Mark's Treatment of the Jewish Leaders*. Leiden: Brill, 1978.

Cullman, Oscar. *The State in the New Testament*. London: SCM, 1957.

Falk, Harvey. *Jesus the Pharisee: A New Look at the Jewishness of Jesus*. New York: Paulist Press, 1985.

Garcia Martinez, Florentino, and Julius Trebelle Barrera. *The People of the Dead Sea Scrolls*. Leiden: Brill, 1995.

Gnilka, Joachim. *Jesus of Nazareth: Message and History*. Translated by Siegfried Schatzman. Peabody, MA: Hendrickson, 1997.

Hengel, Martin. *Was Jesus a Revolutionist?* Philadelphia: Fortress, 1971.

———. *Victory over Violence*. London: SPCK, 1975.

———. *The Zealots: Investigations into the Jewish Freedom Movement in the Period from Herod I until 70 A.D.* Translated by David Smith. Edinburgh: T&T Clark, 1989.

———. *The Pre-Christian Paul*. London: SCM; Philadelphia: Trinity, 1991.

Horbury, William, et al., eds. *The Early Roman Period.* Vol. 3 of *The Cambridge History of Judaism.* Cambridge: Cambridge University Press, 1999.

Jeremias, Joachim. *Jerusalem in the Time of Jesus.* London: SCM, 1969.

Kampen, John. *The Hasideans and the Origin of Pharisaism: A Study in 1 and 2 Maccabees.* Atlanta: Scholars Press, 1988.

McLaren, James S. *Power and Politics in Palestine: The Jews and the Governing of Their Land, 100 BC–AD 70.* Journal for the Study of the New Testament, Supplement Series 63. Sheffield: JSOT Press, 1991.

Mendels, Doron. *The Rise and Fall of Jewish Nationalism.* New York: Doubleday, 1992.

Saldarini, Anthony J. *Pharisees, Scribes and Sadducees in Palestinian Society.* Edinburgh: T&T Clark, 1989.

Sanders, E. P. *Judaism: Practice and Belief.* London: SCM, 1992.

Stemberger, Gunter. *Jewish Contemporaries of Jesus: Pharisees, Sadducees, Essenes.* Minneapolis: Fortress, 1995.

Weber, Max. *Ancient Judaism.* Translated and edited by Hans Gerth and Don Martindale. New York: Free Press, 1952.

Jesus and John the Baptist

John the Baptist as Prophet

As Jesus begins his teaching, John the Baptist is already acknowledged as a great prophet whose words cut into politics in both Judea and Galilee. This is true throughout his ministry and even after his death at the hands of Herod Antipas. From several decades later Josephus offers an interesting insight on John. It is in relation to the defeat of Herod Antipas in a war against Aretus IV, the Nabataean king to the east of Herod's territory.[1]

But to some of the Jews, the destruction of Herod's army seemed to be divine vengeance, and certainly, a just vengeance, for his treatment of John, surnamed the Baptist. For Herod had put him to death, though he was a good man and had exhorted the Jews to live righteous lives, to practice justice towards their fellows and piety towards God, and so doing to join in baptism. In his view this was a necessary preliminary if baptism was to be acceptable to God. They must not employ it to gain pardon for whatever sins they committed, but as a consecration of the body implying that the soul was already thoroughly cleansed by right behaviour. When others too joined the crowds about him, because they were aroused to the highest degree by his sermons, Herod became alarmed. Eloquence that had so great an effect on mankind might lead to some form of sedition, for it looked as if John would guide them in everything that they did. Herod decided therefore that it would be better to strike first and be rid of him before his work led to an uprising, than to wait for an upheaval, get involved in a difficult situation and see his mistake. Though John, because of Herod's suspicions, was brought in chains to Machaerus, the stronghold that we have previously mentioned, and there put to death, yet the verdict of the Jews was that the destruction visited upon Herod's army was a vindication of John, since God saw fit to inflict such a blow on Herod.[2]

John was thus the chief early critic of Herod Antipas's reign. He was a considerable political figure, potentially the one around which an uprising could take place. Josephus's view is one from outside Jesus' circle and offers a removed perspective. The Gospel portrait is more intimate. Jesus and John share significance in the womb and at birth. Their mothers commune together about their sons, as John the Baptist leaps in the womb at the arrival of the pregnant Mary (Luke 1:39–56).[3] Zechariah faces a vision in the Temple about the name and identity of his firstborn as a prophet, rather than a priest like himself. Eventually he declares his son to be "John," the prophet of God, preparing the way of the Lord (1:59–80).

But what is a "prophet"? Prophecy is an important Old Testament tradition, and one to which Jesus frequently makes reference. Jewish prophets called the people and their rulers to God and God's law. They did not fight or try to impose the law, but merely proclaimed it faithfully and took the consequences. They rekindled a sense of God's dealings with the people and brought God's law to the hearts of the people and the rulers. They insisted on people facing God in their lives, and they were political. From Elijah through to Jeremiah, they challenged the rulers of Israel and Judah to walk with God and obey God's law. Nor were they just parochial in their concerns. They addressed the empires of Egypt, Assyria, and Babylon with the word of the Lord, and Daniel's prophecies were honed to the Neo-Babylonian and Persian empires. In part, they were like God's official opposition, commenting on and critiquing government in the light of God's purposes and law. More than just foretelling, they addressed the future in terms that looked beyond human plans to God's deeper way. Man proposes, but God disposes. Sometimes, God proposes and rulers or nations do their own thing, but then folly and judgment inevitably become evident. Prophets carry God's way to the rulers and people.

Because this tradition is partly lost in modern politics, we need to reflect on it as political theology. Throughout much of history, politics has operated on its own terms, normally those of the rulers or elites with power and ideological clout. It is seen as humanly self-defined, as autonomous, autocratic, democratic, or oligarchic. The participants are always preoccupied with themselves and gaining power within the system. But here in the Hebrew Scriptures is an utterly different perspective. The prophets look on politics with God's purview. They hold governments accountable for justice, care of the poor, and peace. Repeatedly, when prophet meets king, the latter is under judgment. The kings threaten death to the prophets, put them in cisterns, or chase them into deserts, but the word of God weighs heavier in the balances, because that is what it is. It insists that things are not the way the rulers see them, and God's perspective is different and authoritative.

John was in this tradition, but it had atrophied. The true prophets—there were also false prophets, who flattered and sought preferment or were just shallow crowd-pleasers—had ceased with Malachi some five hundred years earlier. Why had the prophetic sense of God's word departed from the people during this long era? Perhaps the religious nationalism of the Maccabees ruled out the kinds of criticism dished out by Isaiah and Jeremiah, although they had hardly been popular. Often prophecy was fiercely critical of the nation's people and rulers and regarded as "unpatriotic." It was a tradition of searching rigor, pointing out wrongs, self-indulgence, shallow principles, and injustice.[4] Prophecy did not pander to the people. If the focus is solely on the enemy and defeating the colonial power, there is less space for reflection on God's words of judgment and accountability. For whatever reason, the great external critique of politics on God's terms, really the source of much human healing, was silenced. Yet around the birth of Jesus comes a restoration of the prophetic tradition, but now among the little people. Anna, Simeon, Zechariah, and Mary herself prophesy. Finally, John is to become the greatest of the prophets, the one who will midwife the rebirth of politics on God's terms.

His home is in the south, the Judean hill country, reasonably close to Jerusalem, where his father served in the Temple one or two times a year. He was a kinsman of Jesus, probably a more distant relative than cousin, because it was unlikely that the young Mary was sister to the ancient Elizabeth. Luke tells of Mary coming to her kinswoman, Elizabeth, and of the old pregnant woman feeling her child whoop it up in the womb. "Why am I so favored that the mother of my Lord should come to me?" (Luke 1:43). The inner revealed link in the births of Jesus and John would be shared in both families, but after the scare of the Bethlehem massacre, it would be kept quiet and not known more widely. Because of the distance from Nazareth to Judea, John and Jesus would rarely meet, except perhaps around the time of Passover, when they travel with their families to Jerusalem. The calling of John is precisely located in Luke (3:1–2) to about a year or so before Jesus' ministry began. As opposed to the *priestly* role of his father, John is called by God to a mighty *prophetic* task, as his dad already knew.

John's calling leads him into the desert near the Jordan. The geography is important. He preaches in the desert partly because he will be put in prison if the politicians get their hands on him. John needs twenty miles between himself and those in power to be safe from arrest. He takes on everybody. His message is direct and confrontational: "You brood of vipers!" Snakes, wriggling, all coiled together, venomous. This is addressed to the Pharisees and Sadducees, the Jerusalem rulers (Matt. 3:7). "Who warned you to flee from the coming wrath?" The message cuts into the kind of politics these leaders are pursuing. They are calculating the most expeditous policies for their agenda: a steady growth in Temple and synagogue religion and making deals with the Romans. John brings them up sharply against the purposes of God and shows them that they are under judgment. More than this, he hunts them down. They trust in the superiority of the Jews and their ethnic identity as sons of Abraham. But John, himself a Jew, arrows this ethnic pride with one of the great put-downs of all time: "I tell you that out of these stones God is able to raise up children for Abraham" (3:9). From a Gentile, this would be clever abuse; but from a fellow Jew of priestly caste, it cuts deep. Retreat into ethnic self-righteousness will not work. Thus, John stands outside the system, arraigning them before God.

John's challenge is even more pointed. God is like a man wielding an ax, who has already put it down to the trunk to test the swing and is straightening his arms to wield it. "The ax is already at the root of the trees, and every tree that does not produce good fruit will be cut down and thrown into the fire" (Luke 3:9). You either respond to this warning or run from it. You can feel the blade at your knees. Many do respond. "What should we do then?" the crowd asked (3:10). John replies, angling his responses to different groups in terms of God's justice. "You, rich people, share your clothes and food. You, tax collectors, be honest in collecting revenue, charging only what is required. You, soldiers, don't use your position to rob and extort, and be content with your existing pay" (cf. 3:11–14). Here are practical messages, involving do-able actions, for Sebastene or Roman soldiers and for Jews. They cut at the corruption and wrongs of Jerusalem society. The message soon travels the twenty-five miles or so to Jerusalem. John becomes a stinging commentator for God's ways, and the people begin to wonder if this man might be their leader, their Messiah. He is not and says so, but many people become his disciples and learn of God from him in the desert, away from the center of power. Unlike the ascetic retreat of the Essenes to the south, his directness goads the politics of Jerusalem and also of Galilee. He is a potent influence as the messages filter back to the capital. But then the twist comes.

John's Struggle with Herod Antipas

Herod Antipas was one of the less prominent sons of Herod the Great when he was growing up, which turned out to be safer. At Herod's death, he is one of the chief contenders for the succession under Herod's will and goes to Rome for the verdict of Augustus. After a lengthy dispute among the sons, he is made tetrarch (rather than king) of Galilee and of the separate region Perea. This area east of the Jordan is our immediate concern, because John has backed into it as he criticizes the rulers in Jerusalem. Prophecy doesn't have rules as such, but we could project one precept of safe prophecy: Don't confront too many people at once and watch your back. Antipas commuted regularly to Perea during the time of his long rule, which lasted from 4 BC (shortly after Jesus' birth) to AD 39. But probably during this period something else was going on.

John speaks out against Herod probably while the latter is in Perea. The story is well known. Antipas fell in love with his brother Philip's wife, plotting to marry her while staying with his brother on his way to Rome. There is a debate about which brother because Herod Antipas had two brothers named Philip. Here we presume, perhaps wrongly, that it is his ruling neighbor Philip the tetrarch.[5] Philip was less powerful than his half-brother Antipas. And Herodias, his younger wife, fancied the more powerful Antipas, as he was attracted to her.[6] She left her husband, went to Antipas, and married him. John fearlessly points out that this is wrong. There is discussion about whether his concern is adultery or incest. Herodias is Antipas's niece, but she is actually moving from one uncle, Herod Philip II (or I!), to another, Herod Antipas; so the issue is less likely to be incest. John probably is straightforwardly attacking the ruler's adultery. Herodias has betrayed her husband, Philip. Antipas has stolen his brother's wife, and John tells it the way it is. Many would agree with him. God's law is no respecter of persons. Adultery, cheating on your wife, is wrong for Herod Antipas or for Prince Charles.

The story unfolds. Herod Antipas's first wife, the daughter of Nabataean King Aretas IV, hears about the plot, fears for her own life, and finds a way of journeying to Machaerus and on to her father's territory. The story of the way his daughter has been treated makes Aretas angry, and he declares war against Antipas and defeats him in the incident Josephus reports (see beginning of chapter). When this defeat occurs, we are not quite sure.

The immediate dynamics of the events are quite interesting. Josephus mentions that Machaerus is at that time subject to Aretas IV, and from thence the daughter can travel safely on to Petra.[7] (This is puzzling, because Herod is known to have murdered John the Baptist at Machaerus.) We can surmise that Herod Antipas is not in Perea having a holiday break when John is arrested, but actually facing the acute likelihood of invasion from the east, by an enraged ex-father-in-law, who has already taken over the remote fortress at Machaerus. Antipas perhaps travels down to Livias (Julias), fifteen miles east of Jericho. John has also rebuked Herod for "all the other evil things he had done" (Luke 3:19), and his criticism of the adultery is a threat to Antipas and Herodias. She goads her husband to arrest him. His soldiers swoop on John and take him prisoner. Antipas then fights his way into control of Machaerus, pushing back the attack of Aretas's soldiers across the desert plain. The fortress of Machaerus, the "black fortress," is high up a wadi on the edge of the desert plain of Moab and difficult for Aretas to defend with long supply lines. It is the key military point in the area. After this initial victory, on his birthday, Herod gives a banquet. Mark's Gospel (6:21) notes that his military commanders are there. Clearly, it is a big event, perhaps a celebration after he has retaken the fortress from Aretas.

Whatever these circumstances, Matthew (14:3) makes clear that the arrest is partly a result of the nagging and insistence of Herodias. This is understandable, because if John's criticism sticks, Herodias could be put away. She is acting to protect herself and is under some pressure. Already Antipas is being led by his wife, as he will be in killing John. Some seven years later in the summer of 39, there is a great ironic conclusion to Herodias's nagging. She becomes upset at the way her brother Agrippa is given the title of king in Philip's territory after the latter's death and nags her husband to do more about his own career. Why not go to Rome to seek the title of king, she pleads. Eventually Antipas gives in and they both go to Rome, hoping for preferment. Meanwhile, Agrippa, a nasty piece of work, sends messages to Rome claiming that Antipas is being disloyal to Rome and thinking of mounting a rebellion. As Herod Antipas and Herodias have an audience with Gaius Caligula, the Caesar is fingering these messages. He believes the messages rather than the protestations of loyalty from Antipas and Herodias, and the two of them are sacked on the spot. They finish up, not with the title of king and queen, but by being banished to Lyons in France, at the other end of the empire.[8] Herodias is one pushy, destructive woman.

John is imprisoned. Josephus tells us he is brought in chains to Machaerus.[9] A stairway and dungeon have been found at the bottom of the fortress where John may actually have been held. Antipas goes to talk with him. The Gospel account shows, as one or two other episodes do, that there are Christian followers already in the Herodian camp, for we have a good record of how Antipas feels about John, and it is quite complex. The relevant passage is in Mark:

Herod himself had given orders to have John arrested, and he had him bound and put in prison. He did this because of Herodias, his brother Philip's wife, whom he had married. For John had been saying to Herod, "It is not lawful for you to have your brother's wife." So Herodias nursed a grudge against John and wanted to kill him. But she was not able to, because Herod feared John and protected him, knowing him to be a righteous and holy man. When Herod heard John, he was greatly puzzled; yet he liked to listen to him.

(Mark 6:17–20)

This is inside knowledge. Herod would not make known that he is listening to his prisoner, or even protecting John against his new wife. Machaerus is inaccessible. Someone has provided this information. There are three possible Christian sources for this knowledge. One is Chuza, the manager of Herod's household, and his wife, Joanna. They would probably travel with Herod from Sepphoris and Tiberias in Galilee to Machaerus, near the Dead Sea, as part of the royal household (Luke 8:3). The second is the royal official whose son Jesus has recently healed. He lives in Capernaum and works in either Sepphoris or Tiberias. A third is Manaen, brought up with Herod as a close companion, and part of the church at Antioch some ten years later (Acts 13:1). There may be others; the Herodian world is not hermetically sealed.

We can only guess at the impact John has on Herod. The tetrarch listens to a prophet who directly addresses a range of his own evils. At the same time, John is clearly not partial to Jews, for he criticizes them as well. He has Antipas's respect, and yet the tetrarch finishes by lopping off his head. The story is horrific. Herod has a banquet at Machaerus, inviting "high officials and military commanders and the leading men of Galilee" (Mark 6:21). Herod is holding court here, asserting his dominance in the area. When the guests are wined and dined, Herodias sends out her (and Philip's) daughter Salome to dance. As far as we know, Antipas has no other children, and so this stepdaughter is special to him. She is seductive and extracts a drunken extravagant promise from Antipas. Backed by an oath, he offers up to half of his kingdom. She goes out and says, "What shall I ask for?" Her mother says, "The head of John the Baptist." The girl, fully primed, hurries in to the king with her requirement: "I want you to give me right now the head of John the Baptist on a platter." The guests gasp that a nubile girl can ask for such a thing. Antipas is distressed, but he cannot back down because of his oaths and his guests as witnesses. An executioner goes down to the dungeon with orders to bring John's head back, which he does. As requested, he carries it on a platter and presents it to Salome. She gives it to her mother. John's disciples come, take the body, and lay it in a tomb (Mark 6:14–29). The guests quickly spread the disgusting news. The dance of Salome, the savagery of Herodias, the venom of using your own daughter as a come-on to the drunken Herod—all of this confronts the Jews with the distance between Herodian evil and the goodness of John. He has seemed to be God's righteous person, but he is gone. Evil has again triumphed over goodness.

John and Jesus

The events of John's life follow from his teaching and witness. In the wilderness, dressed in rough camel's hair, John has no relationship with the priesthood or the temple cult. He has made a complete break from his father's way, as his father knew he would. John is a prophet, and his message is prophetically focused. He is not a recluse but is directly addressing the lives of those around him. Yet his message is not just on what is evil in Jewish society, but on opening up the way of God. He knows something of the enormity of God-with-us. When God arrives at the party, he needs to be announced properly. John rolls out the red carpet. He lays out the motorway before God. Maybe when God arrives and starts teaching us, we will be ready, warmed up, sharp, seeing the point. Maybe we will hear the deeper lessons of God. Maybe . . . John is, as his father knew, "the prophet of the Most High" (Luke 1:76). He is proclaiming the Messiah, but not a messiah of the Maccabees, the conquering warrior-deliverer—or is it? John does not really know. He knows his father's prophecy about a "horn of salvation," the ram's horn blown to rally the people, to call them to worship (1:69). The key message for him is this: "For you, my child, will . . . go on before the Lord to prepare the way for him" (1:76). "To guide our feet in the way of peace" did not sit easily with a warrior king (1:79). John therefore is unsure. He is sure, however, about the great words of Isaiah:

> A voice of one calling in the desert,
> Prepare the way of the LORD,
> make straight paths for him.
> Every valley shall be filled in,
>   Every mountain and hill made low.
> The crooked roads shall become straight,
>   The rough ways smooth.
> And all mankind will see God's salvation.
>
> (Luke 3:4–6; cf. Isa. 40:3–5)

All who heard those words would chill, for they would know what follows. There is a great section where God says, "Cry out." Isaiah says, "What shall I cry?" Then the text follows with the theme: "[The people] are like grass, . . . but the word of our God stands forever" (Isa. 40:6–8). Then is commanded the Great Shout, the Good News, the message to end all messages: "HERE IS YOUR GOD!" (40:9). This is where John is. He is the great civil engineer, flattening out the landscape so that Jesus, the Son of God, may properly arrive. He is the fanfare, and he blows like Satchmo.

This goes against the grain of much Western culture, which often emphasizes *our* thinking about God. The inbuilt fallacy of this approach, that the derivative creature can understand the Creator, that Hamlet can understand Shakespeare, is worked out century after century. Even much Jewish thought emphasized how *we* live righteously before God. The cultural direction of all of this thought and living is from humanity toward God. The Scriptures, however, show the converse movement. Rather than saying what we think God to be, we depend on God's disclosure. Rather than presuming that we know what we are, we wait for God to examine us. We depend on God's revelation to us. The God who has created us and the whole natural world, who has given us language, in whom we live and move and have our being—this God defines our existence and can communicate with us. The important flow is God's communication with us, what God reveals to us, not our thoughts about God or ourselves. So John goes before the Lord as the trumpet of the dawn, when the rising sun will shine on those living in darkness and the shadow of death. He is the highway of God's presence with us. An exaggeration? Wait and see.

John rates himself as the less and Jesus as the greater (Mark 1:7; John 3:30). As he makes clear, Jesus' discernment will be far greater than his own. "His winnowing fork is in his hand, and he will clear his threshing floor, gathering the wheat into his barn and burning the chaff with unquenchable fire" (Matt. 3:12). This theme of searching judgment is one that will take time to develop. We are not comfortable with it either. Politicians, for a while, seem to get away with whatever the public will swallow. Whether what is done stands up to the demands of the justice and mercy of God does not usually dominate our thinking, but Jesus will winnow it all as wheat or chaff. Much of human politics and strategy will be swept away on the wind, valueless and forgotten. John has absorbed Isaiah 40 and knows something of what the Creator of the ends of the earth is like. "See, the Sovereign LORD comes with power, and his arm rules for him" (40:10) This is on a completely different level. The enthroned God "brings princes to naught and reduces the rulers of this world to nothing" (40:23). Here is John out in the desert, not through fear, but just in order to proclaim the fulfillment of this great prophecy. "A voice of one calling: In the desert prepare the way for the LORD." Suddenly, there is life in the desert, political life for those who open up to God and trust God. Suddenly, the desert is the center of the political universe. The people know something is going on, but they cannot comprehend the depth of it. John explains it in terms that everyone will understand. "After me will come one who is more powerful than I, whose sandals I am not fit to carry" (Matt. 3:11). He pictures himself as a slave and sees himself unworthy of the menial task. John is below a slave in comparison to Jesus, but a Jew will be slave to none but Messiah. His hearers know what he is announcing and suck in their breaths. Either what is going on here is slightly absurd, two obscure people on another planet, or John is right. When God is here, everything is changed, including our politics.

Jesus and John

Now we hit another great twist in expectation. John's words about Jesus are extravagant. They would fire up most leaders to take control and assume the glory of the role. The power and the glory go together. But Jesus does two things. First, he accepts that he *is* the fulfillment of John's and Isaiah's prophecies. This is momentous, bigger by far than the swearing in of a president. Only someone who is crazed by self-importance can take on the claim "Here is your God" unless it is true. Jesus does accept the claim, but not publicly. As Jesus submits to John's baptism of repentance, probably all the crowd absorbs is that another disciple of John is receiving baptism. He is lowered in the Jordan by John, the water drains off his body, and then the direct presence of the Spirit of God comes to rest on him, as a dove slows its flight to the place where its feet will alight. God directly voices the words, "You are my Son, my beloved, in whom I delight" (Mark 1:11). Here is God's person. Here is the fulfillment of John's lifework. "He must increase, but I must decrease" (John 3:30 KJV). John is like an athlete who has handed on the baton and watches the star who will motor to victory.

Jesus' second response also opens things up. Everything would ordinarily point to self-importance, but Jesus eschews the glory. His relationship with John is one of submission, despite John's protests, and he leaves the water and departs (Matt. 3:14–4:1). The crowds stay with John. This begins Jesus' steadfast determination to avoid popularity, to escape the limelight, to reject self-importance. Here, if you like, is the politician who turns down every television appearance. Far from being engulfed in self-glory, Jesus departs to the desert and self-abnegation, cut off from people, food, and the acclaim he could receive. This is difficult for us to comprehend, especially in a media age. Is it possible for a ruler to be so insignificant? Can political rule be so nondescript, so selfless, that it is not noticed?

> He had no beauty or majesty to attract us to him,
> nothing in his appearance that we should desire him.
> He was despised and rejected by [people],
> A man of sorrows, and familiar with suffering.
> Like one from whom people hide their faces,
> He was despised, and we esteemed him not.
>
> (Isa. 53:2–3)

Suddenly we see that the whole cultural construction of political self-importance may be awry. Limousines, *Air Force 1*, presidential palaces—all such may be unnecessary and even misguided. We begin to see, perhaps faintly, what government without self-glorification might look like.

This level of insight is too much even for John. When he is in prison at the fortress of Machaerus, he thinks (as one does when one's head is in danger) of whether his life holds together. That depends on Jesus. But at this stage, Jesus seems to be doing nothing political. He is just moving around in Galilee, talking of God's rule, and healing people. John wants action, a Messiah who moves into John's own father's prophecy. His escape from prison is at issue. Surely God will deliver him from the evil of Herod Antipas and Herodias, will he not? His disciples maintain contact with him in prison, and he sends two of them on a walking round trip of 160 or so miles—this is no idle request—to ask Jesus the burning question. John has carefully framed it with an edge: "Are you the one who was to come, or should we expect someone else?" (Matt. 11:3). The words press toward, "If you are the Messiah, now is the time. We want some action." Jesus cannot miss the implication. The people have looked to John for deliverance. Now he is in prison, and the question is whether Jesus will take up the role of national deliverer and also free John.

Jesus' answer is measured, and not in the terms John is expecting. The disciples are to report that Jesus is giving sight to the blind, restoring the mentally ill, and curing the sick, in words that echo Isaiah 35 and 61. And then Jesus utters the final sentence: "Blessed is the man who does not fall away on account of me" (Matt. 11:4–6). John is offered no deliverance. There is no messianic hope of the kind John can grasp or understand. There is just the evidence of ordinary people being healed, and Jesus' word that John's business is to stay faithful to him through the coming tribulations. Good will not triumph in his lifetime. As John faces death through beheading, that is all he has.

Yet there is more than that. Jesus honors John and gives the crowd a three-movement verbal concerto in his praise. As John's disciples go back to him with their sober message, Jesus speaks to the crowd about John with three great rhetorical questions: "What did you go out into the desert to see? A reed swayed by the wind?" No. The crowds know they did not. The point about John is that he is God's man, straight and unbending to corruption and injustice. Jesus presses on: "If not, what did you go out to see? A man dressed in fine clothes? No, those who wear fine clothes are in kings' palaces." The question is again answered for them. It's not the pomp and power that counts, but the one who speaks truly. The third and compelling question comes from Jesus: "Then what did you go out to see? A prophet? Yes, I tell you, and more than a prophet." The twice-repeated "No" precedes the final great "Yes." Here is Isaiah's messenger of God, preparing the way of the Lord. Here is Elijah, the one who has confronted kings. Here is the greatest of the prophets born of women.

Yet, Jesus adds, if you grasp the meaning of the rule of God as John faces death through beheading, you will see that the one who is least in the kingdom of God is greater than John. The great rhetorical questions and the rolling statements push the crowd to see the significance of John. Before him are the law and the prophets. With him the rule of God is on the march, though violent people lay hold of it. Jesus pushes them beyond their understanding. "He who has ears to hear, let him hear." But, of course, it is too much to take in (Matt. 11:1–15).

Jesus probes further. "To what can I compare this generation? They are like children sitting in the marketplaces and calling out to others: 'We played you a happy tune, but you did not dance. We sang a sad one, and you did not cry.' You want things on your own terms, but they do not happen that way. Neither John nor the Son of Man is here on the terms you expect and ask for" (cf. Matt. 11:16–19). Already Jesus is shaking the ways in which the people normally respond to the politics of the day. When the shock comes and they hear of John's horrific death, they know that God's greatest prophet has been killed, but perhaps they begin to grasp that he is not the end of the story.

Bibliography

France, R. T. "Jesus the Baptist?" Pages 94–111 in *Jesus of Nazareth: Lord and Christ*. Edited by Joel Green and Max Turner. Grand Rapids: Eerdmans; Carlisle: Paternoster, 1994.

Kazmierski, Carl R. *John the Baptist: Prophet and Evangelist.* Collegeville, MN: Liturgical Press, 1996.

Stegemann, Harmut. *The Library of Qumran: On the Essenes, Qumran, John the Baptist, and Jesus.* Grand Rapids: Eerdmans, 1998.

Taylor, Joan E. *The Immerser: John the Baptist within Second Temple Judaism.* London: SPCK, 1997.

Webb, Robert L. *John the Baptizer and Prophet: A Socio-Historical Study.* Journal for the Study of the New Testament, Supplement Series 62. Sheffield: JSOT Press, 1991.

Wink, Walter. *John the Baptist in the Gospel Tradition.* Cambridge: Cambridge University Press, 1968.

Yamasaki, Gary. *John the Baptist in Life and Death.* Sheffield: Sheffield Academic Press, 1998.

Jesus and Herod Antipas

Jesus' Temptations in the Wilderness

The three temptations Jesus faces in the Judean wilderness have deep political significance. They occur after Jesus' baptism by John. The Spirit leads Jesus into the parched mountains south of the Jerusalem–Jericho road, where Jesus is to wrestle with some of the deepest possible issues. People do not fast forty days for trivial reasons. This kind of fast is a time of unqualified physical weakness. Central to the meditations are his relationship with God and his identity as Son of God. He faces three external temptations: to change stones into bread, to cast himself down from the Temple as a sign, and to receive all the kingdoms of the world if he bows down to the devil. In all three the devil, the father of lies, is involved with Jesus in the construction of falsehood or truth. The interchanges are deep, like moves in chess, hinging on where the roots of truth and falsehood lie. The issues are enormous, encompassing some of the underlying realities of life, and two or perhaps all of the three temptations are political.

After forty days of fasting, Jesus faces the first temptation, to use his miraculous powers in making bread. The tempter comes to him and says, "If you are the Son of God, tell these stones to become bread" (Matt. 4:3). There is nothing wrong with bread when one is hungry. But that is not the real point of the interchange. The temptation means, "Prove yourself. Claim your status as Son of God. Put food first and exercise your power over the natural world." The issue is where the focus of human life should be—on God or on the *getting* business of life. Jesus answers, "It is written, 'Man does not live on bread alone, but on every word that comes from the mouth of God'" (4:4; Deut. 8:3).

In Jesus' response the whole perspective is right. Bread, in its wider sense, is also the stuff of politics. Marie Antoinette was wrong in saying, "Let them eat cake." There is no substitute for bread, and she lost her head. Down through the ages, wiser politicians have understood that bread is political. But Jesus will not give the people what they want and allow the material aspect to dominate. Later he upbraids the disciples for misunderstanding what he means in talking about bread. "You of little faith, why are you talking among yourselves about having no bread? Do you still not understand?" (Matt. 16:5–12). Jesus has just laid out food for thousands, and yet they still stay preoccupied with basics and ignore the bigger picture he is trying to convey. Even in his extremity of fasting, where bread is the most legitimate of all, the word of God and the centrality of God have to come first. Jesus has resisted the temptation in principle and in its most benign form. End of stage 1.

The second and third temptations are both political, interchanged in order by Matthew and Luke, which probably signifies that the order did not matter much. They both involve Jesus being taken to a location that embodies a particular kind of political temptation. The second (in Matthew) is nationalistic. "The devil took him to the holy city and had him stand on the highest point of the temple. 'If you are the Son of God,' he said, 'throw yourself down. For it is written: "He will command his angels concerning you, and they will lift you up in their hands, so that you will not strike your foot against a stone"'" (Matt. 4:5–6; Ps. 91:11–12). Here the devil uses the word of God that Jesus has just affirmed. Again, his status as Son of God is under question. He is merely asked to prove what is true, and to do so in the public arena. Yet, providing the sign is the temptation. The location is the Temple. Herod the Great's plan for rebuilding it, announced in 22 BC, was largely completed in about eight years, with ten thousand workmen and a thousand priests trained as masons and carpenters, because they alone could enter the temple area without defiling it. The Temple was a magnificent piece of work and celebrated with a festival where three hundred oxen were sacrificed. The building contained a quirk. In 1 Kings 6:2 the temple was 30 cubits high, but some ancient versions of 2 Chronicles 3:4 describe it as 120 cubits high, presumably an error. Herod went for a higher version. So, the result was an ancient skyscraper, far higher than other temples of the era, about as high as it was wide. The surrounding courts were extended and magnificent.[1] This glorious skyscraper building, gleaming white with points of gold, was the national shrine for the Jews, as we have seen. The significance of the highest point becomes clear through another event we have already covered. Late in his life Herod the Great erected a gold eagle over the massive front door of the temple. This was a diplomatic move toward Augustus, because the temple of the national god would normally be seen as a rival to Rome and Caesar, and Herod in building it had to be careful not to displease Rome. So the gold eagle was to appease Rome. But it infuriated the Jews. It was seen as an insult to God and an act of desecration.

One day a rumor went round that Herod had died, and immediately some students, prompted by two outstanding rabbis (Judas, son of Sepphoraeus, and Matthias, son of Margalus), scaled the temple, cut the eagle down from its pinnacle, and destroyed it. They were heroes, but Herod came out on his sickbed and lectured the Jews on their ingratitude and lack of respect for him and his Temple. Forty prisoners were executed, and the two professors and two students were burned alive. This gives some feeling for the tension created around the top of the Temple. It was the place where either God rules or Romans rule.

What the devil is inviting Jesus to do is not just some private act of magic. The act of coming down from the top of the temple in front of crowds would show the people that God is among them to save them from Rome and the Herodians. To throw oneself down from here and survive would be *the* sign, the sign that many Jews were looking for, that the Deliverer has come. This is the messianic hope. Like a chess player refusing a crudely offered queen, Jesus responds, "It is also written, 'Do not put the Lord your God to the test'" (Matt. 4:7). He directly claims the title the devil puts to doubt and repudiates the quest for a sign with words from Deuteronomy 6:16, where the Israelites test God after the exodus. The quest for signs and miracles is wrong; to test God is an insult. Jesus later repeatedly exposes these attempts to prove God, to make God subject to what we decide is our validation. End of stage 2.

The third temptation is even more centrally political. "The devil took him to a very high mountain and showed him all the kingdoms of the world and their splendor. 'All this will I give you,' he said, 'if you will bow down and worship me'" (Matt. 4:8–9). This is not just facing a sign that will show Jesus as national Messiah, but the ultimate political temptation of world rule. There are a number of decisive issues hanging around this great temptation.

It moves beyond the nationalist focus of the previous temptation to embrace all the kingdoms of the world. This is odd for a Jew to address, because Jewish thinking is so fiercely nationalistic and the Romans are the world power. The temptation requires a total ambition of the kind only present with Alexander the Great, the Caesars, and a few others. It also requires the kind of arrogance that believes, "I am good for the world. If I ruled the world . . ." Among candidates for benevolent dictatorship, Jesus would, of course, rank top. But his response to the devil shows that all of this is misconception. Jesus insists: "Worship the Lord God, and serve him only" (4:10; Deut. 6:13). This is the crucial political lesson. Many politicians assume that *their* getting to power is the answer: *then* they can do good. Jesus understands that getting to power is not the answer; instead, unqualified submission to God is required to do anything good. The beginning, middle, and end of politics is obedience to God.

Moreover, what the devil offers is worldly power—control plus splendor—the kind of flaunted dominion present within the Egyptian, Macedonian, and Roman empires. The premise is that power is possessed, in this case handed over by the devil to Jesus, if he agrees. Along with the *possession* of power goes self-glorification and splendor—palaces, rich clothes, servants and slaves, gold, hanging gardens, and women. This is the idiom of possessing power and its rewards, found throughout history from Babylon to Peking. Jesus rejects it all in favor of the unconditional worship and service of God. This is not an *a*political principle, but one that changes the inner meaning of political rule. Since the time of Moses, the servant of God, service rather than the possession of power has been an alternative way of approaching office. Because of our Christian heritage, this perspective has become stronger in democratic politics. The fulcrum on which the whole change of conception turns is found here in this temptation. Jesus turns his back on the *possession* of worldly power and unreservedly toward the service of God. Of course, the "possession" of such power is a chimera, our vain self-construction, but it persists in much political activity and philosophy, East and West.

Further, the idea that the devil owns power and that it can be grasped through evil acts, Jesus shows to be an illusion. All who try to accumulate power by evil are here under judgment. Grasping power is not real *power,* but weakness. Power based on evil disintegrates. Solzhenitsyn's prophecy—the great USSR, because it was based on the evil of the Gulag, would collapse—turned out to be true. There can be no real permanence and stability when political rule is not just and for the good of people. Repeatedly, rulers think they can play with evil or use it, but the illusion costs them. Here there is clear-eyed insight. True power is God's, requires unequivocal goodness, and is not at the devil's disposal.

The temptation is also twisted in the condition it lays down for having control of all the kingdoms of this world, a position from which much good could perhaps be done. It is submission to Satan and the evil ways of Satan. This is the route where the end justifies the means, getting to power with evil is justified by the "good" results of being in power. The end justifying the means is more accurately described as the good end justifying the wrong means of getting there. Yet this expedient never works, because the consequences of wrong means remain destructive and do not disappear, and also because the end is always compromised and twisted by the sinner who wills it. Jesus will not take the shortcut, the quick route to power and control. Shakespeare later toys with the same issue in *Macbeth* and *Henry IV* (part 2, 3.1.31): "Uneasy lies the head that wears the crown," says the usurper king. Many of our political problems occur because we do not understand that the evil shortcut does not exist; it is always a cul-de-sac reeking of excrement. "Though the mills of God grind slowly, yet they grind exceeding small; / Though with patience He stands waiting, with exactness grinds He all."[2] Jesus avoids this error and signals the incredible patience of God's kingdom to do only good. There is no more clever a political strategy than right and just living on God's terms.

Finally, the centrality of Jesus' response is unequivocal: "Worship the Lord your God, and serve him only" (Matt. 4:10). Thus, the worship of God, recognition of the rule of God, is the central *political* response and the central political issue. This is the truth to which kingdoms should submit, because with the rule of God comes submission to God's justice. Then the quest for human political glory of one group over another is finally defeated. Only with the full recognition of service of God is the issue of human government resolved. Here, picking up J. R. R. Tolkien's later echo in *The Lord of the Rings*, is the actual journey when the ring of power is thrown into the flaming maw of Mount Doom.

Thus, right at the outset of his three years of teaching, the central political issues have already been settled. Jesus has repudiated national glory and the human quest for power and domination over others as not God's way, as not worthy consideration. The only true political response is to bow before God and obey God. Consistently, Jesus opens up this principle and sees through the weakness of different human political constructions. Even now when we see how the quest for possession of power grips and cripples British, American, Chinese, and African leaders, we realize these conclusions are already way beyond our politics. John the Baptist could scarcely know how wonderfully he has been vindicated.

Jesus in Galilee

With our conceptions of politics, it is easy to miss what is going on. Jesus knows from the beginning that he is Messiah, the ruler of his people. There is no evidence of changes in understanding or growth in self-awareness such as we normally experience. When Nathaniel moves from skepticism—"Can anything good come out of Nazareth?"—to affirming Jesus as "the Son of God" and "the King of Israel," Jesus accepts the affirmation as a matter of course (John 1:46–49 NRSV). Unequivocally, this man believes himself to be God's ruler, yet he moves about Galilee, preaching, healing, teaching, relating, and talking. He starts and finishes with nothing—no power, no popular appeal, not working within groups, not ambitious, not aggressive. How can this be political rule?

This is difficult for us to see. We know Acton's maxim, "Power tends to corrupt and absolute power corrupts absolutely."[3] We cannot think of a ruler without power seen in these terms, one who is also incorruptible. Yet here is a person who is not pre-compromised. As we see things, the rest of us cannot afford the truth because our position, power, party, or purse needs defending, but Jesus can afford it. The politician must get to the top, but here is one who does not dominate or climb. The ruler accumulates glory and servants, but here is one who sometimes does not even have a bed, let alone a palace. Can this be political rule in its proper character? The answer will emerge one way or the other. It is clear that this man with equanimity understands himself to be king, ruler, Messiah, and a man with dominion. As rulers go, he is incredibly cool and self-possessed. He needs and craves nothing; he is free to give rather than grasp.

In chapter 6 we shall look at the central theme of Jesus' teaching, but from the start it is clear what it is. He tells of the kingdom of God. "Kingdom" is certainly a political theme. Jesus teaches about the kingdom or rule of God as something that stands on God's terms with a kind of ultimate authority, a kingdom that requires priority over the realms of Antipas, the Romans, the British Empire, and the United States. What Jesus says right from the start is partly confrontational. It requires repentance, because without the awesome business of laying wrongs before God, there cannot be healing and a good relationship with the Father. He sets out God's terms, and as we might expect, they are not negotiable. Yet he proceeds quite ordinarily. He has access to synagogues; they are there for rabbis to teach, and each village craves good teaching (Matt. 4:23; Mark 1:21, 39; 3:1–6; 5:35; 6:1–6; Luke 4:31–37). Over the last few decades synagogues have grown strongly in the villages of Galilee. The requirements and good news of the kingdom begin to generate opposition from the Pharisees. Jesus' teaching authority and healings anger them. Gradually, as the number of listeners grows and because of Pharisaic hostility, Jesus moves to open-air teaching in the glorious countryside, a move later echoed by Whitefield and Wesley, and the structure of this ambiguous kingdom begins to be articulated.

The ambiguity is important. For example, Jesus moves around healing people—a man who is manic, a woman with fever, those who are paralyzed and diseased, a man with leprosy, and so on. It is clearly his prior concern: Jesus seeks out people who are ill and receives those who come to him. No one at that time or throughout most of human history has seen healing as part of politics. Wars? Yes. Taxation? Yes. Healings? No. That position is still resolutely held in the United States today. Yet, if care of our neighbor is part of just and righteous living, health and healing need to be a concern of the state, as they are now throughout much of the world. In Britain's 2001 election, the National Health Service was the *dominant* issue. So, we have this man walking around, lifting people up, giving them relief in mind and body, exhibiting what God's rule is like, and it includes healing.

Soon the scope of Jesus' way opens out a different worldview. The Sermon on the Mount alone is far bigger in scope than this book, but it too is partly political. Jesus teases at precepts and ways of thinking and shows how they need to be brought centrally in relation to the living God. "It has been said . . . , but I say unto you . . ." is a theme that shows how Jesus reconstructs his hearers' worldview. He is critical of the culture and attitudes of the Pharisees. The Pharisees are making a particular religiopolitical appeal to the local people. As they see it, they know God's law and live the right halakah, the God-given national code of conduct according to their interpretation, and *they* can teach it to others. They know how to pray and do a lot of public praying. They are righteous, giving alms. They fast a lot and are therefore fit to be leaders. They want to establish control over communities. Yet Jesus sees their supposed strength as weakness. Theirs is an acted righteousness, self-congratulatory, making themselves judges. In these respects the central relationship with God, which must have integrity, is compromised. Jesus holds everything in the light of relationship with God. Without it we are all lost, whatever legitimation we construct. With it we are blessed and our house is built on the rock.

Beware false prophets! What you accept as of God matters supremely. Already the winnowing is at work, and those who are cast away on the wind feel uncomfortable and angry. They resent his teaching and the appeal he has to the crowds, who hang on his words and ignore the Pharisees. More than this, Jesus is incisively critical of them. The Pharisees and teachers of the law are rule-bound and caught up in legalism at the expense of the substance of the law. Rather than honoring and caring for the old, they encourage people to divert gifts from their parents to themselves (Mark 7:11–13). Jesus quotes Isaiah: "These people honor [God] with their lips, but their hearts are far from [God]" (Mark 7:6; Matt. 15:8; Isa. 29:13 LXX [Septuagint]). Their teaching becomes caught up in their own formulations. He also warns of those who are hypocrites, making a fuss about helping the poor and praying, but really doing things just for effect, to gain high standing in the eyes of others.

He requires people to do things honestly before God and without seeking popularity, applause, or the moral high ground. Jesus critiques them from a central point of reference: "You have let go of the commands of God and are holding on to the traditions of men" (Mark 7:8). Again, we see Jesus' insistence that the standard for a worthy life is obedience to God. Doubtless, the Pharisees surely feel uneasy at this exposure of their attitudes and motives.

Jesus' analysis is a vertical line judging our own crooked politics. Media pressure toward presentation, reputation, public relations, image formation, and spin-doctoring means that we are not even fighting this battle anymore. The integrity of political action and debate seems lost in the swirl of media opinion. There is little sense of politicians on their knees before God, seeking to discern what is just and good. From today's standpoint it would even seem strange that the Pharisees are prickly under this searchlight, for now appearance is everything, and politicians will even discuss publicly how they should change their image. Image reigns in our political culture. It does not really reign, of course. Real justice and injustice before God actually determine our lives and give running commentaries on the failures of appearance politics. Every image pitch in the media is followed sooner or later by exposure and collapse. The froth evaporates and the bubbles pop. In some situations, newspapers seek to follow the line of Jesus, trying to uncover the realities of a false situation, as with the *Washington Post* and Watergate. Yet, images also flood their pages, and exposure remains mixed with appearances. Root honesty and plumb-line justice before God, the compass point of truth by which we must live, emerges only with the Nazarene.

Jesus also attacks the self-rightness of the leaders. Commentators have asked, "Were the Pharisees really that bad?" It is not the Pharisees as a particular group who are the problem, but the power of this attitude in them *and* in us. The need for political leaders to be right is frightening. Rarely does one admit to making any mistake. Jesus' attack is incisive and cuts through history. Leaders commit the most dreadful deeds with a sense of self-rightness. Bin Laden is just one chilling example in a long line of justified evil. Such self-rightness constructs a distortion: us = good, and them = bad. We become the Moral Majority, the good guys, whiter than right, the cowboys, the true voice of Allah or the "Free World." "They" become baddies, delinquents, Indians, terrorists, infidels, or Communists. At elections, one leader or party is right and the other is wrong—except that the opposition reverses the positions. Elections often present two self-righteous political universes, seemingly untethered to reality and incompatible. Self-rightness dominates political debate, at times in Britain reducing it to a Yah-Boo farce.

In the same way, the Pharisees presume their own rightness and work at it, articulating their ethics and rules into the only acceptable orthodoxy. But Jesus overturns the whole framework. Judging is central to politics. "You judge others and exonerate yourselves; you are trying to get rid of a speck of sawdust in their eye while you have a plank in your own. But this is hypocrisy. Concentrate on your own failings, and you will not have time for much criticism" (cf. Matt. 7:1–5). It is easy to see what Jesus is addressing. The Pharisees are constantly coming to Jesus and criticizing him—for forgiving the paralytic's sins (9:3), for eating with tax collectors (9:11; Mark 2:16), for healing demon-possession (Matt. 9:34), for eating grain on the Sabbath (12:2), for healing a man's hand on the Sabbath (12:10; Mark 3:2), for eating with unpurified hands (Mark 7:2). They actually criticize what is good. This bundle of self-righteous, trivial criticism is probably what Jesus warns his own disciples about. It is yeast; it spreads and infects the whole. Either you humbly address self-rightness, or you hate the person who exposes you. The Pharisees do the latter with Jesus. The rightness of political leaders, made into a competitive industry in the twenty-first century, is suddenly caught in the glare of the headlights. His winnowing fork is in his hand, and it sifts our politics as effectively as those of the Pharisees. The being-right chaff and straw float in media emptiness on the wind into oblivion.

The Sending of the Twelve

Quite early in his ministry Jesus chooses his disciples and sends them out to declare and show the kingdom of God. Jesus' disciples are quite ordinary and disparate; they include a Herodian (Levi/Matthew) and a Zealot (Simon), normally people at loggerheads. They are Jesus' followers or students, and the leader does not make too many demands of them. Nevertheless, the Gospels recount how Jesus with enigmatic instructions sends the Twelve out into surrounding villages and towns in Galilee. Interpreters usually count this sharing of the good news of God's kingdom as the first stage in forming the church. In some sense this is true, but it is also a distinctive mission, with an unusual political focus. Here the disciples go to the little people, proclaiming the gentle rule of God and expecting nothing except welcome or rejection. Other would-be rulers send followers out on conquests, but Jesus sends his disciples out in *peacemaking* under the authority of God. "As you enter the home, give it your greeting. If the home is deserving, let your peace rest on it; if it is not, let your peace return to you. . . . Judgment [will follow]. . . . I am sending you out like sheep among wolves. . . . You will be brought before governors and kings as witnesses to them and to the

Gentiles. . . . When they arrest you, do not worry" (Matt. 10:12–20). This is a mission of peace, quelling the fractious power-seeking and aggression of the political world.[4]

There is reliance not on militarism, money, technology, or earning favors, but on the free giving of the kingdom to others: "Freely you have received, freely give" (10:8). The simplicity of transmission is breathtaking. Yet at the same time, it is divisive: "Do not suppose that I have come to bring peace to the earth. I did not come to bring peace, but a sword" (10:34). This is a root-and-branch matter of commitment and loyalty all down the line. Jesus insists on the (at-present) distant and extravagant metaphor of taking up the cross to follow him—a chilling test of loyalty, recognized as execution by the state. He finishes with a firm focus on simple humanity: "And if anyone gives a cup of cold water to [some]one . . . because he is my disciple, . . . he will certainly not lose his reward" (10:42). What a strange man! What kind of movement is this?

Later, the sending of the seventy-two, probably in Judea, has a similar focus on the rule of God as a pattern of peace settling upon those who accept it (Luke 10). After the event, Jesus' response is one of overflowing joy and praise to the God of heaven and earth, because this way is hidden from the wise and learned and revealed to the little people (10:21). This is a planting, not among the powerful and educated, but among those who are humble enough to hear God's good way. It is a politically significant outreach. After the return of the seventy-two, he says: "Blessed are the eyes that see what you see. For I tell you that many *prophets* and *kings* wanted to see what you see but did not see it, and to hear what you hear but did not hear it" (10:23–24, italics added). This is a different kind of kingdom, spreading slowly through the hills and valleys of Galilee, Samaria, and Judea, a creeping peaceable kingdom. Then, and perhaps even now, it is poorly understood.

Soon Jesus and the disciples are collecting followers in the countryside around Galilee. There are some among Herod Antipas's own staff who relay his responses to news about Jesus. "At that time Herod the tetrarch heard the reports about Jesus, and said to his attendants . . ." (Matt. 14:1–2). "King Herod heard about this, for Jesus' name had become well known. Some were saying . . . But when Herod heard this . . ." (Mark 6:14–16). "Now Herod the tetrarch heard about all that was going on. . . . But Herod said, 'I beheaded John. Who, then, is this I hear such things about?' And he tried to see [Jesus]" (Luke 9:7–9; 23:8). He tries to see Jesus by sending out soldiers to capture him and bring him in. Jesus appears as a messianic threat; indeed, he is one. But the threat is not in the crude terms Antipas envisages. Herod is trying to work out whether Jesus will have to be put to death, as the Baptizer was, to prevent rebellion. Yet Herod also has a strange sense of Jesus' ambiguity. What is he really like? Herod's incomprehension plays through the Gospels.

Against the apolitical interpretation of discipleship often adopted today, the disciples actually do see their position in political terms. Later, Zebedee's wife, flanked by her big boys, comes with an embarrassing request: "Grant that one of these two sons of mine may sit at your right and the other at your left in your kingdom" (Matt. 20:21). The chagrin of the other disciples is not against the political image of the ruler sitting with his two prime ministers, but outrage at *their* presumption in seeking to be first. It resurfaces in the Last Supper. "Also a dispute arose among them as to which of them was considered to be the greatest [most important]" (Luke 22:24). Clearly, the disciples see themselves, in part at least, as political followers. Neither Jesus nor his disciples nor Herod Antipas see Jesus' campaign as apolitical.

Far more powerful, however, is Jesus' response at the Last Supper to this dispute, which mirrors the jockeying for position that happens in most cabinets and governments worldwide. He takes such competition by the neck and states the central principle of service we shall later consider at length. Jesus makes it clear that they do not understand, but at the same time he affirms, nay instates, their political status:

> And I confer on you a kingdom, just as my Father conferred one on me, so that you may eat and drink at my table in my kingdom and sit on thrones, judging the twelve tribes of Israel. (Luke 22:29–30)

This statement is an unequivocal gift of delegated political authority over the tribes of Israel. It needs to be carefully weighed. There are two extremes of interpreting Jesus' statement. One is to be too literal, as often the disciples are (Matt. 16:7). The disciples are not going to take over the Sanhedrin, and they do not. But the other is to be too figurative and noetic. Jesus, with no illusions about the route to the cross, recognizes that the Father has also conferred political rule on him, and he in turn gives it to his disciples. Too much weight can be given to the "Twelve," but it fits the ancient tribal structure of the kingdom of Israel, a pattern of government that expresses God's purpose. The Twelve, the seventy-two, and all subsequent disciples are, it inescapably seems, called also to political discipleship, not to be shrinking violets. They are to go out as peacemakers who, in some sense, rule.

The Feeding of the Five Thousand

It is odd how we ignore aspects of the biblical text. The Gospels clearly recount the sudden expansion of crowds following Jesus. Some say the feeding of the five thousand is an exaggeration. But perhaps the text just tells the truth, giving a rough but accurate estimate. Suddenly, there really are significant gatherings of four and five thousand plus others in northern Galilee. Why do these great crowds emerge at this stage? The Gospels say there are about five thousand men. It is significant that the focus is on men; Matthew adds, "besides women and children" (14:21). These are football-crowd sizes, and it becomes clear that this vast swelling in numbers following Jesus occurs because the word has gone round that this is the messianic Deliverer. What is actually happening can be seen from a significant but neglected verse in the Gospel of John: "Jesus, knowing that they intended to come and make him king by force, withdrew again into the hills by himself" (6:15). This is not a throwaway line. In Galilee there is only one putative king, Herod Antipas, and there can be no other interpretation than that the crowd, following the Galilean Zealot pattern, are seeking for a leader who will overthrow Herod and supplant Roman rule. Moreover, the idea that he will be made king "by force" shows there is some momentum with the crowd. This is a potential uprising in the great Galilean Zealot tradition; some of them have even come out with weapons.[5]

The political and military position of Herod Antipas at this time is interesting.[6] It is possible that news has just come through of the execution of Sejanus in Rome in October 31. Sejanus was Antipas's close ally and was effectively given control by Tiberius as the Emperor retreated to Crete. Now, dramatically, he is shown to be plotting against Tiberius and his other successors and is killed by the Emperor. Suddenly, Herod's political position is shaky. The news comes quickly, and if the feeding of the five thousand is in spring 32, serious instability in Rome would focus people's minds. But there is another more domestic issue. While going to Rome to see Sejanus, Antipas takes a fancy to Herodias, his brother's wife. As we noted earlier, his abandoned first wife, the daughter of Aretas IV, quickly travels back to the Nabataean capital of Petra, southeast of the Dead Sea.[7] When she arrives home, the insult stirs Aretas to quarrel and declare war, partly also over a boundary dispute.

At some time, we are not sure when, Aretas defeats Herod. "In the ensuing battle," Josephus says, "the whole army of Herod was destroyed when some refugees, who had come from the tetrachy of Philip and had joined Herod's army, played him false."[8] Josephus records a Jewish view that this defeat is God's judgment on Herod for executing John the Baptist. "But to some of the Jews the destruction of Herod's army seemed to be divine vengeance, and certainly a just vengeance, for his treatment of John, surnamed the Baptist."[9] So perhaps, not long after the death of John in early 32, Herod Antipas is at war with, and partly defeated by, Aretas (we do not know how many conflicts there were). He also is not on good terms with his cuckolded brother, Philip. As soon as the Galilean Zealots hear of Herod's need to go and fight on his borders, their heads would be up, and they would also be outraged at John's death. It is not impossible that these dynamics are partly behind this great flux of men. Or perhaps the fighting with Aretas occurs later, after a period of tension and nervousness of which the feast at Machaerus is part. Nevertheless, the main dynamic is the death of John. After the Baptist's death, those who have looked to John for deliverance from Herod now turn to Jesus, the one whom John has marked.

Whether or not Herod faces these precise difficulties at this time, the messianic word is going around. How well formed the response is we do not know. Perhaps, it is a vague longing. Perhaps people, some with long-hidden weapons, begin to converge on the supposed Deliverer. This call could explain why this vast crowd is prepared to gather from the surrounding towns and move purposefully around the lake to a remote spot, neglecting their food. They are not just foolish tourists who have forgotten to pack lunch. They know Jesus is on the lake and heading east in a boat moving slowly in a light wind, and they can see the vessel a mile or two out. Crowds stream from towns on the northern shore and race round the north end of the lake to begin the revolution. This is the crystallizing moment in the politics of Galilee for a generation, the rekindled hope from the time of Hezekiah, Judas, and others. As the crowd sees it, neither John the Baptist nor Jesus, great teachers though they are, can face the crunch alone and lead them against Antipas. Jesus needs a show of determined support, before it is too late and Herod wipes him out, too. Will he respond to our call? The hubbub rises as the crowds move round the shoreline, pointing at the boat out on the sea.

Although these uprisings are endemic to the Zealot history of Galilee, Jesus' answer is not even in doubt. Jesus has them eating out of his hands. But to the person who has faced the temptations and who has never sought victories over people, this way is wrong. The terms of God's rule are different. If we are to love our enemies, we must not attack them. The way of peace cannot be paved with war, and Jesus has been teaching peacemaking to his disciples. This ruler has seen through the self-glorifying leader complex; he has nowhere to lay his head. The last thing these harassed and helpless people need is a leader who would take them to death. Some thirty-four years later, Galilee does indeed rebel. The battle is finally fought out on the same lake, and Josephus describes the resulting slaughter in horrific terms:

A fearful sight met the eyes—the entire lake stained with blood and crammed with corpses; for there was not a single survivor. During the days that followed a horrible stench hung over the region. The beaches were thick with wrecks and swollen bodies which, hot and steaming in the sun, made the air so foul that the calamity not only horrified the Jews but revolted even those who had brought it about. Such was the outcome of this naval engagement. The dead, including those who had earlier perished in the town, totalled 6,700.[10]

The figure of those dead nearly matches those who come out to meet Jesus. For one who sees the end from the beginning, rebellion is out.

The feeding of the five thousand is therefore a complex event, with layers of meaning. The journey of Jesus and the disciples across the lake is partly so that the group can mourn John's death, be quiet, and be at peace (Matt. 14:12–13; Mark 6:29–32). They sail slowly eastward, with little wind, beyond Herod Antipas's territory to the northern coast near Bethsaida-Julias. But they are not allowed time to grieve. Crowds with their own agenda follow around the north shore, more than matching the speed of the boat, and eventually funneling toward where Jesus and the disciples will land. Jesus "had compassion on them, because they were like sheep without a shepherd" (Mark 6:33–34). Jesus is beyond their agenda and takes charge of the event. He teaches them with cool, probing principles, requiring immense thought, and thus diverting them from this drive toward a nationalist leader. They have accepted this man as their leader and are willing to lay their lives at his feet. But what he says does not travel the same way. He is focusing their lives on their relationship with God.

As the day progresses, the unease and the clash of purposes become tangible. They think of food, and so do the disciples. Jesus addresses the simple question of faith in God for food, helped by the faithful offering of loaves and fishes from a small boy. Can the people live with this simple trust in God? The Nazarene goes into the fast-food business, and they all sit down, as if for a picnic, perhaps with weapons lying in the grass. Jesus gives thanks to his Father, and the food is distributed, a glorious cornucopia, changing the mood of the vast crowd. The disciples are unable to cope with the situation because the crowd is so big, but Jesus acts as chef and manager, prevailing excessively on the bounty of God. But this too is politics. "Let them have food," is Jesus' direct, slightly imperious focus. Feeding and healing are his concerns, not a Herodian rebellion.[11] However, the crowd's agenda is not done. They hear echoes of Moses, the first ruler of Israel, feeding the children of Israel in the wilderness. Baskets of food are collected for the journey home, five or even fifteen miles for some. Perhaps this is the messianic sign, the prophet who is to come into the world, the Deliverer, the second Moses. Some of the crowd make a clumsy attempt to affirm Jesus as their King (Messiah), the one who will deliver them from Antipas and the Romans.

It is a great meal; many politicians would kill for this skill. Here is a politician who can do nothing wrong. But Jesus closes the event down. The disciples are dispatched and isolated from the event, and then Jesus deliberately dismisses the crowd before going up into the hills alone to pray. Some of the crowd disperse back into the villages of Galilee, arriving home late at night with a wide-eyed story of the day. So, the hope of a national deliverer is repudiated. Jesus turns down the Zealot-leader option when the Galilean crowds lay it before him on a plate. He pursues another lonely and dangerous path. Those who really hear what Jesus is saying know that the gentle rule of God is light years away from the revolutionary Zealot conception. When Jesus leaves the crowds, they are well fed and not being led on to inevitable bloodshed and destruction.

But some of the crowd, perhaps several thousand, stay on tenaciously for the great revolution. Jesus withdraws into the hills. In the dark he approaches the disciples' boat, walking on the water, and he is received into it by his frightened friends. Their fishermen's puzzlement is shown by their estimate that they have rowed three or three-and-a-half miles across the lake in windy and rough conditions. Meanwhile, the crowd believes Jesus has not gone. As John points out, "The next day the crowd that had stayed on the opposite shore of the lake realized that only one boat had been there, and that Jesus had not entered it with the disciples, but that they had gone away alone" (John 6:22). Their logic is impeccable. Therefore, Jesus cannot be in the boat; but they have missed a trick. The dynamics of this sequence is interesting. Many of this vast crowd, intent on insurrection, camp out overnight. They are persistent. Those who set out to accomplish a revolution do not give up at the first setback. Their commitment to Jesus is tenacious. The disciples row *against* a strong wind in the night and land at Gennesaret (Mark 6:53).

Immediately men send word to the surrounding country that Jesus is there; an insurrectionist urgency drives the news. People also bring their sick and are healed. By midmorning news of where Jesus is has reached Tiberias, Herod's capital. Strong westerly winds take boats rapidly from Tiberias and ten miles across to the Bethsaida area, to bear the news. Presumably, news of the possibility of rebellion is rife in Tiberias, and the fact of Jesus' arrival back on the western coast is promptly transmitted to the insurrectionists. Maybe some in Herod's capital city are even involved on the insurrectionist side. Is Herod away in Perea? We do not know. Only with this news do the crowds camping out realize that they have lost the plot and their leader. They plod back round the north end of the lake and try to get their act together. In Capernaum, his hometown, where Jesus has walked from Gennesaret, they find him (John 6:24). They gather round him perplexed, in the center of the village and near the synagogue, about twenty yards from the waterside. A revolutionary movement that loses its leader is going nowhere, and they try to recover momentum.

When they meet, with many of the crowd suffering from a bad night's sleep, Jesus engages them in a discussion that is teasing, even bantering. Previously they had wanted a sign, but he upbraids them for a more basic fixation. "You are not wanting a sign from me, but are just traveling around looking for bread." Ha. Ha. Very funny. The crowd gathers round the man, dozens deep. Then he speaks to their hearts at a deeper level. "Go after food that lasts to eternal life, which I, the Son of Man, will give you." Constantly, he will not respond to their agenda but keeps on bringing up their central relationship with God. They respond with a promising question, "What must we do to do the work that God requires?" (John 6:28). They are thinking of rebellion. Jesus' answer points to himself, which is odd when they are totally focused on him anyway. It engages them at a level where it is difficult to hear properly. Why is he so obscure? "The work of God is this: to believe in the one he has sent" (6:29). To move from doing the work of God to this simple, personal faith is too much. All they actually have to face is that God's "Son of Man" is among them, and relate to him. He is the central truth of life, standing with them now.

Jesus gives too much for them to take it all in. They persist in their agenda and ask for a sign. They have made the link with Moses and manna and descend into abject babble: "What miraculous sign then will you give that we may see it and believe in you? What will you do? Our forefathers ate manna in the desert, . . . 'bread from heaven'" (6:30–31). "What will you do?" Somewhere in their addled heads they think, "Weren't we given bread from heaven yesterday?" But the discussion leaps ahead as Jesus says, "For the bread of God is he who comes down from heaven and gives life to the world." "Sir," they say, "from now on give us this bread" (6:33–34). Jesus then puts the awesome metaphor right under their noses. "I am the bread of life. He who comes to me will never go hungry" (6:35). Jesus places before them the total personal act of coming to him, of becoming a child of God, of receiving eternal life. Can they rethink their agenda? The issue hangs in the air, and then a sense of failure returns. An uprising has gone flat. They have had a bad night. This is just Jesus-bar-Joseph from Nazareth on the hill.

The crowd begins to grumble, struggling with the depth of what Jesus is saying, stumbling at the person who will not take up what *they* have to offer. Jesus pushes them further, teaching what they can hardly comprehend. He claims the astonishing prophecy "They will all be taught by God" as a possible existing reality (6:45). Can people sit around and just be taught by God? There is quite an atmosphere as the sheer difficulty of Jesus' teaching is tossed about among the people. Then he moves into what is incomprehensible to them and possibly to us, that we will directly feed on him and have life through his death. A dying leader will not do. They want a Deliverer. Jesus' larger concern for their life before God will not square with their wants (6:25–59). In these terms, he lets them down, and "from this time many of his disciples turned back and no longer followed him" (6:66). At the same time, as a friend and healer of ordinary poor people, he is the one to whom people flock, and all who touch him are healed (Mark 6:53–56). Jesus' refusal to succumb to their terms is astonishing.

After this event, Jesus withdraws to the mountainous region of Tyre and Sidon, a walk of thirty or so miles northeast through difficult terrain, away from Roman roads and out of Herod Antipas's reach. This is a straightforward response. Jesus has to quell a revolution, and his disciples are in danger of being butchered. The boats return, and news of a crowd of five thousand supposedly planning an insurrection buzzes round Tiberias and must reach Herod, perhaps now back from Perea. This time he will not be inquisitive, but out to kill. There is pressure. The crowds do not give up. In the region of Tyre "he entered a house and did not want anyone to know it; yet he could not keep his presence secret" (Mark 7:24). This is an odd report about someone with a few disciples wandering a long way from home and largely unknown, but it may be explained by the political significance of the event. Presumably, Jesus is finding it difficult to lose these people of fanatical Zealot loyalty. Later, he and his disciples begin a long circle back through the territories of Philip to the area of the Decapolis, partly avoiding Herod's region and partly trying to lose the crowds and the hysteria for revolution (7:31).

Yet people are following him, and once he reenters Galilee, they pick him up. Mark records them as being with Jesus for three days and becoming very hungry. Again, about four thousand are fed, bringing their people for healing, and then Jesus sends the crowds away and leaves by boat for Magdala, or Dalmanutha, a few miles north along the lake from Herod's capital, Tiberias. It was hardly a safe location at the time with Herod so close, but insurrection could not be planned there. Crowds could not gather under the nose of Herod's soldiers. Throughout this great cycle of events, a Galilean uprising in effect tries to press Jesus into the Zealot messianic mold. But Jesus refuses the proposed form and the crowd's conception of politics, letting the pressure dissipate. This is not the rule of God.

There is a postscript. Shortly after this time Jesus says to the disciples, "Watch out—beware of the yeast of the Pharisees and the yeast of the Herodians" (Mark 8:15n NRSV). The Herodians are, of course, the political group against which this revolutionary hope grows. The Pharisees are similarly a power-gathering group, aiming to advance their own position. Perhaps Jesus is also warning against the dominating groups that spawn revolution, both the false action and reaction. Turning down a revolution does not mean supporting the establishment; they too are a danger. Some see revolutions as moments of truth and clarity, but Jesus sees their weakness and the corruption that generates them. Both establishment and revolution are delusive. Jesus stands outside them. No one owns this politician.

Messiah

When the people have departed and only the chosen ones remain, seemingly the nadir of Jesus' political fortunes, the great word is given that Jesus is Messiah. It is one of the strangest political events in history. Messianic crowds have been following Jesus, hoping that he is their Man. They are eventually persuaded to disperse and lose hope. In contemporary terms it is like a candidate who retires from the presidential election race and goes back home to a few supporters, announcing to them that he really will be president. Yet in this case it might be true. Jesus calmly brings the subject up. He asks about the crowd's view of him. "Who do people say the Son of Man is?" (Matt. 16:13). The evidence is that the term "Son of Man" is not much used outside Palestine, later in the NT, or in wider Judaism. Jesus seems to use it insistently as a third-person term for himself (cf. 16:21; Mark 8:27, 31), with an obvious messianic focus in Daniel 7:13.[12] He therefore invites the response of Messiah, because that is precisely what everybody has been saying he is.

Yet the disciples, after what they see as a considerable failure, skirt round the possibility. "Some say John the Baptist; others say Elijah; and still others, Jeremiah or one of the prophets" (Matt. 16:14). In other words, they report all the other great Jewish figures *except* Jesus. They reflect the crowd's disillusionment with the messianic hope, for now they too cannot think of a messianic uprising. Their heads are down. But Jesus insists on a response, asking the disciples: "Who do you say I am?" Simon son of Jonah responds, as though the idea is wrung out of him, far beyond these limiting thoughts of seeming failure: "You are the Messiah, the Son of the Living God" (16:15–16n). Jesus affirms what he says as true, revealed directly by God, and goes on to name him Peter for this revelation. In this knowledge, he will be the rock (*petra*) on which the church (*ekklēsia*) will be built.[13] The Greek meaning of *ekklēsia*, part of the culture of the time, is the congregation or assembly of free citizens that make up the Greek *polis* (city), the gathering of the *dēmos* (people, public assembly); it has a partly political meaning. The focus is on gathered people, not cultic religious activity. These are people who will gather to Messiah, but in the right way. Jesus' messiahship and its affirmation are the rock, the foundation of the people of God. Jesus also gives Peter the keys of the kingdom, with a metaphorical allusion to the civic duty of opening or closing the city gates: the kingdom has an inside and outside (16:17–19).

Clearly, Jesus sees this revelation as epochal for the disciples. But for now it is to be secret. He warns the disciples not to tell anyone and couples it with informing the disciples for the first time that he will go to Jerusalem and be killed and rise again (16:20–21). What Jesus reveals is light years ahead of where the disciples are. The truth cannot be fully told because of the false messianic hopes that are around. The meaning of *Messiah* is far deeper than the Jews, including the disciples, perceive. It not only includes the Suffering Servant themes of Isaiah (cf. 52:13–53:12) and elsewhere, but the issue of what political redemption before God means. It takes on all the failures, crises, suffering, and conflict of which politics is made. Rather than manipulating a few immediate events, Jesus is walking into the eye of the storm, seeing political evil and failure as they really are and addressing them with love. He and his followers must "take up the cross," the ultimate form of expulsion by the political system. So Jesus is en route to Jerusalem, following a way that none will understand, because no one thinks of politics in God's way. Only when they are shown and perceive with the Spirit of God will they see, albeit dimly.

Bibliography

Batey, Richard. *Jesus and the Forgotten City: New Light on Sepphoris and the Urban World of Jesus.* Grand Rapids: Baker, 1991.

Burkett, Delbert. *The Son of Man Debate.* Society for New Testament Studies Monograph Series 107. Cambridge: Cambridge University Press, 1999.

Freyne, Seán. "Bandits in Galilee: A Contribution to the Study of Social Conditions in First-Century Palestine." Pages 50–68 in *The Social World of Formative Christianity and Judaism.* Edited by Jacob Neusner et al. Philadelphia: Fortress, 1988.

Hoehner, Harold W. *Herod Antipas: A Contemporary of Jesus Christ.* Grand Rapids: Zondervan, 1980.

Horsley, Richard A. *Archaeology, History, and Society in Galilee: The Social Context of Jesus and the Rabbis.* Valley Forge, PA: Trinity, 1996.

———. *Hearing the Whole Story: The Politics of Plot in Mark's Gospel.* Louisville: Westminster John Knox, 2001.

Jesus the Messiah?

The Political Messiah?

The idea of Jesus as Messiah is momentous. In this chapter we pause to unpack its significance more fully. Christians follow Jesus *Christos*, the Greek term for *Messiah*. This affirmation is there from the beginning of the church and, as we have seen, is Jesus' self-identification. Christians follow Jesus the Christ. Yet the title is subject to Christian and wider debate. It means clearly something like God's chosen political leader. In all Jewish and Christian thought, the relationship with God is central. Yet this idea is obviously problematic. History is littered with many leaders aspiring to be godlike or god-inspired, from Nero to Napoleon, and most of them have claimed bogus authority and been disastrous. Nor have they cared much to present God truly. If there is such a thing as God's leader, who can possibly produce the goods? Rightly there is skepticism about the claimants.

Another part of the debate is the historic meaning of *Messiah*. What did *Messiah* convey in the centuries preceding Jesus and in the Hebrew Bible? What has it meant in the Judaic and Christian traditions of Messiah? They formed about the same time and have obviously diverged. This discussion especially focuses on the New Testament, because we can now know or substantially guess the messianic views of a variety of different first-century groups, and this scholarship can locate the Gospel meanings more fully.

But there is also a deep-seated Christian dilemma. Although Jesus identifies himself as Messiah and the church has affirmed this down the ages, he was systematically reluctant to be known publicly as such. In the Gospel narratives, Jesus seems like a titled lord who briefly acknowledges his nobility but spends the rest of his life trying to bury it. This phenomenon is normally called "the messianic secret." Why is this pattern discernible in the Gospels, and what does it mean? If Jesus backs away from the political identification of Messiah current at his time, does this mean that Christianity is apolitical?

Or perhaps *Messiah* is a title that is not significant in the same way for early Christianity as among the Jews. It has become more of a surname, like the Smith in John Smith. This is a common view:

> Already by the time of the earliest letters of Paul *Christos* has ceased to be a technical term and has become a name. . . . It is remarkable that in the nearly 400 uses of *christos* in the letters of Paul (most of them written, of course, to predominantly Gentile churches) there is only one clear sense of its use in its original technical sense. . . . So if the term *Christos* tended increasingly to be used simply as a name of Jesus . . .[1]

Talking of Messiah to Gentiles within the Roman Empire is cross-culturally difficult. But does Paul's understanding of *Christos* lose its Jewish content? It hardly seems so. After his conversion, we read that "Saul [Paul] grew more and more powerful and baffled the Jews living in Damascus by proving that Jesus is the Christ [Messiah]" (Acts 9:22). Fifteen years later he is explaining, proving, and proclaiming Jesus as Messiah to the Jews in Thessalonica, in northern Greece (17:2–4). He is doing the same in his final years in Rome, preaching the kingdom of God and teaching about the Lord Jesus *Christos* (28:23, 31). As a Jew, Paul knows exactly what *Messiah* means, and his development is to extend the meaning of *Messiah* to the Gentiles. In his final paeon of praise to Christ in the letter to the Romans, he states who the Messiah of the Gentiles is, quoting Isaiah. Nothing can be clearer:

> And again, Isaiah says,
>> "The root of Jesse will spring up,
>> one who will arise to rule over the nations;
>> the Gentiles will hope in him." (Rom. 15:12)

Paul thus sees an *expansion* of the meaning of *Messiah* and *rule* to the Gentiles, not its neutralization.

Yet always the prior question is whether Jesus' understanding of *Messiah* is political or not. Perhaps the Christ addresses the general human condition and reveals something of God, but without any direct engagement with the state and political rule. Then Christians too will have no special engagement in that area. Key to this issue is the meaning of the Messiah, the Christ, opened up in the Gospels. This term cannot be incidental to the life of Jesus Christ, and this chapter focuses on it.

We must push the terms of the discussion further. Even in some of the more political intepretations of Jesus' life, he is not seen as "fully" political. Some views insist on Jesus being seen as a model for radical ethics formed on God's terms and without compromise. The kingdom of God has political consequences, but it is not directly political in the sense of seeing Christ as a political leader and claiming our prior commitment for Christian politics. This ethical stance is common.[2] Political action is standing in principle against worldly ways, as the great Anabaptist tradition has done through the centuries. But perhaps messianic claims are fully political. Christianity has recognized Christ's rule over the whole of life, but does the title also mean that he is an actual political ruler? In Isaiah's words, is the government really on his shoulder? Is Messiah actually the King, ruler, and political leader in a more direct sense than we usually consider? Do we vote for him or not? In these terms, we consider the Messiah as God's political leader.

Mary and the Coming Messiah

When the angel visits Mary in the small village up the hill, she gives her consent to the conceiving of Jesus. The angel tells her news that is powerfully messianic: "The Lord God will give [Jesus] the throne of his father David, and he will reign over the house of Jacob for ever; his kingdom will never end" (Luke 1:32–33). That call from God is the ultimate call for a Jewish woman, one for which every woman longs. She responds with acceptance and submission. Fairly soon after conception, she goes to the hill country of Judea to stay with her elder relative Elizabeth and share the news of their joint pregnancies, Elizabeth's sixth months more advanced than hers. Elizabeth knows Mary to be bearing Messiah. It is probable that Mary composes the Magnificat while she is a guest in the priestly family, as that family is marveling over the growth of John the Baptist in the old woman's womb. The Magnificat expresses Mary's relationship with Jesus in a wonderful prophetic poem.[3] Mary's words are formed within a tradition that she obviously shares with Zechariah, Simeon, and other men and women prophets. It partly reflects the pseudepigraphical *1 Enoch* 46:

> This Son of Man whom you have seen is the One who would remove the kings and the mighty ones from their comfortable seats and the strong ones

from their thrones. He shall loosen the reins of the strong and crush the teeth of sinners. He shall depose kings from their thrones and kingdoms. For they do not extol or glorify him, and neither do they obey him, the source of their kingship. The faces of the strong will be slapped and be filled with shame and gloom. Their dwelling places and their beds will be worms. (46:4–6)[4]

There are clear parallels, and yet Mary's song is different. It is a womanly prophecy that replaces judgment with mercy and blessing. It stands apart from Zechariah's, which has a focus similar to the Enoch passage, on God's victory and national salvation. Zechariah yearns for "salvation from our enemies and from the hand of all who hate us" (Luke 1:71). These phrases focus on the normal messianic hope. The vision is for someone from the line of David (thus a king) "to rescue us from the hand of our enemies, and to enable us to serve [God] without fear in holiness and righteousness before him all our days" (Luke 1:69–75). But this vision of Zechariah is not realized. Rather, within two generations the nation faced unprecedented defeat. Jesus does not deliver his people in this way. *As a result of* their nationalism and messianic hope, they face the greatest national tragedy imaginable in the destruction of Jerusalem.

When Mary reflects on the child in her womb, her political focus is more universal. "He has brought down rulers from their thrones but has lifted up the humble" (Luke 1:52). This is strange. Suddenly, the old theme of might and conquest is bent to lift up the humble. This is the known world turned upside down. Rulers down, the humble up. It is a revolutionary statement, except that it is not rabble-rousing. Instead, it looks to the mighty forearm of God, to the child in her belly. The contrast is obvious. On the one hand, Herod the Great seems to be running the show through the Roman Empire, with fortresses, soldiers, taxation, fear, and death to his enemies. This is the way of government, the universal way. But as we now see (or do we, in our superpower, missile world?), there is madness in this rule, madness that sends Joseph and Mary down to Egypt just to protect the baby Jesus. The real political sanity lies with the One who will scatter the proud in the imagination of their hearts, as Tyndale put it, before he too was viciously murdered. This word *imagination* must not be lost. Rulers believe in realpolitik, but as Mary says, what they often think is realism actually deceives self and others, because they are proud. Jesus later will destroy false imagination simply by telling the truth. But all of this is beyond any concrete formulation. There is a nagging difference between these intimations of Mary and the prevailing hope. This messianic vision already has its own character.

The Jewish Messiah

But as such, it was only one emphasis in a widely shared hope. The normality of messianic expectation at the time of Jesus is clear. This is conveyed in the Gospels almost incidentally. Herod asks where the Messiah is to be born, and the scribes reply almost as though it is a standard response by referring to Micah 5. Simeon has received an oracle that he will not see death before he has "seen the Lord's Messiah" (Luke 2:26 NRSV). The eighty-four-year-old prophetess, Anna, is fasting and praying for the Messiah's "redemption of Jerusalem" (Luke 2:38, reflecting Isa. 52:9). These people are waiting before God for the coming One, but Messiah talk is far more widespread. People ask John the Baptist if he is the Messiah, almost as a routine question (John 1:19–20). The hope even occurs among the Samaritans (4:25–26). Most revealing is the aimless chitchat of the people:

> "But we know where this man is from; when the Messiah comes, no one will know where he is from." . . . They said, "When the Messiah comes, will he do more miraculous signs than this man?" . . . Still others asked, "How can the Messiah come from Galilee?" (7:27n, 31, 41)

These comments show general popular expectations, crowd talk that makes the search for the political leader intrinsic to the times, almost like discussing who the next prime minister might be. Each political party has its own slant on power and the Messiah. But the evidence from the Gospels and elsewhere is that this background hope and expectation are shared throughout first-century Jewish culture.

The Old Testament history of messianism explains why this is so. Its origin lies with Moses as God's chosen national deliverer, leading the Israelites from Egyptian slavery into freedom. The idea of God's Anointed One emerges with the kings of Israel, especially with David, who loves God's law and becomes the Godward king. As the kings falter, the vision takes shape within the prophets. Its most striking expression is in Daniel, where the Anointed One, the Ruler, is prophesied (Dan. 9:25–27). Daniel struggles with relationships between the rulers of the Babylonian and Persian empires and the Lord his God. There is an account of both Nebuchadnezzar and Darius being brought face to face with the God whose kingdom will never end (Dan. 4, 6). When Daniel has a dream of four beasts, representing four empires, the culmination is the appearance of "one like a son of man" before the Ancient of Days. "He was given authority, glory and sovereign power; all peoples, nations and [those] of every language [served] him. His dominion is an everlasting dominion that will not pass away, and his kingdom one that will never be destroyed" (7:13–14; cf. 7:18, 22, 27). Daniel, himself a high official in the greatest empire of the time, explicitly presents the one like the son of man in political terms. He is the one whom all rulers will worship and obey (7:27).

In postexilic times and apocryphal and pseudepigraphical writings, these themes are being gathered in a swathe of other texts identifying God's chosen ruler. In the book of *1 Enoch* the "pangs of the Messiah" and judgment are graphically drawn. The *Testaments of the Twelve Patriarchs* focuses on the coming together of the twelve tribes into one nation, and the *Psalms of Solomon* focus on the glory of the holy King. *Second Baruch* and other texts have a vision of the rule of God, and *4 Ezra* and the *Sibylline Oracles* lay out the ferment and conflagrations of the final days.[5] The visions are centrally related to God and involve the great or holy King and national deliverance. This literature becomes a deep part of Jewish national consciousness. The views vary in emphasis; none is really apolitical.[6] Some focus directly on the political; others are more apocalyptic, looking for some sudden intervention by God. The Essenes are perhaps the least political, but they still wait for the acts of God and the overthrow of Rome. Here is one of their hymns of messianic hope:

> Get up, hero, take your prisoners, glorious one, collect your spoil, worker of heroic deeds! Place your hand on the neck of your foes and your foot on the piles of the dead! Strike the nations, your foes, and may your sword consume guilty flesh! Fill the land with glory. (*War Scroll* 19.2–4)[7]

In the great rebellion, the Essenes, having been politically passive, join in the war against the Romans (66–70). Neusner and others note that the "Sicarii (dagger slayers) were Essenes turned activists in the heavy days of the war."[8] When the moment comes, their views are also decisively political.

But the literary meanings of *Messiah* are heightened versions of ordinary politics. More normal are a series of individuals who seek to raise a rebellion in the mode of Judas Maccabeus. This pattern occurs from the beginning of Herod the Great's reign through to AD 70. Josephus, scorning those actually not far from his own position to clear himself with the Romans, describes them thus: "Cheats and deceivers claiming inspiration, they schemed to bring about revolutionary changes by inducing the mob to act as if possessed, and by leading them out in the desert on the pretence that there God would show them signs of approaching freedom."[9] But Josephus protests slightly too much. This hope is a far more integral part of first-century Jewish history.

It focuses on God's Deliverer. Jewish history is one of political deliverance. Moses delivered the children of Israel from slavery in Egypt. David delivered Israel into being an independent nation free from control by the Philistines. But the deliverance theme flourished most strongly in the intertestamental period. After the exile, there was a long struggle against the empires of Alexander the Great, the Syrians or Seleucids, the Parthians in the East, and the heavy hand of Rome. If all of these went to sleep, Egypt could be relied on to cast her eyes northward (as in the third century BC; cf. 3 Maccabees). It was a D-day culture, continually looking for liberation from the dominating empire. That was to be accomplished by the Deliverer. The Jewish model was Judas Maccabeus. The Maccabee family started by defending Jews in Galilee and the Jordan valley against the Edomites and Philistines. Judas's father took up the fight against the Syrians and died while exhorting his sons to continue it. Judas became the foremost of them (see 1 and 2 Maccabees).

Judas defeated and killed Apollonius, the Syrian leader, and from then on in true warrior style used Apollonius's sword in all his fighting. Gradually he trained an efficient Jewish army. In 165 BC, Judas and the army won a brave victory at a battle near Emmaus. About a year later another Syrian force under Lysias was formed. Despite this, Judas was able to establish control over Jerusalem and set about rededicating the Temple and restoring its worship (1 Macc. 4, in 164 BC, celebrated at Hanukkah). When the Seleucid leader Antiochus Epiphanes died, Lysias assumed total control. He won a victory just outside Jerusalem and laid siege to Mount Zion, the Temple Mount. Those inside began to suffer intense hunger, partly because it was the sabbatical year, when little food was grown. It looked as though they would have to give up or be slaughtered. Then suddenly Lysias faced a rebellion at home that forced him to make a lenient peace and retreat. It was understood as an act of God, vindicating and marking the Maccabean family.[10]

From then on the Jews were able to continue the free practice of Temple worship on terms of the Mosaic law, right down to the time of Jesus. Even the Romans did not dare to challenge the place of the Temple, because they knew it would invoke vicious war. Thereafter, the Temple and the coming Warrior-Deliverer were bound together in a strong nationalism, presuming that "God, *our* God, will deliver us" (cf. Ps. 67:6). This emphasis was so strong that it prompts the fanatical defense of Jerusalem in 66–70. During Jesus' time it was the focal meaning of *Messiah* for most groups, orientated against the hated Romans and Herodians and toward national deliverance. Overwhelmingly, the people and leaders thought only in terms of a *Jewish* deliverer.

Another element in this cultural package was the importance of the sign. The people wanted a "miraculous sign" that God was with a leader (John 6:30). It was the anointing, as Judas Maccabeus was anointed by his amazing defense of Jerusalem. People were waiting to rally behind the one who was God's person, so that the great miracle of national deliverance could take place. The Gospels are full of Jesus' reaction to the need for a sign. "It is a wicked generation that asks for a miraculous sign," he says. "You interpret the sky and you should interpret what is happening, but you can't read what is going on in front of you. The only sign you will get is the prophet who went asking *Gentiles* to repent and saved the city of Ninevah" (cf. Matt. 16:2–4). This was an infuriating refusal to fit the messianic model of the time. A leader must lead and have God's mark of success and greatness. In all of these respects, therefore, the culture of the time sees Messiah as political—God's leader, king, deliverer, ruler. This is the model portrayed both in the Gospels and in other Jewish literature. One cannot read the term *Messiah* apolitically.

But this still leaves the question of whether Jesus' self-identification is political. Perhaps it is not. Indeed, in many other respects he counters the culture. He is not nationalist. He eschews the role of warrior. He refuses to hate the Romans or to intrigue with them. He avoids the crowds rather than whipping them up. He critiques signs and does not seek power over his people. Jesus stands outside the Jewish messianic culture at every turn.

Jesus and Isaiah's Messiah

From well before Handel, many have recognized that the Old Testament home for Jesus the Messiah is the Suffering Servant portions of Isaiah, as Jesus himself invites us to see. There is debate about whether these are part of messianic understanding in the first century. They do not fit well with the warrior-deliverer motif. The likelihood is that the Suffering Servant theme is rather sidelined and sublimated (though echoed at Qumran in *Thanksgiving Hymns* II–IX). We have direct evidence of this, for when Jesus tries to explain the Suffering Servant role to the disciples repeatedly, they clearly have no terms of reference, which might make sense of it. The disciples, taught about servanthood and the way of suffering, continue to clamor about who will be the greatest (Luke 9:46). Peter speaks for the Twelve in protesting Jesus' predictions of his death (Matt. 16:22). After the resurrection, the two on the road to Emmaus describe their sense of defeat at Jesus' death. With an ironic poke at their slowness to comprehend, the risen Lord shows them how the prophets prefigure this suffering (Luke 24:26–27; cf. Acts 8:30–35). The disciples' inability to comprehend is significant. Within a culture so strongly driven to seek the national deliverer, the Suffering Servant is incomprehensible.

At the same time, the text of Isaiah is the object of much reflection from Qumran to Galilee. The fact that an obscure little synagogue at Nazareth has the scroll tells the story. More important, it is clearly part of Jesus' self-understanding. John the Baptist identifies with Isaiah 40. Jesus reads Isaiah 61 in the synagogue (Luke 4) and bases himself on the quiet servant theme from Isaiah 42 (probably Jesus' words, not just Matthew's interpretation; Matt. 12:16–21). At Jesus' baptism the voice from heaven echoes Isaiah 42:1 (Matt. 3:17). Jesus' words on the road to Emmaus reflect Isaiah 53. These all show Jesus at home in these texts and seeing them as messianic. This has always been recognized as a key fulcrum to Jesus' meaning of the Christ. So, what kind of Messiah does Isaiah present?

Here again, we face the fact that these texts are partly political. The great Isaiah 52:14–15 text says, "My servant . . . will sprinkle many nations, and kings will shut their mouths because of him. For what they were not told, they will see, and what they have not heard, they will understand." The divine ruler cannot be excised from these texts. Alec Motyer reflects on the structure of the book: "The Isaianic literature is built around three Messianic portraits: the King (chapters 1–37), the Servant (chapters 38–55) and the Anointed Conqueror (chapters 56–66). It also shows how each of these portraits is integral to the 'book' in which it is set. Standing back from the portraits, however, we discover the same features in each, indicative of the fact that they are meant as facets of the one Messianic person."[11] A careful reading of the text cannot but conclude that Isaiah's Messiah is also inescapably political.

But far more is involved than this. Before and since Jesus, people have not been able to interpret Isaiah's Messiah. The starting point has to be the unquestionable sovereignty of God the Creator, to whom the nations are like a drop in the bucket or dust in a vacuum cleaner (40:15). The sovereignty of God stands beyond all other political perspectives. Throughout history, political philosophy has moved in many different directions: authoritarianism, dictatorship, the divine right of rulers, the popular leader, individualism, rights theory, and so on—all these locate the meaning of politics within political rule. Few have seen the radical difference and rightness of God's rule over nations and empires. Few have had the vision that the ruthless can be stilled by God (Isa. 25).

Yet more difficult is the idea that the king can also be a Suffering Servant. Deep in this great book is a radical understanding of sin and injustice, a deconstruction of human autonomy and power, a knowledge of love and mercy, and a pervasive sense that God is with us. It requires the self-referencing attitude of the state and politics to be discarded in recognition of their accountability before God. Above all, it requires a complete rethinking of the idea of victory. Throughout sinful human history, conquest has been domination, self-will, glory, and control over others. Such thought forms are endemic to presidents, prime ministers, kings, and people through the centuries. Yet here in Isaiah a different fulcrum is intimated. To win is to fight for the other, the weak, the sick, and even the enemy. To win is to lose, even one's life, steady in love. By his wounds we are healed. The Deliverer is led like a lamb to the slaughter, and he bears our iniquities (Isa. 53). No one can be sure of the actual incarnation of Isaiah's meaning in the Suffering Servant. But here is the prototype for the great hinge of political history in Jesus. It all swings on this.[12]

On the other side of this door, when we actually set out to think farsightedly what a good ruler is, there is no alternative. When control of others, self-glorification, injustice, militarism, and self-serving are seen for what they are and removed, the Isaianic model begins to become unavoidable. All models of the good ruler from Plato onward retain forms of self-indulgence and mistaken human infallibility. Plato, for example, is quite happy to treat women as cattle. The enlightened despot ignores the peasants. The revolutionary finishes up proud and dominating. Most rulers do not have the humility to face the issue of their own weaknesses and have spread their damage around. But humanity always and inescapably needs a humble ruler, a servant.[13] All those would-be dominators will kick against God's stone and be broken on it (Dan. 2:45; Matt. 21:42–44). Handel, weeping his heart out before the *Messiah*, had it about right. Even fat old King George II had some inkling of it when he stood up before his Lord during the "Hallelujah Chorus." Surely, he has born our griefs and carried our sorrows, and the Lord has laid on him the iniquity of us all.

The Gospels seamlessly present this Messiah. He has no presence or power to attract us to him, nothing in his appearance that we should vote for him. He is the kind of person we ignore. He finishes up at the bottom, and anyone who is anything, even his friends, withdraw from him. He is a friend of the poor, the widow, and the sick. He finishes up wearing a crown of thorns. He is led as a lamb to the slaughter and is silent in the face of false accusations. The punishment that brings us peace is upon him. The actual Messiah is so far away from all our preconceptions, including Jewish ones, that by and large we have not been able to take it. When the good ruler comes, we turn the other way.

Here we stop and reflect. In Isaiah and as the Christ, Jesus is the *political* leader. He is the Prince of Peace, the Son of David, the true King of the Jews, and the government will be upon his shoulder. This is not a retreat from politics, but the deepest engagement with it. "He will reign on David's throne and over his kingdom, establishing and upholding it with justice and [right living] from that time on and for ever. The zeal of the LORD Almighty will accomplish this" (Isa. 9:7). Those who follow him therefore give their allegiance to him also as political leader. This is consistently Jesus' self-identification. There is no other way of interpreting his claim properly. He is a radically different leader, but neither he nor the Gospel writers disavow the fundamental truth that he is political leader, God's chosen Messiah, as political as any prime minister or president, though also far more.

Is Jesus Messiah? Unravelling the Enigma

The puzzle of the "messianic secret" now unravels easily. First, we see Jesus clearly unwilling to allow his public proclamation as Messiah. This is no great mystery, for if Jesus proclaims himself as such, he would be taken over by the current popular perceptions and thrust into the role of national military deliverer. He "warned his disciples not to tell anyone that he was the Messiah" (Matt. 16:20n) and effectively deconstructs or slips away from all the situations where he would be cast as nationalist leader. He has to avoid the stereotype because it is part of the great lie. Jesus not only has to be the Messiah; he also has to protect its true meaning.[14]

This is why he so firmly resists the idea of producing a confirmatory sign. He heals those who come to him in faith, but such healing is extraordinary and draws an ecstatic following. Early in his ministry a man with leprosy comes to Jesus and is healed. Jesus orders him, "Don't tell anyone, but go, show yourself to the priest and offer [your thanksgiving sacrifice to God] . . . as a testimony [of your gratitude]" (Luke 5:14). Then we read, "Yet the news about him spread all the more, so that crowds of people came to hear him and be healed of their sicknesses. But Jesus often withdrew to lonely places and prayed" (5:15–16). This obviously was not coyness on the part of Jesus, but his systematic concern to prevent the buildup of messianic fervor. Later the pattern becomes more intense. When Lazarus, known by all in his village to be decomposing, is raised to life, people run around with the news and into Jerusalem (John 11). The Sanhedrin gather and state Jesus' problem from their perceptions: "Here is this man performing many miraculous signs. If we let him go on like this, everyone will believe in him, and then the Romans will come and take away both our place and our nation" (11:47–48). Exactly. It is precisely this sign-giving Deliverer role that Jesus has systematically avoided throughout his ministry.

But the obverse, rejecting the title, does not occur either. For Jesus, his mother, the disciples, the Gospel writers, and Christians, Jesus clearly is the Christ. This is from Jesus himself. We return to the moment when it is made explicit. Jesus leads the conversation.

> "But what about you?" he asked. "Who do you say I am?" Simon Peter answered, "You are the Christ, the Son of the living God." Jesus replied, "Blessed are you, Simon son of Jonah, for this was not revealed to you by man, but by my Father in heaven." (Matt. 16:15–17)

There could be no clearer affirmation. What Peter says is true; it is from God. The answer from Jesus himself to the question at the head of this section is a clear "Yes. Jesus is Messiah." The shape of the discussion shows Jesus deliberately communicating this to his disciples at the time. He opens up the topic, inviting them to address it and know that it is true. There is no doubt that Jesus understands himself as Messiah from the beginning and throughout his life, death, and resurrection. Moreover, Jesus clearly understands his own messiahship as political in this broader sense. He constantly presumes himself to be King or Ruler, even though his style is so different. He enters Jerusalem mounted in a deliberate messianic statement. Zechariah says, "See, your king comes to you, . . . gentle and riding on a donkey" (Zech. 9:9). Thus, he sets up his entry to Jerusalem in a clear allusive statement. The crowd on the road cries out words from the procession of triumph in Psalm 118:26, "Blessed is the king who comes in the name of the LORD!" The Pharisees object, fearing the worst. Jesus responds, "I tell you, if they keep quiet, the stones will cry out" (Luke 19:38–40). Moreover, this is a calm statement of what is the case: no mere triumphalism, for he is on his way to death. Soon he laments for these same people who do not recognize the time of God's coming to them (19:41–44).

Jesus' frequent use of the title "Son of Man" reflects the same truth. The term has been subject to detailed academic reflection. By now, two points are quite clear in relation to its source and Jesus' use of the title. First, as we've seen, the key point of origin is Daniel's vision (Dan. 7). This is so explicitly political, involving the rise and fall of empires, that Jesus' use of the term could not be any less so. Every time he gives himself that title, he is naming his sovereign power and pointing to the everlasting kingdom, where all rulers will serve and obey him. It is a vision that turned Daniel pale, and yet Jesus wears the title like familiar socks, but also with strategic awareness.

The most telling example occurs when Jesus appears before the Sanhedrin. This ruling court has the power of any punishment other than death. They are frustrated because they cannot do the very thing they want to do, which is to have Jesus killed, and this frustration is built into the conduct of the trial. It moves from false evidence, to using one of Jesus' enigmatic sayings against him, to a direct confrontation by the high priest, face-to-face with Jesus, wanting the big showdown. He thrusts his face before Jesus and rasps, "I charge you under oath by the living God: Tell us if you are the Messiah, the Son of God" (Matt. 26:63). The response of Jesus is full of self-control and almost matter-of-fact: "Yes, it is as you say" (26:64; cf. Mark 14:62, "I am"). Jesus teaches that his followers should always tell the truth before God and do not need to swear (Matt. 5:33–37). So he does not swear; he makes his statement from an uncompromising commitment to truthfulness. He has chosen to be silent in the face of earlier accusations, and he chooses to speak now. But what a thing to say! It will lead to his death. Jesus knows it will evince the screaming charge of blasphemy. In Jewish law, this is the ultimate sin. But what follows from Jesus is even more devastating. For he turns the trial from himself to the ultimate judgment of his accusers.

> "Yes, it is as you say," Jesus replied. "But I say to all of you: In the future you will see the Son of Man sitting at the right hand of the Mighty One and coming on the clouds of heaven." (Matt. 26:64)

We recognize the conjunction of Messiah and Son of Man. They are one and the same—God's ruler, God's judge—to whom *they* will have to give account. We also note the worthy way Jesus rules and proclaims judgment in the face of the unjust judges. The Son of Man stands trial as Messiah, fulfilling its content as no one can conceive, and on no other terms than his own. Caiaphas tears his clothes after Jesus' response and is incandescent with rage. He has his evidence, and the rest of the Sanhedrin concurs. They hit Jesus with their fists, spit in his face, blindfold him, and say, "Prophesy to us, Messiah. Who hit you?" (26:67–68n). There is no doubt what is at issue.

Bibliography

Avi-Yonah, Michael, and Zvi Baras, eds. *Society and Religion in the Second Temple Period.* London: Jewish History Publications/W. H. Allen, 1977.

Burkett, Delbert. *The Son of Man Debate.* Society for New Testament Studies Monograph Series 107. Cambridge: Cambridge University Press, 1999.

Casey, Maurice. *Son of Man: The Interpretation and Influence of Daniel 7.* London: SPCK, 1979.

Charlesworth, James H. *The Messiah: Developments in Earliest Judaism and Christianity.* Minneapolis: Fortress, 1992.

Collins, John J. *The Scepter and the Star: The Messiahs of the Dead Sea Scrolls and Other Ancient Literature.* New York: Doubleday, 1995.

Edersheim, Alfred. *Prophecy and History in Relation to the Messiah.* London: Longmans, Green & Co., 1885.

———. *The Life and Times of Jesus the Messiah.* 2 vols. London: Longmans, Green & Co., 1900.

Eisenman, Robert, and Michael Wise. *The Dead Sea Scrolls Uncovered.* Dorset: Element, 1992.

France, Richard T. "Messiah." Pages 987–95 in vol. 2 of *The Illustrated Bible Dictionary.* Edited by N. Hillyer et al. 3 vols. Leicester: Inter-Varsity, 1980.

García Martínez, Florentino. *The Dead Sea Scrolls Translated.* Leiden: Brill, 1994.

Groningen, Gerard van. *Messianic Revelation in the Old Testament.* Grand Rapids: Baker, 1990.

Hengel, Martin. *The Zealots.* Translated by David Smith. Edinburgh: T&T Clark, 1989.

Higgins, A. J. B. *Jesus and the Son of Man.* London: Lutterworth, 1964.

Hooker, Morna D. *Jesus and the Servant: The Influence of the Servant Concept of Deutero-Isaiah in the New Testament.* London, SPCK, 1959.

———. *The Son of Man in Mark: A Study of the Background of the Term "Son of Man" and Its Use in Mark.* London: SPCK, 1967.

Horsley, Richard A. *Archaeology, History, and Society in Galilee: The Social Context of Jesus and the Rabbis.* Valley Forge, PA: Trinity, 1996.

Knohl, Israel. *The Messiah before Jesus.* Berkeley: University of California Press, 2000.

Lewis, Peter. *The Glory of Christ.* London: Hodder & Stoughton, 1992.

Motyer, Alec. *The Prophecy of Isaiah.* Leicester: Inter-Varsity, 1997.

Mowinckel, S. *He That Cometh: The Messiah Concept in the Old Testament and Later Judaism.* Translated by G. W. Anderson. Oxford: Blackwell, 1956.

Neusner, Jacob, et al., eds. *Judaisms and Their Messiahs at the Turn of the Christian Era.* Cambridge: Cambridge University Press, 1987.

O'Neill, J. C. *Who Did Jesus Think He Was?* Leiden: Brill, 1995.

Reymond, Robert L. *Jesus, Divine Messiah: The New Testament Witness.* Phillipsburg, NJ: Presbyterian & Reformed, 1990.

Silver, Abba Hillel. *A History of Messianic Speculation in Israel.* 1927. Repr., Boston: Beacon, 1959.

Storkey, Elaine. *Mary's Story, Mary's Song.* London: Harper Collins, 1993.

Tuckett, Christopher, ed. *The Messianic Secret*. Philadelphia: Fortress; London: SPCK, 1983.

Virgo, Wendy. *Mary, the Mother of Jesus*. Eastborne, UK: Kingsway, 1998.

Wrede, William. *The Messianic Secret*. Translated by J. C. G. Greig. 1901. Repr., Cambridge: James Clarke, 1971.

Yoder, John Howard. *The Politics of Jesus: Vicit Agnus Noster*. Grand Rapids: Eerdmans, 1972. 2d, rev. ed., 1994.

The Government of God

The Kingdom of God

We pull back from the great narrative events and reflect on the political significance of Jesus' teaching about the Kingdom of God. This is not easy. The Kingdom or Rule of God is central to Jesus' teaching and has ramifications that puzzle his contemporaries and later generations. His teaching is the most studied in human history, and that is no accident, for single stories expose the human condition or touch our deepest needs. Jesus knows his teaching is difficult; he re-presents Isaiah 6:9–10: "You will see, but not perceive; you will hear, but not understand" (cf. Mark 4:12 et par.). By calling into question the terms in which his hearers think, Jesus wants to help them move through to grasp what he is conveying. In the parable of the Sower, the word falls on them, and it will either produce an extravagant crop of a hundred, sixty, or thirty times what is sowed; or it will be snatched away by evil, dropped like a fad, or choked by the worries of the world. Hearing and absorbing these Kingdom truths is difficult (Matt. 13:1–23; Mark 4:1–20; Luke 8:4–15). But God is at the center, sowing this seed; this is a Kingdom that grows (Mark 4:26–29). Jesus' teaching on the Kingdom or Rule of God is clearly foundational. Yet the term *Kingdom of God* or *Kingdom of heaven* does not really work in our culture, because the word *Kingdom* is so dated. The United Kingdom is neither united nor a kingdom. Where there are kings, they no longer rule but are ceremonial heads of state. Yet as we have seen with Herod the Great, in Jesus' day kings *are* the government. They run the system: they judge, war, tax, make laws, plan cities, and dictate how people live. Jesus' use of *kingdom* denotes the real and effective *government* of God. This is no withdrawn, otherworldly kingdom.[1] He is talking about God's actual government or rule of our lives as the central truth of our existence, deeper and fuller than mere political government. The subject of most of the kingdom parables is God, and our concern is this: How does God govern?

Still, this is difficult for us and his first hearers to absorb. Jesus moves through Galilee "proclaiming the good news of God. 'The time has come,' he says, 'The government of God is near. Repent and believe the good news'" (cf. Mark 1:14–15). Why is this good news? How can this message change the world? How can it cut into politics? Why repent? The questions come crowding in. Perhaps we need to take our bearings. Many other texts study Jesus' teaching of the Kingdom.[2] Here we are concerned mainly with the political implications.[3] Nevertheless, this is not much less challenging because it depends on the central truth governing all of our existence. Jesus' proclamation of the government of God is the pre-ordering truth of the universe. All of creation is made by God and is subject to God. The government of God is that within which we live. God sends his rain on good and evil alike (Matt. 6:45). We face this truth in any area of life, for all existence depends on God. Although the metaphor of Kingdom is political, the teaching covers everything. Jesus shows the significance of the rule of God in relation to work, status, friendship, marriage, time, food, clothing, healing, money, anxiety, and rest. He addresses prayer, faith, repentance, forgiveness, honesty, and rightness in relation to God. The teaching of the Kingdom is far broader than political, yet it is also political. The rule of God over everything is also God's rule in politics. It is the central truth of political life, the reference point for states, rulers, law, and justice—whether they recognize it or not. Logic requires it. How could the rule of God not apply to states and politics, as though God opted out of this part of our existence?[4]

The Deceptive Teacher

Jesus comes, as Mark says, *"proclaiming the good news of God. 'The time has come,' he said. 'The kingdom of God is near. Repent and believe the good news!'"* (Mark 1:14–15). How can this message amount to anything of significance or reverberate worldwide? Let us examine it point by point.

First, he declares the *good news* of God's rule. Throughout history rulers have been *bad news*. Attila the Hun, Genghis Khan, Bloody Mary, and Idi Amin are not the first people you would invite round the table for a meal. Louis XIV was overbearing, George III was mad, and Ivan was terrible. Rulers are justifiably associated with slavery, heavy taxation, expensive tastes, a tendency to quarrel with neighbors, an addiction to palaces, and asking you to die for them. The rule of many, on the whole, has been a tale of burdens laid on people. Even rulers who have believed themselves benevolent dictators have usually been harvesting the labors of others for their pet schemes—pyramids, a water system for Versailles's fountains, or the Millennium Dome. What really might be good news in terms of political rule is a conundrum, even when today's candidates announce it with wide-smile assurance.[5] In what sense is the rule of God that Jesus proclaims *good* news politically? It is possible that God has a better grasp of human affairs than we seem to have. We wait and evaluate.

"The time has come." Jesus' proclamation seems to be a decisive moment. But is it? As we have already seen in relation to John the Baptist, Jesus' actions do not seem to direct political events. Nor is the impact on first-century world politics great. Indeed, Jesus' ineptness and failure by the standards of twenty-first-century politicians are beyond belief. Most politicians, after feeding seven or eight thousand people gratis, would capitalize on it or at least pass the hat around. Jesus wastes crowds with profligacy. He makes it difficult for his followers. He never takes advantage of big miracles. Jesus does not court allies and ignores the main sources of power in his day. Being, as Isaiah accurately put it, "despised and rejected" is hardly the recipe for an aspiring presidential candidate. This is not decisiveness as we understand it. But our reaction calls into question our own view of time. What is decisive?

The government of God coming among us could be the greatest event in political history; perhaps the greatest ripples do not require the biggest splash. Our mistake would be to expect epic events like conquering Europe, Pearl Harbor, or building the Great Wall of China. We may look to Hannibal or Lenin, but historians understand that change is more complicated than that. Indeed, our expectations may be our mistake. What if the government of God among us is far deeper and more subtle in the changes it effects?[6] At first, everything seems the same, for the Creator gives summer and winter, and rain falls on good and evil alike. The change comes as tyrants fall away, peace steals across continents, justice is done, mercy replaces vengeance, and serfs are lifted up. This would be decisive—the deconstruction of old perceptions and the new consciousness of God's way. It could be the pivot of history, but not in-your-face with armies and the biggest gun in the West. It could take centuries or even millennia to unfold, but in the end it will be decisive.

Nor is Jesus decisive in terms of leadership and power. We think of politics in terms of wars, presidents, leaders, and power. In that sense we are elitist, even media elitist, looking to charismatic figures to shape events. Even our democracy is elitist, defined as the business of choosing politicians who can sort things out for us. We ask the politician, "Can you solve the crime wave?" "Yes," says the politician, "we will have more police." But, of course, the only practical way of sorting out a crime wave is substantially to end crime. Because of our mental closure, we do not even think of this possibility. For centuries people have offered and sought simple top-down, magical solutions, approaching the concrete mixer with a spoon, but the government of God churns deeper into people's lives. And this explains Jesus' style. Can ordinary teaching, life lessons, good living, exposure of hypocrisy, and patience change politics? Yes, they can and have, in many Christian-influenced cultures.[7] Because kingdom politics stays with ordinary people, it can solve problems that other philosophies cannot reach. A politics for the demos focuses less on leaders. It shows ordinary people that the time has come to love justice and walk humbly with their God (Mic. 6:8). It changes politics by conviction rather than control. Maybe it could be decisive.

When Jesus proclaims, "Repent and believe the good news," he signals the way of entering the kingdom, and it is a strange one. "The kingdom is near." It nudges you. It comes to you like a gentle and respectful traveling salesman. Most kingdoms are territories, defended by walls, armies, or custom posts. Often you are in or out by birth. In God's kingdom the boundaries are different. To enter you repent and believe the good news about living with God; you agree to live life on God's terms. Entry is by choice, not by imposed rule. Disciples go out into towns, villages, and cities and offer entry. Perhaps it happens through meetings, friendship, missionaries, or just reading about Jesus. "Do you accept the rule of God or not?" There is invitation and response. You can do it or not do it now, reading this book. Jesus' manner is open, because people are genuinely left to choose their direction. The rich young ruler goes away sad but unchanged. The wheat and weeds will grow together until the end of the age. Here is a kingdom without domineering, control, or defenses. God does not need to be assertive. We are created with responsive freedom, and we enter the kingdom or we do not. This certainly differs from other political cultures, where religiopolitical compulsion is normal. It was so in the Roman and other empires. Far Eastern rulers required conformity. Some Islamic regimes formed the idea of conquering on God's behalf and compelling observance of Shariah.[8] State socialism overthrew capitalist regimes and became controlling single-party states. Max Weber, who studied many states, even defines the concept thus:

"The term 'political community' shall apply to a community whose social action is aimed at subordinating . . . through readiness to physical force, including normally force of arms."[9] Within these perspectives, compulsion is the name of the game. In the middle of all this is a strange culture of people who are voluntary members of a kingdom. Please come along and sing choruses! "Would you like to come to church? The choice is yours." True, since Constantine many Christians have been subverted into control and establishment. Yet that pattern comes from elsewhere, not from its leader.[10] Christ rejects political stratagems like imposed control because God does not rule that way.[11] Jesus offers the gentle rule of God; people are met as persons free to accept or reject. They can pray or not pray to God: "Your kingdom come."[12] This is a voluntary kingdom, and who says you cannot have one?

Nevertheless, some see Christianity as imposed and dictatorial. There is evidence for this in established churches, religious wars, the Crusades, the Inquisition, and sundry other events. Christians have also moved into the controlling mode of a religiopolitical state, suppressing the rule of God for their own rule, a serious error that they should address. Often, of course, these patterns have involved politicians using Christianity. But this view does not come from Christ's teaching. He eschews all control and domination, even playing with the idea, blowing up the balloon, and then letting all the air escape. Political control is always a "yoke." It implies slavery. Seeing the beast of burden trundling along each day is the most obvious parallel with the common lot of the politically dominated. Jesus is political without trying to control people's responses. He picks up the idea of political rule and fills it with new content in the love-fullest invitation of all:

> Come to me, all you who are weary and burdened, and I will give you rest. Take my yoke upon you and learn from me, for I am gentle and humble in heart, and you will find rest for your souls. For my yoke is easy and my burden is light. (Matt. 11:28–30)

The shoulder ache melts away. Here is the opposite of imposed control. We are *invited* to take the yoke, rather than having it jammed upon us. The gentle rule of God means that no human institution can properly claim domination over us.[13] All the systems of domination—whether temple- or magic-based, Confucian, Islamic, Absolutist, Fascist, or Communist—which claim political control are dethroned.[14] God rules, and politicians merely hold limited office. This Kingdom is the root and branch of political freedom.[15] Thus, the Quakers did not take their hats off to politicians, lest the latter get the idea that people were beholden to their ilk; instead, people and judges should quake before God. When God rules, nobody else does.

In the end, people changing their hearts, minds, and attitudes is *the only feasible political method*. Jesus pithily understates it: "The government of God is like yeast that a woman took and mixed into a large amount of flour until it worked all through the dough" (cf. Matt. 13:33). The spreading of the Kingdom is as everyday as that. Here, as Jesus teaches his local people, the profound political revolution starts. In its own way it is good news, decisive, and unforced. It has, in part, worked in subsequent history. So, when the deceptive teacher strolls through Galilee meeting people and doing nothing of great note, we should not be deceived. It is momentous. It signals a different way of life and of politics.

The Offense of the Kingdom of God

There is another aspect of this Kingdom that deserves reflection. As Jesus intimates, it also causes a good deal of offense. Jesus expects it and even gives it quite directly. He goes to eat with a Pharisee who criticizes him for not washing his hands according to the Jewish purification rites (Luke 11:38). Jesus responds with a robust attack against the hypocrisy of outward appearance. An expert of the law, clearly expecting better treatment, answers him, "Teacher, when you say these things, you insult us also" (11:45). For good measure Jesus turns and attacks him, pointing out that his kind put burdens on people that they cannot really bear and do not lift a finger to help them. Jesus exposes the position of experts in the law. They have recently erected marble tombs and monuments, honoring the prophets and reverencing the great prophetic traditions, as they see it. But Jesus reverses their loyalty: "The prophets of old who spoke God's words were killed by people who wanted to silence them. You build tombs and thus validate that process of murdering God's messengers. You are in the tradition of those who persecute God's prophets and want them dead." Not surprisingly, both Pharisees and teachers of the law take offense (Luke 11:47–51). Jesus is no wind sock. The requirements of God are sharp-edged and cannot be watered down. "Repent" is subversive: "God says you have it all wrong, and you need to publicly admit it." We dress up apologies, retain mental reservations, and see them as social accommodation, but the call to repent does not bend. "What you are doing is actually wrong; accept that you are wrong before God." Thus, "Repent!" is diamond sharp. Those who will not make the move are offended by the requirement. Submitting to God on God's terms upsets many rulers. John, the messenger to Antipas and Herodias, lost his head. Jesus' message will drive leaders to kill.

We see this offense laid out in one of the parables of the Kingdom. Jesus is teaching the people in the temple courts and is confronted by the Chief Priests, Sanhedrin, and elders—the corporate rulers of Israel. They are smarting and try to face Jesus down. After a skirmish that they lose, Jesus presents them with the parable of the Tenants: A man planted a vineyard, did a lot of work to it, rented it to tenants, and went on a journey. At the time of harvest, he sent his servants to collect his share of the produce, the rent. The tenants seized his servants and beat one, killed another, and stoned a third. He sent other servants to them, more than the first time, and the tenants treated them in the same way. Last of all he sent his son to them, saying, "They will respect my son." But when the tenants saw the son, they said to each other, "This is the heir. Come, let us kill him and take his inheritance!" So they took him, threw him out of the vineyard, and killed him (cf. Matt. 22:33–39).

Jesus then asks, "What then will the owner of the vineyard do to them?" The crowd is pre-programmed for the answer, and it is interesting how the Gospels variously report it. In Matthew the crowds themselves reply: "He will bring those wretches to a wretched end, and he will rent the vineyard to other tenants who will give him his share of the crop at harvest time" (21:40–41). They state the justice of the case. In Mark and Luke Jesus states the inevitable conclusion, perhaps reiterating their murmurings, telling them what they already know. "He will come and kill those tenants and give the vineyard to others." The crowd cries out, "May this never be" (Luke 20:16; Mark 12:9). As they hear this, the rulers go pallid. They are tenants, not owners of the Temple. They know the piles of gold that lie inside. The prophets of God have come and have been ignored, and Jesus is telling the Temple rulers that they have not given God his due. The Son has come, and he is shortly to be killed. Then the tenants will be killed and the vineyard given to others, presumably Gentiles. In case they have not understood, Jesus adds, "Therefore I tell you that the Kingdom of God will be taken away from you and given to a people who will produce its fruit" (Matt. 21:43). The rulers cannot repent; they are livid, knowing that Jesus has spoken this parable against them. They look for a way to arrest him, to be rid of this irritation.[16] As Jesus presents it, the offense is not *from* God; the offense is *to* God.

The structure of the political offense is asking rulers to submit to God rather than be self-referencing. This process does not begin with Jesus; it fills the Old Testament, as rulers operating from presumed self-sufficiency or autonomy stand against Yahweh's judgments and justice. The list stretches from Pharaoh to Caesar. The issue sticks in the throats of rulers: "God rules, and you are accountable." Nebuchadnezzar is recorded as eventually swallowing the pill: "Now I, Nebuchadnezzar, praise and exalt and glorify the King of heaven, because everything he does is right and all his ways are just. And those who walk in pride, he is able to humble" (Dan. 4:37). The message of Daniel is that human rulers either submit to God, or they rebel in their own pride. Even many of the kings of Israel and Judah, knowing God, still stand and fall in their own pride. The prophets insist on exposing them. Elijah, Elisha, Isaiah, Jeremiah, Amos, and the other prophets pinpoint kings, elites, nations, and empires that turn from God's ways into their own. They warn. They lay out the consequences of injustice, of turning from God's law, of having a false faith in alliances or the nation or the Temple. They show cultures that are self-referencing rather than open to God. Carving this message into history has provoked the deepest confrontation. It involves rulers laying down their arms and power before God, yet they often will not do so. They fight, attack, evade the message, or punish the messengers. And, indeed, the messengers have sometimes not presented the requirements well enough.

Yet in another way, this offense is strange. Why were Christians thrown to the lions? Why have good, law-abiding Christian citizens been persecuted in Russia, Eastern Europe, Nazi Germany, the Middle East, Sudan, Indonesia, China, and many other countries?[17] Christian terrorists do not feature much worldwide. For the most part Christians do not rock the boat and cause political disturbances. Yet they are locked up for just preaching the gospel or singing hymns. The real offense lies in the message to the politicians: "God rules and you do not." They cannot stomach that. Pharaoh, Nebuchadnezzar, the Caesars, Napoleon, Stalin, Hitler, Mao, and others turn against respecting God's reign. If they are accountable, they have no power on their own terms. They assert their own power over others to do harm, imprison, kill, but that is only proximate power. The only real power we have is to do good in obedience to God. Jesus uncompromisingly lays out this level of the issue to his disciples: "Do not be afraid of those who can kill the body but cannot kill the soul. Rather, be afraid of the One who can destroy both soul and body in hell" (Matt. 10:28). Accordingly, Jesus faces the Chief Priest and Herod without fear, and the parasitic power of destruction is exposed for what it is—bullying. Yet the offense of the message must be eradicated. Those who say "No" to the rule of God are trying to tame the message. "Christianity has nothing to do with politics," they say. "If you say, 'God rules,' you break our rules," they teach, and many Christians learn to be suitably servile; but the gospel message never is servile. It cuts at the power of the evil and self-important. It is the thumbtack on the throne.

Jesus helps the disciples see confrontation and offense as part of Christian Kingdom experience. "Do not suppose that I have come to bring peace on earth. I did not come to bring peace, but a sword. For I have come to turn 'a man against his father, a daughter against her mother, a daughter-in-law against her mother-in-law—a man's enemies will be the members of his own household'" (Matt. 10:34–36). These cases are graphically presented as examples of the confrontation between the rule of God and other powers. The disciples will be flogged. "On my account you will be brought before governors and kings as witnesses to them and to the Gentiles" (10:18). Jesus warns the early Christians of the consequences of this ultimate political divide. Indeed, they are to take the principle further: "Blessed are you when men hate you, and when they exclude you and insult you and reject your name as evil, because of the Son of Man. Rejoice in that day and leap for joy, because great is your reward in heaven. For that is how their fathers treated the prophets" (Luke 6:22–23). This is not inviting Christians to a persecution complex, although some of us weakly take it this way. The phrase "Son of Man" with its political weight from Daniel says otherwise. Jesus is pointing out that persecution surrounds God's rule. The offense of the prophets was to face the rulers with God's justice. Offense is normal, part of the package; it is to be borne with joy. It is the persecutors' problem and not yours. So the dividing line is laid down—a humble response to the living God or self-serving politics.

The Subversive Government of God

The government of God goes beyond offense; it subverts, as we noticed at the beginning of this book. It sets up a different way. The gentle rule of God pulls down all kinds of existing powers and structures that glory in themselves. God does rule. "Perhaps," the gospel whispers, "we do not need wars, weapons, rulers in palaces, leisured elites, and those who run bloated governments for their own purposes. Our rulers can serve. National and ethnic rivalries may cease. Political and economic slavery can end, and the security costs of terrorism fall. People and nations can be forgiven and fresh starts be made before God. Corruption can be replaced by honesty, the meek can inherit the earth, and justice can be done." Ordinary people, when they are allowed to hear, find these messages appealing, especially if they have suffered war, faced the oppression of rulers, or been downtrodden by self-important politicians. This subversion transforms perspectives. For decades the Great War was a matter of victories, medals, and glorious sacrifice. Serving and dying for king and country were the ultimate good and seemingly validated by

God. But that was not the last word. Superseding "for king and country" was Edith Cavell's Christian saying, "Patriotism is not enough. I must have no hatred or enmity towards anybody."[18] The bereaved are told that war was worth it. Then Joan Littlewood's *Oh! What a Lovely War!* (1963) unmasked some of the self-importance and incompetence of the ruling military and political class. A deeper awareness of the tragedy of World War I emerged when we identified arms dealers, inadequate rulers, militarism, imperialism, and groups with closed minds. Now we see, in the main, how this war was an error that blighted most of a century. The glorious "official" version has died. Gradually the message seeps out: "The emperor has no clothes." And the established position dies. But at the same time, political establishments and power brokers defend their carefully constructed positions, often trying to compel agreement.

H. G. Wells describes the subversiveness of Jesus:

> In view of what he plainly said, is it any wonder that all who were rich and prosperous felt a horror of strange things, a swimming of their world at his teaching? He was dragging out all the little private reservations they had made from social service into the light of a universal religious life. He was like some terrible moral huntsman digging mankind out of the smug burrows in which they had lived hitherto. In the white blaze of this kingdom of his there was to be no property, no privilege, no pride and no precedence; no motive indeed and no reward but love. Is it any wonder that men were dazzled and blinded and cried out against him?[19]

To some this might seem a bit strong, but it broadly fits the evidence. The power structures of Jesus' day are carefully constructed and well established. The Temple is a vast, moneymaking structure, already forty-six years in the building, but Jesus looks to its destruction (John 2:20; finished in 64, destroyed in 70). The Roman Empire seems mighty in power, but Jesus is prepared to say to Pilate: "You would have no power over me if it were not given you from above" (19:11). This is a rather dismissive attitude to the Roman Empire when your back is open and bleeding flesh, and its representative has your life in his hands (19:1–2). The Pharisees need to be honored by men, but Jesus parodies their search for approbation. Herod Antipas wants to be entertained by the captive Jesus and plies him with questions, but Jesus does not bother to answer him (Luke 23:8–9). The High Priest interrogates Jesus. The Christ's reply is the uncompromising epitome of public justice: "I have spoken openly to the world. I always taught in synagogues or at the temple, where all the Jews come together. I said nothing in secret. Why question me? Ask those who heard me. Surely they know what I said" (John 18:20–21). The directness and sense of public accountability are clear. Yet when Jesus says this, one of the officials strikes him in the face. "Is that any way to answer the High Priest?" he demands (18:22). Well, actually, we say, it is exemplary. Jesus refuses to bow to the false sense of authority bound in the position of the High Priest. "If I said something wrong, testify as to what is wrong. But if I spoke the truth, why did you strike me?" (18:23). This man Jesus gives no validation to the use of power constructed outside God's purposes. People may claim authority in different ways, but they do not have it in truth, and his kingdom is of truth, not privilege (cf. 18:36).

The claims to pumped-up political authority usually occur through existing patterns of power and entrenched positions, or perhaps because of the ownership of property and wealth. Ideologies have been constructed validating the ruler's position, from the fantastic regenerative myths of Egypt to modern mass popular support. Many rulers presume, as they did in first-century Jerusalem, that they have the right to dominate the system or run things their way. Other political leaders use Christianity and presume its compliance with their policies and views. They appoint suppliant church leaders, quote biblical passages that suit them, and have an occasional church service to give credence to their position. The establishment develops "doctrines" like the divine right of kings or the anointing of the monarch, which are supposed to give divine sanction to whatever may be done. Others may say that Christianity really means saluting the flag and is to be identified with the American way of life.[20] These agendas try to use the Christ and the rule of God to their own purposes. "God is on our side" becomes a national orthodoxy. Legitimacy is constructed and built up through ceremonies, morality dodges, rules, and regulations until the presumption is that the establishment rules. But do these claims hold? Do power, military might, property, elitist performance, and popular support satisfy and impress God? Jesus stands obstinately against them because he has already seen through the myths and will not allow the kingdom to be bent to another end. "The kings of the earth lord it over one another. Not so with you" (cf. Matt. 20:25–26; Mark 10:42–43; Luke 22:25–26). Not so with Jesus' true followers, in truth. On Jesus' terms we are all in our underpants and without privilege before God. Christian leaders, too, come under the searchlight. Why have they supported empires, wars, exploitation, and religious conflict? Some Christian leaders say "Thus saith the Lord" and talk a load of rubbish. The history of Christian establishment is largely compromised and under judgment.[21] But far wider than this, Christianity asks of all rulers, "Do you act in justice and truthfulness?" The gospel subverts the structures that are not open to God. Christ exposes spurious authority like a splayed ox.

Suddenly the *ownership* of politics is gone. Often rulers come to believe their own politics; power is theirs. But Jesus stands against the possession of worldly power. As the final confrontation of the cross approaches, the chief priests and elders of the people, the effective rulers in Jerusalem, angrily ask him by what authority he is operating, for he has cleared the Temple of commercialism. They have the established authority of the Temple, the high priesthood, and the Torah, and they resent Jesus' intrusion into their power structures. They believe they have this power from God and are very conscious of their own authority. His seeming authority challenges theirs, and they rap out the questions: "By what authority? . . . Who gave you this authority?" (Matt. 21:23). But Jesus requires an answer of them. "Was John the Baptist's message of God or with merely human authority?" (cf. 21:25). They could not answer because of their own relationship with the crowd and their refusal to hear John. Their pathetic "We don't know" is met by Jesus' refusal to answer the question about his own authority (21:25–27). They are left bereft of any sense of their possession of power and do not like it. Shortly Jesus will say, "Therefore I tell you that the government of God will be taken away from you and given to a people who will produce its fruit" (cf. 21:43). There is no possession of authority, only obedience to God. Jews, Romans, Christians, Americans do not have ownership of any system. The God who rules "will rent the vineyard to other tenants who will give him his share of the crop at harvest time" (21:41). Politics on God's terms subverts. We are conditioned to accept the rulers and subjects, high and low, mighty and weak, patricians and plebeians, citizens and slaves, middle class and working class, lords and commoners, the underclass and the Third Estate. But the kingdom plows through them, bringing down those who claim their own authority and lifting up the humble.

It is the poor who inherit the kingdom of God, because the rich and powerful are too proud to enter. They have been issued invitations, but they do not turn up. Jesus was well aware of the dynamics of this process. It comes out in Jesus' pithy sentence recorded in Luke: "The Law and the Prophets were in effect until John came; since then, the good news of the [government] . . . of God is proclaimed, and everyone tries to enter it by force" (16:16 NRSV). What does this mean? Jesus is not speaking against the Law or the Prophets (16:17), but he is signaling a change. Before John and himself, rulers owned the "kingdom." They owned the land, often owned slaves, and kept everybody in their places. The laws of the elite defended the kingdom. But now the crowds just walk in, past the guards. The rabble are storming through the gates and pushing their way into God's kingdom. You don't need tickets! As Paul put it, "Not many of you were wise by human standards; not many were influential; not many were of noble birth. But God chose the foolish things of the world to shame the wise; God chose the weak things of the world to shame the strong. He chose the lowly things of this world and the despised things—and the things that are not—to nullify the things that are, so that no one may boast before him" (1 Cor. 1:26–29). It is a subversive Kingdom.

The Structural Place for Politics in Life

The biggest subversion of all is to dethrone the ruler and politics and put them in their limited place under the sovereignty of God. This change is at the fulcrum of world political history. To identify the issue, we have to begin by recalling the overwhelming structure of the ancient world's cultures. Politically, they were ruler-dominated cultures: the ruler, often with the help of priests and religious myths, provided the total worldview for its citizens. Archetypal was the Greek city-state: the polis, and its goddess in the acropolis, defined the society and its members. Athena personified the city-state, and in worshipping her, the citizen was engaging in a political act. Ernest Barker describes the structure: "Religion was an aspect of the political life of a political society: it was no other life and it entailed no other society. The sphere of the Greek city was not limited by the existence of an association [such as a local church] claiming to be its equal or superior."[22] Here, politics, the Polis, was the religion. The dominance of the Acropolis and the Parthenon, surrounded by small buildings, was awesome. People lived beholden to the state god. Greek thought generally worked within this assumption. Plato's *Republic* is a political reconstruction of the order of the polis. His *Statesman* coins a word we often use, but its meaning conveys the underlying frame of reference. Barker sums up its focus: "Some who bear command are sovereign, without any superior, and their commands originate with themselves; others are under authority and the commands which they issue are commands which have been issued to them. The statesman belongs to the former class."[23] Here is the sovereign, the self-ruler, taking his place in political philosophy. From the same perspective, Aristotle later sweepingly defines man as a "political animal." The ultimate framework for a society is supposed to be found in the political. The political is total; it has the character of a total cultural system.[24]

This Greek model merely reflected the pattern found throughout most of the ancient world. The state, the ruler, defined the whole society and required worship, often with supporting systems of magic, rite, myth, and idolatry. Before the Greek city-state, the culture of Minoan

Crete centered on the palace at Knossos. Earlier within Greek culture at Mycenae and Tiryns, citadels emerged that circled up to the central palace. In other cultures the central focus was the place of rule, from which people were seen to receive their identity. Of the four great early civilizations known, at least three had this political form. We do not know much about the Indus Valley cultures, but Egypt, Mesopotamia, and China were civilizations clustered round the sacred places of the ruler—the palaces and pyramids, the palace-city, ziggurat, or Shang Palace. Ur, Nimrud, Babylon, Ninevah, Persepolis, Susa, Zhengzhou, Anyang, Thebes, and other ruler cities all have the same structure of making the ruler the focus of worship and controller of religion. We recognize here the Babel principle (Gen. 11), where the tower of rule gives identity to the people. Its later outworking occurs in Babylon, Assyria, Egypt, and the other biblical empires. In these the ruler is worshipped as legitimized by myths. There is Pharaoh as a god on earth, and we read of Nebuchadnezzar's golden statue (Dan. 3). In the Old Testament is a presentiment of what we now discuss. Abraham leaves Ur with its great ziggurat, and in faith seeks a city with foundations, whose architect and builder is God (Heb. 11:10). The Israelites leave Egypt and its Pharaoh to go out into the desert as the people of God, who commands, "Let my people go, so that they may worship me" (Exod. 7:16 et passim). Their leader is called Moses, the *servant* of God. Shadrach, Meshach, and Abednego do not bow down to the ruler-god image of gold and are delivered (Dan. 3). The prophets denounce the self-referencing kings and empires in the name of God (e.g., Amos 1–2). The tension between the sovereign rule of God and the political religion of the ruler is evident throughout Old Testament history.

By the time of Jesus, not much has changed. Rome, though it has different foundations, is a politically defined culture. The Roman state defines citizenship or slavery, worship, and law, and it operates with an overwhelming sense of control. At the time the empire is moving fast toward worship of the divine Caesar.[25] Gaius Caligula goes on a self-as-divinity spree throughout the empire, erecting massive statues of himself all over the place.[26] The issue really blows up in June AD 40, when Jews at Jamnia (Jabneh), west of Jerusalem and near the coast, tear down an altar erected to the emperor. He goes ballistic and orders that a statue of Zeus wearing Caligula's own face be put in the Jerusalem Temple (cf. 2 Thess. 2:4). The Jews are ready to sacrifice their whole nation to stop that action. Fortunately, Caligula was dissuaded by Agrippa, then died and the order died with him.[27] Even before Caligula, the empire was self-believing. The city of Rome specified "civilization," and to be a Roman *civis* (citizen) was the defining glory. Its gods were civic. Not worshipping them was a crime against the state. In this sense Rome had the same structure as the ancient Greek polis, as had the Macedonian Empire of Alexander the Great between the two. The Jews, of course, strongly opposed the worship of Caesar and wanted the worship of the God of Abraham and Isaac to be upheld. They were inheritors of the great tradition where the ruler was subject to God, answerable to God's law and God's prophets. Yet this was largely a failing tradition. The rulers had often been self-referencing and tried to suppress the prophets and the requirements of justice that were laid on them. Sometimes they became God-is-on-our-side rulers. As we have seen, the Temple was close to the Acropolis in its conception of a national required center of worship and rule. Jewish state religion was more religious and less state-focused than the Roman or Greek system, but in its statecraft and manipulation, it was not so different. There was a *system* that dominated people's lives in a religiopolitical sense both from Rome and in the Jewish reaction.

Jesus is entirely different. He requires true subordination to the rule of God, in which the state and its ruler are banished from overall control, political and religious. People live before God and not within the conception of the state or the ruler. Living before God demythologizes the whole ethos of dominating politics. People are free to live before God as they choose. Politics is pushed into a limited place, and there is room for friendship, science, children, discussion, prayer, the arts, fishing, and walking about, meeting people. The Pharisees want to dominate people's lives with their religio-political rules, but Jesus shrugs them off. In this Greek sense of the word *polis*, Jesus is anti-political and anti-totalitarian; he refuses the state or the ruler the possibility of defining the meaning of life. Only the Creator does that, and the ruler must be put in his place. Within this perspective we are the people of God, not (Aristotle's) "political animals." In this sense a lot of Christians and indeed many people everywhere feel anti-political. They resent the idea of political control over their lives. They would do well to look to the person who has really fought this battle. "Don't fear rulers," Jesus said. "They can only kill you." They did kill, but he still did not fear them, and for good reason. "Fear God and then you will have nothing else to fear" (cf. Matt. 10:26–31).

Deconstruction is a postmodern word, but it describes how Jesus undermines the structure of the ruler-centered religio-political system. This single person gently puts Rome in its place under God, unthinkable at the time, but its true place. Before it has an inkling, its decline and fall have taken place. He also takes on the Jewish system when no one can think outside it, presaging the destruction of the Temple, rebuking the ruler-priests, and freeing people from imposed burdens. They are only to fear God and not the threatening ruling classes. He frees the relationship with God from its state cultic requirements and deliberately moves into people's ordinary lives with no sense of political control, for always the word of God can be accepted or rejected. Abraham Kuyper got to the nub of the issue when he said, "When you bow the knee to God, you bow it to no one else."[28] God's kingdom is good news because it shows that politics is our servant. Thus, Jesus deconstructs ruler- and state-centered cultures and opens up the truth that human beings live first before God, who has created them, and not as animals of the state.

To subvert this great mythical political system in world history is no mean task. And, indeed, it has not been fully done. In the later history of the world, and especially Europe, the ruler or state that gives meaning has reasserted itself. Statism, nationalism, state Socialism, and Fascism—all have tried to reassert the primacy of the state, with destructive effects. This is no accident. Greek and Roman thought drifted back into Europe during the Renaissance and "Enlightenment." Italian city-states partly mimicked their Greek counterparts. Leaders asserted their "sovereignty." Despotic, autocratic, "self-powered" rule emerged. The Prussian State grew in self-regard and power. Enlightenment thinkers gave an underlying political meaning to society through concepts like Enlightened Despotism or the Common Will. In the French Revolution the rule of the people became the defining tyranny.[29] Napoleon crowned himself and tried to wrest French society into his own conception. Then Hegel asserted philosophically the overarching significance of the state in the life and thought of German and wider culture. All of these developments, an important part of European political thought and ideology, were premised on a state-defined view of society. In an ironic twist the atheist Marx seemingly rebelled against it, looking to the withering away of the state. But the actual revolutions of Lenin and Stalin embodied state totalitarianism at a new level. In Italy and Germany Fascism replicated the same, though with a far-right ideology, and Hitler proclaimed the thousand-year Reich with religious fervor. On the other side of the world, Mao planted the same model back in the great civilization of China, dominating the lives of a billion people. Again, the total domination of the state/ruler/politics over the whole of life is asserted and takes its toll in the deaths of millions in modern world history. Often it is cruel beyond belief.

We see how deadly serious is this great historical confrontation. The Nazarene stands against the absolute rule of the state and against its claim to define the meaning of life. He is brought before rulers and will not bow, but serenely teaches the prior rule of God. The temptation to control all the kingdoms of the world, the totalitarian vision, is dismissed at the beginning of the journey (Matt. 4:8–10). Jesus shows that we all live in God's creation, not in the mythical constructs of the States' men.

Yet, the word is out. Jesus' low-key proclamation of the rule of God restructures the fundamental meaning of politics, which all too often has been construed in Greco-Roman terms. As Jesus taught it, the rule of God has deep structural consequences. First, it subordinates the state to God and to the law. The principle of the rule of law properly understood requires ruler and ruled to submit to God's precepts of justice, respect, and neighbor love. Autocracy, arbitrary rule, and double standards are out. Second, the ruler-god is unacceptable. Rather, the political rulers are officeholders, with required standards of service and patterns of accountability—people who must never look down on their fellows. Third, totalitarianism, or political control of all areas of life, involves the state pretending to possess powers it does not properly have. We live before God, not the state, and the latter is limited to upholding God's justice and not to undertaking the control of people's lives. Fourth, it makes a society pluralist, where family life, work, religion and church, education, the arts, community all have a place before God and are not to be controlled or swamped by the state. A vast body of Christian political thought, often ignored, elaborates this alternative.[30] It is no accident that a series of great Jewish and Christian political theorists like van Prinsterer, Acton, Tolstoy, the popes, Arendt, Maritain, Popper, J. L. Talmon, and others expose totalitarian control. The Kuyperian and Catholic traditions have in part shaped the understanding of institutional pluralism present in modern European politics.[31] The dichotomy is vivid and basic, worth considering in this diagrammatic form:

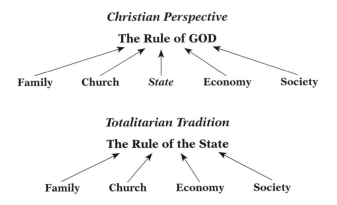

Christian Perspective

The Rule of GOD

Family   Church   *State*   Economy   Society

Totalitarian Tradition

The Rule of the State

Family   Church   Economy   Society

The contrast is deep and pervasive. God has created us to live. There are ways to live and institutions with deep significance in our lives, and we all live freely before God, with no state system controlling our lives.

This Christian truth shows that the society-wide dominance of the state is mistaken at several levels. *God* rules, not the state. The state is fallible and needs a higher system of accountability. The state is partial and does not supply the overall perspective on life. State or political control of other institutions wrongly politicizes them. The state also has no superior status. Within this perspective a political paradigm is not adequate for understanding what family, education, work, and the arts are about. Yet this perspective does not validate church control of the state, the medieval model. When the state and rulers impose the myth of their ultimate rule and try to give a political meaning of life, idolatry is taking place.[32]

As Jesus saunters through the countryside and teaches the actual rule of God, no one and no institution else, he expels fear of rulers from his disciples. "When they arrest you, do not worry. . . . Do not be afraid of those who can kill the body but cannot kill the soul. . . . So, don't be afraid" (Matt. 10:19, 28, 31). As he does so, the ruler-god, the state myth, the political domination of life is dethroned. This is the dethroning of the throne. In the other system, rulers inherit the earth. Here, the meek do. In the other system, rulers enslave mind, heart, and work. Here, rulers serve and work for others. Jesus' submission to his Father is self-effacing (John 15:10). Our reaction is to say that this man is not really a politician, but actually we are seeing the quiet tail that wags the barking State dog.

These Christian truths have partly penetrated our political culture. In some sense the ruler is under law and accountable, subordinate and obedient. Historically, autocracy has slowly been tamed and disarmed. There is a heavy reaction to Totalitarianism. We now hold rulers to account through constitutionalism,[33] opposition parties, the press, and the people. This is good, but we may have lost the underlying truth of the limited range of rulers and their place subordinate to God's law. As the West has become more secular, the focus of accountability has become, not God, but the people: their material needs, whims, likes, and dislikes. These are, of course, in principle equally as arbitrary and autocratic as self-referencing rulers are. The necessary humility, submission to the law, self-questioning, and subordination to God's purposes remain unconsidered at elections as people assume their self-validating dominance. Within this pattern both the people and the political leaders lose the space to submit themselves to what is right and good. Those deeper principles are lost in the clamor of electoral wants and party assertions to represent the people. This is a crisis of late-Western popular democracy. Yet the deeper underlying accountability set out by Jesus remains and decrees our need of a paradigm shift.

Further, the principle of the rule of God over all of life limits the place of the state to a part of it. Almost unawares, we have accepted Jesus' granting of freedom. His story is of friends, healing, walks, parties, weddings, and funerals. One of the nuances of Jesus' thinking is the way he depoliticizes problems. You have harmed your neighbor; sort it out now, before court. You want to discuss divorce; the problem is hardness of heart. Politics is put in its limited place. Even when facing the final political confrontation, Jesus' concern is more to teach his friends about God's relationship with them. Politics is subsequent; the relationship with God is everything. And anyhow, this is what life is really like. God-given life involves eating, sleeping, learning, friends, travel, families, and discussion; it is not politically defined in the ways Fascism and state Socialism have tried to pretend. There is now an understanding of the limited and partial place of politics. The removal of its dominance from other areas of life is one of the marks of the West.[34] Slowly, and with setbacks, work, family life, science, trade, religion, the arts, news, and education have been prized away from political control. They are liberated to stand in their own integrity before God, whether they realize that to be so or not.[35]

Yet the liberal version of this transition is that the individual has gained autonomy from the state. This is not only an impoverished understanding of what has happened; it also has produced in Western postmodern culture an institutional fragmentation of marriage, family, school, community, and nation that may invoke its own new statism.[36] Christian political theology leads to neither of these. The state, like other institutions, has its limited purposes within the rule of God. Politics and the state are one aspect of life lived in relation to God and must know their place. They are a sphere of life, but not the whole. This Christian principle can be known as a conscious and articulate basis for all of political life. Or we could lose it again.

It is still not even established in many parts of the world. Communist totalitarianism remains in China. A substantial proportion of Islamic countries are committed to totalitarian political control, especially over religion, education, and family life. Religious, family, and educational persecution is now systematically justified in terms of a politically imposed Shariah. This will probably be one of the biggest threats to world peace in the twenty-first century. It is currently an issue in the Sudan, Indonesia, Afghanistan, Pakistan, Saudi Arabia, Egypt, Algeria, and elsewhere. At a less acute level, the move from the European Community to the European Union is partly a change from open national community relationships (the original Christian Democrat vision of Europe) and toward a required overarching political structure. We may be trying to politicize Europe and establish some political myth of union, which will emerge in a new kind of imperial history.[37] This may be a danger. In numerous other regimes throughout the world, the party, the military, and the leaders proclaim their salvation stories and claim a central role. The mythical character of Nkrumah, Kenyatta, Eva Peron, Mao, Pol Pot, Saddam Hussein, and many others is evident. They claim to be national saviors but burden their citizens with their own glory. The Christian liberation that comes from putting politics in its place is still unheard throughout much of the world. It could spread again.[38]

The Politics of Justice

At the same time, the rule of God requires justice that is vested in an institution. Christ validates God's law (Matt. 5:18–19), due procedure (Luke 17:11–14), the state or Moses' seat (Matt. 23:1–2), and even the position of Pilate. Nothing passes away from the Law and the Prophets. The Old Testament institutions of judging, restitution, and just rule are not dimmed in the new government of God but gain an added priority. "Seek first God's government and righteousness" (cf. 6:33). "Hunger and thirst for righteousness" (5:6). The Hebrew word "righteousness" cannot be privatized and is best rendered as "justice-with-right-living." Nowhere does Jesus rebel against the institutions of justice of his day. He fully reflects Paul's later statement that the governing authorities are established by God and are to be respected (Rom. 13:1). The cure of leprosy needs validating by the priest if other people are not to be put at risk. Christ requires that move from the lepers he heals, though he had no brief for priests (Luke 17:11–19). Now we can see what the Gospels reflect and Christian and secular thought has often distorted or misstated. The rule of God is prior to political institutions and formative for them, just as God's law pre-formed the Jewish state. This is not validation of the state in its own terms, but on God's terms. Jesus and Paul lay claim to the Roman state on God's terms. Pilate asserts his power to crucify Jesus, presuming that Jesus will be impressed by the fact. But Jesus insists on Pilate's dependence on God and not the Roman Empire. "You would have no power over me if it were not given you from above" (John 19:11). Paul echoes Jesus' point later when writing to the heart of the empire: "For there is no authority except that which God has established" (Rom. 13:1). This involves critique, exposure, and holding the institution to the law of God, not some unqualified acquiescence. Jesus requires a fair trial and will not answer false accusations. Paul insists on proper trial, not mob rule. Zacchaeus is led to perceive that he must follow the Mosaic pattern of restitution. The leaders are held to account and judged for their failures, because the Christ insists, without violence or any compromise of loving and just living, on holding the state to its God-given task, no less and no more. Christians submit to the state, but on God's terms and not the state's.

Nor is this understanding of the state reactive or reactionary. It is easy to take as given the practices, culture, and compromises of the existing state. But Jesus does not so do. God's rule is not the reaction, the antithesis, but the thesis—the way the state is meant to be.[39] It has principles and operates with a sense of what is important. It takes motives seriously. It is merciful and generous. It weights toward reconciliation. Its inner structure is antibehavioral, focusing on the substance of relationships and justice. In the deepest sense, the calling of the state is first and last to God's ways, not to the wayward reactions of history. In the next chapter, we move beyond the central principle of the government of God to look at some of the structural principles of this kind of state.

Conclusion

Jesus proclaims the Kingdom of God as a truth governing our existence. We enter it by faith in him and as people who willingly submit to the ways of God. Entry requires repentance, personal and communal. Living on God's terms requires the laying down of self-pride and self-referencing politics. Could it really be anything different? Politically, this kingdom stands on its own terms, ruled by the self-effacing One, practicing mercy, justice, and the care of the weak. It stands against self-worshipping kingdoms and ruler-gods, requiring sooner or later that they bow their knees to God. As Daniel prophesied, this Kingdom will grow, gradually eclipsing the mighty political empires of the world. It insists on being good news, and it controls no one. As Jesus moves through Galilee, a powerless pedestrian, living and teaching this Kingdom, a new kind of politics is planted on the earth. All the myths of ruler self-validation are thrown in the air and float away as chaff. What remains is living in this good Kingdom, exploring its ways, and loving its citizens and its enemies. But this is difficult for both the rulers and the ruled. Overwhelming evidence shows the failures of rulers and the inadequacies of the people. What good government might be is a deeply intractable problem, and to that we now turn.

Bibliography

Barker, Ernest. *Greek Political Theory*. 1918. Repr., London: Methuen, 1960.

Beasley-Murray, G. R. *Jesus and the Kingdom of God*. Grand Rapids: Eerdmans, 1986.

Beyerhaus, Peter J. *God's Kingdom and the Utopian Error: Discerning the Biblical Kingdom of God from Its Political Counterfeits*. Wheaton, IL: Crossway, 1992.

Bratt, James D., ed. *Abraham Kuyper: A Centennial Reader*. Grand Rapids: Eerdmans, 1998.

Chiltern, Bruce D., ed. *The Kingdom of God in the Teaching of Jesus*. London: SPCK; Philadelphia: Fortress, 1984.

Dodd, C. H. *The Parables of the Kingdom*. Rev. ed. London: Nisbet, 1961.

Ellul, Jacques. *The Politics of God and the Politics of Man*. Translated by Geoffrey W. Bromiley. Grand Rapids: Eerdmans, 1972.

Gutiérrez, Gustavo. *Essential Writings*. Edited by James B. Nickoloff. London: SCM, 1996.

Heslam, Peter S. *Creating a Christian Worldview: Abraham Kuyper's Lectures on Calvinism*. Grand Rapids: Eerdmans, 1998.

Kuyper, Abraham. *Lectures on Calvinism*. Grand Rapids: Eerdmans, 1931.

O'Brien, David J., and Thomas A. Shannon. *Catholic Social Thought*. Maryknoll, NY: Orbis Books, 1992.

Ridderbos, Herman. *The Coming of the Kingdom*. Edited by Raymond A. Zorn. Translated by H. de Jongste. Philadelphia: Presbyterian & Reformed, 1962; St. Catharines, ON: Paideia, 1978.

Runner, Evan. *Scriptural Religion and Political Task*. 1961. Repr., Toronto: Wedge, 1974.

Talmon, J. L. *The Origins of Totalitarian Democracy*. London: Secker & Warburg, 1952.

Temple, William. *The Kingdom of God*. London: Macmillan, 1913.

Willis, Wendell, ed. *The Kingdom of God in Twentieth-Century Interpretation*. Peabody, MA: Hendrickson, 1987.

Wright, N. T. *Jesus and the Victory of God*. London: SPCK, 1996.

Jesus' Political Principles

Political Principles?

Principles do not always characterize government, but they seem to mark the understanding of the government of God that comes from Jesus' teaching. Principles are directions, signposts, showing the way we must follow. They require us to submit our lives to this way of seeing things, and to understand what the principles require of us. They imply some humility and accountability, and a willingness not to see ourselves as exceptions. Christian principles are bigger than the individual or group and in some cosmic sense reflect the purposes of God. This is the cost that makes principles of universal significance rather than egocentric and small-minded. Nor are they simple: they play into our lives at a level beyond rules. Jesus' principles are reflected in parables, teaching, or action and have a long development in the Old Testament. Grasping their significance may be a lifetime's work; they require understanding. All of them have their roots in our relationship with God. The study in these next two chapters can be no more than introductory, trying to identify at a basic level these themes in Jesus' teaching. Again, we step back from the Gospel narrative and think about these principles slightly more systematically.

Principles are probably not fashionable in a postmodern era, where pragmatism, economic power, and what suits particular groups tend to dominate political culture. Yet, the rhetoric of principles hangs around. We talk of the land of the free, democracy, the rule of law, liberty, equality, and fraternity. But by now these principles either float in the ether or have too many exceptions to bite in much of political life. The West supports democracy and dictators who have oil. We accept equality in voting—one person, one vote—but if he can get away with it, one man will happily pay himself a thousand times more than he would pay an employee. Principles are therefore devalued currency. Those who hold them are likely to be shortchanged. But that is not the end of the story, for living without them is a horror. Gradually life disintegrates into forms of anarchy and self-pleasing that destroy relationships and nations. Indeed, the decay of principle should perhaps be our greatest political fear. The underlying question therefore remains: Are there political principles that do not decay, that last beyond human failure and self-pleasing?

Here, there is a need to understand the roots from which a principle grows. They are not free-floating. A principle like "equality" means different things in different cultures, whether Christian, Liberal, Marxist, Capitalist, or Muslim. For example, Christ's teaching that one must die to self addresses inequality generated by the selfishness that liberalism or capitalism might tolerate. Some will find any principle of equality irksome. Principles are not mechanical rules; they address our lives and politics from different faith perspectives. Christian principles require us to submit to God. They interweave the personal and political. Christian principles hold up the activities of states and international bodies to examination, generating acceptance or opposition. Tyrants often do not like them, self-righteous rulers oppose them, and despots oppress those who hold them because they insist on God's way. With this background, we look at how principles unfold in the teachings of Jesus.

Broadly speaking, we can separate principles into two clusters. First are those growing out of more general human relationships that play into politics. Second are those related specifically to the process of government.[1] In this chapter we look at the first group and reserve the next chapter for the second cluster. The principles in this chapter are especially important because politics grows in a wider culture and relates to life. Political science cannot be studied as a closed system. All the time, the broader pattern of life shapes the particular institutions and acts of politics. Here we look at some of the transforming principles emerging from the teaching of Jesus.

All People That on Earth Do Dwell

For most of human history, only the rich and powerful have had a say in government, while slaves, serfs, and soldiers have been demeaned.

A phrase like "cannon fodder" dreadfully implies that the ruling elite have regarded soldiers as expendable. There have been many ideological vindications of the "important" or elites, and on the other hand many dismissals of those who can be killed or ignored. The ancient Brahmanic development of caste or the modern social Darwinian idea of a super-race allowed people to be untouchable or obsolete. The pattern is ubiquitous. The Chinese literati are superseded by the Communist party member, and the Western aristocracy gives way to the so-called meritocracy. We now inhabit a world where the importance of all people is more often proclaimed but perhaps without much conviction. In the West, the successful or the powerful tend to be more important than the rest. From Orwell's *Animal Farm* the words "All are equal, but some are more equal than others" resonate across cultures.[2] Despite the "importance" of all people, millions are killed in war and famine. The principle of respect for all people is still far from being fulfilled. In light of this checkered history, Jesus' principle emerges with rigor because it is consistent in facing up to the full costs of respecting all people. Already, the Old Testament principles are strong, standing against slavery and allowing no political or wealthy elites. God has created all people and is no respecter of persons; God does not give higher status to one than another. But this teaching is taken to a new level in the words and actions of Jesus. In his mother's words, Jesus has "lifted up the humble" and "has sent the rich away empty" (Luke 1:52–53). He deems every person important in his teaching and shows it by all his actions.

Jesus' teaching makes this clear. The government of God is for every person: all are made in God's image. The principle emerges clearly in the three kingdom parables of the lost—the Lost Sheep, the Lost Coin, and the Prodigal Son (Luke 15). The chapter sets the scene. Tax collectors and sinners, the despised of Jewish society, gather round to hear Jesus. The Pharisees and teachers of the law make disparaging remarks, muttering about the kind of people Jesus welcomes and eats with. They think in exclusive terms. Then Jesus tells three parables against them and against the idea that anybody is expendable. It is a thorough, cumulative riposte, requiring his hearers to move outside their self-importance and see something of the heart of God.

"Suppose one of you has a hundred sheep, and loses one of them. Does he not leave the ninety-nine in the open country and go after the lost sheep until he finds it?" (15:4). By now they know Jesus' mode of teaching. He is talking of God, the God who goes after people and finds them. "And when he finds it, he joyfully puts it on his shoulders and goes home. Then he calls his friends and neighbors together" and asks them to rejoice, too (15:5–6). This is the welcome in the Kingdom for any sinner who repents. Who are the lost? Not, seemingly, the Pharisees and teachers of the law, the righteous who (claim they) do not need to repent. God is out and about, looking for the overlooked, outsiders, excluded, and poor. Suddenly the structures of importance wobble. God is giving first attention to the group that the proud scorn.

Then the second parable rolls out: "Suppose a woman has ten silver coins and loses one. Does she not light a lamp, sweep the house and search carefully until she finds it?" (15:8). The parable involves another level of onslaught. To understand what God is like, they have to imagine themselves as a woman—they who thank God daily that they were not born a Gentile, a woman, or a slave. In Jesus' telling, the woman is not the object but the acting subject. They have to think like a woman in order to understand what God is like! Again, Jesus emphasizes God's rejoicing at the lost being found. This is no cold academic equality, but a warm love full of God's initiative.

Finally comes probably the greatest story ever told: "There was a man who had two sons. The younger one said to his father, 'Father, give me my share of the estate.' So he divided his property between them. Not long after that, the younger son got together all he had, set off for a distant country and there squandered his wealth in wild living" (15:11–13). He becomes the prodigal son, mirroring the way people and cultures journey away from God. Things do not turn out as he thought. What begins as attractive finishes as pig swill. The son is himself degraded by the process, until he even longs to eat the food of pigs, the food of unclean animals. Then he comes to his senses and is able partly to see that this is a wrong direction. He seeks to be admitted back home as some menial servant, recognizing his unworthiness and aware of his wrongdoing, but not conscious of the ache of love that dwells in his father's heart for him. He drags his wretched self home across the hills. But his old father has been scanning the hills day by day. He sees the speck and is out to meet him, running and throwing his arms round him and kissing him. The son's apology is swallowed up in his father's rejoicing and the insistent need for a party of celebration. There is the lavishness of grace, not dampened by what the son has done. "'Quick! Bring the best robe and put it on him. Put a ring on his finger and sandals on his feet. Bring the fatted calf and kill it. Let's have a feast and celebrate. For this son of mine was dead and is alive again; he was lost and is found.' So they began to celebrate" (15:22–24). Jesus insists that God desires to be reunited with us all; we are his children, whatever is said and done. The most wretched is welcome as son or daughter.

The irrelevance of the Pharisees' and teachers' carping compared with God's welcome must have them blanched in their small-mindedness. It is not what persons deserve or whether they are wealthy and important that counts, but God's obsession to find us and bring us back within his love and care. God's creation is for all. We self-righteously define out the undeserving, unemployed, immoral, wasteful, or excluded, but God does not do so. The stories show the ordinary sheep, the coin, and the wretched son as special. Our Father God is the initiator of the welcoming, loving response. God looks for us with compassion as we wander aimlessly over the hills like lost sheep. The woman searches avidly for the insensate coin. Nothing else comes first. God does not despise anyone whom he has created. The Father is a doting old man with a white beard, longing for us to be back. The status consciousness of the Pharisees is engulfed in this inclusive love of God. Then, in the story of the Prodigal Son, Jesus includes a gracious invitation to the Pharisees. He talks of the elder son, more than slightly disgruntled by his brother, who then also is engulfed in the warm embrace and tenderness of his father. "My son, you are always with me, and everything I have is yours" (15:31). If the Pharisees have softened to that word—and in the parable the response is left open—they too can walk into the kingdom and join the party, but most of them do not.[3]

Every person is important. A woman who has been bent double for eighteen years comes to Jesus and is healed on the Sabbath. The synagogue ruler indignantly tells the people to go away and be healed on normal workdays, but Jesus angrily opens up the infamy of this response: "You would put yourself out for an animal on the Sabbath, so should not this daughter of Abraham be set free from this infirmity?" (cf. Luke 13:10–17). The crippled woman stands tall, the leaders are humiliated, and the people are delighted: the worth of one is the worth of us all. The Gospels detail how every kind of outcast is shown to be worthy of the love of God. Jesus, the Messiah, finds a man cutting his body in the tombs and heals him. He stops with lepers cast out of their villages. He has a long chat with a Samaritan woman passed on as an inadequate wife by five men and clearly despised. He heals a man who has been lying on his back for four decades in a covered walkway, hoping for alms and a cure. He stops for a noisy, blind beggar whom people want to silence and heals him. He praises a woman for her faith, one who has long-term menstrual bleeding and is regarded by others as unclean. He heals a man who has been blind all his life. The blind, the mute, the mentally ill, the infectious, and the outcasts converge on this man because they find in him the welcome of God. They know he loves them. Even on the cross, as Jesus is naked and gasping with terminal pain, he tells the nearby thief that he too is welcome in the kingdom (23:43). God, the despised ruler, welcomes those who are of low estate and treats them as the so-called great are treated.

There is an iron structure to this teaching of Jesus. It reflects the two great commandments that he presents as basic to the human condition. "Love God with all your heart, soul, mind and strength and your neighbor as yourself" (cf. Luke 10:27). Love God and love your neighbor. Because we are all created in the image of God and beloved of God, we are worthy of love and respect. God *commands* us to love one another. If we do not love God, then our love for our neighbors will dissipate. If we do not love our neighbors, then where is our love of God? If we love God, then we will love all made in God's image. There is no escape from these fundamental truths about human existence. In the light of this, we see how evil it is that people should bemuse themselves into despising both the Creator of the universe and their neighbors; but so it is, and the two are not unrelated.

That God's government is not exclusive or status-bound cannot be misunderstood because Jesus gives it another twist. He points out that the self-important *exclude themselves* from God's kingdom. A man Jesus is eating with says to him, "Blessed is the man who will eat at the feast in the kingdom of God" (Luke 14:15). To eat at God's feast is the greatest privilege a Jew can imagine. The Pharisee believes he is voicing a sublime, blessed thought, the great reward the righteous seek, and presumably one with which Jesus cannot possibly disagree. But Jesus' reply shreds this sense of uplift. He describes the great feast, the banquet of God. But the great and the good do not bother to come to this feast; they are too busy and full of excuses. Important people are too busy to come to God's feast because they have other things on their minds. The self-important can't be bothered with God, who after all has some claim to importance. But God is not proud: "Go out quickly into the streets and alleys of the town and bring in the poor, the crippled, the blind and the lame" (14:21). Even that does not fill the house. The messenger is sent out into the highways and byways where the lepers and outcasts are, to invite them to come in, so that God's banqueting house will be full (14:23). Thus, God's government and concern is for all—except those who are self-excluded by their importance and self-righteousness, a problem which may be ours.

This principle is a bedrock truth of the Kingdom. God is no respecter of "special" persons and is a respecter of all whom he has made. It cannot be otherwise. Therefore, the law should privilege no one, and all should have equal access to it. This means votes for all and not just the select few. It means the end of partiality toward the rich and famous. But this is not merely some limited kind of political impartiality. Jesus' emphasis is on God's pro-active care and the breaking down of privilege. On this view the state seeks out those with needs. It is a perspective that finds the sick and provides for them, that incorporates the poor in communal wealth, that honors the full status of all citizens and even those beyond the state. Hence, this principle chisels at political establishments. In the parable of Lazarus, the rich man lives in luxury every day, looking for favorable treatment from Father Abraham even at his death. But Jesus shows that in God's greater economy, things do not work out this way. As the rich man ignores his neighbor, so he himself is now ignored. The chasm created by his self-importance cannot now be crossed, and he is in torment. There is judgment attached to privilege (16:19–31).

More positively, Jesus teaches another parable of the Kingdom. The kingdom is like a landowner who goes out to hire workers to work in his vineyard and agrees to pay them a denarius a day, the standard rate. Workers come at six in the morning, at nine, at noon, at three, and at five, the later ones obviously unable to obtain work earlier, but all are hired. Then at six in the evening the employer lines them all up to be paid and gives each a denarius. "That's not fair," say the early workers. "We've worked hard all day and deserve more than you have given to these last workers." But the landowner replies, "Friend, I am not being unfair to you. Don't I have the right to be generous with my own money?" (cf. Matt. 10:1–16).[4] So Jesus insists that God is beyond our limited and distorted notions of what we deserve, relating in generosity and grace, lifting up the poor. As Moltmann notes, Christ deliberately focuses on the subjected, oppressed and humiliated people, on the "nonpersons" dehumanized in our human relationships, to instate them in the Kingdom.[5] This is not a benign equality, but a dynamic, redressive one.

"The last will be first, and the first will be last" (Matt. 20:16), Jesus repeats insistently about the great shake-up. The government of God changes inequality to equality. Here is also laid down the awesome respect due to children, who live before the face of God (18:10–11). This principle of all people moves way beyond that of respect for life[6] but includes it. If the government of God dwells so fully over each person, precious beyond belief, then politics must never eliminate the person. Jacques Maritain, the great Catholic political philosopher, developed the term "personalism" to describe a Christian political perspective in which people are always first.[7] The gospel is opposed to the horrors where people are treated as expendable. Jesus insists on the commitment that a *person*, not even people in general, come first, whatever the cost. This sanctity of human life we still learn from Jesus.

The Christian principle of respect for all has had a slow and compromised development, but it has been present. Gradually serfdom and slavery have disappeared. Torture has been opposed. The poor and the sick have been helped. Wealth as a basis for political participation was attacked by the Levellers and others and has slowly eroded.[8] Democracy, giving more respect to people in the structure of government, initially grew in Protestant countries.[9] Yet the principle has been secularized into a variety of weaker forms. The Enlightenment tried to formulate human rights without reference to God. Liberalism manufactured self-serving individual rights, like the right to happiness. Marxist theories of class exploitation exposed the double standards of the bourgeoisie, but then sought to eliminate them and killed them by the tens of millions. Socialism developed an understanding of the citizen, who lived on the terms of the state.

These ideologies are like branches, cut off from the trunk and its roots, with leaves going brown. They have histories of partial inadequacy and collapse. The tree matters. Christians have often left their understanding implicit, but it should not be so. Thus, the central formative reference to God was in the end left out of the Universal Declaration of Human Rights, though obedience to God shaped many of those who formed it.[10] Nor is our history an impressive march of progress in this area. There is not much change on slavery between Gregory of Nyssa and Wilberforce or Lincoln. Millions have been wiped out in and by most major countries of the globe in the name of one form of exclusivism or another. Threats to respect for all people scream across the world at the beginning of the twenty-first century in wars and rumors of wars not the least from the United States.

The New Testament vision is clear, as Peter explains: "I now realize how true it is that God does not show favoritism but accepts people from every nation who fear him and do what is right" (cf. Acts 10:34–35). Beyond that, "You shall not kill" and "Love your neighbor" are required. The Kingdom insists on those conditions of accountability. All people are required to live on God's terms or exclude themselves. They are not the self-serving demos but the demos of God. These terms end exclusivism and the deaths of the expendable. Paul gives the theme an additional twist: "God chose the weak things of the world to shame the strong. He chose the lowly things of the world and the despised things—and the things that are not—to nullify the things that are" (1 Cor. 1:27–28). As opposed to oligarchies, aristocracies, Plato's philosopher-kings, elites, and cognoscenti, the rule of God knows no excluded people. The Master teaches, "For he who is least among you all—he is the greatest" (Luke 9:48). Rendering that principle fully operative is still far from complete in Western democracies, let alone areas where many people are disrespected and downtrodden. Nevertheless, God still backs that principle. In some areas it has thoroughly brought the demos into a share of power; yet everywhere all of us riff-raff stand in created integrity before God and therefore also in the state, whether rulers realize that or not.

The Principle of Peacemaking

The seeming normality of war dominates modern history. Estimates vary, but in the last century something like 160–200 million people were killed by internal and external wars, an unthinkable evil.[11] The Holocaust is part of a universal pattern. Something like 5 percent of all deaths in the last century were wartime killings.[12] We think of murder as an occasional heinous crime, but killing—it's the same to the victim—has been done to one in twenty of the human race throughout modernity. Fighting and the necessary slaughtering of people is repeatedly advocated by so-called civilized countries, most recently by the Bush and Blair administrations.[13] Hatred of enemies is normal, encouraged by propaganda machines of national self-rightness. Peace, even in the limited sense of no war, is a vague modern hope. In the last fifty years the West has merely been able to push wars out of its territories, at least until September 11, 2001.

This level of warfare is not new. Historians talk of the Hundred Years' War, pointing out that people were not fighting *all* the time. War has been the normal state enterprise, for the Caesars, William the Conqueror, Henry V, Napoleon, Lloyd George, Lyndon Johnson, and George W. Bush. The soldier has had great status with the ruler, and sometimes they have become the rulers. It is not a great leap from Julius Caesar to General Gautieri or General Eisenhower. Military dictators have been a special feature of the last century, often with self-endowed medals: "Well done, sir," he says, patting his own chest. Against this background, Jesus' principle of peacemaking is somewhat strange. The rulers and generals are for war, but Jesus is for peace. Clearly, it is not as simple as this, but there is an insistence in the teaching of Jesus that we must try to hear.

Peace is often seen as a kind of glow word, which we can lay hold of through a piece of paper or a negotiation that ends years of conflict. We long for a state of peace in international affairs, cities, and families. But Jesus' principle is dynamic, not merely a state of being. His insistence is on *peacemaking*. He says, "Blessed are the peace*makers*, for they shall be called sons and daughters of God" (cf. Matt. 5:9). Peacemaking is not magic; as Jesus lives and teaches peacemaking, it is a great costly positive principle. Peacemakers must move back across the divide of hostility. "Love your enemies and pray for those who persecute you," commands Jesus (5:44). The Son of God requires us to go through barriers that have hitherto led to war, and to be *for* the enemy, for their good, to be in the clinch of love and hug the Russian bear. This approach is costly, as the Gospels show. It leads to persecution and insults, but it breaks the causal law of evil with the power of the love of God.

We know what this means directly from Jesus. He has his back welted and opened by the thong, thorns pushed into his head, his face covered in spittle, his arms and feet impaled to the cross, and is naked except for blood. After that, his words are, "Father, forgive them, for they do not know what they are doing" (Luke 23:34). That sentence comes from a place no one else has ever inhabited. We see where peace*making* goes. It redefines the situation, going beyond evil, and necessarily involves God, because this conflict must be laid before the God who sees beyond it with love and grace. It is often a cosmic jump in the human imagination. The Normans, Huns, British, Spanish, Germans, Russians, and Taliban are our enemies. Yet they and their children need not be. We can love them, think for their good, and be faithful to them, whatever the circumstances. This principle wins victories over war and vendetta.

Where reluctantly there is war, it ends and is marked by goodwill. Understanding that lesson after the First World War probably would have avoided the Second.[14] With patience and love of enemies, we could probably avoid most wars. Forgiveness overwhelms the weak cycles of retaliation, but not with any sense of self-righteousness. Jesus requires us to say, "Father, forgive us, as we forgive those who trespass against us" (cf. Matt. 6:12). He requires that we recognize the symmetry of sin and forgive in accord with the terms of our membership in the Kingdom. With the focus on our own failings, the self-righteousness of enmity must wilt. Always, this is peace on God's terms.

When Paul, talking with magnificent irony, urges us all to put on the armor of God, it is equipment that cannot hurt anybody. In Tyndale's translation, we are commanded to stand "shod with shoes prepared by the gospel of peace" (Eph. 6:15). Peace walks and travels across hard ground. With such equipment Christians can stand against and defeat evil, using patience, love, humility, forgiveness, righteousness, the sword of the Spirit (Word of God), and prayer to slowly overcome the divisions of humankind (6:10–18). We dwell in the steadfast love of God against all the antipathies of hatred and revenge. We stay at the Christmas party, which means no return to the trenches (cf. the 1914 Christmas truce in World War I). It is beyond us, yet ours by faith because "the punishment that brought us peace was upon him, and by his wounds we are healed" (Isa. 53:5). This also is Jesus' principle of government.

Peacemaking occurs way before the crisis. It sees over the fence and understands the point of view of the other. It confronts what is wrong before it builds up into an insoluble dilemma. It turns the other cheek when wrong has been done, rather than retaliating and getting locked in tit-for-tat escalation. It does not go for defense but stays with the attacker. It moves beyond being right or being wrong into exposing everything to the truth, including our own failings. It forgives and therefore removes offenses from relationships. It focuses on what is good for the other in a way that transcends barriers. Peacemaking is for those who are so secure as sons and daughters of God that they can make peace.

Occasionally, it has been fulfilled. Black Christian Americans patiently saw beyond their abuse in and after slavery by immature white neighbors and persevered to create a nation of peace. Christian Democrats and others constructed a peaceful Europe after World War II, burying national rivalries in a greater sense of Christendom. Jimmy Carter's patient work with Egyptians and Israelis was in the mold of his Master, and it has held. Germany has moved from being the scourge of Europe to one of its primary peacemakers. Mandela and Tutu, with others, have made peace across a great divide in South Africa. Yet we still have vast amounts to learn from Jesus. We practice peacemaking with hypocrisy. We try to stop conflict but sell arms. We abhor war, except when we want to fight. We preach peace to others, but at the drop of a hat wage war ourselves. Making peace is often still on the drawing board, or picked up suddenly, after years of neglect. The seduction of hatred and impatience still turns out to be too strong for weak leaders. To receive wrong and submit it to God is to heal history, but we are novices in the process. Nevertheless, the gentle imperative and actions of the Messiah will not be gainsaid, and the Way creeps forward.

Dwelling in Truth

Similarly, the relation between truth and politics is ambiguous. For much of history, only military power has seemed to matter. Often, too, rule has been surrounded by myths—some architectural, as the pyramids, the Parthenon, Versailles, and the White House all testify. Other myths have been odd—Romulus and Remus as founders of Rome, the German myth of the "stab in the back" after World War I, and the idea that the British are reasonable. Ruler mythologies, like the Divine Right of Kings or Evita, abound. More insidious still is the way propaganda shapes public opinion to the requirements of leaders; lies can succeed for a while if they are shouted loud and often enough. Further, opposition is often quelled by media management; those who are publishing the truth can be discredited, silenced, or eliminated, as they have been in state after state.

Truthfulness has often been an absent or unwelcome guest in politics. Yet it is inescapable. At one level, it was probably Hitler's inability to face quite immediate truths that lost him the war. In our own times, the importance of truth is partly recognized structurally and by intent. Political parties contend to some extent for what they believe to be true, and as such they appeal to the electorate. The media have a keen commitment to unmask the lie and expose the deception. We have hearings, inquiries, and commissions to find out what might be obscured. We distrust those who "are economical with the truth."[15] This ambiguous reality is made more complex by the fact that right motives are not enough. Most of us, honestly believing something to be true, have had its falseness exposed to us, even twenty years later. The issue is vast in scope, but we can see why respect for truth is now built into our politics, at least in part. Yet, really, we may be further away from it in our politics than we were a decade or a century ago. T. S. Eliot's line "Human kind cannot bear very much reality" is insistently true (*Murder in the Cathedral*, part 2).

Jesus' teaching about exposure to the truth is one of his major themes. He speaks these words to Nicodemus, a politician and member of the Jewish ruling council: "This is the verdict: Light has come into the world, but [people] . . . loved darkness instead of light because their deeds were evil. Everyone who does evil hates the light, and will not come into the light for fear that his deeds will be exposed. But whoever lives by the truth comes into the light, so that it may be seen plainly that what he has done has been done through God" (John 3:19–21). This theme of exposure/light/truth/goodness versus hiding/darkness/lies/evil occurs constantly. "For there is nothing hidden that will not be disclosed, and nothing concealed that will not be known or brought out in the open" (Luke 8:17). Jesus takes up the theme later, directly in relation to the exposure of political leaders. Beware hypocrisy, he says: "There is nothing concealed that will not be disclosed, or hidden that will not be made known. What you have said in the dark will be heard in the daylight, and what you have whispered in the ear in the inner rooms will be proclaimed from the housetops" (12:2–3). This understanding of the power of exposure to the light runs through the Gospels. What is hidden will be exposed. The truth will out. It is a strange and compelling theme.

At one level, to walk this way is dangerous. John the Baptist told the truth and lost his head. The prophets, Jesus points out, whom you pretend to venerate, were killed and imprisoned to silence them. And he adds, "You are the descendants of those who murdered the prophets" (Matt. 23:31). Those who tell the truth often suffer at the hands of the powerful. All over the world today, good men and women are arrested, in prison, or murdered because they have been brave enough to expose the truth and discomfort rulers. Amnesty International deals with thousands of cases. Truth is precarious. Whistleblowers suffer. Those who know the truth are silenced. Shortly before his death, Jesus told the people,

You are going to have the light just a little while longer. Walk while you
have the light, before darkness overtakes you. The man who walks in the
dark does not know where he is going. Put your trust in the light while
you have it, so that you may become [children] . . . of light. . . . I have
come into the world as a light, so that no one who believes in me should
stay in darkness. (John 12:35–36, 46)

These words have deep political import, but it is not clear what they
mean. Is truth, "the light," this precarious?

It seems to be so. There is a battle between truth and much political
power. To tell the truth to others, the electorate, and oneself is difficult.
There are choices of truth and falsity all the time. The issue of truth in
politics is crystallized in the great final early-morning confrontation
between Pilate and Jesus, and for a while we dwell with it. Pilate is
conscious of his overwhelming Roman power. The Roman governor is
in control but confronted by the mass of the Sanhedrin, perhaps sixty
or so of the seventy-one, coming as a formal deputation with Jesus
as captive. They want him killed. They are obsequious, submitting to
Roman law and rule, a thing they really hate. The charges they level
against their captive reflect it: "We have found this man subverting our
nation" (Luke 23:2). With ingratiating loyalty they are implying that
Jesus is a revolutionary against Rome. It is untrue, as we have seen, and
the leaders know that Jesus is not treading the Zealot path. "He opposes
payment of taxes to Caesar" (23:2). In an obvious formal sense this too
is untrue, for they have just spectacularly failed to trap him into making
precisely this pronouncement (Matt. 22:15–22). Jesus has relativized
and even dismissed Roman sovereignty, but they have no grounds for
this second statement.

The third charge is the key one. For the Sanhedrin the claim of Messiah is a central blasphemy. They cannot stomach the possibility that
the Son of God stands before them, though they sense it might actually
be true. To Pilate the issue is presented politically: Jesus "claims to be
Messiah, a king" (Luke 23:2n). This, of course, is the clinching argument
to Roman authorities, who have closed down the title of "king" by their
direct rule and see anyone claiming it as treasonous. This statement
is deeply true, but not in the sense that the leaders mean or as Pilate
understands it. They know Jesus is no Zealot insurrectionist and they
are deliberately lying. They say it because Messiah insurrectionists are
the bane of Roman governors and have to be put down. Pilate is being
fed an automatic reaction. He is not fooled for a moment.

The awkward national leaders are left outside Pilate's palace, formerly
King Herod's palace, so that they will not be contaminated and become
ceremonially unclean, hardly a compliment to Pilate as he takes Jesus

inside to question him. He suspects that the charge leveled against Jesus is motivated by jealousy and poses the central Roman question: "Are you laying claim to be ruler of this nation? Are you king of the Jews?" Luke's summary of the event involves a complete non sequitur: "King of the Jews?" "Yes." "Not guilty!" (23:1–4). John shows the actual complexity of the development. When Jesus is asked whether he is king of the Jews, Pilate probably expects him to say "No" because it is a damning question. Instead, Jesus focuses on what Pilate understands by the question.[16] He asks whether the question comes from Pilate or the charges of his Jewish accusers (John 18:33–34). It is odd to discuss the complexities of meaning in the middle of such a trial, but Jesus does it. His answer must respond to Pilate as the latter understands the situation. Jesus presses toward a truthful discussion even though his life is in danger. Pilate is clearly irritated by this and tries to get his answer: "I'm not a Jew. Your people handed you over. What is it that you have done?" (cf. 10:35). Even here, Pilate is probably presuming that Jesus will say "No" to the kingship question or will slip by it. But Jesus insists on telling Pilate of his kingship and the nature of the Kingdom of God (10:36). Pilate goes back with some surprise to his original question and flounders with the complexity of what Jesus reveals to him.

Suddenly, Jesus presents to Pilate a Kingdom based on testifying to the truth. It is one of the most astonishing statements ever made: "You are right in saying I am a king. In fact, for this reason I was born, and for this I came into the world, to testify to the truth. Everyone on the side of truth listens to me" (10:37). "Testify" involves giving witness. It is a strong legal term. Aside from the sheer fearless honesty of the statement, in that situation condemning himself to death, it presents this peculiar reality of a Kingdom constructed around truth. Such a kingdom is unthinkable, not previously envisaged. How would such a kingdom be run? Why would Jesus lay claim to such kingship? How can truthfulness define a kingdom? Then and now this focus for rule is deeply countercultural. But the prisoner could be right. Submission to the truth could be the only proper basis for rule. If in the end all truth is God's truth, only by bowing to the truth can government be properly shaped. When tested, Pilate is one who cannot live the truth. He knows and thrice declares Jesus to be innocently accused, but condemns him to death, albeit with great personal struggle (Luke 23:4, 14, 22).

This truth principle has deep detailed content. One dimension of it is Jesus' concept of hypocrisy. This moves beyond the idea of truth as verbal or propositional.[17] *We* must add up: our lives must be consistent, God-seeing, and pure of heart (Matt. 5:8). There should not be dissonance between words and actions, between appearance and reality, between motive and word, between yesterday and tomorrow, between principle and practice, between public and private. Truth penetrates everything. Jesus' words—"They do not practice what they preach" (23:3)—about the Jerusalem politicians hound every politician through history. John Major's Conservative government, which championed a return to traditional moral values, was cremated on the corruption and sleaze of its members. The U.S. government and people have strongly condemned terrorism after September 11, 2001. Yet for several decades many American Irish people and politicians have supported terrorism in Northern Ireland, killing and maiming thousands of people. Most of the IRA funds and three-quarters of the discovered arms caches have come from the United States.[18] The hypocrisy remains unconfessed. The truth lies there, often hidden, but it does not go away. The kingdom of truth has staying power beyond all our posturing. We were better to show it respect.

Jesus draws on the great prophetic tradition of exposure to the truth before God, from whom nothing is hidden (Jer. 16:17; Heb. 4:13). Elijah, Elisha, Isaiah, Jeremiah, Amos, and Obadiah were some of the prophets who spoke God's awkward truth to corrupt rulers and cultures. Even today some of this is breathtaking in its honesty. Isaiah looks at the corruption and extortion that mark the ruling classes. But, he points out, women obsessed by their appearance, image, and self-indulgence help to create pressure for this. They will be a stench, bald, and filthy, says Isaiah (ch. 3). Few of us would dare thus to address women who have been led by commerical pressures into vast, silly, conspicuous consumption. God's law and God's word for people and organizations strip away excuses, self-justification, and self-importance.

There is granite solid honesty. Finally, Jesus becomes the fulfillment of the prophetic tradition, the truth that sticks in the gullet, the stone on which leaders stub their toes, the awkward one. Of course, the line continues through history, even among those who do not fully own its source. As Nathan exposed David, so the *Washington Post* exposed Nixon. But one recent event does not touch the depth of the issue. Only before God and in this man Jesus is all exposed. The lie does not work, but we are all tangled in it. We cannot lie to others without telling a (different) lie to ourselves. Our move to deceive others actually deceives ourselves, and we are all deceived. Day by day politicians in London and Washington hide things from us.[19] We are all victims of the weapons of mass deception. Against this, Jesus offers us the Spirit of truth, the One who knows us better than we know ourselves and can carry us beyond self-deception (John 16:13). We do not possess truth or own it, but to our deepest good we can submit to it, albeit incompletely.

This principle of Jesus contends with many formulations in political philosophy.[20] Often truth has been seen as the possession of one political group—Plato's philosopher kings,[21] enlightened despots,[22] the Hegelian state, or Marxist revolutionaries.[23] Or it may be constructed around the sociopolitical position of a group. Brahmans validate the caste system,[24] landowners claim the sanctity of private property, and capitalists honor the unqualified virtue of profit.[25] There are forms of pride about truth. The rationalist believes there is no value outside his own thinking,[26] or the intellectual that his construction should shape the world. Indeed, the great modernist dilemma is the presumed human ownership of the truth, validating its totalitarian imposition on all. In the early twentieth century, propaganda emerged as a prime means of this imposition.[27] At other times politicians construct truth around the self-affirming image of party or leader.[28] At another level people see truth as embedded in the way the system runs—some esoteric knowledge of the state's operation, the process of gaining power, competing groups, or some idea of the democratic process.[29] The modernist dilemma posed by the idea of the human possession of truth has recently led to a deep postmodern scepticism.[30] Is it possible for any kind of public truth to emerge? These debates require questions of truth to go beyond politics into issues of worldview. They require us to address human sinfulness and its impact on veracity, and they ask whether humankind can, without God's help, find any place of truthfulness. They reopen Jesus' analysis of self-deception. Only the Nazarene leads us beyond these political misconceptions of truth to the possibility of honesty before God.

Yet, this principle of Jesus now weighs on us. Newspapers and interviewers expose corruption, often with great normative commitment. There is nothing hidden that will not be revealed. After centuries where the inner closet and smoke-filled rooms have characterized the decision-making process of politics, planning the overthrow of Richard II, or organizing an attack on Pearl Harbor, we have and laud transparency and openness. Covert deals are now leaked to the media. There is a principle of "open government." But the principle cuts deep. Media exposure is not the same as the principle of Jesus: exposure to the truth as a pattern of submission and openness to God. The latter is radical, more like the prayer of David: "Search me. . . . Test me. . . . See if there is any offensive way in me" (Ps. 139:23–24). This clearly is more demanding than the odd media question or scandal. It requires inner and public honesty, the willingness to submit what we think, say, and do to deeper scrutiny.

Such a commitment challenges self-righteousness. It makes politics more sober and less sure of itself. It heeds the judgment and warning: "You are like whitewashed tombs, which look beautiful on the outside but on the inside are full of dead men's bones and everything unclean" (Matt. 23:27). It distrusts party and national collusions to lie. It seeks light on our errors before we become entrenched in them. Such commitment scrapes paint off the cover-up. The words reverberate: there is nothing hidden that will not be revealed. The irony of Nixon organizing his own Watergate exposure conveys a deeper sense.[31] The truth principle and its Lord will rule by default or by submission. How much better to live open to the Spirit of truth.

Integrity or Popularity?

These principles probe like searchlights, eventually revealing everyone, even those who try to hide. Popularity has been important in politics long before democracy became widespread. But being popular is not per se an adequate political end, because the population is as likely to be as evil or unprincipled as the rulers are. The state is normally expected to provide justice better than many of its citizens' current values.[32] Nevertheless, the "rule" of the people and the people's support have since 1779 often been seen as the foundation of politics and the meaning of democracy. It is the demos rule validated by Rousseau's "general will"—what is best for society. Actually, of course, this position is deeply problematic. Von Prinsterer, Talmon, and others point out the links between populism and totalitarian tendencies; the ruler who embodies the "will" of the people, proletariat, or *Volk*, and can seemingly do no wrong, actually does most wrong.[33] The popular ruler manipulates, simplifies, and constructs what the people want.

There are structural reasons for this. If the people are supposed to embody politics, they *become* the government, the law, the authority of the system. Whatever they say goes. But what they say will be incoherent, containing the normal flaws of human sinfulness and self-idolatry. Though the place of the people in politics is important, a demos-driven model relies on a false god, and it must fail, as it has in revolutionary France, Russia, Argentina, and many other polities. Yet now it is more widespread than ever. Find out what the people want and, in order to be elected, re-present it to the voters—lower taxes, war, high consumption, cheap public services. The result has often been policy that has seesawed and been inconsistent and mass indulgent. Pre-election bribes have been common. Politics gradually shallows to a people who are self-referencing and self-pleasing in their political participation. The problem is not that ordinary people take part in electoral politics, but that they are self-centered in the process. A slice of the electorate plays out the theme "Our will be done." The reference point is not justice, what is good, or the needs of others, but the demotic self with all its sins. In order to be liked or supported, many politicians have traded their principles for acceptance by public, party, or peers. Jesus addresses this structural problem of popularity in terms that are still utterly astonishing and were more so at the time.

The characteristic Roman response to popularity was to put on spectacular events for the masses. The Colosseum, hippodromes, and amphitheaters were places of gory games filling the masses' minds and validating the rulers. They were populist bribes. But this model does not have much success in Judea. Here the Romans remain a colonial power, and the chief route to popularity is hating them. The Zealots command crowd-whipping support, far more powerful than the plodding righteousness of the Pharisees, who want to be popular through their good deeds. Amazingly, Jesus turns away, on principle, from every popular move. Here is a man who can draw crowds, who heals, who holds people on his every word, and who inspires love. Everything points to overwhelming popularity, but almost perversely, he acts the unpopular part. We have seen how he turns down the temptation to provide the people's sign from the top of the Temple. He further castigates those who seek such a sign, calling them a "wicked and adulterous generation." Yes, agreed. There is no sign that can properly validate God, but one may object that there is no need to condemn one's own generation *so* completely; they might take offense.

The Roman and Herodian tax collectors are hated as traitors, but Jesus parties with them and becomes their friend; it is like an American presidential candidate hanging out with child molesters, hardly a good electoral move. The people love the Temple; Jesus talks about it falling down. The Jews see themselves as people of faith and hate the Romans. A centurion (who has good relations with the Jews from building a synagogue) has his servant healed by Jesus. But Jesus' praise goes further than it needs to: "I tell you, I have not found such great faith even in Israel" (Luke 7:1–10). To commend a Roman centurion for *faith* is one up the nose for the Jews surrounding him. Further, Jews hate Samaritans; Jesus mixes with and praises them. Jews hate Gentiles; Jesus also holds them up as examples of faith. He criticizes his supporters; a sympathetic crowd is labeled an "unbelieving and perverse generation" (Matt. 17:17). John records how when the disciples are offended and grumbling about the hardness of his teaching, Jesus goes on to give yet more offense, so that many of his disciples turn back and no longer follow him.

Then occurs an astonishing interchange, which should be the apotheosis of this great antisocial trend. Jesus, with the crowds melting away in the face of some unbelievably difficult teaching, asks the Twelve, "You do not want to leave too, do you?" (John 6:67). We cannot directly hear the tone, which might be plaintive. But his subsequent response to Peter instead suggests that it is forthright. When Peter answers with a fulsome affirmation, Jesus in turn replies, "Have I not chosen you Twelve? Yet one of you is a devil!" (John 6:70). This is hardly an endearing response to the faithful remnant of his followers. Yet the trend continues, and at the end the crowds choose Barabbas, the insurrectionist, over Jesus, and the final journey to the cross is a lonely business. Even there, an amazing interchange takes place. On the way to Golgotha, women mourn and wail for him, presumably with real sorrow. But he quickly takes them beyond their sympathy and warns, "Do not weep for me; weep for yourselves and your children," for a time of catastrophe is coming (Luke 23:27–31). This is not a man who sets out to win friends and influence people. He does not need to be liked. He does bless babies, but only when it is unfashionable.

Why this extraordinary anti-populism? Earlier, when the crowds flock to him, John records Jesus' reaction: "But Jesus would not entrust himself to them, for he knew all [people]" (John 2:24). His actions constantly show the same pattern. Jesus tells those he heals to go away and tell no one, so that the crowds are not whipped up. John notes, "The man who was healed had no idea who it was, for Jesus had slipped away into the crowd that was there" (John 5:13). Luke says, "The crowds . . . came, . . . but Jesus . . . withdrew" (5:15–16). When the crowd of five thousand wants him to be leader, he just walks up into the hills and leaves them (John 6:15). The sense of avoiding popularity is palpable. Mark says, "Jesus commanded them not to tell anyone. But the more he did so, the more they kept talking about it. People were overwhelmed with amazement. 'He has done everything well,' they said" (Mark 7:36–37). In the Sermon on the Mount Jesus opens up the underlying insight. "If you do these things to be seen by others, whether donations, fasting, prayer, or anything else that gives you approval, you finish up living before them, rather than God" (cf. Matt. 6:1–18). Then self-righteousness and hypocrisy will emerge. The only real issue is our walk before God. In modern parlance, Jesus insists, "Always integrity; never popularity." This is not any old integrity, but life fully accountable to God. Obey God consistently and do not be lured into the hypocrisy that follows from seeking approval. This is so far beyond our grubby views of integrity that we can scarcely take it in.

Jesus' commentary on popularity has big implications for democratic elections, for the self-worshipping demos turns out to be a false idol.[34] The demotic self constructs law in its own image. Divorce can be a matter of self-will, and children can be abandoned. Sex is self-serving or commercial, not a matter of shared love, covenant, or commitment. Trade is selfish. Markets exploit, pushing prices below subsistence for primary producers. Consumption is self-serving, polluting, wasteful, and image-based. Politicians dish up permissive legislation on a conveyor belt of increasing indulgence. The so-called end of ideology is found in this one-dimensional, self-pleasing demos.[35] Within the ethos of giving people what they demand, the United States declares global warming not to exist and spurns the Kyoto Protocol, because the people must have their cheap fuel. Electoral popularity contests where "I smile and you vote for me" avoid considering what is right and good. There is a dangerous kind of media-induced shallowness emerging in democratic politics.

How can the electorate and candidates conduct campaigns of integrity and principle? Concern for this seems to be slipping away from us like a riptide.[36] If the deepest value our politicians have is being liked and *being voted for,* we have a degenerate system.[37] Often we have most to learn from those who do not say what we like. For example, few politicians have dared state the real costs of global warming and third-world poverty. Few advocate that we address them before floods and famine overwhelm us.[38] When they do, they may be right and speak for our good, but it is political death to say what people do not want to hear. In the deliberate unpopularity of Jesus, we see the principle's weight. At his trial the leaders play with hatred of the Romans and are suddenly massively popular themselves, but the payday comes when that hatred sends Jerusalem into a frenzy of rebellion leading to the death of a million people. In the end popularity has too high a price.

Power, Freedom, and Weakness

The word *power* seems close to the center of politics. Most political leaders have been powerful, and "getting to power," and hanging on to it, seems to be the preoccupation of many democratic politicians. Political theorists from Machiavelli onward have been preoccupied with the concept.[39] Duverger reflects thousands of modern theorists when he describes political sociology as the "science of power."[40] Great political philosophers like Hobbes, Burke, and Acton have wrestled with the *problem* of power, for such it has often seemed.[41] But in a sense, the issue hits the road with Nietzsche, for whom power becomes central to the redefinition of humankind away from Christianity. He begins his study *The Anti-Christ* with an aphorism: "What is good?—All that heightens the feeling of power, the will to power, power itself in man."[42] Nietzsche continues, "That the strong races of northern Europe have not repudiated the Christian God certainly reflects no credit on their talent for religion—not to speak of their taste. They ought to have felt *compelled* to have done with such a sickly and decrepit product of *décadence.*"[43] Nietzsche sets out the issue fairly well and heralds a movement to faith in power that has shaped much of the subsequent history of Europe. The *Wehrmacht* of the Nazis finally flowered into the superpower confrontation of the late twentieth century, where the "flower" is expressed in multiple-headed nuclear missiles.[44] This is no idle issue.

In the Gospels, we are presented with a perspective on power so radical and disturbing that few have understood or come to terms with it even today. Jesus attacks the very notion of power as *control over*. Throughout human history, men have sought to control others, seeing that as the way to make their own lives more affluent, secure, and free from work. Conquest, enslavement, control systems, state-buttressing taxes, docile populations, and manipulation have been normal parts of this cultural complex. Its costs are staggering. Human history is littered with castles, wars, slave-trading, refugees, impoverishment, futile work, destruction, spy systems, bombing, and other systems of effort that have resulted from the human need for *control over*. England loses its oaks to make battleships. Chechnya is flattened in a fight for control. Hitler devastates the lives of hundreds of millions in a need to dominate. Bombs are the most efficient way of wasting power ever invented. Although we may focus on the worst examples, the acceptance of *control over* is ordinary in the lives of many people and states. But what if this idiom is a great human mistake? This unthinkable truth Jesus presents.

It is not easy to grasp it. John's witness was to one who would be "more powerful than I" (Matt. 3:11). This man, strolling through villages, does not come across as a political ruler—no retinue, soldiers, orders, servants, or bossiness here, but a complete absence of control. Modern powerful leaders sometimes go for a walkabout to meet the people, but for Jesus, this was daily business. Because he had no *power over,* there was no fear or distance from the people. He showed that financial, military, popular, and organizational control is unnecessary, that God's rule is a gentle and unobtrusive business. The deliberateness of Jesus' position shows in his entry into Jerusalem. Throughout the Roman Empire, the idiom of the triumphal return is understood and accepted. The great general, returning from the wars in which the barbarians have been defeated, would ride into Rome to the acclaim of the people. He rides high on a magnificent horse, followed by trophies of war, and leaders who have been taken as slaves trail manacled behind. Throughout the empire great triumphal arches were constructed to mark the return. The Arch of Titus in Rome built about AD 81 shows the treasures of the Jewish Temple sacked a few years earlier. This idiom Jesus deliberately subverts. He follows the pattern set up by Zechariah in an oracle.

See, your king comes to you,
Righteous and having salvation,

Gentle and riding on a donkey,
On a colt, the foal of a donkey.
I will take away the chariots from Ephraim
And the war-horses from Jerusalem,
And the battle bow will be broken.
He will proclaim peace to the nations.
His rule will extend from sea to sea
And from the River [Euphrates] to the ends of the earth. (Zech. 9:9–10)

Thus, Jesus insists on riding into Jerusalem on this young animal, with his feet scarcely off the ground. The foal is small and immature, potentially frightened by the crowds but reassured by having its mother alongside (Matt. 21:2–3, 7). At the deepest level this triumphal entry is fitting for the one who comes in the name of God and enters Jerusalem, but it is also a parody of the conquering hero. This is the nonconquering hero almost paddling the small pack animal into Jerusalem, a deliberate political counter-statement.

What, then, replaces power as *control over?* For those who have suffered control and domination, there is the experience of freedom. Jesus makes a great offer: "My yoke is easy and my burden is light" (Matt. 11:28–30). But this is no magic offer. Its costs are also weighed: if the weak are to become free, the powerful must become weak. They must discard and deconstruct their systems of control. "Blessed are the poor in spirit, for theirs is the government of God" (cf. 5:3). "Blessed are the meek, for they shall inherit the earth" (5:5). Being free from *control over* is actually a blessing. Ending military domination, slavery, class control, elitism, demanded honor, and labor as drudgery is not just good for those who suffer, but also for those who dominate and bully. They can know good relationships rather than intimidating and dishonest ones. Citizen Kane can be loved. Empowerment forgives debt, supports the weak, and refreshes the downtrodden. It brings down rulers from their thrones and lifts up the humble so that both can have a party. It slims the fat and fills out the thin. With the breakdown of control comes the empowering of the weak. Or better, empowerment comes when, before God, all of us, whether weak or strong, once more have response-ability in our lives and can dwell in the gentle power of the Holy Spirit.[45] Each person's response ability dwells in his or her unique relationship with God. Political control gives way to something deeper—the Word and ways of God opening up lives to the power to do good.

This meaning of freedom in the Gospels goes deeper than just non-imposition. It is not self-referencing, as seen in modern liberalism and individualism, with subjects doing what they want. The truth that we are made to love God and our neighbor makes these relationships part of our freedom. Self-referencing freedom ends as self-slavery. It also sees the state and law as an encumbrance. Liberation from those who enslave and control is part of the good news, as South American theology has shown,[46] but it is not liberation into do-what-you-like liberalism.[47] Nor is freedom something we naturally possess, because people are slaves to their own sin, corrupting their relationship with God and tying themselves to corrupt ways and false political moves. Indeed, freedom from sin is the greatest human need, for as Christ teaches, from the human heart come murder, immorality, theft, false witness, and many other sins (Matt. 15:19). Our freedom, in this self-centered sense, generates most of the problems with which politics grapples. Christianity, following the teachings of Jesus, sees freedom as much more than grabbing autonomy. "I did it my way" is the recipe for failure, because sin enslaves and damns our possibility of an open response to God (Gen. 3; Rom. 7). The inadequacy of liberalism is found in the fact that its idea of freedom does not address human self-indulgence. The evidence in the West is that much "freedom" devastates the lives of others.

The astonishing claim of Jesus is that people are only free in the truth of his teaching and through his liberation. The Son will set you free to dwell before God (John 8:31–36). Freedom depends on the Messiah, the saving one, drawing us to the radical center of human freedom before God. It requires sin to be addressed. Nothing is imposed, and we are free to accept or reject Messiah, but the need is palpable. To the leaders of his day, Jesus probably seems libertarian because he departs radically from the impositions of the Pharisees. But the freedom he offers requires the surrender of human self-centered freedom to God, in service of whom freedom will be found. There is a problem within us of enslavement, not generated by others.

Outside Jerusalem, Jesus faces the Pharisees and other political leaders complaining at his disciples for not observing the law. They are an early law-and-order brigade, tut-tutting at those who do not conform. Jesus attacks their focus. They think of observances, but the structure of observance is already distorted by their self-referencing. They talk up gifts to themselves and minimize gifts to elderly parents. They nullify the Word of God because their hearts are not right. Out of the heart comes good, or all the things that corrupt, and "every plant that my heavenly Father has not planted will be pulled up by the roots" (Matt. 15:1–20, esp. v. 13). Freedom from control by others is an issue, but it grows from the deeper one of self-enslavement to sin. It is a problem beyond politics but dominating politics, and Christ has it also in view.

The book of Revelation is visionary and difficult, yet it does touch on the end of political control. Jesus is frequently described as "the Lamb on the throne" (e.g., 5:6). Often the significance of this visual metaphor is related to sacrifice, and the Lamb is described as the Lamb who was slain. But the simple meaning is no less important: a Lamb on a throne? How daft! This innocent creature that harms no one occupies a throne, normally filled by tyrants and those whose trade is raw power and predation. The Lamb on the throne "ba-aa-aas" at the power system. The gentle rule of Jesus has overcome and judges the rule of kings, princes, generals, the rich, and the mighty. Recognizing this in the middle of persecution and a dominant, vicious Roman Empire is almost impossible, but slowly the good news that the Lamb is on the throne has filtered out and brings real political freedom. "Hey! You mean we do not have to be afraid of our rulers?" What a revelation that is to human history! "You mean the meek are not weak?" So far and further this man goes in offering freedom to the powerful and the weak. Truly, we are out of control.

Reconciliation

Why does Jesus, living when he does, not confront the Roman Empire and free the Jews? Surely, that would be a good thing to do against the evil oppressor. After all, Christians have "just-war" theories. Given the evil of the oppressors, why does Jesus not heed his followers, mount an insurrection, and overthrow the Romans? There are some sixty chapters in the Bible with a very negative view of empires, so why not address this injustice and free the captives? Yet as we have seen, Jesus does not raise an army and attack the Herodians and the Romans, and he is not fighting on the side of the Jews, his own people. What is happening here?

It is interesting what frame of reference we construct for addressing an issue. One frame looks at the immediate ethics of war and whether it is justified or not. Frequently groups within the same nation will disagree in their conclusions. Another considers colonialism and its evils and looks for liberation. From within a nation another looks at the unjust acts of other nations with righteous indignation. Colonial powers, whether Rome or "Great" Britain (that silly title), see the benign value of their rule, bringing "civilization" to other nations. They reveal the arrogance of power and its inability to think in other than its own terms. In most wars, both sides are convinced they are right and that their god is with them. Patterns of self-justification and ethnocentric rightness are built into conflicts. The Roman Empire was not much different in structure from the British Empire, but the British were quite happy to believe for two centuries that they were God's gift to their vassal nations and fought uprisings with moral rectitude. "O bother, the natives are restless again." We have to "take up the White Man's burden, . . . to serve your captives' need" (Kipling, 1899) and settle the squabbles. History is full of bloody confrontations where hostile forces, with varying degrees of right on their side, have warred, killed, and maimed. In Gulf War I, the Western Allies were "right" in that Kuwait was illegally invaded, but they finished up killing over one hundred thousand Iraqis. How right is that?

There are deep problems with self-vindication politics. Its underlying perspective is *Us good / You bad.* Cowboys/Indians, Freedom/Communism, Romans/Barbarians, the Brits/the Bosch, Peace-Loving Nations/Terrorists. Self-rightness drives the divide. Decateur's toast—"Our country, right or wrong!"—is precisely the problem. In truth, both sides normally have faults they contribute to the situation; a wrong reaction will be justified by the wrong received. It is lobotomizing to read the self-righteousness of Sein Fein's or al Qaeda's literature. But the dynamic is far deeper. There is a tendency to see long-distance faults and ignore those at home, a moral hypermetropia. Ex-colonial nations have rightly judged the imperial power, but often their subsequent self-government has been a failure. The United States, rightly independent of Britain, was soon embroiled in a bloody Civil War, and many African countries have seriously failed in self-government.

Self-vindication often goes with failure. It allows us to ignore our own faults and exaggerates those of the enemy. Scapegoating, another stage in the process, retains the enemy as the problem and can last for centuries, as it has in the Balkans. The human ability to identify enemies and become convinced that only the enemy is wrong is rampant. But Jesus stays outside this position, offering himself as friend of Roman, Jew, Samaritan, and Greek. This stance has a cost because it requires criticizing your own side and deconstructing its self-righteousness. For centuries, Jews have felt Jesus to be anti-Semitic, and there is systematic evidence that supports the case. Gentiles are praised. Those who are children of Abraham are told that they have become children of the devil (John 8). Jesus deliberately deconstructs all the self-glorying and self-righteousness in Jewish ethnic identity. Is this anti-Semitism?

No. The logic of Jesus' position is incontrovertible. Reconciliation is possible only when ethnocentrism is broken. Americans can be properly reconciled with the Russians only when they know they are, in part, international self-righteous bullies incapable of seeing anyone else's point of view and blinded by self-congratulation. The British can properly relate to the French only when they recognize they themselves are loutish and inarticulate, with a degenerate culture and a grossly unjustified self-regard. Jews and Gentiles cannot truly live together within ethnic self-rightness. Jesus begins the great deconstruction of ethnocentrism two millennia before the word arrives. It is the cost of reconciliation, and the cost is paid in Jesus' refusing to flatter his own people, as most of us do. It generates racist and nationalist hate toward him. The Jews and Romans are sworn enemies. Here for a while they come together to hate him. The Romans provide the means of execution, crucifixion: a deliberate string-them-up-to-make-the-others-behave death. The Jews provide the victim. Nevertheless, this man has done no evil. He is the best thing that ever happened to Romans and Jews, and yet both collude in his death. The writer to the Hebrews (or Jewish Christians) adds the last poignant word from within his ethnic ethos:

> The high priest carries the blood of animals into the Most Holy Place as a sin offering, but the bodies are burned outside the camp. And so Jesus also suffered outside the city gate to make the people holy through his own blood. Let us, then, go to him outside the camp, bearing the disgrace he bore. For here we do not have an enduring city, but we are looking for the city that is to come. (Heb. 13:11–14)

Here is a touching picture of people prepared to be seen with Christ, even at the level of unclean offal, rather than clinging to their chief ethnic ritual. This bathetic eclipse shows the weight of ethnic identity. The Romans and Jews are no different from any other race. We all swagger behind our barriers, not just of nation, but also of race, gender, class, and age. In the name of our self-rightness, we repeatedly do evil. One has seen the problem and carried it, and with his stripes we are healed. Paul, previously a Jew of the Jews, describes how Jesus has destroyed the barrier, the dividing wall of hostility. Jew and Gentile are made one, reconciled in peace. No longer are we foreigners and aliens to one another but fellow citizens from all races in the kingdom of God, a worldwide dwelling in which God lives by his Spirit (Eph. 2). If you hold the hands of enemies in steadfast love, you will be ripped apart. But that is not the end of the story.

Reconciliation is a rediscovered principle. Perhaps it first came back nationally when France, Germany, and other combatants who endured repeated wars and conquest moved after the Second World War into national friendship. Christian Democrat leaders like Adenauer, Schumann, Maritain, and De Gaspari saw a community of nations reconciled into a European partnership, and they worked and prayed for it. Now many of the national frontiers have all but disappeared. Egypt and Israel were deeply sworn enemies. In October 1973 they engaged in a bloody and costly war. In 1978 Sadat, Begin, and Carter inaugurated the Camp David Accord, ending some thirty years of hostility; the reconciliation has lasted for at least two decades.[48] The rapprochement between the USA and USSR, hopefully seen more wisely than as a triumph of the United States, has blessed us all. The conflict in Northern Ireland totters toward reconciliation, bedeviled by the whiff of ingrained self-rightness. In South Africa the Truth and Reconciliation Commission has embodied the principle of making a rainbow out of black and white.[49]

The dynamic power of this principle has scarcely dominated world politics, but it is emerging strongly. States are apologizing for earlier wrongs. Unthinkable visits are made to bridge gulfs of alienation. Countries are learning to see from the other side and recognize the depths of the offense they have created. The principle of reconciliation builds bridges where none existed. It is, in Jesus' unforgettable words, to "do to others as you would have them do to you" (Luke 6:31). The principle heals the world, changes opposition into empathy, and is powerful beyond what we have yet tried.

Reconciliation comes from God, who "causes his sun to rise on the evil and the good," and is "merciful" and "kind to the ungrateful and wicked" (Matt. 5:45; Luke 6:35–36). Here is a vantage point above pettiness, seeing with some of God's magnanimity. Nor is it merely a "nice" principle. We know what it means by seeing Jesus stripped naked and nailed through his flesh to the cross, howling out the words, "Father forgive them, for they know not what they do" (Luke 23:34). It entails suffering. The victory of reconciliation is where nobody wins and everybody does. It is no casual option, but a requirement. Jesus tells his disciples to pray, "Forgive us our sins as we forgive those who sin against us" (cf. Matt. 6:12; Luke 11:4). Again, the logic cannot be gainsaid. Those who will not forgive reject the principle and the God of the principle. We are tied into God's terms. "For if you forgive men when they sin against you, your heavenly Father will also forgive you. But if you do not forgive men their sins, your Father will not forgive your sins" (Matt. 6:14–15). So the way of reconciliation is Jesus' required way. "Forgive seventy times seven" (cf. 18:21–22). If you have created offense, *you* take the initiative to settle it: "First go and be reconciled to your brother" (5:23–26).

The early Christians knew that Jesus in his own body had reconciled enemies, making two one and bringing opponents to God and one another. He is the reconciler, the one who broke down the hardest dividing walls of hostility, by loving and forgiving through the wall (Eph. 2). The politics of reconciliation are on Christ's agenda, and they will roll.

Stewardship

Many political debates are about ownership. In Britain, there has been a hundred-year altercation on public and private ownership between every government and opposition. It is as predictable as the tides—nationalization followed by privatization, followed by re-nationalization.

In the West ownership and possession have often been seen as an absolute right, to be defended by law and established as one of the "rights" alongside life and liberty, although it didn't quite get into the Declaration of Independence. The sacred ownership of capital and the error of state intrusion have been articles of faith in much of the laissez-faire West. Economic thinking has been polarized into these two options—private ownership or state Socialist ownership; there seems to be no other possibility. Nor has this theme of ownership and possession been as straightforward as many think. Much property was the result of conquest. English Enclosure Acts led to common land being arbitrarily taken by the landed classes in patent theft. Marx rightly pointed out that much capital accumulation was achieved by exploiting workers. Monopolies allowed another form of expropriation from consumers. The possession of slaves and grabbing land from the Indians have hardly been uncontroversial. Crises, like the 1929 Wall Street crash, called into question capital ownership.

In the face of these, a naive faith in private ownership is absurd. But above all, the complexity of the modern economy has shown how inadequate and crude is the idea of possession. Land, property, and resources have multiple uses. In one sense the worms and birds also own the land. Economic activities have horizons beyond immediate owners, and the complexities of intellectual property, for example, move outside simple notions of "It's mine." Moreover, the very notion of ownership engenders errors; the idea that a company can *own* a genetic modification, when the word *modification* points to all they have been originally given in a genetic code, suggests that we have more thinking to do.

Hence, it is surprising that more attention has not been given to this next theme in Jesus' Kingdom teaching. Deliberately and repeatedly, Jesus teaches *stewardship*. The underlying truth lies in the status of what we have been given, ultimately by God and often by others. We do not have any absolute claims to it. God says, "The world is mine, and all that is in it" (Ps. 50:12; cf. 24:1). When we recognize the ownership of God, human economic activity takes place in relation to God and with a sense of our limited leasing of resources and the responsibilities they entail. The meek inherit the earth, not the owners and possessors. We face a crucial question: What will we do with what we have been given?

Jesus' Kingdom parables explore the theme. "There was a man who had two sons . . . and said, 'Son, go and work today in the vineyard'" (Matt. 21:28–32). "There was a landowner who planted a vineyard . . . and went away" (21:33). "Again, [the Kingdom will be] like a man going on a journey, who called his servants and entrusted his property to them" (25:14–30). Always God is the owner and we are to identify with the stewards. The parable of the Rich Fool points out the error of a man who believes in his own possessions. Jesus concludes: "This is how it will be with anyone who stores up things for himself but is not rich toward God" (Luke 12:13–21).

The Prodigal Son receives property but wastes it in the expression of his own autonomy (Luke 15:11–13). Bored with this straightforward presentation of the same theme, Jesus flips it to commend the person who gives away what he does *not* have in the parable of the Dishonest Steward. The boss calls his steward in and gives him the sack because he has been inefficient. The steward asks himself, "What should I do now?" Then he has an idea. He calls in his master's debtors and cuts their overdraft by half while he has the chance. His ethics may be a bit wobbly, Jesus says, but he has a better idea of stewardship and sharing than some of you (Luke 16:1–15). And the flipped parable is saying something more: we all do not own what we retain or give away. Constantly, Jesus reiterates the theme of being entrusted with resources and using them wisely before God and in relation to our neighbors. Will you be faithful with what you have been given?

Jesus states the principle that really shapes political economy. Some Christian economists, notably Goudzwaard, have seen that stewardship is fundamental to the discipline, not ownership, money, or trading.[50] What we have is given by God,[51] by previous generations, by the research and development of millions of workers, from the resources of other countries. To construct supposed islands of absolute ownership or deserved reward on these continents of gift and interdependence is a myth. Really, most of us tacitly acknowledge that property has multiple uses and that we are temporary stewards. We know that God's creation, which we must respect, is the foundation of the economy. We know ecology matters, that we add and subtract value to existing stocks, and that common wealth is vital. Neoclassical economics may be living in some kooky universe,[52] but stewardship of the creation is the sine qua non of economic activity. Nor will the idea of capitalism save us. Western economies run on responsibility, not on capital as something-in-itself to be worshipped.[53] Germany had its capital destroyed mercilessly in 1939–45, but it was back on its feet in a decade. Business and economic life should show responsibility before God and toward our brothers and sisters for using the resources we have been given. A "talent" is a great big slab of resources and capital, and it is on loan from God. We are all tenants for the Lord of the land. Capital merely sits atop a big column that does most of the work.

By contrast, Jesus' focus on stewardship sheds light on a great sweep of issues. The word *environmental* means "around us" and puts us at the center. Stewardship of the earth puts God first and requires different priorities in caring for the creation, its land, animals, energy, sea, and plants. If we are stewards for later generations, our economic decisions do not gather round instant gratification. If we regard God and our neighbors, common wealth is often more fruitful than private wealth. Really, the West cannot avoid living by the principle of stewardship, not ownership. We do better if we promptly acknowledge Jesus' teaching and the deeper accountability structure of political economy.

The Poor and Compassion

The Kingdom parables also teach direct neighbor love and compassion. The Good Samaritan cares for the man in need and does not pass by on the other side. Jesus' words to his interlocutor, "Go and do likewise," leave him freedom to do so or not and yet have the character of a command (Luke 10:25–37). This is God's way: we are commanded to love our neighbors as ourselves. Nor is this just a private matter. It is interesting that the idea of private charity and generosity has often been used *against* state welfare. The pressure has often been from those who want their own taxes to be low. But charity and generosity can also be expressed through taxes and a state welfare provision. Clearly, if the rule of God covers both personal and political, as it must, then compassion and care should both be expressed in personal and political life, especially when care is most effectively and efficiently provided publicly.

And indeed, that is what has happened. Those who are ill are in need, and a National Health Service is a political expression of meeting that need with compassion, and even, following the example of the Good Samaritan, with a generosity of spirit. Here countries differ in their responses. The Netherlands, Germany, and Scandinavia have had high standards of provision as a matter of national policy. The United States has had much more of a "look after yourself" mentality behind its provision, which leaves many struggling and causes heavy costs to society.[54] Britain, after having good provision, was mean for more than two decades, preferring lower taxes and private affluence. Now it is paying in lower standards of healthcare provision, which we hope will be improved.

More than this, however, we learn from Jesus' acts in the Gospels both the richness of care and its inner structure. Jesus meets the needs of an extraordinary range of people—the sick, the mentally ill, lepers, widows, the disabled, the paralyzed, the possessed, the blind and dumb, the crippled, the poor, the bereaved, the hungry, the mute, the epileptic, the fevered, and the dying. Indeed, many hospital and care agencies have grown simply from following one of Jesus' patterns of healing. This was the source of generation of the British Welfare State.

"Granted that the Kingdom of God is something more than a Christian social system," said R. H. Tawney tartly, "we can hardly take the view that it is something less."[55] Care of the sick, insane, old, blind, deaf, abused, injured, and disabled has gradually been built into the British system of government, together with the myriad of voluntary agencies that also provide care.[56] This care is to be responsive, addressing the needs where the people are, and meeting them as persons. Yet a fuller pattern of personal care is also offered. People need to know God, the forgiveness of sins, and the indwelling of God's Spirit. These too are addressed by Jesus. The healed are to know that "the Kingdom of God has come upon you" (Matt. 12:28).

There is something still deeper in all of this. Our dominant idiom is often of *our* help to the poor. Jesus teaches that the poor and poor in spirit are independently blessed. He comes "to preach good news to the poor" (Luke 4:18; 7:22). This remains obstinately different from some patronizing blessing or trickle-down effect. "Woe to you who are rich, for you have already received your comfort" (Luke 6:24) jars against this idea, for the patron is benevolent and self-satisfied. Obstinately, Jesus seems to assert that the poor, with the good news of the Kingdom, are in a good place. They have integrity before God. They have the richness of living with God. They bless the rich. Try going for half an hour without being blessed by someone who is, or was, poor. We cannot. The poor have made our coffee, shoes, house, and clothes. They have given; we are parasites. They are not snared with the cares of this world, and in God's eyes they should have the same wages as everybody else.

A materialist culture often assumes that the poor cannot be blessed, but often there is more joy in a small African village than you will find on the whole of the London Underground. Compassion to the poor is not providing for the undeserving, but returning resources to those robbed of them over the years. It is God's Jubilee (Lev. 25; Luke 4:18–19, 21). Christ does not allow a moralist response to the beggar, leper, or invalid. Invalid is precisely what none of us is before God. Western materialism has *taken* third-world resources, labor, scenery, energy, and crops even as it believes it is giving. The government of God blesses the poor and poor in spirit (who do not exploit, look down on their neighbor, demean the lives of others, and grab for themselves). To share with them or to be them is our gain. There is no paternalism when we acknowledge one Father of us all.

Our failures in compassion carry on—a poor record on aid, inadequate welfare, bad provision for those with disabilities and for the needy old. The failures are personal and political, but in both personal and political life the insistent words of Christ in the parable of the Good Samaritan return: "Go and do likewise" to those in need. They direct us across national and international politics. They require us also to live by the standards of the poor and poor in spirit.

Political Toleration

The issue of toleration is a global political concern. Throughout much of history, political rulers have been happy to dictate to their subjects what they should believe, religiously and politically. Ancient Rome, Greece, China, Japan, Egypt, and South American civilizations had rulers who claimed to be godlike, demanding worship, or a state religion and priesthood validating the process of government, which people were expected to accept. Nebuchadnezzar's requirement that people worship his image under sufferance of death typifies many cultures (Dan. 3). Nor is this pattern only ancient. Indeed, the twentieth century seems one of the least tolerant in history. Totalitarian regimes in the USSR, Italy, Germany, China, and elsewhere required a political and religious response from citizens; dissidents were killed or imprisoned. More recently, in a ring of countries round the Middle East, Islamic Fundamentalist parties are insisting on imposed Shariah and working toward a state-imposed religion.

Even in the West we discover that liberal and consumerist views proclaiming freedom have actually often ruled out opposition and effectively imposed their views by funding, blanket advertising, media control, and silencing opponents. Consumerism is spread every fifteen minutes on television through advertisements in the biggest propaganda campaign that the world has ever seen. Product logos echo the mark of the beast (Rev. 13:16–17). Christians have also been part of the problem of required conformity. Since Constantine, Christianity has sometimes been politically imposed. More often the established church has cozied up to the state and enjoyed being validated by it. But this pattern has receded in recent history, and more usually Christians are persecuted for their faith.[57] There is an extremely powerful set of cultural attitudes undermining religious and political toleration; yet many in the West claim toleration as a deep commitment. What is going on here?

Before we return to the Gospels, let us review the history of toleration. Broadly speaking, the dominant ideology of toleration now is liberalism. It insists that individuals should be free to think what they like, religiously and politically. This is seen as an absolute right, prior to any state activity, grounded in the individual. Though we may agree with this view, it is actually a latecomer to the scene. Nor does liberalism provide an understanding of how the state should treat different religious and political groups, because it has no philosophy of the state, except one of minimalism. The real toleration debate occurs within Christianity, especially since the Reformation. Broadly speaking, there were two positions: Conformist and Nonconformist. The former involved alliances between mainly Catholic churches and rulers throughout Europe, alliances that established certain kinds of religious practice and control. Its conformist character can be judged by the fact that church leaders had Tyndale politically murdered for producing one of the greatest ever translations of the Bible.

Luther initially, then Anabaptists, Calvinists, Puritans, Quakers, Levellers, Mennonites, and all kinds of other groups of Nonconformists broke this control. They argued that people should be free to worship God without the trammels of the state, because the state has no jurisdiction over human worship and faith. Two hundred and eighty-two Englishmen were burned at the stake for this cause. Cranmer wrote a recantation under duress contrary to his heart; he famously held his writing hand into the flames first as he was executed in 1556.[58] The Tudor and Stuart church establishment maintained control through to the Commonwealth, and after the Restoration, but the argument was lost. The *Mayflower* had sailed to Massachusetts, seeking freedom of worship. Figures like Roger Williams and William Penn proclaimed liberty of conscience.[59] They argued that a Christian is to receive his salvation from Christ alone and not from any other authority. The civil authority has no power to ordain articles of faith or establish any religion.[60] In England under Cromwell, censorship collapsed. Milton's *Areopagitica*, a great tirade to the English Parliament for the liberty of unlicensed printing, remains forever unrefuted. We do well to hear a sentence or two from his pen:

> When a man hath bin labouring the hardest labour in the deep mines of knowledge, hath furnisht out his findings in all their equipage, drawn forth his reasons as it were a batell raung'd, scattered and defeated all objections in his way, calls out his adversary into the plain, offers him the advantage of wind and of sun, if he please; only that he may try the matter by dint of argument, for his opponents then to sculk, to lay ambushments, to keep a narrow bridge of licencing where the challenger should passe, though it be valour anough in soldiership, is but weaknes and cowardise in the wars of truth. For who knows not that Truth is strong next to the Almighty; she needs no policies, nor stratagems, nor licencing to make her victorious, those are the shifts and the defences that error uses against her power.[61]

This is not toleration as weakness, but truth "contending in the marketplace." Hundreds of cheap newspapers, 722 in 1645 alone, poured off the presses during the Commonwealth.[62] After 1660 the establishment tried to put the genie back in the bottle, and for a century and a half Nonconformists and Catholics were not fully tolerated by the state. But the principle of religious liberty and toleration was forged well before Liberalism and the First Amendment to the United States Constitution.

The Christian inspiration for this emergence of toleration is deep and structural. Christianity is the religion of *faith*, the process whereby I freely give my assent to the object of my belief or commitment. Faith cannot be coerced. If it is, it is not faith. The Bible is full of persons who do, or do not, respond in faith to God. Hebrews 11 gives us a view of faith as shaping human history. Because faith, by default or positively, is our response to God, it cannot be gainsaid or overridden by the state. Second, Christianity shows that God does not control belief. Since before Babel people have been able to think as they please, in belief or unbelief. Most of biblical history is a record of human waywardness, by rulers and ruled, but God gives sun and rain to good and evil alike (Matt. 5:45). The ruler has no competence to dictate or shape human faith. The Bible gives no warrant for the ruler taking on the mantle of God and judging people's faith and lives. Because the prior relationship of all humankind is with the Creator, political dominance of that relationship is illegitimate.

Jesus underlines that freedom. A less coercive ruler there has never been. He faces and accepts opposition. Disciples are free to leave or disagree, and many do leave when they do not get their Zealot leader. The Gospels contain no hint of compulsion or direction of belief, even though, as we have seen, Jesus understands himself to be ruler. His rule does not mean coercion of belief; he does argue, contending for what is true, critiquing leaders, but without doubt, he does not coerce. The English, it is said, love a loser (despite their often arrogant and domineering history). Perhaps there is something to this, because losers do not control, or at least not very well. Here is the loser whose followers desert him and who is finally without worldly domination and dying on a cross. Nowhere in all his relationships is Jesus involved in anything like pressure, threat, or coercion. His final command to his disciples, "Love one another as I have loved you," is to those who have voluntarily submitted to his way (John 13:34; 15:12).

Jesus' dismissal of intolerance is summed up in an incident as he walks through Samaria with the disciples on the way to Jerusalem. Messengers go on ahead to get things ready for Jesus, but the Samaritan village does not welcome them because they are heading for Jerusalem (Luke 9:51–56). Presumably, Samaritans have sensibilities about their cultural enemies and want their own local temple to have loyalty. The disciples, glorying in the power of their leader, burst out, "Lord, do you want us to call fire down from heaven and destroy them?" (Luke 9:51–55). But Jesus turns and rebukes them for this immature and misplaced reaction. The rule of God dwells with people; it is not imposed on them, even or especially by God's ruler. The wheat and the weeds will grow together to the end of time.

But political tolerance is not, nor can it be, an understanding that all views are equal, or even that no views should be criticized—a kind of "neutral" political correctness. Along with political tolerance goes the highest concern for truth claims. What people think may actually turn out to be false, self-indulgent fantasy or based upon false premises. Whether this is the case matters, and the Gospels are full of face-to-face confrontations about truth. Jesus identifies his kingship with testifying to the truth, no less. Groups gather to Jesus, discuss or dispute, and go away. What is right and true and central to belief is addressed by debate, not compulsion. Nowhere is there political control. Truth meets error, exposing it rather than imposing something. God does not control belief. Nor does Christianity sanction state-imposed belief, though Christian history since Constantine is partly dogged with that failure.[63]

The state is not the Christian vehicle for revelation. Indeed, it often fails and needs revelation rather than meting it out; historically, the prophetic tradition carries revelation to the state. Nor indeed is it the state's task to be the institution of faith; that is the job of the church and has been throughout Christian history. The ultimate sanction of the church is only to excommunicate and leave things to God's judgment. Centrally in Christian history, faith is a matter of belief accountability before God and not conformity to the state. Indeed, the history of Christian mission, nonconformity, dissent, and evangelism is seeped in toleration. The person-to-person transmission of faith without political, military, or organizational pressure is the mode of the Christian gospel. These principles have shaped Christianity and world history. They give the foundation for a principle of toleration.

Perhaps the deepest political expression of the principle of toleration comes from the Dutch Kuyperian understanding of institutional democracy and pluralism. It reflects principled differences of belief, not just in politics but also in schools, business, the media, and churches.[64] Even in the Netherlands this is partly lost in a flaccid liberalism that insists on privatizing belief. But faith differs publically for all of us, and it is a public matter involving elections, media, business, and education. Only Christianity understands the dynamic of faith as a public democratic process. Sadly, Christians have sometimes been intolerant, hang on to vestiges of establishment, or fail to express their faith in public life. Thereby they allow the strong Christian and nonconformist principle of toleration to atrophy. But they have no grounds for so doing, and the overwhelming impetus of Christianity has been against religious control and for political toleration and expression of faiths. The Founder allows all their way, whether it is the rich young ruler, not prepared for some sacrifice, or lepers caught up in their healed bodies. The tolerance is palpable. Even the Temple traders are soon back to their business.

For the last hundred years or so Christianity has faced religious persecution in a number of world cultures, perhaps beginning with the Boxer rebellion in China, but also in Fascist, Nazi, Communist, Maoist, and even Democratic Socialist regimes. It is time people face the question of why this persecution has occurred throughout much of the modern world. In Europe, Asia, and Africa, regimes have set out to marginalize Christianity and exclude it from the public domain and public debate. It is a sorry record.[65] Over the last fifty years Christians have been handicapped, degraded, and killed in a number of Islamic regimes; most notably, something over a million were killed in the Sudan. The cost of voluntary acceptance of the government of God has grown as these regimes claim primary allegiance and attack the politics of the Galilean. The offense of the gentle Kingdom of Christ engenders hostility in the face of this intolerant political ideology. No less serious is the dogma of neo-liberalism that claims world hegemony for its consumerist way and writes other views out of the script through belief in the sovereignty of the individual or commercialism. Companies try to take over our minds. The English language is now partly owned by companies who have commodified it.[66] The contrast is with Jesus' radical insistence on the awful freedom of all of us.

Conclusion

The principles of Jesus undergird political thinking and attitudes. They require openness to God and create an architecture for political life. They are not too easy to tease out, especially if they do not accord with normal politics. Yet their indwelling of Western politics is deep, from both Christians and the cultural heritage. Often they are partly shared, perhaps without any sense of their source and author. These people are, as Jesus describes them, like birds nesting in the tree of the rule of God, not really caring where they are or knowing the tree in which they roost. But the tree and the roots matter because these principles find their basis, their true expression, and their fulfillment in the person of Jesus. Too often they have been adulterated or lost, and darkness has covered areas of political life for decades or more. Perhaps the only real political progress is as these branches produce their proper fruit. In the last century, empire, Fascism, State Socialism, and other secular corrupters of these principles led humanity into the worst century of war, intolerance, and devastation on record. We would do well to see how precious these principles are and how deeply we depend on the One who gives them.

Bibliography

Brailsford, H. N. *The Levellers and the English Revolution*. Edited by Christopher Hill. Nottingham: Spokesman, 1983.

Carlson-Thies, Stanley W., and James W. Skillen, eds. *Welfare in America: Christian Perspectives on a Policy in Crisis*. Grand Rapids: Eerdmans, 1996.

Eide, Asbjørn, et al., eds. *The Universal Declaration of Human Rights*. Oxford: Oxford University Press; Oslo: Scandinavian University Press, 1992.

Gutiérrez, Gustavo. *The Power of the Poor in History*. Translated by Robert R. Barr. Maryknoll, NY: Orbis; London: SCM, 1983.

———. *Las Casas: In Search of the Poor of Jesus Christ*. Translated by Robert R. Barr. Maryknoll, NY: Orbis, 1993.

Moltmann, Jürgen. *The Way of Jesus Christ: Christology in Messianic Dimensions*. London: SCM, 1990.

Mouw, Richard J. *Uncommon Decency: Christian Civility in an Uncivil World*. Downers Grove, IL: InterVarsity, 1992.

Nietzsche, Frederick. *Twilight of the Idols/The Anti-Christ*. Translated by R. J. Hollingdale. Middlesex: Penguin, 1990.

Runner, H. Evan. *Scriptural Religion and Political Task*. Toronto: Wedge, 1974.

Sandoz, Ellis, ed. *Political Sermons of the American Founding Era, 1730–1805*. Indianapolis: Liberty Fund, 1998.

Wolterstorff, Nicholas. *Until Justice and Peace Embrace*. Grand Rapids: Eerdmans, 1983.

8

Jesus' Statecraft

In the last chapter we looked at a range of broader principles in Jesus' teaching, reflecting on their political content and implications. In this chapter we look more directly at his teaching on political rule and the structure of the state. In a prodigious sense Jesus embodies God's political rule. He is Messiah and the King of the Jews, even while moving about the countryside having trouble with accommodation. Nor is this emphasis a latter-day interpretation; it is reflected in many of his sayings, for example, about law. Law is crucial to the structure of all states. We elect legislatures to pass it. Manifestos are normally expressed in terms of proposed laws. Nowhere has the law been more important than in Jewish society, where Torah is loved and seen as the basis of understanding and the identifying character of Jewish society. Since Jesus' valuation of it is equally high, we are astonished by his claim in the Sermon on the Mount: "Do not think that I have come to abolish the Law or the Prophets; I have not come to abolish them but to fulfill them" (Matt. 5:17). This makes us uneasy. It seems too big a claim that the whole law can be embodied and find its ultimate fulfillment in one person. But that is unequivocally what Jesus means. The wider claim to be God's embodiment of political rule has to be tested in the outcome. What do we learn about the state and political rule from this man? Surprisingly, it is a question that has scarcely been asked in this direct way.

Perhaps it requires another level of awareness and vindication. Jesus is saying, "If you want to know what the state is like in God's terms, look at me." Well, we are and will do so in this chapter, but it is difficult to grasp such a big claim or to know in what terms it will be answered. As a result, the content of this chapter has a character that is worth trying to describe at the beginning. The principles in the last chapter presented great alternatives: domination or freedom, conflict or peace, possession or stewardship. People swing one way or the other—the way of the world or the way of God. In this chapter, somehow, we are closer to the hinges of the door, the fulcrum around which this door will open. Here, in some sense, we may come to learn centrally what political rule is about and learn God's ways of seeing things. From these lessons flow constitutional and political principles that we still barely see or understand.

The Servant Ruler

Throughout history, domination and control have marked political rule. Conquerors, lords, fiefs, and barons have dominated their territories and people. In the last chapter we looked at Jesus' insistence that the government of God lifts up the weak and brings down the mighty. But actually, there is something going on deeper still; it concerns the very structure of politics, addressing what the ruler is for. The focal event where it emerges is riveting. James, John, and their mother approach Jesus requesting positions of glory in Jesus' kingdom for the brothers. Their concern is real. All three are thinking in terms of some kind of messianic victory that will establish Jesus' position in Jewish society. Jesus has had a powerful following, and as he comes to Jerusalem, it builds up again. To everybody's amazement and the horror of the chief priests and Pharisees, Lazarus has been raised from the dead. The possibility of Jesus' political triumph seems to be realistic. Given Jesus' popularity and reputation, the disciples believe the journey to Jerusalem is the vindicating one. As they understand it, nothing else can be possible. In this sense, they are right, for Jesus enters Jerusalem to massive acclaim at Passover time. But in order to hold this position, they have had to ignore or suppress what Jesus actually said about his suffering and death. Perhaps Zebedee's wife takes the lead in seeking the best for her boys as she bustles up to Jesus. The structure of her thinking is hierarchical and overwhelmingly normal for politics; she wants reflected glory. Rumor has it that politicians still think about cabinet positions and preferment. James and John are set on glory and position, sitting on the right and left of Jesus, the conventional view of gaining subordinate power (Matt. 20:20–21).

Jesus does not allow them to sit with this way of thinking. Instead, he takes them on a terse journey. The request is made to sit with Jesus.

He responds, "You don't know what you are asking" (20:22). They are out of their depth. What they are asking has eternal significance. It reaches out far beyond events in Jerusalem to the issue of God's rule throughout human history. To be worthy of these positions would involve deep service and loyalty that they will not be able to give. "Can you drink the cup I am going to drink?" They are thinking of glory, but the reality will be Jesus' suffering and death. The cup of bitterness and death is Jesus' focus, and they have not faced it. Can the disciples even enter into what this means? Of course not. They have no awareness of the truth and reality of Jesus' death. They are miles behind. The answer actually given by the two disciples may mean a number of things. Yet the reports of these conversations are often so tight that it is possible to hear the nuances and psychological reactions. They are putting themselves forward, and once they have begun to do so, they have to carry on. And so they answer, "We can." We can drink of your cup. Perhaps they are partly embarrassed by their mother and looking for a route that would justify their request. Possibly they have also opened up to something like empathy. Jesus has been steadily telling them he is going to die, and now, when he responds to their request in these terms, they are shamefully aware that their focus has been solely on themselves.

But Jesus does not respond to their assertion that they can share his death. When he goes through his arrest and trial, the disciples flee. The straight answer to his question is that they cannot share the cup with him. Jesus does not respond to what they say, but to the truths behind this situation. When they have experienced his death and resurrection, these disciples will know it is for them. They will then drink the cup, remembering Jesus' death and knowing that the persistent love and grace of God are more powerful than human sin. So Jesus corrects himself and then continues: "You will indeed drink from my cup, but to sit at my right and left is not for me to grant. These places belong to those for whom they have been prepared by my Father" (20:23). The issue is removed from their consideration or anybody else's, not denying Jesus' rule, but by a sense of the far greater significance of the government of God. After this reply, the group dynamics fizz as the other disciples are angry at the self-glorification and status-seeking of James and John. But then Jesus moves to the great universal political statement on servanthood.

In a few sentences, he turns the whole meaning of world politics upside-down and inside-out. We do well to savor these words many times. Jesus calls them together and says:

> You know that the rulers of the Gentiles lord it over them, and their high officials exercise authority over them. Not so with you. Instead, whoever

wants to become great among you must be your servant, and whoever wants to be first must be your slave—just as the Son of Man did not come to be served, but to serve, and to give his life as a ransom for many. (Matt. 20:25–28)

We cannot treat this as just a principle, for the focus is centrally on Jesus. Looking to him, we see the Servant King. The Servant has come, and those seeking to be great must be like him. The principle is breathtaking. The rulers, the glory-takers, the lording people are wrong. Now the self-serving structure of political rule is dismantled. "With you," he says, "these positions involve service and slavery. The people do not serve the rulers, but the rulers serve the people." The rulers are our servants, called to act for our well-being. It is not in the temporary demos rule of a slave-ridden Athenian society that the origins of democracy lie. Rather, it is built on the rock of this text through the albeit muddled history of the Christian faith. Here in human history we encounter the Servant ruler as the truth about politics.

We commonly ignore how fully this principle has been absorbed into our view of politics. The hinge has swung, albeit slowly through vast tracts of history. In British history Oliver Cromwell (before and after he became head of state) signed himself in his letters, "Your most humble servant," "Your affectionate servant," "Your faithful and most obedient servant," "Thy dear friend and servant," "This is all—but that I am ready to serve you and rest, Your loving friend."[1] It is quite clear from his writing and actions that he saw service as his prime motivation and thus added his swing to the hinge. We now have civil (usually) servants. Tony Blair announced service of the British people as the criterion by which New Labour's tenure of office would be judged.[2] We keep our prime minister in a terraced house to show him his place as our prime servant. A "minister" is a servant, one who acts as the agent of a superior. Especially in the Protestant West, rulers have been made accountable to the people they serve to see if their contract should be renewed. Elections decide whether the servants will be re-employed. Many politicians spend themselves in working for us, in duty and beyond the call of duty. Jesus' "not so with you" has been widely learned, although quite a few political leaders are still too full of themselves. This radical principle of service probes our motives and structures in politics as in the rest of life. It exposes self-serving bureaucracies, groups seeking power for their own ends, and those who want to be served and live off the work of others. Indeed, the most searching examination of government organizations is this: Are they built for service? It shows the sham of past leisured elites, whose aim was to be served. It points to the overwhelming solid worth of love and service as the basis for all political rule.

But it also requires submission to the one who is the Servant and to the government of God. In an extraordinary juxtaposition John exposes the conjoined reality of Jesus' power and service:

> Jesus knew that the Father had put all things under his power, and that he had come from God and was returning to God; so he got up from the meal, took off his outer clothing, and wrapped a towel round his waist. After that, he poured water into a basin and began to wash his disciples' feet, drying them with the towel that was wrapped around him. (John 13:3–5)

John locates in Jesus' head these two seeming opposites—Jesus' universal power and his service. Knowing his power, he was house-slave to his disciples. The King is the slave. In authority he says: "I have done it; you do it." As servants of Christ, we serve, or else our motives are self-validating. As Jesus says in another kingdom parable, "So you also, when you have done everything you were told to do, should say, 'We are unworthy servants; we have only done our duty'" (Luke 17:10). It is our job just to obey the Son of Man, but the sublime irony is that when we obey, we discover that God does everything for our good. Now political rule is shaped only by love, and the curse of political domination is removed.

This question can be asked of every branch and organization of government. Does it serve or require service? Long ago the Israelites were warned about rulers who would require chariots, weapons, cooks, vineyards, grain, taxes, cattle, and slavery (1 Sam. 8; cf. Deut. 17:14–20). The list is slightly different now, but the issue is the same. Self-serving government eats into the lives of the people. A serving government works at what is good for its people. Thus is the chaff of misgovernment winnowed out.

Political Office

The term "political office" reflects an emphasis in Jesus' teaching that continues from the Old Testament. Often rulers and military leaders have done things their way. They rule as they rule. Yet throughout the Bible from the time of Moses there is an understood tension between the actual occupants of positions and the Godward understanding of what those positions entail. This reflects the fact that politicians, as sinners, will fail properly to fulfill their role. The point of reference is therefore not what they do or are, but what they should do before God, their office. At times, Moses did not live up to the standards of his office; he was exasperated or disobedient, though he was known as the servant of God. Later, kings like Saul and Ahab were effectively sacked because of their failure to walk faithfully and obediently before God. The prophets held them to account.

There was another side to this distinction. Defining the office meant that the proper requirements of statecraft could be learned and upheld in various political offices—judge, king, elder, and so on. It allowed politicians to be educated and built understanding. Magistrates were to be impartial, observe rules of evidence, avoid bribes, operate by precept, and learn the law. Soldiers, as John the Baptist points out, are not to use physical force to extort for themselves. Within this perspective, developed by the prophets throughout Israel's history, the officeholder is accountable to God to observe norms and faithfully fulfill the office (1 Sam. 10:25; 12:1–5, 14). Now, this sense of office is such a normal part of Western political life that we are shocked when an officeholder fails and faces resignation, impeachment, or dismissal. That they should not resign or brazen it out against the norms of office is even worse, because this is placing themselves above the norms of office. There are spectacular examples of failure in office. In Britain the Deputy Prime Minister Reggie Maudling resigned after implication in the Lockheed bribery scandal. In the States, Nixon resigned to avoid impeachment; Clinton was exposed, impeached, then acquitted in his Senate trial. But far more ordinary questions of probity in office arise every day, essentially shaping the quality of government.

The theme is rooted in the Gospels in Jesus' understanding of submission and accountability. Many rulers have pleased themselves and expected their will to be fulfilled. Their egos were at the center of the exercise of power. But with Jesus the central relationship is with God and fulfilling the required tasks: "Who then is the faithful and wise manager, whom the master puts in charge of his servants to give them their food allowance at the proper time? It will be good for that servant whom the master finds doing so when he returns" (Luke 12:42–43). Jesus describes himself as completing the work the Father gave him to do (John 17:4). The deepest accountability before God requires doing the assigned tasks to the full: "From the one who has been entrusted with much, much more will be asked" (Luke 12:48). This central dynamic of office, or calling, far deeper than just doing what the boss says, defines the character of all political work. The desire to be a faithful servant to God and our neighbors allows us to work out what the best norms of office are, to have professional and complex government, defining the norms of specialized governmental tasks. It is the foundation of all offices of state and is reflected in a vast group of people who faithfully fulfill and develop their assigned offices. It has enriched the polity beyond our knowing.

The Lord of Law

We have already briefly looked at Jesus' claim to be the fulfillment of the law. But as we approach this claim, what is our own slant? In the West we both know and do not know the importance of law. We have absorbed much from Christian and Roman traditions. We mouth law-and-order slogans at elections. Probably the dominant understanding of law today is sociological: it is what we happen to agree about and codify as state rules. In a self-serving way, we have respect for the law, but we seldom hear in a comprehensive way the Christian meaning of law. It is background belief, part of the collective subconscious, but ignored for most practical purposes, like getting our own way, engaging in litigation, or considering legislation. Yet really, state law is in an uneasy place. Criminality is normal and even chronic in many domestic and international situations. Policing absorbs vast quantities of resources. Administering law is often a bureaucratic and procedural nightmare. I remember sitting for most of a day in Wood Green High Court, hearing an extended discussion of whether a transvestite should be allowed to appear in the dock in women's clothes. More than this, areas of *lawlessness*, Durkheim's *anomie*,[3] appear in people's psyche and within society more generally; there are no-go areas, mafias, delinquents, underworlds, criminal fraternities, terrorists, and fraud subcultures. Corruption is creeping back into areas of life. Law often seems so complex that ordinary people cannot understand it. At another level, liberal, positivist, and sociological interpretations of law compete, and lawyers, wanting to be affluent and busy, encourage litigation. The police are often angry at the legal obstruction of justice, as they see it. This is a messy brew, and yet we know it is better than the breakdown of law observed in some countries past and present.

So, let us approach law with some firmer distinctions. There are two main Western views of state law.[4] The first is Roman. It developed through governing the empire as an expression of political sovereignty. It was the product of *jurisdiction*, with the emperor as the source of law and authority. Later codifications, partly influenced by Christianity, developed more order and consistency to this rule. Within this perspective, state law is primary; it made "civilization," since the rabble was included within the order of the *civis* (citizen). Essentially, therefore, Roman law was state control of people's lives to make and keep them civilized. By contrast, in Jewish and Christian understanding, state law is secondary.

Primary is the law of God, which defines in a pre-political sense what is right and good in human society. The Ten Commandments have this form, identifying basic principles of life; none of them is politically focused. "Honor your father and mother" (Exod. 20:12), as the other commandments, is pre-legislative, deeper and more penetrating than legislation that defines subsequent issues of injustice.

The broader Mosaic precepts and the teaching of the prophets open law up further: neighbor respect, worship of God, mutual care and support, marriage, employment, no idolatry, a welcome for aliens, family integrity, and obedience to God—these are developed as living principles. What is right or good in all these areas of human relationships then informs state law. It is expressed in judicially and politically generated statutes supporting these right ways of living before God. State law grows from this deeper understanding of God's law, insofar as the state discerns it. The state's task of upholding justice requires additional political norms like impartiality, public evidence, and recompense. These also appear within the Mosaic law. Through its history Israel often failed to uphold the law of God or to develop adequate state law. During the period of the judges, the people "did what was right in their own eyes" (Judg. 21:25 NRSV). Later kings ignored important laws. Rehoboam's use of slave labor split the kingdom (1 Kings 12). Hezekiah kindled a return to the law, but it too was spasmodic, and the character of law remained inadequately understood. The prophets were its guardians against the failures of rulers, people, and legislation, but prophets were scarce in the centuries before Christ.

From his first appearance, Jesus seizes the existing legal traditions and shakes them like dead rabbits. But this is not an attack. He has not come to attack the law but to honor it as God's way. He does not attack the Pharisees and Scribes for their love of Torah, but goes beyond them. Not a jot or a tittle will pass away (Matt. 5:18). He comprehensively affirms and upholds the law of God. Yet Jesus' understanding of the significance of Torah is more radically centered on God and the inner meaning of justice and love to others than the Pharisees' view. As such, this inner meaning of justice and love is the foundation of the state, what leaders must thirst for and pursue single-mindedly. It is the government of God, giving us understanding of living with integrity interpersonally and in society. It needs to be understood at a deeper level than the behavioral ways of the Pharisees and teachers of the law. In the Sermon on the Mount, Jesus expects God's law to be communally taught and honored. Those who undermine it for others are failing. The law is to be obeyed; it is fundamental to our whole existence and will last through human history. We depend on it for self-knowledge. To teach the law is central to human life (Matt. 5:17–20). This root-and-branch affirmation of the

Law and Prophets will not be gainsaid. The rule of God occurs through God's law directly engaged with the human heart.

This is no mere affirmation of the status quo. Jesus wants ordinary people to have a deeper commitment to the law than the legal scribes and teachers. This law dwells in truth and is not arbitrary, a theme of Psalm 119, because it shows the way we are created to live before God and in relation one to another. It is our very selves, intrinsic, not imposed. God's law defines our good selves. Love, justice, marital faithfulness, not grabbing from our neighbors—these are not addenda to life; they are life. Above all, Jesus insists on our relationship to God and neighbor as central to law. When asked by an expert in Jewish law what the greatest commandment of the law is, Jesus replies with the great central commands, "'Love the Lord your God.' . . . 'Love your neighbor as yourself.' All the Law and Prophets hang on these commandments" (Matt. 22:35–39). Jesus bows the great Deuteronomic Shema to vibrate in our "cello" lives (Deut. 6:4). These are commands, because this is what life is like. They can't be ignored, even if we try. They are central to existence because the Creator defines the great overall drama of life. They bring "abundant" life; this is what is good for us—to live on God's terms, because God created us (cf. John 10:10 KJV). It is that simple. In this sense law can never be reduced to obeying rules or state-required behavior because it indwells all of life. Centrally, life involves submitting to the God of the law.

The statements of the Gospels require us to think carefully about the meaning of God's law. It cannot be equated with morality, which actually is an eighteenth-century Enlightenment creation embodying the idea that reasoning subjects can (inerrantly) work out what they should do from reason, nature, self-interest, or benevolence. God's law defines us. It reflects our created purpose, the paternalism of God, the care of a parent. Through it we grow in understanding, but we never get beyond it. At twenty, forty, sixty, and eighty, we are still learning not to covet or use the name of God to our own ends. It is law that requires thought and priority. Ethical reflection follows from it. Mercy and justice are prior to but shape procedure or penal policy.

This perspective requires that state law, as a secondary form, responds to, and draws its central direction from, God's law. It is easy to miss this in the Gospels because it is a view shared by Jesus, Pharisees, and the elders of the people, but it is there. The debate is merely about how God's law is expressed. And God's law has been a deep formative principle in the partly Christian West. Our state law fallibly represents the God-given ways we are called to live, personally and politically.[5] Continually, the structural difference between God's law as the law of life and state law invites reform. But this reform does let the state pretend to be infallible, as sometimes happens with Shariah law and other statist conceptions. That is a crude category mistake that identifies the law of God with the law of the state. The state, its officers, and subjects may be far from the law of God. Rather, Christianity seeks for the reform of state law in the light of Gospel principles. Legal reform becomes a normal part of politics. A reformist tradition has existed since the time of the Reformation and continued in evangelicalism. It searches out the inadequacies of state law and tries to embody deeper, better principles in the law of the state. Fair elections, the abolition of slavery, proper care of the mentally ill, good working conditions, a fair wage, the prevention of child abuse, and many other reforms are part of this Christian tradition. But it all essentially grows from the teachings and life of Christ. Incessantly, Jesus points out that the law is compromised by legalism, hardness of heart, distortion, hypocrisy, lack of mercy, and poor principles. State law needs reforming in a way that goes beyond itself to what is good and just. It is subordinately and fallibly instituted to uphold what is good. This kind of Christian legal reform, bringing legislation into line with the best insights of the law of God, is the backbone of Western legal development. We would be fools to ignore it.[6] By contrast, secular views—seeing subjective wants, the practice of lawyers, or sociological agreement as the basis of law—import and legitimize all kinds of human failings. Jesus, in the great prophetic tradition, sees the rulers, whether the elders, Herod, or the Pharisees, as necessarily responding to the law of God, and state law as evaluated in its light.

This central truth leads Jesus to several devastating attacks, first on those who seek to own the law and use it for their own purposes. This is a sustained and penetrating critique. Mainly, those involved are out for money and power. The law is used as a control mechanism. "You can ignore your duty to care for your parents as long as you give us a tithe. You have failed to observe the law and should give an offering to us. The temple is God's place, and you should support it" (cf. Mark 7:9–15). Jesus confronts this great self-serving system and faces it down. "God's law is for us, not against us. The Sabbath rest is our blessing, not a burden. You experts in the law! Why are you tying burdens to people's backs, when they should not be carrying them?" (cf. Luke 11:46). Thus Christ gives a critique of those who seek to own the law and shape it with partiality—hey presto, producing ersatz laws that favor themselves.

It is not difficult to see these New Testament cases replicated by later groups—landowners, establishments, the monarchy, lawyers, bureaucrats, men, the churches, politicians, and business. Who produces a law that someone should be hung for stealing a sheep? Why, landowners, of course! Who has a vested interest in the complexity of law, in guilty people pleading innocent, in long trials? Why, lawyers! Who produces laws for the establishment of religion? Why, churchmen and ayatollahs! Who toughens antimonopoly law? Not the East India Company or Microsoft! There is a decisive difference between God's law, which is *for* us, and the misuse of law, which various interest groups have perpetrated for their own ends and *against* the rest of us. Jesus exposes the self-serving constructors of law, and the same searchlight shines on us.

Jesus also attacks legalism. This is the process where the law is so dominated by the legal process that it loses touch with God's central truths for human relationships. "Why do you worry about Sabbath-breaking when a person needs to be healed?" (cf. Mark 3:1–6). "You neglect the weightier matters of the law like justice and mercy, and concentrate on nonessentials" (cf. Matt. 23:23). "You focus on a legal rule, like that concerning divorce, but ignore the greater principle behind the rule—the unity of marriage—because you are hard of heart" (cf. 19:8–9). "You even detach the legal rule from its meaning. The purpose of the Sabbath law is to give people rest, but you even forbid hungry people to pluck corn and eat. You ignore the Mosaic law, are inconsistent, and make innocent people guilty. You make a fetish of the Sabbath, but the Son of Man is Lord of the Sabbath" (cf. 12:1–8). Those who simply follow rules and ignore the deeper principles of love, mercy, and justice distort God's law and try to detach legislation from it. Seeing any law outside its relationship with God distorts its meaning. So Jesus flushes out legalism and shows its silliness. But the virus returns. Legalism, litigation, the use of law as a weapon, interminable process, and legal wrangles—these are still with us. Lawyers, perhaps, spend much of their time arguing for and guarding their indispensibility. We can therefore ask whether the legal profession distorts law in ways that harm people. Does legalism get in the way of justice? Do we penetrate to the norms and principles that should shape the formulation of legislation? It is odd how little discussion today occurs on substantive principles of law, rather than legal procedure.

Finally, Jesus attacks self-rightness. In every society there is a powerful tendency driving some to define themselves as good—the moral majority or minority. These powerful ones come to own the law and reconstruct it in their own image. Landowners decide that enclosing (or stealing) common land is acceptable. Tax evasion for the rich is institutionalized. The good ones elevate their own way and look down on others, who are the deviants, the underclass, the ne'er-do-wells, the unskilled workers, and sinners. Jesus attacks those who "were confident of their own righteousness and looked down on everyone else" and exposes their bias (Luke 18:9–14). "Two men went up to the temple to pray." Of course, they think. That is what every good Jew does. One is "a Pharisee and the other a tax collector." As Jesus says it, they are all hooked by their own judgment of the tax collector. All he must do is reel them in. The Pharisee prays, thanking God that he is not like this tax collector or a whole range of other wrongdoers. Jesus then has him say what we would normally only think: "These are all the good things I do!" Out in the open, the emptiness and self-congratulation rotting his heart and social relationships are revealed. It prevents him knowing God or himself. The exposed self-righteousness withers. In contrast, the tax collector beats his breast and says, "God have mercy on me, a sinner." So Jesus finishes, "I tell you that this man, rather than the other, went home justified before God. For everyone who exalts himself will be humbled, and he who humbles himself will be exalted." So Jesus flips over self-rightness and cooks the pancake on both sides for us to eat too.

These are some of Jesus' critical perspectives on law. Deeper still is his positive impact. Because of his commitment to teaching all people the depth and significance of the law, we can see the full possibility of a *law-abiding* society, intimated since the time of Moses, and also developed by later Judaism in its love for God's Torah. Ordinary people's right living must surpass the Pharisees to enter God's rule. In the Sermon on the Mount, Jesus links acts and motives, so that we are not performing but subjectively wanting and understanding what is good (Matt. 5:21–48). It is interesting how we react to this law-abiding model. Some see it as unduly idealistic or even as too ordinary. Yet, political models of the autocratic imposition of law do not work, and this model remains the successful and dominant model in world history. Communities of right-living people who need no policing and know what is good for everybody are wonderful. We, too, depend on people who carry the law in their hearts at traffic lights, in relation to the property of others, and in concern for their neighbors. "Thou shalt not steal" is the only way to run an efficient society; there is no other model on offer (Exod. 20:15; Eph. 4:28). Where people love and submit to the law, do not twist it, are not legalistic, and are not self-righteous, there is a law-abiding society. It is a good one, and Jesus so taught the people. The state has less work because people govern themselves before God. It may work well or badly; yet this is the model we enjoy living in and whose breakdown we fear. It is the model that largely tamed the wild West. Once more, we are more beholden to the Nazarene than we care to admit.

Jesus also insists that law is *for us,* as people. Again, this is an amazing cultural transition. Imposed law is for the ruler. Privileged law burdens the many with the requirements of the few. Religious law gives power to priests and magicians. But Jesus does two things that undermine all these cultural constructions. First, the law is a law of love *for* people; it is for their deepest good, just as it is good for a baby to learn to walk. Their needs for healing, to eat, for respect, for forgiveness and restoration—these all dwell in the law. To want the good of others is a great but underutilized ambition. God's law is not an ass, messing up people's lives. It does not damage and hurt. Jesus faces those who are in the synagogue to see if he would heal on the Sabbath and thus break their (traditional) law. His reaction states the principle. "He looked round at them in anger and, deeply distressed at their stubborn hearts," healed the man's shriveled hand, leaving it completely restored (Mark 3:1–6). Still, we face the many examples of laws not for people, but against them, because they are formed for some other reason or to benefit some special group. But predominantly, we know laws that are for us, in which we dwell with security and by which we are loved.

Yet equally, God's law is not mere individual morality, or what any particular group thinks or likes. It is not rooted in what *we* decide is good for us. There is a long history to this human-centered process in the West. We have thought up and declared rational a variety of political moralities—enlightened despotism and self-interest, utilitarianism, revolutionary Socialism, national self-interest, the Nazi *Volk* ethic, and hedonist consumerism.[7] Such moralities have been self-serving in a variety of ways and done much damage. Christians often are the ones who have most strongly struggled against these self-serving moralities, but they have often been overwhelmed. Love and respect for neighbor, for enemy, for other nations and races have been jettisoned in favor of local moral priorities such as landed wealth, revolution, national expansion, or self-centered pleasure. Christ addresses ethnic self-regard, egocentric hardness of heart, or love of mammon (wealth) as not God's way (Luke 10:33; Matt. 19:8; 6:24n NRSV).

The government of God is, not surprisingly, on God's terms and not to be supplanted by humanist self-constructions. In this study, we cannot look at the full architecture of biblical law. But the transformation is radical. Jesus presents a general sociology of degenerate moral subcultures. "It has been said to you . . . , but I tell you . . ." recounts patterns where the Pharisees have adjusted the direct normative content to suit the way they live, as we all adjust our morality to suit our own practice (cf. Matt. 5:21–48). Adulterers conclude that adultery is not wrong, warmongers that theirs is a legitimate war, thieves that this theft is fine because life is not fair, and the hateful that others deserve it. Degenerate moralities are rooted in self-justification, and Jesus does not allow them to remain. "You are the ones who justify yourselves in the eyes of men, but God knows your hearts. What is highly valued among men is detestable in God's sight" (Luke 16:15). Christ does not cook principles until they are mushy, but keeps them firm in the searching love of God.

All this reconstruction of law—requiring it to dwell in the love and justice of God, and bringing the political leaders to account in relation to the government of God—is undertaken by the Man who declares himself its fulfillment. Thus, when disciples pick and eat corn within the gleaning laws of the Old Testament but breaking the Pharisees' fixation on the Sabbath, one of the Ten Commandments (Exod. 20:8–11), the Pharisees upbraid Jesus. His response plummets hawklike on their position. He points out that the greatest king of Israel, David, and the priests in the Temple broke the same rule and remained innocent. Then he adds, "The Sabbath was made for man, not man for the Sabbath. The Son of Man is Lord even of the Sabbath" (Mark 2:23–28; Matt. 12:1–8; Luke 6:1–5). Yes, we see, laws are for us; that is their point. They are humane. This we see, but what does it mean that this man is Lord of the law?

The law of Christ is not even the Christian understanding of law and grace,[8] but something prior. In Jesus, the law is never impersonal. He does not allow the law of God to be separated from the God of the law. Here is the law of life and of blessing. Those who hunger and thirst for righteousness will be filled with it and experience the blessing of goodness. Jesus is the person who gives law rather than imposing it, but he gives it on his own terms. And those terms are surprising by all our normal political perceptions of law. The Lord of the law turns out to be blessing for all who seek good; he gives and defines blessing. Those who really seek the law with purity of heart find the Beatitudes of Jesus and the Jesus of the Beatitudes. "Blessed are those who hunger and thirst for right living, for they will be filled" (cf. Matt. 5:6). They know the joy of dwelling with God their Father.

The Rule of Law and Constitutionalism

These two concepts do not come fully grown from the teaching of Jesus; they developed more in Western Protestant culture,[9] but they are formed in the Gospels. The rule of law is a principle saying that no state executive power is above, or can claim immunity from, the precepts of the law. Rulers still frequently put themselves above the law because they feel they are right. George W. Bush claimed the right to eliminate Saddam Hussein's regime because he believed it was evil; yet in so doing, Bush ignored due process in the United Nations. Other rulers are habitually autocratic and arbitrary in their government. For them, the law must be tamed or used to their own ends and with their own appointees. The fight for independence and the authority of law as distinct from the whims of the ruler is long and complex in Western democratic history. Essentially, it has been waged by those who recognize that the law of God is not to be made the pawn of the ruler, but that rulers must subject themselves to it.

The issue is best conveyed by an interchange between the autocratic King James I and the Puritan Lord Chief Justice, Sir Edward Coke. Coke speaks roughly as follows:

> "True it is, please your Majesty, that God has endowed your Majesty with excellent science as well as great gifts of nature: but your Majesty will allow me to say, with all reverence, that you are not learned in the laws of this your realm of England, . . . which is an art which requires long study and experience before a man can attain to cognisance of it. The law is the golden met-wand [measuring rod] and measure to try the causes of your Majesty's subjects, and it is by that law that your Majesty is protected in safety and peace." King James in a great rage said, "Then I am under the law which is a treason to affirm." The Chief Justice replied, "Thus wrote Bracton, 'The King is under no man save God and the law.'"[10]

We are all indebted to this and many other such "treasonable" statements against autocracy. Yet it is still with us. We have Berlusconi passing a law in the Italian legislature to exclude himself from the effects of law. In contrast, Jesus' affirmation of the primacy and preeminence of the law is repeated, emphatic, and fairly conclusive: "It is easier for heaven and earth to disappear than for the least stroke of a pen to drop from the law" (cf. Matt. 5:18). But of even greater weight is the action. The one who knows himself to be the Son of God and who embodies the law submits to a Jerusalem legal process that he knows to be deeply flawed and unjust. Given his miracles, it is easy to accept that at any point he could pull out. Indeed, Jesus makes the point at his arrest: "Do you think I cannot call on my Father, and he will at once put at my disposal more than twelve legions [72,000 in terms of Roman soldiers] of angels?" (Matt. 26:53). He goes to trial by complete volition, as one who submits to both the law of God and state law. This attitude of subjection to law is the deepest human base for the rule of law and constitutionalism.

There are two essential moves in constitutionalism. The first is that the rule of God requires rulers (and people!) to acknowledge the limited power of rulers. Hence, the ruler does not have competence to control other areas of life, and within the state the ruler has limited offices. The second is that no one is to put oneself above or outside the just government of the state and its rules. These rules may have a proximate weight of wisdom, like restricting the terms of the presidency or the separation of powers, but primarily they are bringing officeholders into the humility of office, allowing the goodness of law to flood their activities and be reflected in due process and transparency. Jesus' insistence on everything being revealed, his affirmation of the Mosaic pattern where people live under the given law of God, and his emphasis on obedience to God—these all set the terms of a constitutional state. Its historical emergence in seventeenth-century Puritan England and New England is another exciting study. It is not difficult to see the tree growing from the sapling. Those who submit to the rule of God honor both law and the institutions of law. They know that no one, including themselves, may claim to be an exception to, or be beyond, the rule of law.

The Judge and Justice

Similarly, the Judeo-Christian tradition of justice has a deep structure. Justice precedes the state and goes back at least to Cain and Abel. It involves treating other people in all aspects of their relationships according to God-given norms. Clearly, it could be complex, but Jesus will not let the issue get away from us. His radical, unavoidable statement is clear: "Do to others as you would have them do to you" (Luke 6:31). Every hurt and sensibility of unfairness we feel contributes to a working understanding of justice. The reliable move is to have a stronger sense of justice for others than for ourselves, but few of us get there. Jesus relentlessly removes the self-pleading structure of *our* justice. His response to a question on divorce law is to move beyond the precepts of the Mosaic code. Marriage is a union of husband and wife, and the man who asks for divorce has hardened against his woman enough to try to dispose of her. That is unjust, and much of the practice of justice is degenerate in the same sense. People turn from God and construct "rational" and other perceptions of justice that are self-justifying, partial, and argue from idolatrous conceptions. One of the great tasks of the prophets was to reconstitute a sense of justice among the people. Unfair trade, extortion, militarism, patriarchy, inequality, exploitation, slavery, sexual abuse, monopolies, and unfair taxes grow on sleepy consciences. The prophets awaken us to be fair to them. Jesus says we must even love our enemies (Luke 6:27). This is no cozy bargain, a tit-for-tat arrangement, but a requirement to stand up for the other even though they will not repay us. It is not just negative but involves actively helping, showing mercy, doing good, and loving the other (6:27–36).

It is no external political imposition, as the liberal tradition of jurisprudence often implies, but part of our created existence because we are members one of another. Biblical justice is justice-with-righteousness; the two words are really interchangeable, involving being right with God, ourselves, others, and the rest of creation. In the Beatitudes, we are to hunger and thirst for it. Even when people are persecuted for following it, they are still blessed because they are right with God. But the state is particularly the institution that administers it. From the time of Moses onward, dealing out judgments to the people, the business of deciding what is just, has fallen to the state, to the magistrate. The state's first calling is to be beyond partiality. Astonishingly, the Mosaic law requires trials to be conducted without favoritism to the poor, taking for granted that there should be no partiality to the rich (Exod. 23:2–3; Lev. 19:15). Our idiom of "blind justice" focuses on impartiality in trial. Impartiality is an important biblical principle growing from the understanding that God is no respecter of persons.

Nevertheless, impartiality sometimes becomes the overriding conception of justice, a rather negative and limited one. Jesus' emphasis is on "loving justice," marked by compassion, mercy, and powerful commitment to others. This is not justice addressing wrongs abstractly, blind to the people involved, but outgoing justice for them. Jesus upbraids the Pharisees because "you neglect justice and the love of God" (Luke 11:42). Loving justice is the foundation of Christian understanding. It is different from the modern liberal view that injustice occurs only when one wrongs another *individual*. Such a view validates indifference and externalizes responsibilities. Jesus critiques this orientation when he is addressed by an expert in the law and replies with the parable of the Good Samaritan. He asks the expert on the law, "What is written in the law? How do you read it?" They agree that the law requires us to love our neighbors as ourselves. Therefore, it is not good enough to pass by on the other side and avoid helping a needy person. The Samaritan has compassion and starts a health service. "Go and do likewise," Jesus commands (Luke 10:25–37). Justice is loving-people related, and not liberal-people indifferent.

God's justice inheres all relationships, but particular relationships have their own normative structure. Thus, there is justice in areas like marriage, family, work, animal care, and education. Jesus accepts and explores these. Divorce cannot be discussed neutrally (Matt. 19:1–9). To cheat one's partner or someone else's partner is unjust. Not to pay a proper wage is wrong. Overworking an animal, unfairly punishing a child, or teaching error is unjust to the other person. The Mosaic law carefully defines work, property, marriage, exchange, tort, immigration, debt, welfare, punishment, and land in terms of precept and justice. They embody deeper values and principles.[11] This law calls for people to give priority and respect to others in all institutional relationships; justice is meant to occur within and between institutions. The Mosaic law, for example, prohibits the state from sending a man to war or having "any other duty laid on him. For one year he is free to stay at home and bring happiness to the wife he has married" (Deut. 24:5). It would be unjust for marriage to be dominated in this way by the state. Hence, the state, as it develops through the history of Israel, is the institution that is to uphold public justice in these other institutional areas. Throughout his teaching Jesus reflects this wider concept of justice.

There is an even more pointed issue in relation to biblical justice. The state is called before God to be just. It is accountable as to whether it is just or not, and Jesus holds the rulers of his time to account. His critique goes to the heart of the matter. The lawyers and leaders have "neglected the weightier matters of the law—justice, mercy and faithfulness. . . . You blind guides! You strain out a gnat and swallow a camel" (Matt. 23:23–24). This strategic point opens up many levels of governance. The state is failing if it does not address the powerful when they are unjust. The state is often partial toward its own faults. The establishment can ignore what is really wrong and veer off onto incidentals and symptoms. The directness of justice can be strangled in a thousand qualifications. The rich can buy off verdicts against themselves. Ideologies can blind people to injustice. Those who want to strangle reform sideline the great issues of injustice in the political system. All these failures and more are implicit in Jesus' critique of the justice of his day. The same political reflection should be part of the normal contemporary Christian response, carrying on the work done by the Israelite prophets of staying centered on God's ways of loving justice.

Another element in Jesus' teaching, prefigured in the Old Testament, is the emphasis on recompense and the restoration of relationships.[12] Justice sees the trust that has been broken and seeks to heal it. It re-creates the wholesome relationship, rather than countenancing a fragmented society.[13] With Jesus' encouragement Zacchaeus goes back to the Mosaic law's emphasis on restitution. He offers to return four times the amount he may have wrongly exacted. To be just is to want to right wrongs and restore good relationships (Luke 19:8; cf. Exod. 22:1). If someone wants to sue you, be generous to them, giving them more than they want, so that you go beyond "an eye for an eye" to real reconciliation (Matt. 5:38–40; cf. Exod. 21:23–25).

There is no end to the surprises that come in Jesus' teaching and responses. Justice normally requires a judge. Indeed, later we shall look at Jesus as judge in his final public pronouncement. But before that he almost presents a model of justice without judges, by examining and addressing why we go to formal judgment. A man shouts out, "Teacher, tell my brother to divide the inheritance with me." Jesus refuses to take up the role of judge over another. "Man, who appointed me an arbiter or judge over you?" He then responds by saying, "Watch out! Be on your guard against all kinds of greed!" (Luke 12:13–14). Litigious greed is no small Western problem. But deeper still, he addresses the way judgment is formed within the soul. "Don't judge others that you be not judged yourself" (cf. 6:37). The human tendency to judge others and excuse oneself lies behind the need for judgment.

We rush to the judge when we are wronged but not when we are the offender. If we were faster off the mark to settle matters as offenders than as victims, the courts would be emptied because a good sense of justice would dwell in our souls (12:57–59). Our attitudes must be reversed, so that our conscience is sensitive to the wrongs we perpetrate before others' wrongdoing. If we have spiritual self-judgment, there is no need for the judge and the magistrate. In the Sermon on the Mount, Jesus completely overturns normality. Everybody worldwide goes to the courts to get their injustices rectified; the *prosecutor* precipitates the process. But, says Jesus, make it the reverse. Not when you have been wronged, but when your brother has something against you or you have wronged him, rush to him, settle matters, be reconciled, and restore the relationship. Let *offenders* push the system of putting things right (Matt. 5:23–26). The conflicts of life can be treated proactively. "Love your enemies" (5:44). "Be reconciled" (5:24). "Blessed are those who hunger and thirst for the justice of others" may be a good paraphrase of Matthew 5:6. Here is an astonishing insight that cuts across our assumption of litigation as normal. It could radically change our court, policing, penal, and insurance systems.

Again, Jesus embodies justice. Matthew applies Isaiah 42 to Jesus. Probably, they had studied the scroll together. God says, "My servant . . . will proclaim justice to the nations. He will not quarrel or cry out . . . till he leads justice to victory" (Matt. 12:18–21). What a strange idea! Normally one side or the other wins a victory—the Coalition or Iraq, Celtic or Rangers. But here justice is the victor, and the quiet one will bring it to pass. The weak will not be broken. Nobody will be snuffed out. Here is the referee whom nobody notices as he walks off at the end of a good match.

The Judge of All People

Judgment is a deep reality, though it can be seen superficially. Some people see it as God's vindictiveness. Others hear the words "an eye for an eye" and think they have an intellectual grasp on the Christian tradition of judicial judgment. Actually, a biblical understanding of judgment sees it as far more deeply entwined in the human condition. All our actions in daily life and history have a significance that continues to reverberate through our lives. This is true of big historical events like world wars, migrations, the development of weapons, and the siting of cities. It is also true of personal events like striking up a friendship, having a child, letting go of bitterness, or reading a book. The outcome of the way we live is for good or ill, albeit in complex ways, and judgment is part of that process. The question is where our judgments grow. God is *for* us, for *our good,* and encourages a deep character of good in our lives involving love, truth, faithfulness, mercy, justice, and wisdom. That is the way God calls us to live and make judgments. But often we live with hatred, fatalism, myths, lies, foolishness, and vengeance. Then we are under judgment, the consequences follow, and they often are awful.

In the last century the Stalinist camps, the Holocaust, the World Wars, and countless other wars and mass atrocities show the horrific things that we have done to one another because of poor judgment. We have done them. Jesus' teaching warns against such misinterpretation. Often, in our flaccid view of judgment we see our cruelty as linked with those who suffer: "They deserve what they get." Thus evil thinkers have always said. Jesus points out that the sufferers often do not deserve the punishment. People ask him about some Galileans whom Pilate has killed as they were sacrificing their offering, perhaps a Zealot group at the Passover. Surely this was judgment, wasn't it? Jesus berates their superstition: "Do you think those eighteen poor people who had that tower in Siloam fall on them were under judgment? Of course not! But you, unless you repent, you too will perish" (cf. Luke 13:1–5). His repeated "Woe to" statements are for those who do unjust things to others, not for the victims.

Throughout the Bible and especially in the Gospels, judgment involves facing truth. It puts us face-to-face with realities so that we see them truly and without evasion. The deepest reality is our relationship with God, where the goodness of our life does or does not dwell, and is or is not made evident. Either we face what is true and just or we run from it. Jesus warns of judgment for anyone who is angry with his brother or sister, anyone who insults, who causes and does not settle an offense, who lusts (Matt. 5). The one who causes children to sin, who does not forgive from the heart (ch. 18), who does not answer God's call (ch. 22), and who does not provide food, clothing, and care for the needy (ch. 25)—such a person is under judgment. The selfish rich (Luke 16) and those who turn to kill God's Son (ch. 20) are under judgment. There are many things going on here beyond our normal reactions. Elites often judge ordinary people, but here it is the rich, the adults, and the dominant who are especially under scrutiny. Why this emphasis on judgment for all, judgment that goes to the root of our existence and the meaning of our lives? It is because the terms for life are not negotiable: loving God and loving your neighbor as yourself are required. To warn is to clarify: "For judgment I have come into this world, so that the blind will see and those who see will become blind" (John 9:39). Shut your eyes if you dare.

Jesus then goes a stage further. An Old Testament emphasis in judicial process is recompense or restitution for wrongs done. If you have stolen a sheep, pay back four, or if you still have the original animal, repay double (Exod. 22:1–4). Recompense establishes again the right relationship and heals the breach between neighbors. Jesus emphasizes it strongly. His focus is on all of us as wrongdoers, generating conflict and creating wrongs. If somebody wants to sue you, because of a wrong they believe you have done, pursue them and find out what is wrong. Empathize. Offer compensation and see beyond the limited retributive idea of an "eye for an eye" (Matt. 5:38–42). Much of the first part of the Sermon on the Mount sets up the way in which relationships can avoid judgment and judicial conflict. Then Jesus builds further in the great attack on the self-righteousness built into judgment of others. To judge others is to give God the basis for judging yourself. You are partial, judging others for what you yourself do. Remove hypocrisy and the city of judgment would be flattened (7:1–5). We all are corralled by this critique of self-made judgment.

But all of this is scarcely preparation for Jesus' final set of public pronouncements, recorded in Matthew 25. There are two parables, those of the Ten Virgins and the Talents, and the final statement of judgment. The parables have urgency. "Be ready! Think ahead. Sort out what you are doing with your life. Recognize your accountability to God. Don't be foolish by not seeing the consequences and outcome of the way you live. For you will regret the outcome, the judgment. Concentrate on your relationship with God." At the end of these parables (containing far more than is covered here) comes the final public statement, "When the Son of Man comes in his glory . . ." (25:31). This is a direct statement, not an elliptical parable. "All the nations will be gathered before him, and he will separate the people one from one another as a shepherd separates the sheep from the goats" (25:32). The locus of judgment is love or indifference, care or neglect. The second great commandment, "To love neighbor as self," is also the first commandment. "To act for the least of these my brothers, is to act for me, the King, the Christ" (cf. 25:31, 34, 40). We are judged in terms of our love for Christ expressed toward the "least" of his brothers and sisters, beyond all human distinction and gradation. "Love me! Love my friends!" "I was hungry and you gave me nothing. . . . I was a stranger and you did not invite me in. . . . I was sick and in prison and you did not look after me." This is the unequivocal statement of the Ruler, the King, the Judge. When we face him, we find the Son of God has identified with all of us, even the least. Perhaps we see what we have overlooked, either to weep or be glad before God.

God's Gentle Ruler

These principles do not stand by themselves; they are given by and cohere in the ruler, and the ruler both speaks with and has authority. This is not the authority of imposition, military force, or autocracy, but one arising from the truths of human existence and the nature of politics. Here is a strange ruler, recruiting members of his kingdom voluntarily, but insisting on a certain kind of government. It penetrates to truths about war, peace, law, and justice, showing us how we are meant to live. It calls us out of the ideologies that have dominated much of our political history. It leaves us free for all of our lives, inescapably so *until judgment*.

We know what we really suspected all along, that God cares for all of us, even the least, and calls us to do the same in our politics. We know that we must abide in God's law, act justly, love mercy, and walk humbly with our God (Mic. 6:8). And we find that the Ruler is uncompromisingly gentle, deconstructing all the systems of domination that we experience and disbursing blessing. This is the government under which we are invited to live. The Ruler turns out to be a self-effacing servant. We find the law recast for us, and justice is structured on the basis of love. Such a ruler is not remote or difficult to accept. When we see this rule properly, it gladdens our hearts—but it does not go down well with everyone.

Bibliography

Anderson, Norman. *God's Law and God's Love.* London: Collins, 1980.

Boardman, John, et al., eds. *The Oxford History of the Classical World.* Oxford: Oxford University Press, 1986.

Bratt, James D., ed. *Abraham Kuyper: A Centennial Reader.* Grand Rapids: Eerdmans, 1998.

Brunner, Emil. *Justice and the Social Order.* Translated by Mary Hottinger. London: Lutterworth, 1945.

Carlyle, Thomas, ed. *Oliver Cromwell's Letters and Speeches.* 5 vols. In *Collected Works of Thomas Carlyle.* 3d ed. Vols. 14–18. London: Chapman & Hall, 1849.

Dengerink, Jan. *The Idea of Justice in Christian Perspective.* Toronto: Wedge, 1978.

Denning, The Rt. Hon. Lord. *The Influence of Religion on Law.* London: Lawyers' Christian Fellowship, 1989.

Dooyeweerd, Herman. *The Christian Idea of the State*. Translated by John Kraay. Nutley, NJ: Craig, 1968. Repr., 1975.

Kaye, B. N., and G. J. Wenham. *Law, Morality and the Bible*. Leicester: Inter-Varsity, 1978.

Lindars, B., ed. *Law and Religion: Essays on the Place of Law in Israel and Early Christianity*. Cambridge: James Clarke, 1988.

Marshall, Christopher. *Beyond Retribution: A New Testament Vision of Justice, Crime, and Punishment*. Grand Rapids: Eerdmans, 2001.

Marshall, Paul. *Thine Is the Kingdom: A Biblical Perspective on the Nature of Government and Politics Today*. Basingstoke: Marshalls, 1984.

Mouw, Richard J. *Politics and the Biblical Drama*. Grand Rapids: Eerdmans, 1976.

Runner, H. Evan. *Scriptural Religion and Political Task*. Toronto: Wedge, 1974.

Skillen, James W. *Christians Organizing for Political Service*. Washington, DC: Association for Public Justice Education Fund, 1980.

Westminster Conference. *The Christian and the State in Revolutionary Times*. Huntingdon Cambs., UK: Westminster Conference, 1975.

Yoder, John Howard. *The Christian Witness to the State*. Newton, KS: Faith & Life Press, 1964. Repr., Scottdale, PA: Herald Press, 2002.

Jesus as World Ruler

What Makes a Ruler?

In one sense, we know what a political ruler is. We learned about them at school. Julius Caesar, Genghis Khan, Charlemagne, William the Conqueror, Elizabeth I, Louis XIV, Pitt the Younger, Bismarck, Hitler, Woodrow Wilson, Charles de Gaulle, Mikhail Gorbachev, Margaret Thatcher, Nelson Mandela, and Tony Blair are rulers. They define political eras for us. But there are complications in this simple picture. We can handle the fact that effective rule has moved from kings and queens to presidents and prime ministers. We also recognize that rule is more dispersed than it used to be. Cabinets, parliaments, commissions, and departments are now part of more complex patterns of rule. But political rule and rulers are always there—obvious, the center of attention, the White House as important, on television and running the country.

Yet it is more complex than that. Different views of rule compete. Rule used to be a status conferred by blood. You *were* the monarch by birth; bastards were out, and Henry VIII killed wives for an heir. Royalty was a matter of hereditary family rule. Still, quite a number of countries in the Middle East remain dynastic. Yet at other times it was not so at all. Legitimate hereditary heirs were swept aside by military conquest. Heads rolled, and the leader with an army moved in to take control. Again, military might as rule still operates widely through the world today; worldwide, about 140 military regimes operated in the last three decades of the twentieth century.[1] More recently, rule has been focused in popularity. Peron, Reagan, Thatcher, and Kohl were in power because, for a while, people voted strongly for them personally; we could call it populism. Other leaders mainly represented the parties for which they stood and were elected on that basis. Attlee, Major, Brezhnev, Adenauer, and Moi have been strong party people. Within democracy, it is often seen that elections confer the authority to rule. The basis, or legitimation, for rule has thus varied quite radically in a short time. Even this understates the problem. Political leaders have held sway, but in a short time they are discredited and gone. The leader boasts and—poof!—he is no more. Nixon and Clinton have been triumphantly returned to power, but through misdemeanors are soon discredited or even slipping from office. Chancellor Kohl is embroiled in party corruption and sinks. Ideologies like Communism, the divine right of kings, aristocratic title, and Fascism come and disappear, spinning their own twists to the meaning of rule. So, what is the basis of ruling? Now, and always, this has been one of the key issues of politics and of life.

In a sense, Jesus has the unbeatable trump card at this point. To be the Son of God is to have quite an overwhelming claim. But though it may well be true, Jesus does not use this card. The Gospel writers, Matthew and Luke, emphasize the genealogies, Matthew going back to David and Abraham and emphasizing the kingly line (Matt. 1:1–17) and Luke pressing a stage further by going back to Adam in establishing Jesus' universal significance (Luke 3:23–38). But Jesus does not pull status—the ultimate status. The Philippians' hymn gasps awe at Jesus' humility:

> [Jesus] made himself nothing,
> Taking the very nature of a servant,
> Being made in human likeness. (Phil. 2:7)

As we have seen, this is not shyness or a withdrawal from the business of power. It is the far deeper issue of being true in person to God's rule. Here is the rule of God—gentle, not using people, blessing the poor and meek, letting the rain fall on good and evil, probing the hearts of men and women, loving, serving, suffering. Here is your king, prime minister, president. No longer is the question the legitimation of rule, but the character of God's rule as the gentle Lamb on the throne, deconstructing human domination and oppression. We learn that human oppression is unnecessary and abhorrent to God. We are ushered into the throne room and find that the king took our coat at the door.

Suddenly, we see the great trick of sinful human history. Later, when Pilate takes Jesus out bound and flogged to the crowd and offers them their king, they are incensed. Through a concoction of circumstances and attitudes, they turn down the ruler who is good and without oppression. The chief priests' words ring out, "We have no king but Caesar" (John 19:15). They actually refuse God's ruler and opt for Tiberius Caesar, their implacable enemy, in order to put Pilate on the spot. The Caesars were deified as a way of enhancing their political status above the masses and the Roman Senate, and because the Roman state was a civic god. The costs of Roman rule were at times unbearable, yet the priests actually shout for it! Thus, throughout human history the oppressors have been appointed and supported, and the true gentle rule of God has been ignored. What fools we are, what utter fools!

When we probe the issue, there is also the question: What do rulers do? They can sit on thrones, but that seems a bit pointless. They can make laws, run the country, fight wars, engage in diplomacy, give titles, sort out the economy, restore order, and service gossip, but what *should* they do? This is far from clear. Some philosophies aim to roll back the powers of the state. Others give it new responsibilities. Human history has seesawed between the kind of total government represented by Mao and Khomeini and the noninvolvement of mad George III or Calvin Coolidge. Is government big or small? The point of asking these questions should already be clear. If Jesus is a ruler, he throws stereotypes on such a scale that we must be awake to our own preconditioning. We try to respond. Jesus was born in a stable, not a palace, we sing. But already the difference is romanticized. Do we really believe that a ruler need not be at the center of glory and power? Could the president of the United States live in Idaho or the British prime minister in Rochdale? Nor must we make this question fanciful, because Washington, Canberra, and Bonn were chosen with some insight as capitals precisely because they were not self-important cities, perhaps under the influence of Christ's example. When we take on this man, the systems and conventions are shaken.

The self-effacing character of Jesus' rule is not an accident; it arises from the nature of the government of God. The requirement of good and just living brings us all into government, with callings, responsibilities, and contributions. And this is part of modern democratic history. The titular ruler has been engulfed and superseded by ministers, legislators, and other workers at government. In the deepest sense the government becomes *our* government, and the idea of "ruler" becomes, in part, obsolete. Again we find the self-effacing One offers the definitive commentary on what is good about our age. In a sense, Jesus has worked himself out of a job. The inner structure of his rule destroys its conventional understanding.

Claims to the Title

Throughout history legitimacy, the title, or the crown has been key to rule. Indeed, much political history has presented a key issue: Does Christianity support monarchy? Already in the Gospels a more complex argument emerges. The Son of God is the King, the Ruler, but none of the conventional modes of legitimation are the basis of the process. As we have seen, the title to rule often comes through popularity, conquest, party support, or dynastic validation. Jesus steps back from these processes. Indeed, the Gospels show a contrast between the concern of everybody else as to whether Jesus is king of the Jews and his own serene walk, revealing what it is to be God's ruler. The scene is set at Jesus' birth as the Magi reach Jerusalem and ask: "Where is the one who has been born king of the Jews? . . . We have come to worship him" (Matt. 2:2). There is uproar from the jealous Herod, prepared to murder his own sons on the issue of succession to the title, and all Jerusalem is disturbed. "Bethlehem is the place," say the Scribes, consulting the prophets, and they are right. Herod's uneasy validation from Caesar Augustus is challenged. He sets out to kill the rival, but in God's purposes he fails. The story is gripping. This is no young pretender, and the three wise men have grasped it right. The genealogies back to King David, the greatest king in Israel's history, give an immediate Jewish legitimation. To the Gospel writers, being the son of David is to be in the royal line. They are portraying the king of the Jews.

Nevertheless, the Gospels show no time when Jesus bothers to assert his position as king of the Jews in the usual way. Instead, there is the steady insistence that the one who rules is the one who serves—radical, putting the whole process of rule on the operating table. Only before Pilate, when the statement will mean his death, does Jesus say he is king of the Jews. Then, at the crucifixion there is a petulant row between Pilate and the Chief Priests. Pilate has written the superscription "JESUS OF NAZARETH, THE KING OF THE JEWS." The chief priests are livid that the reality they have fought to keep under wraps is now expressed, even though Jesus himself is impaled on the cross. Probably as the cross is being raised, the Jewish leaders race the quarter of a mile to Pilate's palace to upbraid him and point out the blasphemy. But he would not budge: "What I have written, I have written," he says. "That's one in the eye for you. I'm on his side," he implies. It was a multifaceted statement. Pilate uneasily believes that Jesus is a king embodying truths he cannot access. The chief priests say he isn't, but Jesus has affirmed he is, in one sense, king of the Jews. Pilate has a disturbing empathy with Jesus and is happy to contradict the chief priests. More fully, Pilate's earlier weakness in front of the crowd is reflected in petulance now. Now he will stand up to the chief priests. Moreover, crucifying the "King of the Jews" also shows his power and loyalty to Rome in suppressing insurrection. The Gospel writers' perspective is different. John records this row (19:19–22), but for him and the other Gospel writers, the *truth* of the statement is the key thing (Matt. 27:37; Mark 15:26; Luke 23:38). Jesus, even on the cross, is the king of the Jews. The title is his, from beginning to supposed end. Yet, discussion at this level has not even begun to grasp the point. We are addressing God with us. Something far deeper than legitimation is going on here.

World Ruler: The Deconstruction of the National King

We are used to national rulers. France, Britain, Senegal, Malaysia, and Argentina have their rulers, as nations have throughout recorded history. Occasionally, there have been times when a world ruler has threatened to emerge. Alexander the Great set out on a swathe of conquest, swooping through and subduing much of the known world. For a while the Roman Empire looked as imposing. There have been other conquerors, such as Napoleon. There has even been the era when much of the world map was colored the pink of the British Empire. These patterns of conquest are the nearest we come to world government, and they are almost the only terms in which we can think of it. Christianity does, however, offer something different. After the resurrection, Jesus comes and says to his disciples: "All authority in heaven and earth has been given to me. Therefore go and make disciples of all nations, baptizing them in the name of the Father and of the Son and of the Holy Spirit, and teaching them to obey everything I have commanded you" (Matt. 28:18–20). This is a comprehensive claim. It involves worldwide sovereignty. It is globalization two thousand years early. To the non-Christian, this is a bit threatening. Why should we Westerners, British, Muslims, Socialists, Russians, Chinese, and Iraqis submit to this man?

The answer partly lies in the kind of world leader Jesus turns out to be. We have already encountered Jewish nationalism. Though the Zealots were the most avid example, almost all the groups had the same underlying commitment to their nation. When the Jews were subdued by the Romans, they retained their ethnic identity and sense of superiority as God's chosen people. To be Jewish, as to be American, British, or French, was great. The Jew thanked God each day that he was not born a Gentile, and today many other races are prepared to "thank god" that they are not of another race. Yet Jesus repudiates nationalism and ethnocentrism structurally. The true cost of being international is to withdraw from all the expressions of national righteousness and

199

superiority that mark Judaism, as they mark other nationalisms. The irony of being the king of the Jews pursued to death by your own subjects underlines how heavy the cost is. We need to perceive the extent to which the early Christians effectively became stateless Jews, outside their national culture.

More than this, the Messiah is killed for the nation. We know enough about the plot to kill Jesus recorded in John 11:45–53 to see this. Jesus has raised Lazarus from the dead; many, not surprisingly, believe in him and become his followers in a surge of popular interest. This is reported back to the Pharisees. They and the chief priests call a meeting of the Sanhedrin, the central Jewish religious and political body. What understanding of Jesus have they formed? It is of Jesus as a threat to the Jewish nation. Our initial reaction may be "But that is unfair." But actually, it rightly responds to what is going on. He is threatening national pride and a nationalistic agenda at a fundamental level. The chief priests and the Pharisees say, "What are we accomplishing? Here is this man performing many miraculous signs. If we let him go on like this, everyone will believe in him, and then the Romans will come and take away both our place [the Temple] and our nation" (11:47–48). This is their nationalist argument and why they perceived Jesus' miracles a threat. Actually, they are a threat to no one, though the Pharisees' response seemed realistic in their own terms. "This man will have the effect of so undermining the Jewish nation that the Romans will be able to eradicate our identity completely," they think. Jesus is the supposed enemy of the nation. Then Caiaphas, the High Priest that year, comes up with his justification for murder. The sixth commandment is to be put aside. You can hear his tone of voice as he insists that there is a sacrifice to be made: "You know nothing at all! You do not realize that it is better for you that one man die for the people than that the whole nation perish" (John 11:50). If the Jewish nation is to survive, this man must die. The conclusion is fundamentally wrong, but it is the obvious one. Perhaps in these words we can hear the echoes down the centuries of millions whose deaths have been justified by what is good for the people, the nation. The World War I poster said, "Your country needs you," but it could have added, "to die." Inestimable evil has been carried out in this name. This argument is the stuck record of history. But the gloss John rightly gives to those words is odd. He presents a man who does not understand what he is thinking as he comments on Caiaphas's words:

> He did not say this on his own, but as high priest that year he prophesied that Jesus would die for the Jewish nation, and not only for that nation

but also for the scattered children of God, to bring them together and make them one. (John 11:51–52)

John's mind moves from the national focus to the international people of God scattered in many nations. He clearly has learned and adopted Christ's frame of reference.

Here is the answer to the enigma of the trial. Why would the people prefer Barabbas, a third-rate insurrectionist, to this person who could really be their leader? Their response, like political responses throughout history, is nationalist. Jesus is not nationalist. He not only repudiates the role of national leader; he also attacks ethnic identity to its very roots. This is so marked that Jews down the ages have believed that Jesus was anti-Jewish. What they should see is the most systematic principled attack on nationalism and ethnic identity there has ever been, anti-American and anti-British in the same way as anti-Jewish, attacking the evils of nationalism and god-claiming racial superiority two millennia before Fascism emerged. Here is the real enemy of the Aryan super-race and the deepest friend of the Jews.

The pattern begins locally, early in Jesus' teaching, when he visits the synagogue at Nazareth (Luke 4:13–30). Jesus has probably moved with his family away from Nazareth to Capernaum, but he is known as the person from his hometown, Nazareth. He is already famous throughout Galilee as an outstanding rabbi, a powerful healer, and one who receives universal praise. The obvious thing is to return to his hometown, teach well, and receive the obvious acceptance and acclamation that would come to the local boy. Indeed, this is what happens. Jesus takes a scroll of the prophet Isaiah, perhaps one he has often handled and read before, moves down to what we call Isaiah 61, and reads the great manifesto of restoration written there. Let us hear it (slightly paraphrased):

> The Spirit of the Sovereign God is on me,
> because God has made me ruler
> to bring good news to the poor.
> He has sent me to bind up the brokenhearted,
> to proclaim freedom for those taken captive in war,
> and release from prison for those whom the king hates,
> to proclaim God's Jubilee release from debt. (cf. Isa. 61:1–2; Luke 4:18–19)

This manifesto is a lovely promise of gladness to the poor and down-trodden, and even here in this village perched above Sepphoris, it is a political event. Sometimes readers assume that the people of Nazareth take offense when Jesus appropriates to himself this prophecy of Isaiah by saying to them, "Today this Scripture is fulfilled in your hearing"

(Luke 4:21). But this is not the dynamic of the events. After this, the text records that they all spoke well of him and were amazed at the gracious words that came from his lips. They would welcome God's Deliverer. What happens next is astonishing. Jesus, when it would have been so easy to do the opposite, actually seems to provoke their opposition. They ask, "Isn't this Joseph's son?" probably meaning, "This Jesus is impressive." Mark adds, "Where did this man get these things?" (6:2–3). But Jesus seems to be deliberately antagonistic: "Surely you will quote this proverb to me: 'Physician, heal yourself! Do here in your home town what we have heard that you did in Capernaum.'" It is almost as though he refuses to perform for the home crowd, to be the darling of his people. Yet the next words are devastating:

> I tell you the truth. . . . No prophet is accepted in his home town. I assure you that there were many widows in Israel in Elijah's time, when the sky was shut for three and a half years and there was a severe famine throughout the land. Yet Elijah was not sent to any of them, but to a widow in Zarephath in the region of Sidon. And there were many in Israel with leprosy in the time of Elisha the prophet, yet not one of them was cleansed—only Naaman the Syrian. (Luke 4:24–27)

Why does Jesus focus on two cases where God's miraculous power was directed at Gentiles rather than Jews, at two pagan neighbors to the northeast and northwest of Galilee? The challenge is direct. No prophet of God is accepted in his own town, because the underlying attitude of the people is stubborn. Their stance is, "You perform for us, and we will believe you." But that is a form of pride. God responds to those with faith, even outside Israel, not to those who turn their back on God's word and prophets. God's good news, proclaimed by Isaiah, is for Gentiles who say yes, rather than for Jews who want God on their own terms. Jesus says all this to his local Jewish neighbors gathered in the synagogue, people who have been abhorring Gentiles all their lives. It is impolitic, as we say, and infuriates them! They react, drive him out, and try to push him off a bluff at the edge of the village. Their fury and the self-fulfilling prophecy measure the problem, a problem that recurs in racism and nationalism worldwide.

A yet more total confrontation occurs in Jerusalem (John 8:12–48). Jesus has gone up to the Temple for the Feast of Tabernacles, the harvest feast. There is a great swathe of teaching and discussion at the end of which Jesus proclaims some of the great "I am" statements his followers so readily affirm. "I am the light of the world. Whoever follows me will never walk in darkness but have the light of life. . . . Then you will know the truth and the truth will set you free" (8:12, 32). The Pharisees cannot face this and respond by attacking and arguing: "We are Abraham's descendants and have never been slaves of anyone. How can you say that we shall be set free?" (8:33). Normally an appeal to Jewish status cannot be gainsaid, but Jesus pursues them, calling in doubt their lineage from Abraham and more or less calling them bastards, as they readily understand. Jesus gives them only two possibilities. Either they are children of God, in which case they would love him because he presents God-given truth, or they are children of the devil, because they are buying into lies and murder (8:34–47). Suddenly, being a Jew counts for nothing. All are brought under the single criterion of hearing, or not hearing, the word of God. Their response to this movement outside their ethnic certainties is to spit out racial abuse: "You are a Samaritan and demon-possessed [mad]" (8:48).

Time after time Jesus emphasizes the same theme. When the Roman centurion's servant is healed, Jesus says, "I say to you that many will come from the east and west, and will take their places at the feast with Abraham, Isaac and Jacob in the kingdom of God. But the subjects of the kingdom will be thrown out, into the darkness, where there will be weeping and gnashing of teeth" (Matt. 8:11–12). It is difficult to overstate how insulting this is to the Jews present; though caught up in such a miracle, they can hardly express what they feel. The theme continues. Without immediate provocation, Jesus pronounces woes on the Galilean villages of Korazin, Bethsaida, and even Capernaum, in which many of his miracles have been performed. Here are people who have seen God's power, but they do nothing and just carry on in their own ways. The prophetic "Woe to . . ." points to the judgment they face. Jesus even compares them unfavorably with Tyre and Sidon in Syria. Turning the screw further, he compares Capernaum with Sodom, the great city of doom (Matt. 11:20–24). Ethnic self-congratulation is scythed away. Everywhere, always, for all racial groups, the issue is their repentance and relationship with God. Jesus doesn't speak against foreigners and praise his own people, the endemic attitude of tribes and nations everywhere. Instead, he speaks against his neighbors and for the foreigners. He knows exactly what he is doing. Jesus locates evil with *us* rather than *them*, the ethnic outsiders.

Again, Jesus warns about presuming identification with Abraham, Isaac, and Jacob. He is going through the towns and villages, teaching on his way to Jerusalem. Someone asks, "Lord, are only a few people going to be saved?" "Well," says Jesus, "look to yourselves. It's a narrow door, and there is a house owner not very different from myself. When the door closes, you can crowd around, pleading familiarity, but the judgment will be that you are evil. The house owner will say, 'I don't know you or where you have come from. Away from me, all you evildoers'" (cf. 13:22–27). Familiarity, being a New Yorker, a Londoner, an American, or an Arab counts for nothing. "You yourselves will be thrown out. People will come from east and west and north and south, and will take their places at the feast in the kingdom of God. Indeed, there are those who are last who will be first, and the first who will be last" (13:28–30). Against the domestic elite, Jesus commends the Good Samaritan for neighborliness and care, a wounding rebuke. These and other comments entirely explain Jesus' unpopularity. To run down your own nation, especially in its presumed area of superiority, its faith, does not invite a warm response. Why does Jesus do this? When we reflect on the worldwide problems of tribalism, racism, and nationalism, from genocide to a white policeman kicking a black person on the ground, perhaps we gather some inkling of how deeply we must disown our own to know the radical equality of all before God.

There is another level of Jesus' trans-nationalism. Although the Gospels make it clear he is king of the Jews, Jesus is far more arrogant than merely to seek this title. The difference in levels of consciousness heaves with irony, especially in one incident that occurs during Jesus' final time in Jerusalem. John records that earlier in Jesus' ministry "others asked, 'How can the Messiah come from Galilee? Does not the Scripture say that the Messiah will come from David's family and from Bethlehem, the town where David lived?' Thus the people were divided because of Jesus" (John 7:41–43). By now, probably, news has begun to leak out about his birthplace and lineage. Both the crowd swarming round Jesus on his entry into Jerusalem and the children in the Temple praise him as "the Son of David." At the time of Herod the Great, being a son of David has been deadly; now it is a massive potential asset. The obvious response for an aspiring king is to say, "I was born in Bethlehem, and I can trace my lineage back to David." But Jesus does none of this. Instead, he has the crowd agog. Quite deliberately, he trumps the significance of being a Son of David (Matt. 22:41–46; Mark 12:35–37; Luke 20:41–44). He asks, unprompted, how the teachers of the law can say that the Messiah is the *Son* of David. This questions unquestioned orthodoxy: of course, the Messiah is the Son of David. Isaiah's great prophecy is enough to establish that:

> [The] Prince of Peace . . . will reign on David's throne
> and over his kingdom,
> establishing and upholding it
> with justice and righteousness
> from that time on and for ever. (Isa. 9:6–7)

Why does Jesus kick against the whole fulfillment of biblical prophecy in himself? He sets up a conundrum. The nature of the challenge is to quote Psalm 110, where *David* acknowledges the lordship of the Messiah. "If David calls the Messiah 'Lord,' how can Messiah be his son?" The unanswerable question has the effect of raising the Messiah's status above that of David, the national king. The Son of God is not merely the Son of David. This is no mere question of a dynastic line, but of God's validation of Messiah beyond any national dynasty. Jesus, jokingly, pushes the issue beyond ethnic pedigree into one of the universal rule of God. The crowd bays and chortles at the logic, but something far deeper is going on. The king of the Jews is claiming a wider title and has in part been given it in Christendom down through the ages.[2]

No less astonishing is his attack on the Temple, worse than an Athenian attacking the Parthenon. On the one hand, he affirms it as God's house, the place of proper worship; but on the other hand, he predicts its destruction. The initial statement after Jesus first clears the Temple is ambiguous. In response to a demand for a sign, Jesus gives a messianic sign: "[You] destroy this temple, and I will raise it again in three days" (John 2:19). This was absurd. They would never think of destroying the Temple.[3] Everyone had watched with pride as each great block of stone, often bigger than a garage, was painfully moved, taking years of engineering. "We'll try to move it twelve cubits before lunch." The Temple's destruction was more unthinkable than that of the World Trade Center. To state it was to attack the national center of Jewish faith, treachery of the deepest kind. But the remark is deliberately unfocused, aiming to be misunderstood. Jesus even insists on the playing out of the double entendre: he speaks elliptically of the Temple as his own body. They hear the destruction of the Temple; he talks of his death (2:20–21). He is understood to be saying that he will destroy the Temple. It even comes up at his trial, with the high priest frenetic at this possible attack on the great cultic edifice. Jesus does not bother to rebut the charge. *For after all, he is replacing this great national focus with his own crucified body.* So far, he stands outside and deconstructs the nationalism of the ages. This is the full cost of being ruler of the nations, and he pays it.

But Jesus also displaces and deconstructs Temple worship. It is relativized in his talk with the Samaritan woman: "A time is coming when you will worship the Father neither on this mountain, nor in Jerusalem. . . . Yet a time is coming and has now come when the true worshippers will worship the Father in spirit and in truth" (John 4:21, 23). Later, as he leaves the Temple with the disciples and is asked to look back at its beautiful, glowing stones, Jesus prophesies that not one stone will be left on another; every one of them will be thrown down. This was almost literally fulfilled. In 70, the temple was razed, but some of the retaining wall for the Temple Mount remained; its western part is called the Wailing Wall. In substance, its fulfillment was fearfully met in the Romans' determination to destroy this central symbol of Jewish nationalism. At a deeper level, the Christian liberation from cultic Temple worship has allowed the worldwide spread of an open response of worship to God. Ironically, some Christians and many tourists reconstruct churches and cathedrals as cultic temples, against the great freedom of Jesus' good news, as though the God of the universe can only be greeted at a church door.

The key to seeing this deconstruction of ethnic identity occurs when some Greeks come to worship at Passover in Jerusalem, wanting to see Jesus. They contact Philip, from the more Greek area of Bethsaida-Julias in Galilee, who in turn comes to Jesus, announcing their presence. What the latter says in reply seems at first unconnected to its precedent: "The hour has come for the Son of Man to be glorified. I tell you the truth, unless a kernel of wheat falls into the ground and dies, it remains only a single seed. But if it dies, it produces many seeds. . . . But I, when I am lifted up from the earth, will draw all people to myself" (John 12:23–24, 33). How can his death be glory, and what is the link between the Greeks, this single seed dying, and the subsequent proliferation? Then it becomes clear. Jesus, prompted by the arrival of the Greeks, people outside Jewish culture and life, states the inner connection—the ethnic death, killed by his own national leaders, and the universal reconciliation across ethnic barriers. As a result, the early church, against all its own inclinations and cultural preoccupations, finds that Jesus draws people of every tribe and nation in the most astonishing cosmopolitanism of all history (cf. Rev. 5:9–10). The battle against ethnocentrism has already been fought, and the church becomes "the rainbow people of God."[4]

Again, the underlying logic is unerring and devastates our ways of thinking. There is a vicious bent of self-righteous national partisanship that has shaped human history. We have only to think of the thousand wars of nation and empire reflecting this deep ability to see ourselves as right and the other nation as wrong. It is burned into our national psyche by hatred, intellectual constructions, interpretations of history, previous conflicts, and required loyalties. The person who sees the depths of this problem and attacks it will be very lonely; he might even be killed for "the sake of the nation." But without him, the redemption of humankind is not possible. Here, in the systematic repudiation of all nationalisms, is also our salvation, if can we but see it: Jesus—gentle *world* ruler.

The Cost of Rule

There is a whole level of noncomprehension in our overall response to Jesus' rule. We think of rulers coming to power, of chosen leaders, and of power battles, but what does God think? Our focus is on rulers and their policies and solutions. But God sees the complex problems of human sin and evil that bedevil all political structures—control, greed, exploitation, racism, self-glory, manipulation, sheep-like populism—all of these problems are laid bare in the Scriptures and the teaching of Jesus. The problem is therefore always deeper than *who* is in control. There is a problem in the nature of rule, and the relationship between ruler and ruled. When we draw back and think, political rule is deeply problematic. Moses has to deal with a stiff-necked people. Historians look at countries locked in tragedies that take decades to unfold and be resolved because of the attitudes of the people. In recent times Yugoslavia, Rwanda, Ireland, and Afghanistan have been chronic examples. Each state and its rulers face their own intransigent populations, generating problem after problem. Modernist political analysis that sees rule just as a matter of who gets what, when, and how, have veneered the question of rule. When the surface cracks, deeper problems emerge, as they always have and as postmodern political theory is beginning to recognize.

These arise from the sins and injustices of the population generally. Rulers who focus on their own performance, but ignore what is happening in the lives and hearts of the populace, come and go like windblown foam. The deeper business of politics lies with the problems and injustices in the body politic. Shakespeare grapples with it in his great histories:

> We are all diseas'd;
> And, with our surfeiting, and wanton hours,
> Have brought ourselves into a burning fever,
> And we must bleed for it. (*Henry IV* 2.4.1)

By default or with intent, the ruler engages with these. In Britain, Blair has a load of problems, which mainly we are, though it has become rude in a democracy to point out that the demos are the problem. The United States' population is fat but believes it is in glowing health. Many problems in the body politic are beyond solution, cancerous, morbid, and sclerotic because people refuse to change. Nowhere is this issue seen more clearly than in the Gospels, where the ordinary greed, self-serving, hatred, love of money, and other sins in the lives of ordinary people are laid bare. As there, so everywhere. Many political leaders, after years of struggle and attempted reform, see how meager their efforts have been compared with the weight of direction coming from the body politic. We might observe the movement of the political tip of the iceberg, but really, the flow of its mass in the unseen currents is the reality. To change the analogy, most "leaders" are sliding on the slurry of their subjects' sins. Crime, fraud, exploitation, aggression, and greed come from people. We are the problem.

Jesus is the ruler who sees this ambiguity of rule, who dwells so fully with the people and their sinful problems that he plumbs the depths of the political problem. In chapter 12 we look at the route to the cross and see Jesus staying with the problem to the end, having already identified it fully. At the very time Jesus is recognized as Messiah by Peter and affirms his confession, he sets out the prospect—suffering, trial, execution, and resurrection—because of the sins of the people and the supposed rulers. Here is political rule that addresses people as they are and does not put an elitist or paternalist gloss on it. With our prejudices, self-interest, and conflicts, we yet are moved beyond our incomprehension to know that God is with us and for us in the heart of our human problem. Here is the ruler who carries the problems of his people and his people's sin. Even when the good ruler is being slaughtered, he is for us. Even when callous political hate mutilates his body, Jesus prays, "Father, forgive them, for they do not know what they are doing" (Luke 23:34). This kind of politics is different. Here, God buys the house riddled with dry-rot to lovingly restore it. Here, God marries the old discarded prostitute. Here, Pilate the vicious flogger is loved. Many rulers ask their subjects to die for them. Here, the ruler carries the subjects' failures to his own death. Here, the worst in politics is held in the love and grace of God. God does not just meet evil with good, but also with love for the evil ones. Here is redeeming politics.

Jesus is quite clear in facing it. Though the issue has been with him for a long time, in the garden of Gethsemane, Jesus finally is in anguish and sweating profusely. His words to the Father focus the issue: "[Dear] Father, if you are willing, take this cup from me; yet not my will, but yours be done" (Luke 22:42; cf. Matt. 26:42; Mark 14:36). This cup has nothing to do with the Last Supper or Communion; it is the chalice of death. It is even the poisoned cup which the king fears and has tested by his wine taster, but which Jesus here faces knowingly. The route to flee is easy, but it is unthinkable. In the will of God the Father, the evil is to be endured and carried alone. Finally, we know God is with us as we thrash in our sin.

Even at this point, God's love is on God's terms. It is not a shallow accommodation to evil or a limp acceptance of wrong. Nor does it allow people to negotiate with God. The response of faith and obedience is required. As Jesus is processed through court, we are judged, for the events are part of the common currency of humankind. Pilate would fare well in comparison with a hundred twentieth-century political leaders. Politics on God's terms is not just a casual option, but the unavoidable reality. "When the Son of Man comes in his glory, . . . all the nations will be gathered before him, and he will separate the people from one another as a shepherd separates the sheep from the goats" (Matt. 25:31–32). Even now, we really know that nothing less than this searching way will do. The current responses do not go deep enough. Beauty parade democracy does not address poverty, the arms trade, environmental destruction, family failure, or consumerism. Ordinary people are hard-hearted, enjoy hating, destroy families, exploit workers, create addiction, construct holy wars, make weapons, practice corruption, accumulate unearned wealth, and ignore their neighbors' needs. We are a far bigger problem to govern than we acknowledge. Westerners swallow self-deception like hamburgers. Politicians say, "You are wonderful people." But we are not. These responses evidence weak leadership; they are lies fed to mindless gumps.

By contrast, to stand before this ruler is to find the place of truth. By osmosis deep lessons slip into our history. This gentle rule, far from being weak, is actually strong. The one who turned down ownership of the kingdoms of this world sees the deep structure of rule. He binds nations together. He blesses the poor. He changes missiles into wheelchairs. He heals the brokenhearted and lifts the burdens from the harassed. Jesus silences the bigot. But the cost is unbearable. Who, knowing what they are, would/can govern this lot? Nobody else can really do the job. Ask leaders who have reached the point of thinking about the issue, and they will tell you that they cannot. The word *Savior* has been cheapened, mainly because we do not even see the problem. We brew poison, unknowing, on tap. Jesus drinks it, knowing. He is the ruler who carries the burdens of his people to his own death.

God's Gentle World Ruler

Here, then, for acceptance or rejection, is the gentle world ruler. This is not a worldwide superpower, because this man does not control. His program involves no military conquest or imposition; he comes as a man of peace and allows open voluntary responses. There is no bureaucracy and legalism. This rule takes place, or does not take place, in the hearts and lives of people everywhere.

But this ruler is no soft touch. He insists on his own terms of government. He deconstructs all the privileges of wealth, race, and nation. Being an American or a Jew counts for nothing; indeed, it is to be scorned.

Jesus insists that we move from ethnocentrism into true relationship with God and our neighbors. He is no local hero, but the ruler of the nations. He names injustice and hypocrisy. What he requires cannot be mollified into self-serving politics. Though we try to reshape the pot, it has been fired and is as hard as iron. Sooner or later, we will bow our knee to God's gentle ruler.

Yet the Christ is not only the ruler who governs, but also the one who carries his people. This is the most difficult of all to conceive. Popular democratic politics looks for the crowd-pleasing leader, the one who does what the people want. But Jesus has realized what is wrong with the people. They are a sorry lot, trapped in their own failures, but still he loves them. He is the Sovereign Lord who gathers the lambs in his arms and carries them close to his heart. He is the ruler on whom we lay our insoluble burdens. Jesus is so far beyond us that, as we follow the journey to Jerusalem, we will never really catch up.

Bibliography

Barth, Karl. *The Church and the Political Problem of Our Day*. London: Hodder & Stoughton, 1939.

Derbyshire, J. Denis, and Ian Derbyshire. *Political Systems of the World*. 2d ed. Oxford: Helicon, 1996.

Edersheim, Alfred. *The Temple: Its Ministry and Services As They Were at the Time of Jesus Christ*. London: Religious Tract Society, 1874.

Jeremias, Joachim. *Jesus' Promise to the Nations*. London: SCM, 1958.

O'Donovan, Oliver. *The Desire of the Nations: Rediscovering the Roots of Political Theology*. Cambridge: Cambridge University Press, 1996.

Tutu, Desmond. *The Rainbow People of God*. London: Bantam, 1995.

Watson, Alan. *Jesus and the Jews: The Pharisaic Tradition in John*. Athens, GA: University of Georgia Press, 1995.

Williams, Eleazer. *Good News to the Iroquois Nation: A Tract, on Man's Primitive Rectitude, His Fall, and His Recovery through Jesus Christ*. In the Iroquoian language. Burlington, VT: Samuel Mills, 1813.

Jesus and Taxation

Economic Background

This chapter is a slight detour from the main narrative. It addresses a particular issue, a part of politics that we can easily marginalize in our focus on Jesus. But this area, as many others, is a concern of Jesus; it features strongly in the Gospel texts. The Gospels do not give a systematic treatise on the subject. Yet it was one of the chief issues of Jesus' day and recurred directly in his life, teaching, and relationships.[1] Here, as a slight aside from the central narrative, we taste some of the subtlety and depth of the Master by bringing together events and teaching where taxation is involved.

In an earlier era, Herod the Great collected his own taxes and then paid a lump sum levy to Rome. It was not an exact process but depended on bullying and the maintenance of fear. Herod was generous to Rome and generated high income for himself, both at the expense of the taxpayers. The considerable costs of the rebuilt Temple, ostensibly from Herod's purse, were of course raised from tax revenue, as were the costs of his other fortresses and palaces. His taxes were heavy and a source of the Jews' frequent complaints to the Romans. The Herodian tax system was based on military dominance. These revenues were not coming back to the people as health, education, and welfare provision; instead, they were going to support the Roman Empire, military occupation, and Herod's private expenditure. Yet in another way they were an important part of the economy. After all, Jews would be employed as builders, servants, laborers, and skilled artisans by the Herodians and given the minimum wage of a denarius a day. Herodian towns like Sepphoris, Tiberias, and Caesarea would be part of this tax-funded establishment, partly separate from the native economy. It left normal people poor and would have seemed a much more oppressive and important part of life than tax does to us today. It made poverty fairly normal.

Taxes were taken in kind and by coin. We need to see the overall structure of the subsistence and exchange economies. "Transactions" could be carried out through exchange, obligation, or mutual giving. Many workers, for example, would be given food and be part of the household. Money would be needed for a limited range of transactions—more distant trading, paying hired workers, some market transactions, and taxation. There were four kinds of money in general circulation: Roman, Greek, Herodian, and Jewish. Different groups accepted different kinds. The Jewish coinage of shekels and lepta was not very significant either in trade or overall. At the time, they were not being struck, and therefore a limited stock was available. Judas received thirty silver coins, likely Tyrian shekels, about four months' pay (Matt. 26:15; 27:9) and the price of a slave (Exod. 21:32). Only Tyrian coins were acceptable at the Temple; hence, the need for money changers there.

Greek coins were universally traded and widely used by Jews. The Greek silver drachma was a day's pay, like the Roman denarius (Matt. 20:2, 9) and the lost coin in Jesus' parable (Luke 15:8–10). Four drachmas made a stater, and a hundred drachmas made a mina, about three months' salary. In another league was the Greek talent, about 0.75 million drachmas, or sixty times a mina, a vast amount, roughly what we would think of as a million pounds (wages for more than fifteen years of common labor). The gigantic amount in Matt. 18:24, ten billion pounds, is an important feature in Jesus' parable.

The Roman coinage consisted of the silver denarius, worth about the same as the drachma, and the aureus, a gold coin worth twenty-five denarii. Roman coinage really revolved round the taxation system, and the Jews did not like it very much. Coin was issued for work and goods the Romans bought and then required back as taxation, funding the structure of empire. Now you see it, now you don't. Jewish hatred of coins bearing the head of the emperor grew from both their flouting of the Second Commandment and the feeling of enslavement to Rome and the Herodians.

Tax revenue was either used locally or repatriated to Rome, a process that kept the economy permanently depressed. Herod the Great had received something like 5.4 million denarii a year. After his death in 4 BC, the split of tax-earning revenue was about 3.6 million to Archelaus, 1.2 million to Antipas, and 0.6 million to Philip. By the time of Agrippa in AD 41–44, the combined revenue to the kingdom had gone up to 12 million denarii. This reflected a general pattern of population growth and economic improvement throughout Jesus' life, especially in Galilee. Agricultural improvement and the absence of serious war probably allowed the betterment. But this made the taxation only slightly less oppressive.

Roman and Jewish Tax

Changes occur in the taxation system after the death of Herod the Great; it then becomes a tripartite system for Judea, Galilee, and Philip's territory. The Romans exercise direct control in Judea after Archelaus is removed. Their own direct tribute or taxation demands are higher, but they have removed the Herodian level of expenditure. The development of Caesarea as a Roman center away from Jerusalem comes out of this expenditure. Who collects these taxes is an interesting issue. Goodman suggests that the Sanhedrin collect Roman taxes, but that would seem to compromise their Jewish identity and popularity too much, and hence is probably not the case.[2] The Sanhedrin could too easily siphon away some of the taxes, too. Probably the Romans are retaining overall control but operate either through Jewish publicans (tax collectors) or a more direct administrative system, backed if necessary by Samaritan soldiers.[3]

Moreover, because taxes are so unpopular, it is more sensible to administer them from places like Caesarea or Jericho. Perhaps Zacchaeus is close to the center of the national system, administering Jerusalem's tax from Jericho. This fits the notoriety of the Jerusalem–Jericho road for robbery and may explain why Zacchaeus lives on the Jerusalem road out of Jericho, near the revamped Herodian Winter Palace complex.[4] Collection takes place with occasional intimidation, perhaps through the threat of the sword or burning people's homes.[5] Samaria is under the same regime, but because many of the enforcing soldiers are Sebastenes, less hostility is generated. Taxation resentment may well be behind some Judean hostility to the Samaritans.[6] This direct system of Roman taxation probably lasts until Agrippa I becomes king of Judea, Galilee, Perea, and Idumea (AD 41–44), when he reclaims collection.[7]

In Galilee, Perea, and Gaulanitis, the taxation system probably remains controlled by the Herods. Matthew would be employed by Herod Antipas as a tax collector, not directly by the Romans. The money and crops are gathered into Tiberias, Sepphoris, and the other Herodian cities, from which the required tribute is passed on to Rome. Most people are poor because they pay a bundle of taxes to the Romans and Herodians; it is one of the basic conditions of life. Taxes are not a matter of ethical debate; of course they are wrong, but the people can do nothing to change them. They are normal. Tax collectors and soldiers move in and require payment. Resistance to taxation is an act of insubordination, bringing rapid reprisals like house-burning from soldiers; its possibility hovers in the Galilean consciousness for decades.[8] The total Roman-Herodian tax take is probably 20 percent or more. (This level does not seem too high on our current incomes, partly because a lot of it is returned to us as benefits. But at subsistence levels without benefits, it is very heavy.)[9] Because Galilee is quite a fertile area, the population is not pushed to the edge by all these demands. In AD 17 Judea and Syria complain to Rome about their burden, but not Antipas's territories. They put up with it, but they are poor.[10]

In both Galilee and Judea during this period, Jewish taxation has emerged as a rival to the Herodian-Roman system. With the building of Herod's Temple and the establishment of a new Temple elite, the High-Priestly families, the Jews are able to grow their own indigenous tax system. It is technically voluntary since it is not enforced by soldiers, but it involves strong socio-religious pressure. It is a growth industry, reflecting the immense success of the Temple as a cultic place of worship. At the same time, the Pharisees also try to establish a system of income. It seems first to involve encouraging tithing. The Pharisees tithe herbs as an example to their peers, who probably find some of their tithing a burden but are taught that it is part of righteous living. They also claim levies around the principle of Corban, a gift devoted to God, to establish their own economic well-being.[11] This is partly in competition with the Temple tax. Both groups rely on national sentiment to keep the money rolling in. Broadly speaking, the Jewish taxation system is growing in clout and effectiveness during the period, and the people of course view it more positively than the hated Roman tribute and Herodian taxes. Thus, during Jesus' life there are competing tax demands from Jewish and Herodian-Roman sources. The load is a real burden.

Taxation would substantially structure class relationships. Those with direct or indirect access to taxes (or pressured offerings)—the Herodians, Romans, and tax collectors on the one hand; and the priestly group, Pharisees, and Sadducees on the other—are rich or relatively well-off. The rest get by as fishermen, builders, shepherds, or hired workers. There are also some traditionally rich landowners and traders, but in large measure the class divisions exist around these transfers by taxation. Movement of money is largely from the poor to the rich, exacerbating existing patterns of poverty and wealth. We can see these divisions represented in the Gospels. Nevertheless, they can be seen in terms too absolute. Many of the Jewish tax collectors may be quite poor, eking out a living above what they pass on to the Romans. The centurion in Capernaum is rich but generous to the Jewish people (Luke 7:4–5). Jesus has some contact with a Herodian household, at Sepphoris or Tiberias (Luke 8:3). The overall impression is that although these groups are partly distinct in power, wealth, and ideology, substantial contact is present, with some intermingling class dynamics as displayed in the Gospels. Jesus does not have a class location that angles his message, as some commentators have tried to argue.[12] Indeed, we see overwhelming evidence of his amazing ability to cross and deconstruct these class and status divisions.

The Different Taxes

The taxes have a number of different forms:

- The land tax, the *tributum soli, arnona,* or tribute of the soil, was collected from the landowners by traveling tax collectors backed by soldiers who may carry out their own extortion (Luke 3:14). The landowners are rich, and it is easy to collect from them. Tenants pay in kind or through their rent. If payment is not made, dwellings could be torched or other reprisals taken. The land tax amounts to a quarter of the crop and animals every two years—12.5 percent of the annual crop except in the Sabbatical Year, when the land was fallow.[13] If there is an insurrection or trouble, it is also claimed in the seventh year. This tax is therefore in kind and directly taken into Antipas's storehouses in Sepphoris or wherever. It falls more heavily on the rural than the urban population.
- The tribute, poll, or head tax is based upon a census and is a specifically Roman institution. The census at Jesus' birth shows the development of this form. "In those days Caesar Augustus issued a decree that a census should be taken of the entire Roman world. (This was the first census that took place while Quirinius was governor of Syria) [a problematic identification because he seems to have been procurator later]. And everyone went to his own town to register" (Luke 2:1–3). People are named and located, and the head tax is required of them. Tax collectors take their own cut and know who the locals are. To escape from the head tax is to be a marked person, on the run.
- Levies are taken at crossroads, on property, on salt, on sales, and on income. Once a tax is declared as legitimate, it is sold to a tax collector, who exacts whatever he can from the locals under that dispensation. Off-road traveling became a way of dodging these

levies. Clearly, there is often local wrangling and much ill feeling at these rather arbitrary demands.

- The Temple tax, a levy throughout Israel and beyond, is collected by the priesthood and channeled back to the temple elite at Jerusalem (Matt. 17:24). It is a half-shekel or two-drachma annual tax, more willingly paid because it does not go to either the Herodians or the Romans. It has often been taken up communally when Jews from villages go up to the festivals, when contributions are voluntary. Money changers are needed because the Temple accepts only Tyrian coins to ensure a reliable silver content. More recently, it can be collected locally by agents of the Temple hierarchy. The amount is not inconsiderable. A few years after Jesus' crucifixion, Pilate commandeers the sacred treasure of the Temple sacrifices and uses it to construct an aqueduct 23–50 miles long to bring water into Jerusalem. The Jews protest and are clubbed down in a vicious attack.[14] Miles of aqueduct constructed of stone do not come cheap.

- Corban and the tithe are the remnant of the Old Testament legal provision. The Temple party and the Pharisees are trying to resurrect it as a way of funding themselves, as a provision that goes more to meeting their own needs than fulfilling its original purpose of providing for the poor.

Perhaps we have to revise our view of Jewish taxation, though our information is poor. If something between 2.5 and 3 million Jews worldwide are paying the two-drachma Temple tax,[15] the revenue is about half the amount the Romans raise.[16] When we take into account the substantial gifts to the Temple treasury and other religious levies, the total Temple income is likely to be three-quarters or more of Roman-Herodian taxes. This is surprising. If in addition we add the funds raised by the not inconsiderable number of Pharisees, we see the size of Jewish taxation. It weighs almost as heavily on the population as the Roman-Herodian system, contributing to an overall levy of 40 percent or more on relatively poor people.[17] In a largely subsistence economy, such taxation dominates money transactions. With this background, we see the extraordinary development of Jesus' position in relation to the range of taxing groups and the taxes themselves. This begins with the cleansing of the Temple.

Cleansing the Temple

The Passover is the greatest Jewish feast, and thousands come to the Temple on the understanding that they can bring gifts and make sacrifices in order to receive a blessing. To sacrifice is to be right with God. It is bonanza time for the treasury, surrounded by religious pressure and superstition. There are thirteen treasury boxes in the Women's Court of the Temple, and the money changers and those offering sacrificial animals gather in the Court of the Gentiles. To give is to have god's favor, and the more one gives, the greater the favor (but cf. Luke 21:1–4). In this respect, Herod's Temple is closer to Greek temples in meaning than to the Jewish Holy of Holies. This is a great moneymaking business, which gives the high-priestly class its wealth and status. Foreigners and natives pay large sums in several ways. First, visitors change their money into whatever is required to be put into the treasury. The didrachmon (two-drachma piece) is the annual Temple tax, but there likely are required coins or Temple tokens. Schürer indicates that Tyrian high-quality silver coins are required. They can be changed at a premium, brought back from the treasury, and recycled to tomorrow's visitors. The poor widow's mite is two lepta, Jewish coins (Luke 21:2). The money changers mark up heavily, especially to foreigners. Gentiles cannot go into the treasury area, and perhaps their money is put in for them, or at least some of it.

Sacrificial animals brought into Jerusalem every day are sold at exorbitant prices. Mary and Joseph's two pigeons or doves thirty years before were bottom of the range but still expensive (Lev. 12:8; Luke 2:24). Sheep and cattle are for the very rich, and the sellers are either franchised by the Temple priests or directly controlled by them. Then money set aside for God is poured into the treasury coffers. The rich put in large amounts (Mark 12:41–44). This is a magnificent moneymaking Jewish system.

John records Jesus' controlled and authoritative intervention—overturning tables, scattering money, and reasserting the Temple as his Father's house. Animals flee the Temple area with their owners trying to regain control. We can hear the intensity of the moment and the glorious pandemonium of animals. Somewhat surprising is the response to this outrage, for the Jews seem partly to acknowledge the correctness of his position. The sacred Temple has been encroached by this noisy commercialism. They ask for a sign to validate Jesus' authority, but they seem sheepishly to recognize how the worship of God is being used to extort money. Jesus' incomprehensible and enigmatic answer leaves the event hanging. "Destroy this temple, and I will raise it again in three days" (John 2:19). "Destroying the temple is the last thing we would do," they mutter. "What is he talking about? It's taken forty-six years to build thus far, and he talks of rebuilding it in three days! Is he mad?" (cf. 2:20). But the weight of the attack stays. Jesus retains moral authority over the Temple area after the event and throughout his three years of ministry. Moneymaking in the name of God is suspect and dishonest, as is the Temple party who exploits it. This system dishonors God, and uneasily people know this is the case.

Matthew, the Tax Collector

Somewhat later Jesus calls Levi the son of Alphaeus (Matthew, as later called; Matt. 3:9) from his tax collector's booth (Mark 2:13–17). Levi follows Jesus and therefore deserts his tax business, probably a customs levy on the international road from Damascus, where it passes at the top of Capernaum. We can almost identify the spot where he set up shop. Jesus then goes to Levi's house and eats with him and his friends. Already the effect of this is complex. A defector from the hated Herodian system would immediately raise interest and hopes. It arouses great public support. But to eat and chat with the whole ostracized group of tax collectors whom Levi knows is to go beyond the pale, to mix with those whom the "righteous" deplore. Jesus counters firmly, deconstructing this self-righteousness and identifying with the tax collectors and sinners. "If you want me, this is where I shall be," he says in effect. "It is not the healthy who need a doctor, but the sick. I have not come to call the righteous, but sinners" (Mark 2:17).

Matthew, not surprisingly, remembers the event more fully in his own Gospel, including Jesus' words: "But go and learn what this means: 'I desire mercy, not sacrifice'" (9:13). With God's mercy, Matthew and the other tax collectors are able to respond to the God of love and escape from their role. Matthew and his friends already know that tax collecting is extortionate. He has no problem recognizing the sin. He is branded. But Jesus, on God's behalf, extends unconditional mercy. Matthew receives it, holds a party, and becomes one of the twelve apostles (Matt. 10:3). So, already, we have ambiguity. The Jesus who attacks the tax system also mixes with the tax collectors.

The Good Samaritan and Health Provision

So much has the West absorbed of Christian culture that it often cannot see its dependence on Christian principles. Modern taxes, for example, are often *for* us. They fund health, education, welfare services, and other compassionate provisions. To those who have lived with colonial extortion and self-serving state taxes, this kind of focus for taxation is a revolution. Yet this is the revolution that we in the West have been through, to some extent. The parable of the Good Samaritan is a paradigm for the meaning of taxation (Luke 10:25–37). Jesus tells of a man robbed and left dying on the Jerusalem–Jericho road. Three people come by: a priest, a Levite, and a Samaritan. The first two are from the taxing classes, but they do not care. The Samaritan cares for the victim, takes him to an inn, and funds his recovery. "Who acts as neighbor to the mugged man?" Jesus asks in an unavoidable way. When the answer comes, he says, "Go and do likewise." It remains our inescapable duty.

Taxation can be an expression of the nation's system of care and neighborly love. Through taxes, we are true neighbors to our neighbors. Here Jesus, in speaking with the expert in the law, lays out the motive that can drive a positive view of taxation. It can be an expression of love, not just a process of state imposition. Now, through our choice of governments, paying taxes is largely a democratic voluntary act. In 2001, the British electorate voted parties proposing higher taxation; previously they had done the opposite. Jesus' appeal in the parable of the Good Samaritan is to obey God's command to love our neighbor as ourselves: "Go and do likewise" establishes the principle of providing for the sick and injured, meeting their needs.

This parable has been a signpost down through history. The Benedictines and other caring orders, the early provision of charitable hospitals, monastic infirmaries, care of lepers and the insane, medical schools, midwifery, the nursing profession, and other areas—all of these are Christianly shaped. In London, medieval Christian hospital foundations like St. Thomas's and St. Bart's shaped sickness provisions. During the eighteenth century foundations motivated by the evangelical awakening sprang up. Westminster Hospital was explicitly founded on the teaching of the parable of the Good Samaritan. Thomas Guy of Guy's was a devout Baptist, and the London Hospital was similarly inspired. Charitable provision generated more than one new hospital or dispensary a year between 1700 and 1825.[18] Nursing, associated with Florence Nightingale and Edith Cavell, had strong Christian inspiration. The Christian Medical Movement went with and as missionaries to plant embryonic hospitals worldwide.

This welfare movement has shaped Western medical culture and been incorporated into the normal taxation processes of Britain and other countries. Even where health provision is done through individual insurance, other forms of welfare and communal provision provide the main meaning of the taxation system. This great parable acts as a signpost for societal organization. Indeed, it could be said that a nation is defined as a unit where a decent level of neighborly care is reflected in the political structures.[19] Here, therefore, is a positive communal sense of provision through taxation.[20]

The Temple Tax

While in Galilee, Jesus responds to the Temple tax. The Galileans face heavy Herodian taxation. Now they are asked to pay the Temple tax—half a week's wages (Matt. 17:24–27). The Temple rulers are intent on expanding their power and sweep out into Galilee, picking up those who can contribute more revenue, for God is worshiped in the Temple, and every Jew should contribute. As agents of the High Priest, the collectors of the tax come to Capernaum. They have to establish the validity of this collected tax for all, and they know that the key to this is whether Jesus will pay. Everyone knows where he is.

It is an amazing scene. Jesus sits back in a small courtyard and changes the taxation systems of the world without lifting a finger. We know what happens down to the last nuance. They are in Peter's house, yards from the docile edge of the lake, close to the center of the village. This is on the east side of the synagogue, in a tightly packed, slightly fishy spot. The house incorporates two courtyards, built of dry stone walls probably above head height. Already heralded, the collectors arrive at the entrance away from the lake and ask for Peter, who goes out to meet them in the small north yard. They will not come into the house to collect taxes (cf. Deut. 24:10–11). But this is not a private meeting. They know Jesus is there, probably because the courtyard is filled with talking and listening people. When they announce themselves, the talking quiets as the people gather to Jesus to hear the drama. The question comes with an edge. These tax collectors are intruding on a relaxed gathering, and also, as the collectors suspect, there is the clash of two worldviews. "Doesn't your teacher pay the temple tax?" (Matt. 17:24). They are out to collect Jesus' tax in Peter's house. Will Jesus pay?

The Temple tax is collected from each adult male. These are insistent and rich people, expanding their domain throughout Galilee, and the tax is an imposition on poor people. But God is worshiped in the Temple. How will Peter respond to the collectors' pressure? He blusters: "Jesus will pay." On the other side of the wall, there is now silence. Jesus hears Peter's predicament, and the echo of Jesus' words "One greater than the temple is here" (Matt. 12:6) flits through several minds. As Peter comes in to collect the money, Jesus pre-empts the situation and speaks immediately to Peter in front of him, with the guests gathered round and the tax collectors over his right shoulder on the other side of the wall. "What do you think, Simon?" pulls Peter out of his predicament into Jesus' question. "From whom do *the kings of the earth* collect taxes—from their own sons or from [others]?" (17:25). Everyone can hear where this is leading. Peter gives the programmed answer, "From others." But already the implications of the carefully phrased question roll out like a red carpet. This is a statement not about *the kings of the earth,* but the greater statement about God. "Then the sons are exempt." The kings' sons never pay taxes. Of course they don't.

The soundless bomb bursts. The sons and daughters of God are beholden to no one to pay taxes. Jesus sits there with folded hands and boots out worldwide oppressive taxation—empires, the feudal system, and this draining system of Jerusalem religious power. Already Herod Antipas is trying to kill Jesus, and after this, the Jerusalem powers will plot for the same. To rebel against the Temple tax is to institute civil war. The sweet knowledge that God does not operate with the servile slavery of taxation mixes with panic. The enormity of the truth sinks in. We live freely before God and are not pawns dominated by the taxes of the powerful.

Into the silence of people's thoughts, Jesus speaks more words: "But so that we may not offend them . . ." They listen on the other side of the wall. Is this Jesus climbing down, making a U-turn? Are these words a good principle, but really, back to business as usual? No. Jesus carries on with absurd instructions for Peter to fish for the four-drachma coin. Suddenly everyone bursts into talking and laughter and pours out round the corner down to the waterfront near the slight promontory. They stand around joking about Peter not being able to catch a fish, *half* expecting another miracle. Jesus does not even bother to go out of the house the short distance to the waterside. "Go to the lake," he says, and waits. The tax collectors and the small crowd gather.

Peter, defending his reputation (4:18), is not long in catching a fish with hook and line, just beyond his own backyard. It comes in. Normally, fish are just thrown on a heap, but this one is grasped on the line, probably by one of the crowd, and its mouth pried open. *The coin is there in its gaping mouth!* There are cheers, claps, and laughter as the precise coin is handed to Peter, who then formally passes it on to the Temple tax collectors, paying Jesus' and his own tax. The air is electric. "God is with us. God has provided his own tax!" The Temple and its tax are dismissed, and the truth is out. The God who does not exact taxes has provided the money for this one. God's money for God's house—what could be fairer than that! It is not the automatic condition of humankind to be taxed by tyrants. The tax collectors move off; they have probably had enough for one day. The sons and daughters of God are free. When you bow the knee to God, you bow it to no one else.

As the crowd files back noisily into the stone-walled courtyard, killing themselves with laughter and slapping their thighs at the stupendous event, they look at Jesus, smiling at them, bringing them face to face again with God. They bathe in the reality of living as children of the Father. They recall with awe the miracle and fight for time to absorb all this. The ripples have traveled a long way before they reach us. We live after feudalism has lost out to the steady God-fearing rise of the peasants. The proud empires leeching subdued populations have gone. The work-and-financial servitude of State Socialism has come and largely passed. Ceauşescu with his great palace and Emelda Marcos with her hundreds of shoes have faded away. Still there are petty tyrants out to subdue and milk the people. But the word of the Lord remains. In this year of grace of our Lord, we live with the principle of taxation and church giving as our contribution to the commonwealth, not as the automatic imposition of tyrants on a servile population.

The Tax System and Forgiveness

Although the meaning of the parable of the Unmerciful Servant (Matt. 18:21–35) is abundantly clear, its vividness comes from its focus on taxation. Jesus talks about a king who wishes to settle accounts with his servants, and a man who owes ten thousand talents is brought to him. Commentators discuss this figure as exaggeration or error,[21] but its contemporary referent would of course be the chief tax collector's take, effectively for the whole realm, even for the Roman Empire. Josephus mentions a figure of eight thousand talents as the total tax take for Syria, Phoenicia, Judea, and Samaria.[22] In our terms, this is the chancellor of the Exchequer calling in the head of Inland Revenue to pay up billions of pounds, and the latter, the chief tax collector, cannot pay because he has been appropriating funds for himself. As Jesus paints the Roman Empire's operation, Peter and the other people are spellbound. This is one hell of a crisis, unbelievable. The king's servant has bungled the tax system of the whole Roman Empire. The man faces enslavement of his whole family, but the surprise is that he is not instantly killed.

Yet the man begs for time to pay. He is on his knees before the emperor. He cannot pay, and the only question is what will finally happen to him. Even here Peter and the other listeners would be agog. The possibility that this tax collector would mount a massive bout of tax collection throughout the empire flits through their minds. They can see the next move. But Jesus is playing with them. The king "took pity on him, canceled the debt, and let him go" (18:27). Jesus whips the carpet from under their feet as they think, "What! You can't do this.

You can't just cancel a debt of ten billion pounds! Don't be crazy. That's preposterous!" "Who's telling this story, you or me?" he implies. Behind the words, they hear the Roman Empire wobbling and maybe echoes of the generosity of God.

While they are still struggling with this, the story takes off again with the cruel reaction of the king's servant. The man who has been treated so exorbitantly generously turns out to be mean. He goes out and beats up a man who owes him a relatively small amount. This is the normal savage world of tax collecting and extortion, but against the background of this astounding generosity, it is severe beyond belief. He is called to account and punished, and the dire warning is issued: "This is how my heavenly Father will treat each of you unless you forgive your brother from your heart" (Matt. 18:35).

The message is relentlessly clear, to Peter and all of us. We who have been greatly forgiven should forgive seventy times seven. We are always in debt to God. The Scottish version of the Lord's Prayer reverberates: "Forgive us our debts, as we forgive our debtors." The parable rocks the system. This king is one who is prepared to wipe out the entire Roman burden of taxation. The forgiveness from God turns out to be bigger than the whole Roman tax burden. Nobody can be in any doubt where this is leading. Here is a lump of Gruyère cheese where the hole is bigger than the lump. No cheese. No taxation. What a Kingdom!

Zacchaeus

Then we come to Zacchaeus (Luke 19:1–10). The journey to Jerusalem leads through Jericho, the "City of Palms." It has fortified walls, an amphitheater, a palace and gardens, and is now dominated by the Romans, who enjoy it away from the intensity of Jerusalem. Jesus passing through the city is an odd public event, his national stature pulling out the crowds and perhaps some curious Romans. By this stage he has a reputation for converting tax collectors. Zacchaeus is a chief of tax collectors. We know he is seriously wealthy. He may be collecting from the rich balsam plantations or organizing the collection of the national poll tax and land tax for the Romans in Jerusalem and Judea. Jericho is an obvious safe holding place for these accretions of money from Jerusalem, once the road between them is negotiated. Zacchaeus is hated but secure in this location.

He runs ahead and climbs the easy-branching sycamore-fig, because he is short and the crowds will obscure his sight if he stays on the ground. Jesus comes along with the noisy throng, who are praising God after blind Bartimaeus is given his sight (18:35–43). Suddenly in the euphoria, Jesus looks up and calls Zacchaeus. His name means "the just," "the pure," and seems a mockery.[23] Everybody knows this man. He is notorious. This is a far bigger social gap than the calling of Matthew.

But Jesus' approach is to welcome him, to cross the hostile barrier and request hospitality of Zacchaeus. The whole company, including quite a few gate-crashers, move into Zacchaeus's property, and it becomes a public place. His house is lavish, with a courtyard, palms, water, and bathing. Zacchaeus, thus asked to give rather than get, welcomes Jesus. But suddenly the crowd lurches from praise to hostility and grumbling that Jesus can consort with this pariah figure in his lush villa. Their erstwhile hero is now consorting with the enemy. They hang around, chafing but still enthralled by Jesus.

Inside, the spiritual revolution takes place. Zacchaeus knows, or comes to know, Jesus' normative position, reflecting the Mosaic law of recompense. Either as Jesus sits as guest with him, or outside in front of the crowd, Zacchaeus says, "Look, Lord! Here and now I give half of my possessions to the poor, and if I have cheated anybody out of anything, I will pay back four times the amount" (19:8). This is astonishing change for Zacchaeus, involving huge sums of money and heavy claims, and reflecting the Mosaic law on stolen sheep or cattle (Exod. 22:1). It is also dangerous because it undermines the whole Roman system. The crowd goes ecstatic. This move reinstates the Mosaic pattern of just interpersonal relationships and reduces the status of Roman tax collection to theft. It leaves the Roman system in free fall, and as we note in the next chapter, Jesus has to act quickly to prevent uprising and bloodshed.

The Second Cleansing of the Temple

Many commentators link the early cleansing of the Temple in John 2 with the later event recorded in the Synoptics (Matt. 21:12–22; Mark 11:15–25; Luke 19:45–48). Yet they are different in many respects. First is the incident of Jesus cursing the fig tree, which then withers. This is a gratuitous act, having nothing to do with the tree. It really is a reflection on the incident in the Temple courtyard, which follows in Mark but precedes in Matthew. The tree bears no fruit and must die. The Temple system bears no fruit and must die. It sucks in and is parasitic, a den of robbers. Further, the tone is different with this incident. The earlier one, with a whip of cords for driving out animals, was a rout. But the second one is an occupation, clearly the beginning of an extensive time of teaching in the Temple area. There is the same upending of the tables, leaving the moneylenders scrabbling for their money on the floor. If you love money like this, it puts you at a disadvantage. This time Jesus quotes Isaiah 56:7, with its focus on the inclusiveness for eunuchs and foreigners. He deliberately heals the blind and the lame in the Temple (Matt. 21:14). Children come into the Temple area and dance around, praising God, and Jesus settles down to do some teaching.

It is a beautiful transformation from exclusion to welcome. Those with physical deformities were normally not allowed to go into the central Temple court, but Jesus here makes them good and well. Children, who are normally ignored and excluded, come praising God and shouting, "Hosanna to the Son of David" (Matt. 21:9). Suddenly money is banished and all are welcome in the Temple of God. Lest the point is not clear, as Jesus teaches them, he says, "Is it not written, 'My house will be called a house of prayer for all nations'?" (Mark 11:17; Isa. 56:7). Rather than being the Jewish ethnic cult place, it is purged of taxation and exclusion and becomes the place where all may meet God. What has been a place of sharp practice becomes one where the praise of children sounds to God. The chief priests and teachers of the law are livid. They know they have to kill this man.

God and Caesar

The next day, the Pharisees and the Herodians set out to trap Jesus on the question of Roman taxes (Matt. 22:15–22; Mark 12:13–17; Luke 20:20–26). During the time of Herod the Great, these two groups were opponents, not allies, but now the Pharisees have become establishment enough to line up with the Herodians. All Jesus' enemies are now gathering, and the ploy is to deliver him to Pilate to be killed. They know that Jesus recognizes Roman taxation as unjust, as does every Jew. It is not even an issue. After all, the news about Zacchaeus has just zapped through Jerusalem. They set about making Jesus say so, and then he can be eliminated. The question comes, clothed in flattery and requiring the answer they want: "Is it right to pay taxes to Caesar or not?" (Matt. 22:17). It is a good question. If Jesus replies "Yes," he loses all credibility with the people; if "No," he is clapped in prison immediately.

Jesus first opens up the hypocrisy of their question: "Why are you trying to trap me?" (Matt. 22:18). This is not particularly insightful; everybody knows what is going on. Then he responds and, naturally, his words reflect the trap: "Show me the coin used for paying the tax" (22:19). They bring him a denarius. Already they are compromised, because coins bearing images of Caesar should not be brought into the Temple area, though they are probably piled up by money changers each day. The next questions seem daft: "Whose portrait is this? And whose inscription?" (22:20). Everybody knows that it is Tiberius Caesar. Jesus is not asking for information but is feigning ignorance and indifference. He probably does not even take the rather small coin, but leaves it sitting in the palm of the man who has brought it. The inscription everybody would know is "Tiberius Caesar Augustus, son of the divine Augustus." This is Caesar's claim of divinity and an insult to Jews, especially in the Temple area. But Jesus requires an answer to his question "Whose?" They reply "Caesar's" as though they are giving Jesus information he does not possess. Then comes the great verbal coup: "Give to Caesar what is Caesar's, and to God what is God's" (22:21).

It is like a game of chess, the small sacrifice and then the mate. The small coin goes to Caesar, but every Jew would have to acknowledge that since everything belongs to God (e.g., Ps. 24:1), everything else goes to God. Technically, the Herodians and Pharisees cannot charge him. This is game, set, and match to God, with Caesar eliminated. Or to retain the earlier metaphor, Jesus takes the Roman emperor with a pawn. Here something magnificent has happened. In the middle of the Roman Empire's oppressive taxation system, Jesus requires that all issues of tax be laid before God and God's requirements of justice and help for the poor.

This great denouement has reverberations. Heavy taxation arising from the opulence of the political leaders, overlords, or colonial powers has dominated much of history, including even the twentieth century. Jesus' statement puts this extortion in sharp relief and requires a review of taxation that we in part now carry out and still need to. The prior question is what God requires. All the priorities of the Mosaic law reverberate. Do taxes serve the people, especially the poor, or do they line the pockets of elites? Care of the poor, widows, neighbors, and aliens is what God requires. On this hinge our whole perspective on taxation swings. It is no longer about ruling powers and their petty demands, but about the sweeping requirements of God (cf. Rom. 13:7–10).

It is sad that some people and latter-day representatives of Caesar are too literalistic to hear what is going on. They claim that this text is some kind of quid pro quo, as if Jesus is saying, "Caesar should get his bit, and God should get his. That's fair, isn't it?" It is as though Jesus is proclaiming a balanced dualism. Are we so thick? The crowd at least sees the point. "When they heard this, they were amazed" (Matt 22:22).

The Widow's Mite

Finally, there is the incident that economists really love. Jesus and the disciples watch a poor widow put two small coins (lepta), a sixty-fourth of a denarius, into the Temple treasury (Luke 21:1–4). Jesus counts the value of this money in relation to her income. Her offering, given out of poverty, is great. Others who are rich give a very small proportion of their wealth. Implicit here is the analysis of regressive and progressive taxation, defined in terms of the proportion of income going for tax. We can almost hear, "from each according to his ability, to each according to their need," a view of taxes where needs and resources are weighed (cf. Matt. 25:15; Acts 2:45; 4:34–35). A progressive tax is where the richer give a higher proportion of their income because they can afford it and have a lot left over. Often today the rich have found political ways of making sure that their level of taxation is low. Astonishingly, for many years now the richest fifth of the British population have been paying a smaller proportion of their income in taxes than the poorest fifth.[24] In technical terms, it is regressive. Jesus sees beyond absolute levels of giving and honors the poor widow. Our own tax patterns still do not incorporate this insight.

The Deeper Commentary

Jesus presents a critique of the meaning of taxation deeper in scope than his contemporaries can possibly understand. They merely groan at the impositions of Rome and the Herods. They support or mistrust the Temple and Pharisaic levies, but they do not see the whole system in relation to God. Jesus moves his disciples into the freedom of living as sons of God. Tax is given by consent, not as a sign of bondage. Through parables of God's rule and forgiveness (spoken *and* acted), Jesus deconstructs the Roman tax collection system, whether at the level of paying taxes to Caesar or by the redemption of Zacchaeus and other tax collectors. He shows the self-serving falseness of the Temple system of taxation and accumulation. Jesus relativizes money values and brings everything into relation to God and the question of how we serve and care for one another.

It has taken something like two thousand years for these principles to seep into government and taxation policy, but there is no historical inevitability about this process. Even now, these principles are often unfulfilled or partly unraveling. Still state militarism and conquest dominate budgets. Still elites construct their own gravy trains and tax payoffs. Even now, individualism is moving the West away from mutual provision and care into selfishness and distrust, and we are losing a humane society to isolation and predation. We generate tax expenditure that manages problems rather than addressing neighbor needs. Like the people of Jesus' day, we see the scene but do not really perceive what loving God with all our hearts and our neighbors as ourselves actually means for taxation. So we still count taxes as a burden rather than as an expression of love.

Bibliography

Bauckham, Richard. "Taxing Questions: Jesus on Taxation." Pages 73–84 in *The Bible in Politics*. London: SPCK, 1989.

Carter, Warren. "Paying the Tax to Rome as Subversive Praxis: Matthew 17:24–27." *Journal for the Study of the New Testament*, no. 76 (December 1999): 3–31.

Fiensy, David. "Leaders of Mass Movements and the Leader of the Jesus Movement." *Journal for the Study of the New Testament*, no. 74 (June 1999): 3–27.

Goodman, Martin. *The Ruling Class of Judaea*. Cambridge: Cambridge University Press, 1987.

Grant, F. C. *The Economic Background of the Gospels*. London: Oxford University Press, 1926. Repr., New York: Russell & Russell, 1973.

Hagner, Donald A. *Matthew*. 2 vols. Word Biblical Commentary. Dallas: Word, 1993–95.

Hoehner, Harold W. *Herod Antipas*. Grand Rapids: Zondervan, 1980.

Malina, Bruce J., and Richard L. Rohrbaugh. *Social Science Commentary on the Synoptic Gospels*. Minneapolis: Fortress, 1992.

Stauffer, Ethelbert. *Christ and the Caesars*. Translated by K. Smith and R. Gregor Smith. London: SCM, 1955. Esp. 112–37.

Thiessen, Gerd. *Sociology of Early Palestinian Christianity*. Philadelphia: Fortress, 1978. Esp. 42–45.

The Journey to Jerusalem

It Doesn't Make Sense

Any politician or political commentator reading the account of Jesus' journey to Jerusalem will be deeply worried. It does not make sense. True, in the north, Herod Antipas is in control, and he would be quite happy to arrest and probably kill Jesus. He has a working alliance with the growing Pharisee group, who also want to be rid of Jesus. But in the north if there is no confrontation, it is possible to develop support and survive. Jesus is not running from the north; instead, he sets his face to go to Jerusalem. In the south, Pilate enforces Roman rule but leaves the Pharisees and the Temple party to run daily Jewish business, apart from collecting taxes. Here both groups want to kill Jesus because he is a major threat,[1] though his popularity makes this difficult.[2] The Temple system in Jerusalem is a rich and powerful establishment. The high-priestly party, controlled by Annas, has enormous wealth and has bribed friends in the Praetorian (Roman) guard so that they can operate with increasing autonomy. To move head-on toward this opposition is dangerous. Further, if you are making a political move for leadership, you have to do it properly, and the right way is to create a power base that can grow. Jesus does not do this. He sets out on an extended journey, with women and other supporters in his entourage, but without a policy for power. No first-century politician relies on women. In these terms, every move is a mistake, a failure. But clearly, Jesus operates on different terms.

From the beginning, he has warned his followers that he is going to be killed, that he will effectively lose. His journey is full of healing and teaching, but he has a strong commitment, it seems, to alienate his followers. Popularity can only be bought at a price he will not pay. The disciples sense some possibility of their power as leaders in Israel, but it will come to nothing, or nearly so. His political strategy seems to operate on a plane none of his contemporaries understands. Yet Jesus clearly knows what is happening. He has watched John the Baptist go to a prophet's death and discerns the kind of people he faces. He has X-ray vision of the motives and strategy of the Pharisees, Herodians, and Temple party. Why this extraordinary, deliberate journey to Jerusalem?

The answer is difficult to state, but it might be something like this. Jesus is going to the seat of political and religious power. Jerusalem for Israel is like London for Britain or Paris for France, only more so. This journey can be seen as a confrontation, but it is not so in the normal sense of the term. In the Sermon on the Mount Jesus describes Jerusalem as "the city of the Great King" (Matt. 5:35). Here the great King comes to the city, which is really his, bringing the truth of God, exposing it to what is good and just. He will bring the God of the Temple to the Temple of God. He will *not* be participating in the structures of political control and manipulation, though he will be submitting to them. The coming is done tenderly. Jesus weeps over the city. He is soft toward it as a hen is with her fluffy little chicks. The journey raises a key question: What will Jerusalem do with Jesus? In this sense the Lord, apart from his teaching and care of his disciples, is passive in the process. The activity surrounds conspirators, crowds, and authorities. The answer is grim, but it must be given, one way or the other. In effect, Jesus will travel to the heart of the political evils in the system and find those evils directed at him, without him participating in the evils. This is the astonishing reality. Here is political evil in its normal forms—power struggles, alliances, manipulation of the people, the shallowness of the populace, brutality to prisoners, lying about opponents—but Jesus does not participate in any of it. With love and sadness, all is exposed. We realize that Jesus' noncorruption, deeper agenda of truthfulness, and forgivingness are already in place at the beginning of the journey. He is open-eyed as he walks into trouble.

We also recognize something that hardly needs saying, except that it has so much racial abuse around it. It is not ethnically significant that the Jewish political leaders act as they do. For centuries these kinds of activities have been going on in Rome, London, Paris, Washington, Moscow, Peking, Karachi, and Berlin. There is nothing particularly significant in Jesus being killed by *Jewish* leaders, but at times anti-

Semitism seems to have fueled this pattern of blame. Ironically, Fascists who especially mount this ethnic attack have committed atrocities far worse in scale and were in thrall to racist doctrines. The death of Jesus is like the death of millions worldwide, perpetrated through political evil. It evidences a human problem, not a specifically Jewish one, nor is Roman participation some kind of damnation for Italians. British, Americans, Ugandans, and Australians have political murders aplenty on their hands, not so different from this one. The Jews are supposed to be close to God, but so were Americans when they killed a hundred thousand Iraqis and armed Indonesia to wipe out the East Timorese. There is, sadly, nothing exceptional about political murders. In this case, the uniqueness comes from the one who is murdered, who confronts the Jewish state and all states with the goodness and love of God.

In this sense, it is a universal journey. Every polity on earth is riddled with power-seeking, control, privilege, extortion, and injustice. Indeed, much of humanity sees politics as endemically evil. We intone Acton: "Power tends to corrupt and absolute power corrupts absolutely."[3] Or less precisely we say, "It's a dirty game, politics." The sinfulness of politics is not just in Jerusalem, but also in London, Washington, Moscow, Babylon, Tehran, and Beijing. Can anyone walk into politics retaining one's purity, being just and incorrupt? It is a big question, and historians rarely answer in the affirmative. Yet Jesus did so walk, and the terms on which he conducts his politics therefore matter to all of us. Here we have the good politician, and that alone makes him unique.

Preparing the Disciples

Nevertheless, there is more to it than even this. Something like a year before the crucifixion, Peter has declared that Jesus is God's Messiah. Jesus prepares the disciples for what is going to happen: "The Son of Man must suffer many things and be rejected by the elders, chief priests and teachers of the law, and he must be killed and on the third day be raised to life" (Luke 9:22). Jesus often tells the disciples things they do not understand, and this is one of them. Their level of non-comprehension must be vast. They must try to confront the fact that Jesus—the Messiah, no less—will not be a national political deliverer but another kind of political ruler. It is beyond their understanding, as it is still largely beyond ours.

The tension in Peter's confrontation with Christ is clear. Jesus explains that he must necessarily suffer, be killed, and be raised from the dead. Peter cannot hear these words and berates Jesus, with passion. He has just fully understood that this man is Messiah, and no Jew can stand to hear of the Messiah's death. It is an excruciating thought: "Never, Lord! This shall never happen to you!" But Jesus in turn rebukes Peter: "Out of my sight, Satan! You are a stumbling block to me; you do not have in mind the things of God, but the things of men" (Matt. 16:22–23; cf. 4:10). How startling is the polarization of the two men who have seemingly just been in such unity. Partly, it shows the gulf between their views of politics: one still with the national deliverer, the other on a different plane, following the consistent path present since the temptations.

What Jesus then says is difficult to live with: "If anyone would come after me [the Messiah], he must deny himself and take up his cross and follow me" (16:24). Politics has always been about victory, success, vindication, being right. Every politician has his victory celebrations. But here is repudiation, suffering, self-loss, and the ultimate political condemnation. The place of the self is crucial. Whoever wants to gain his life, make it, and enhance his ego, that person loses it; but whoever loses his life for the Christ will find it. Shakespeare echoes this self-emptying when Richard II finally stands unkinged in Pomfret Castle dungeon, waiting to die:

> But, whate'er I am,
> Nor I, nor any man, that but man is,
> With nothing shall be pleas'd till he be eas'd
> With being nothing.[4]

Jesus, however, is not faced with being nothing through defeat; instead, he makes himself nothing. The temptation is to do politics as men do politics rather than as God does them. "What good is it if a man gets power, gains the whole world, yet forfeits his soul, his probity, his standing before God?" (cf. Matt. 16:26). The means never justify the ends. Only the good will do. The Lord in principle rules out crossing the line where expediency compromises integrity. Philosophically, once this point is stated, it can never be gainsaid. Anyone who is prepared to sink his soul for political gain is a fool; he has already lost himself and everything he might gain. But we have seen it all—lies, bribery, exaggerated claims, false messages, wars to gain popularity, rulers chopping rivals. We ordinary people can see the costs of vaulting ambition. Like Macbeth, often the ruler is dead while crowned. But the point probes further into every corner of our human egos, where the self cuts us off from God and does evil to others. From Clinton's silliness to Mussolini's chest-thumping, the ruler's ego will be found out. But then here is this man who made himself nothing, and we can learn best from him.

The personal point is also an attack on political systems, for there is much in political rule that is ego-construction and self-glorification embedded in thought. Good local insights are turned into self-validating ideologies. The ideological failures of Marx, Jefferson, Bismarck, and Thatcher show by what they glory in—the working class, revolution, independence, enlightenment, the state, Germany, private enterprise, Great Britain. We can see the ego problems of political philosophy. Where we build and construct our Babel, there is the uncritical place for sin to work. So overwhelmingly normal is the egocentricity of politics—breeding war, creating offense, generating divisions lasting centuries—that we cannot step outside it. Here Jesus in a few words declares war on this kind of politics: "What good will it be . . . ? What good will it be . . . ?" Self-made victories do not produce good. The temptation to gain all the kingdoms of the world, or even one of them, is not worth the candle. It is the great deception down through human history. Shakespeare, no mean political theorist, with breathtaking brevity describes the great political problem. Hamlet picks up the skull and muses, "This might be the pate of a politician . . . one that would circumvent God."[5]

But Jesus does not stop there. Beyond his death, and the need for ego to die, he talks of ultimate judgment. He says to his disciples, "I, the Son of Man, will judge each person with God's accounting, according to what they have done, neither more nor less" (cf. Matt. 16:27). Power does not count, but only God's judgment of what is truly good or evil. Jesus does not make this journey to Jerusalem as some kind of victim, but as the judge of all the earth. We now may have an inkling of what this is all about, but the disciples then must be clueless. It involves ways of thinking incomprehensible to them and even difficult for us. This man is not as we are.

Moses and Elijah

However, three of the disciples have some chance of seeing the bigger picture. It is difficult to know what to make of the transfiguration, whether it is vision or actual appearance. The disciples see Moses, Elijah, and Jesus. We can imagine what it would be for a Jew to see Moses, the one who received the law from God, the founder-leader of the nation. Moses is the archetypal politician, the one who dwells in the covenant between God and Israel and on whom the nation depends. Elijah, no less, is the founder of the prophetic tradition, the one who is the scourge of kings. Both are people who dwell with God more deeply than they relate to their people. They represent the authentic response to God, the pattern of true obedience to God throughout Israel's history.

They are called forth by Malachi's prophecy right at the end of the Old Testament, the final word of the prophets: "Suddenly, the Lord you are seeking will come to his temple. . . . But who can endure the day of his coming? Who can stand when he appears?" (Mal. 3:1–2). The drama shortly to happen in Jerusalem is judgment. "So, I will come near to you for judgment. I will be quick to testify against . . ." (3:5). The refiner's fire, the winnowing of good from evil, the process that burns away all the small, selfish, sinful, unjust aspects of our lives. What will it leave? The arrogant, the evildoer will be stubble, burned as by a furnace on the day of the Lord. This is what the threesome is about. Malachi goes first to Moses: "Remember the law of my servant Moses, the degrees and laws I gave him at Horeb for all Israel" (4:4). Moses is here as the porter of God's laws to the people. The disciples know that. They also know why Elijah is here. "See, I will send you the prophet Elijah before the great and terrible day of the LORD comes" (4:5). Elijah is the sign of the great choice between the prophets of God and the prophets of Baal. He is the great "or else" of history. "He will turn the hearts of parents to their children, and the hearts of the children to their parents; or else I will come and strike the land with a curse" (4:5–6). Either children and parents will be together, healed of sin, and go out jumping and kicking with joy, like calves let out from the winter stalls—or the curse of evil will happen. This is the great clarifying moment, not one of magic, but one when falsity is revealed for what it is.

Here "the sun of righteousness will rise with healing in its wings" (4:2). The great shimmering light of God will spread. The almighty God jokes: "Test me . . . and see if I will not throw open the floodgates of heaven and pour out so much blessing that you will not have room enough for it" (3:10). "But you have said, 'It is futile to serve God'" (3:14). The choice hangs in the balance: Serve God, remember Moses and Elijah, and listen to the One whom God has sent—or go your own way. The disciples are dazed. This is too much to take in. Then comes the voice, "This is my Son. . . . Listen to him!" (Matt. 17:5). The words are redundant to these Jews who have just seen Moses. Of course they will. But the listening must be much deeper. Many claim to be heirs of Moses and do not listen. The winnowing of Elijah has already occurred with the coming of John the Baptist, and the Son of Man will also suffer like the Baptist. Before people wake up, the day of the Lord will arrive. The actual response to God's way is two dead bodies, one decapitated at a party and the other crucified on a hill. They will kill the Son of Man. Yet now these privileged disciples see the source of Jesus' government over Israel in Moses and Elijah. They are confused beyond imagining, but they know they must listen to Jesus.

Jesus and the Locus of Truth

Jesus' journey to Jerusalem is just as Christians have always seen it. He heals and teaches and tells stories. He meets ordinary people and ministers to them, whether they be lepers, sisters, an epileptic, or little children. Again, we must guard against unduly politicizing Jesus or the good news of God with us. He hosts meals, sits in the sun, extracts Martha from housework, and raises Lazarus from the dead. He clearly has the Creator working for him. Never are relationships sacrificed to the political. Little children whom the disciples want to marginalize in their own self-importance are brought center stage. Nevertheless, this journey is also political. It gathers elements of what it means to be the Messiah. This is going to be a power confrontation, but between two different understandings of power, and one must prove to be false. Jesus gives substance to the gentle power of God. Can it actually be that this gentle kingdom is what the whole world has awaited and has not seen? Can this be what Plato, the pharaohs, Confucius, and Cicero were looking for (Luke 10:24)? Jesus tells the disciples it is, but they scarcely know what they have.

The disciples cannot make the paradigm shift. They struggle with different universes of discourse. Status, position, and glory are endemic in much human thinking. The disciples are already concerned with greatness. Alexander the Great, the great Maccabees, and outstanding leaders gather those who pick up reflected glory. Similarly, position in Jesus' entourage is an issue for the disciples. It crops up in Capernaum. Jesus patiently explains that the first must be last. He deconstructs greatness with a little child. "Welcome and honor this child, and you have God as your guest" (cf. Mark 9:33–37). "When you sit at table, go to the bottom seat and you might be promoted or you might not" (cf. Luke 14:10). "For everyone who exalts himself will be humbled, and he who humbles himself will be exalted" (14:11). But the issue will not lie down. There is an element of gaining power from closeness to the powerful, an idiom throughout history. James and John, as we have seen, vie for position. Jesus asks, "Can you drink the cup I am going to drink?" (Matt. 20:22). We hear the deeper meaning, but we may miss the more superficial joke. Each king, especially a Herod, has a cupbearer by his side who tastes his drink first to establish whether it has been poisoned (cf. Gen. 40; Neh. 1:11). The disciples are jolted from their self-concern into facing the possibility that they might be poisoned! But this idea flits past and the deeper significance of drinking the cup, though unknown to the disciples as yet, is presented to them.

Along the way, Jesus also teaches his disciples to handle a fairly straightforward sense of opposition. This is culturally interesting. Many

Christians are so busy being nice that they cannot disagree with anybody. The idea of forming a Christian political party fills them with fear because they might have to oppose other groups. Others are automatic conformists. Many in opposition are strident, self-righteous, revolutionary, or destructive. Good opposition is difficult. Jesus both teaches it and shows how necessary and constructive it is. He also shows how to move beyond partisanship, to "love your enemies, do good to those who hate you" (Luke 6:27). The disciples are worried about a man who is "not one of us," but Jesus responds: "Whoever is not against us is for us" (Mark 9:40). He also states the obverse: "He who is not with me is against me" (Matt. 12:30). Hence, this is not a passive but an active definition of opposition. More widely, Jesus both precipitates and teaches opposition. To coin a word, he antithetes (provokes an antithesis): "As the crowds increased, Jesus said, 'This is a wicked generation'" (Luke 11:29). People flock to hear him, and he tells them they are under judgment because they have not repented. They have probably given no thought to repentance at all. It is as awkward an idea then as when some nutty evangelist proclaims it on street corners now—unheard, wrong in tone, but still voicing a word basic to the human condition. When faced, repentance is not nutty at all. It is a sober way to address what is wrong, and Jesus deals heavily in the currency of repentance. A Pharisee invites him for a meal. Suddenly Jesus is upbraiding him for neglecting justice and the love of God, and for being hypocritical (Luke 11:42–44). It is a deeply wounding attack. Foolishly, the experts in the law pop up their heads and say, "Teacher, when you say these things, you insult us also" (11:45), and so Jesus turns on them. He contrasts the presented adulation of the prophets with the actual history of Old Testament murder from Abel to Zechariah, who was stoned to death in the courtyard of the Temple by orders of wicked King Joash. "Those whom God sends are rejected, and you in this generation will be held responsible for it all" (cf. Luke 11:47–51). It is not a convivial meal. The Pharisees and teachers of the law leave it furious, fiercely opposed to Jesus' exposure of what is wrong and seeking revenge. Jesus deliberately polarizes the rule of God and the kingdoms of darkness, murder, extortion, and covert evil. Either he is wrong or he is right, not just for them, but also for us. Perhaps, as a culturally flaccid generation, Western Christians have much to learn of good principled root-and-branch opposition.

Jesus' underlying argument is clear. It is laid out in one of the earlier confrontations in Jerusalem (John 8:31–47). Either we are children of God, and come to the light to test our motives and actions with God's Spirit, or we are children of the devil. Of course, many protest at this polarized view of good and evil. Other philosophical positions abound: "Really, we are neutral and externally influenced by various degrees for good or bad." Or, "There is a good guy in each of us waiting to get out. At our core, we are really good, unless we are Russians, aliens from outer space, or bin Laden." Or, "Perhaps humanity is like the curate's egg, good and bad in parts." Or, benignly, "We live quite good lives, really, with occasional mistakes." Jesus' position is uncompromisingly different. When we are not open to God, submitting to the Spirit of truth, we belong to the father of lies and are going to produce evil fruit. Human beings serve God or another master, and become slaves to one or the other, possibly changing within a short time. For a while during the Enlightenment, people believed that a rational or educated mind produced good people. But most of us now know, whether we are in politics or not, that our spirits can easily be gripped by evil, individually or collectively. Either God on the one hand, or mammon, the devil, and idolatry on the other—this is not an overly dramatic polarization. Truth is contentious, and mealymouthed; accommodating Christians weakly trying to fit in with the culture of the day have often been prepared to bury it. Their leader is not.

Triumphalism and the Ten Minas

The approach of Jesus to Jerusalem has a heightened sense of drama. Already the Pharisees, teachers of the law, and the Temple party are treating Jesus as a redoubtable enemy. The rumor has gone around that they are trying to kill this man. Many of the vast Passover crowds have come out to the region east of Jordan to link up with him. His stories and teaching are carefully reported and fizz from one group to another. Lazarus has been raised from the dead in a miracle, defying all human experience. As the event gets back to Jerusalem, a meeting of the Sanhedrin is called to try to cope with Jesus. They obviously feel he is too hot to handle. Caiaphas, the high priest, recommends his death and easily carries the vote. We know that Joseph of Arimathea does not consent (Luke 23:51) and probably neither does Nicodemus (John 19:38–39), but otherwise the vote is likely overwhelming. But they are not sure how they can do it; it is after all not in their power to kill, and they need a charge that will warrant execution. In Perea Jesus has been throwing out parables challenging the structure of life, and now he moves across Jordan into Jericho. This is a Herodian city, a place of affluence. It has four protective forts, a theater, and an amphitheater, a warm paradise of palms and fragrant balsam. Jerusalem Jews look down on it as pagan and extravagant.[6] One (or two) blind men receive their sight, calling "Jesus, Son of David," and the crowds zing with expectation (Matt. 20:29–34; Mark 10:46–52; Luke 18:35–43). The journey threatens to become a procession of triumphal acclamation through Jericho and out the other side toward Jerusalem, near the Herodian palaces and the abode of Zacchaeus. We have already looked at the strategic position of Zacchaeus, perhaps as a chief tax collector for the Jerusalem region (Luke 19:2). As he repents of his Roman role and is reinstated as a son of Abraham, the spreading news is greeted by cheers and free drinks. The stage is set for the returning national hero, the one who will sweep all before him. Except it is not to be.

As the crowd leaves Jericho, Jesus tells them a parable. Most of this book relies on widely accepted exegesis; here the interpretation is slightly different. The scene, recorded in Luke, occurs after the salvation of Zacchaeus and is a significant event. The conversion of a chief tax collector who will return his ill-gotten gains seems to herald the collapse of the Roman system. It is like the Inland Revenue or the Internal Revenue Service going on strike. The crowd, already bubbling and massed, moves into a frenzy of anticipation. We know this because it is explicitly given as the reason for the parable. He tells them this parable *"because* he was near Jerusalem and the people thought that the kingdom of God was going to appear at once" (Luke 19:11, italics added). You cannot speak more plainly than that. We have the reason for the parable, and its content should reflect this reason.

The similarity of this parable of the Minas to the parable of the Talents has normally meant that this required interpretation is ignored. Some say that it is the same parable sloppily recorded in two different versions. Others transfer the meaning of the parable of the Talents (told later in Jerusalem) back to this parable. But the differences between the two parables are striking and multiple. For example, the sums of minas are "petty," worth only 2 percent of the talents. Further, what Jesus actually says is notably different.

> A man of noble birth went to a distant country to have himself appointed king and then to return. So he called ten of his servants. . . . But his subjects hated him and sent a delegation after him to say, "We don't want this man to be our king." (Luke 19:12–15)

Everyone hearing this would know exactly what Jesus is retelling. He is describing their political system. The distant country is Rome. Archelaus, Herod Antipas, and Philip, the three boys of Herod the Great, all scurried off to Rome to try to get bits of the kingdom after their dad died (4 BC). Archelaus especially had trouble. He hoped to be a popular king, but ratification from Rome was required. An uprising in Jerusalem at the Passover resulted in him sending in the troops and killing three thousand people. Every Passover this horror would be remembered, and hence, he was hated. He then went to Rome, and there was a long hearing, during which a delegation of fifty came from Jerusalem to Rome to accuse Archelaus of the massacre and say, "We don't want this man to be our king." With other witnesses before Caesar Augustus, Antipater similarly accused Archelaus, his stepbrother.[7] The delegations wanted direct rule from Rome. When the Romans heard that message, they knew that the citizens were serious. Eventually, Archelaus was promised the title of king if he proved capable of that position. He came back, not mightily pleased with the opposition he had encountered in Rome. He was the most brutal and tyrannical of the Herodian brothers, as Mary and Joseph well knew. And he had a local reputation in Jericho, restoring a magnificent palace there, constructing an aqueduct to bring water to palm groves, and seven miles north of Jericho building a new village of Archelais, humbly named after himself.[8]

The locals can pick up Jesus' references, and instantly they are in the parable. There is one other aspect of this situation of which we need to be aware. Archelaus, following Herod the Great's lead, eliminated landowners by bringing vast tracts of property, especially around Jericho, under his direct and indirect control. Goodman sums up the change after Archelaus's fall in AD 6:

> Finding no natural landed elite in Judaea but needing the co-operation of local rulers of some kind for their administration to work successfully, the Romans elected to entrust power to those Judean landowners who did exist, regardless of whether such men could command any popular prestige. These men were the creatures of Herod who had been granted land and position within the state since 37 B.C.[9]

These landowners, the Herodians, are the hated ones, now linked to the Romans, part of the group Zacchaeus has just deserted. The structure of Jesus' parable now becomes clear. Zacchaeus, the chief tax collector in Jericho, has just been converted. The Jews are looking for the great deliverance. But Jesus tells them this scarcely veiled story about Archelaus, the local bad guy, of the way he rewards his cronies and punishes those who tell the truth. Moreover, the main part of the parable recalls the case of Zacchaeus. We tend to assume that the idea of "taking charge of ten cities" is just normal predemocratic despotism, but outside the Herodian cities, there were no despotic rulers of this kind. Taking charge of cities means taking charge of them for taxation purposes. The parable, not surprisingly, describes tax farming. These are not people receiving cities for themselves as some kind of benevolent reward, but gathering money mainly for the king and for themselves through the Roman-Herodian tax system. The whole parable sets out the Herodian-Roman tax-farming system with its injustices. "I am a hard man, taking out what I did not put in, and reaping what I did not sow. . . . I tell you that to everyone who has, more will be given, but as for the one who has nothing, even what he has will be taken away. But those enemies of mine who did not want me to be king over them—bring them here and kill them in front of me" (Luke 19:22–27). Zacchaeus might be converted, but the system will go on like this. This is no metaphor of God's kingdom, but a direct warning against the belief that liberation is imminent. It also exposes the character of the Herodian-Roman system. This dominating system requires people to serve it, and if you don't fit in or if you try to overthrow the king, he will kill you, coldly. It is a savage but realistic commentary on the tax farming. The parable mightily dampens the celebrations over Zacchaeus. Triumphalism dies. Luke pithily adds, "After Jesus had said this, he went on ahead" (19:28), on the ten miles or so up toward Jerusalem, going up into the complex hills, perhaps off road, until he comes to Bethany, where he stays. When your leader has warned that you are likely to be killed in cold blood, it takes the spring out of your steps. Jesus is not offering triumphalism and says so. He does not want followers who will be killed.

The insurrection does not start. Even the triumphal entry into Jerusalem is calmer. When Jesus goes through his trial and crucifixion, he is the only one who is killed, apart from Judas's suicide. The parable speeds before Jesus into Jerusalem, where he gives it its final great twist as the parable of the Talents. As Luke 19:11 declares, Jesus' story and warning make sure that the triumphal entry into Jerusalem is without bloodshed.

The Triumphal Entry into Jerusalem

It nevertheless is a great political event. The entry of a ruler into the capital city has to be big—crowds, soldiers, triumphal arches, political gestures, victory wreaths, and acclaim. Triumphal arches in Roman culture are for the conqueror coming home—the Trajan, Marble, and Admiralty arches, and L'Arc de Triomphe in Paris—useless, but full of the glory of empire. But this entry into Jerusalem is Jewish rather than Roman. Here, rather than a conqueror, is hope of the Deliverer—God's chosen Messiah. The royal family, the Herodian line, is pro-Roman, and even they have now been replaced by direct Roman rule. The Deliverer will come, and Jesus, despite his ambivalence, could be the One. The people know he outshines John the Baptist, and now there is news of Lazarus being raised from the dead. The great popular surge that Jesus has been trying to quell—the belief in a sign, the great rallying call to

God—effervesces round Jerusalem. The crowds gather, even as hundreds of thousands pour into the city for Passover, in this great period of ferment.

Jesus' actions are deliberate and counter-cultural. They are designed around Zechariah 9:9–10. The triumphal leader generally comes on a war horse. He must be imposing, dragging slaves and defeated leaders in his train. Jesus, by contrast, chooses the foal of a donkey, which would scarcely take his feet off the ground. The weight of the Zechariah prophecy hovers over what Jesus does, taking away war horses and chariots and breaking the battle bow. Here is One who commands peace to the ends of the earth.

The dynamics of the event are key. Jesus is lodging in Bethany, probably at the house of Simon the leper (or ex-leper). He is on the final stage of his great journey to Jerusalem with his band of disciples, including the accompanying women. They have a bit of a party. Martha, Mary, and the raised Lazarus are nearby, and the village is seething with scouts from Jerusalem, gawking at him and asking questions. Jesus probably moves from Martha and Mary's house to escape the publicity. A leper's house is a good place to avoid tourists. At a dinner in Jesus' honor, Mary lathers pure expensive nard on his feet, drenching the house with the smell in an enthusiastic expression of love (Matt. 26:6–13; Mark 14:3–9; John 12:1–8). What would you not do for the One who has brought your brother back to life? In the midst of all this celebration, Jesus sends the disciples ahead to the village of Bethphage, and their instructions occupy the Gospel writers. This is possibly because there are people about who are out to kill Jesus; at some level they are a hunted group. There is also a need to prevent development of a revolutionary head of steam. This event can lead to the deaths of thousands. The tethered donkey and its mother are to be brought, with a promise of their return, secured by the fact of Jesus' need of it. Jesus travels from Bethany to Bethphage, probably off-road on the rocky terrain, and avoids the buildup of the event. Even so, when he mounts the foal of the donkey, with its mother traveling alongside to keep the young animal unworried, the adulation quickly mounts (Matt. 21:6–10; Mark 11:6–11; Luke 19:34–44).

The people gather, spreading their cloaks on the road in a great gesture supporting his kingship (as for Jehu; 2 Kings 9:13). To have this person's baby donkey walk over their cloaks is a sign of honor. They cut palm branches as signs of deliverance (cf. Rev. 7:9–10) and spread them, too, on the uneven road. They begin to chant, and their words take up the great victory chant of Psalm 118, the psalm of festal procession, resonating with great themes: "The stone that the builders rejected has become the chief cornerstone . . ." (118:22). "Open to me the gates of righteousness" (118:19). But they focus on "Blessed is the one who comes in the name of the Lord" (118:26). The cries also give praise to the Son of David. This is a celebration, not an insurrection. It rings with truth. To the city of the Great King, the King has come. The Pharisees who try to rebuke Jesus and the crowds have it wrong (Luke 19:39). This is God's chosen one, come to bless the city. The people want the simple succession, a man of the house and lineage of David, proclaiming his messiahship and establishing himself as their ruler. They grow in number, and the shouts become resonant. "Peace in heaven!" "Hosanna in the Highest!" *Hosanna*, the great cry meaning "Save now," proclaims the insistent messianic moment. The script is written: the King is coming.

But as the descent toward Jerusalem begins from the Mount of Olives, the script falls apart. Jesus is deeply troubled, descends from the foal, and begins to lament and cry. This is both a heartrending sob and also a prophetic lament, the recognition that what will now happen will be a failure for the city. Corporately, Jerusalem is about to miss its great opportunity, to make the wrong choices at every level. There is an awesome shadow in Jesus' final warnings:

> If you, even you, had only known on this day what would bring you peace—but now it is hidden from your eyes. The days will come upon you when your enemies will build an embankment against you and encircle you and hem you in on every side. They will dash you to the ground, you and the children within your walls. They will not leave one stone upon another, because you did not recognize the time of God's coming to you. (Luke 19:42–44)

This seems a clear reference to the destruction of Jerusalem forty years later, though such foresight is humanly unthinkable. In 70, from April to September, the Romans laid siege to Jerusalem, starving the inhabitants who gathered there. The people generally and the Zealots in particular looked for a miraculous act from God that would deliver them from the Romans, the same kind of messianic hope that Jesus himself confronted. Josephus comments that in the final slaughter the streets ran with so much blood that it put fires out.[10] He estimates that 1.1 million people were killed. The Temple was burned and razed to the ground despite the orders of Titus, Emperor Vespasian's son. Some say this uncanny prophecy must have been added later, but this will not do because it fits the whole narrative. This is the time of God's peaceful coming, and it is not recognized. The one who sees the tragedy is not heard.

This lament is not merely a prediction but a warning, trying to open the eyes of the people concerned. It is not even a process of blame. The horrific wrongs are perpetrated against the Jews, not by them. But it is a warning against national confrontation and triumphalism, like the parable of the Minas. It takes the evil of the evil seriously and confronts what may be unthinkable. More than that, it sees future political disasters rooted in the present. Jesus requires us to see what is happening now, for its peace or long-term bitterness. Political foresight and discernment across decades matter, and the structure of national messianic hope is vain and destined for failure. Josephus only sees the problem as it later unfolds. Here its spiritual roots are laid bare.

Throughout, Jesus' emphasis is on peace. Even those who don't know more of Jesus' teaching and miracles know that whatever is going on round these two donkeys is not an insurrection. "The things that make for peace" remain unknown, hidden (Luke 19:42 NRSV; cf. Zech. 8:16 NRSV). Even when told, the people cannot see. There is a gulf between Jesus' way and the people's. They quieten. As Jesus talks to the city below them, the crowd can all too easily imagine what Jesus describes. Perhaps they think of the Romans. They are forced to think of defeat. Echoes of Isaiah and Jeremiah abound. "You will be defeated, because you are not right with God. You have not recognized the time of your visitation from God." Jesus' woe is imprinted on the crowd. The descent continues, but the triumphalism drains out of the immediate group.

Yet this entry is also problematic at another level. Jesus is coming to an imperially controlled capital. We may ask, "Why did Jesus not more directly oppose the Romans?" It is a difficult question. Perhaps, it is partly unlocked by Gandhi in a "Confession of Faith" he wrote in 1909 while especially under the influence of the Sermon on the Mount and Tolstoy. In relation to British colonial control, he said, "If British rule were replaced tomorrow by Indian rule based on modern methods, India would be none the better, except that she would be able then to retain some of the money that is drained away to England."[11] Ignoring Gandhi's more quirky ideas, the point stands. Removing colonialism does not penetrate any country's deepest condition, and ex-colonial countries still suffer with their own ills. If the move against colonialism, usually nationalist, is merely reactive, and the basis of a country's political formation is not itself just, it will continue to flounder. In his own way Gandhi sought to build the integrity of India for independence. In this and other areas, so much of our politics is reactive, often justifying further wrongs and failures. Jesus sees beyond the immediate wrongs to the full picture, and how full it is.

This lament is soon engulfed in the momentum of the mass. John records how crowds surround Jesus to the extent that the Pharisees feel defeated: "You see, you can do nothing. Look, the world has gone after him!" (John 12:19 NRSV). The rest of the day Jesus spends with the disciples in and around the Temple crowded with Passover visitors. They go out to Bethany in the evening, walking the two donkeys and returning them to their owner on the way through Bethphage. To those closely involved in the day, the contrast between the messianic hope of entry into Jerusalem whipping through the crowds and the lament over the city must be disturbing and difficult. This is a deliberate political non-event.

Bibliography

Edersheim, Alfred. *The Life and Times of Jesus the Messiah.* 3d ed. 2 vols. in 1. London: Longmans, Green & Co., 1906.

Geldenhuys, Norval. *The Gospel of Luke.* London: Marshall, Morgan & Scott, 1977.

Goodman, Martin. *The Ruling Class of Judaea.* Cambridge: Cambridge University Press, 1987.

Kinman, Brent. *Jesus' Entry into Jerusalem: In the Context of Lucan Theology and the Politics of His Day.* Leiden: Brill, 1995.

Schürer, Emil. *The History of the Jewish People in the Age of Jesus Christ.* Vol. 1. Edinburgh: T&T Clark, 1973.

Jerusalem and the Cross

Jesus and Political Evil

The last days of Jesus' life in Jerusalem give us an unrivaled understanding of political evil. Jesus' confrontations are direct and uncompromising, and he faces a variety of corrupt and distorted responses. They are not unusual in so being. Most political history of every era, including today's, reads roughly the same. Yet here each person, structure, or act stands out exposed by the light of Jesus' comments and acts. Let us identify some of the forces at work. There is the shallow populism of the masses, welcoming Jesus into Jerusalem on a wave of instant appeal, but without any real commitment to him and his way of politics. Their support evaporates like the morning dew when the leaders manipulate them. Thousands hear his teaching, but it does not dwell with them and bear fruit. A confrontation with Pilate, and they are readily swept up to speak against him.

In the Temple, the great symbol of national identity, avid moneymaking continues. Annas and his family's quest for money and profit corrupt the worship of God. Moreover, the Chief Priests and those running the Temple are prepared to kill to maintain their system. They are angry and already set on a course leading to Jesus' death. The Pharisees are slightly different, removed from power, but also frustrated and aware that Jesus the Rabbi can cut through their teaching like a hot knife through butter. They think they need to oppose Jesus' teaching in the Temple. Many influential ones accept the Temple party's conclusion that he must die. For most of the others, rabbinic debate is to be won, and submission to God's law is recessed in their thinking. Thus, the political leaders of the day gather to plot against the person who is threatening their power and control. *Why* they are so threatened is sublimated. The plotting is secret, and it has the aim of killing Jesus, eliminating opposition, without reference to what is just or true. False witnesses are used, and expediency is everywhere.

Nor is this even the story of groups of good people overwhelmed by the system. Crowds shouting support evaporate and become complicit in the murder because their vision is already corrupted into simplistic national messianism. The disciples are partly looking to their rise to power and fade away when they perceive they are in danger. Peter vehemently denies his relationship with Jesus. Judas goes further and betrays him. Why does Judas do so? The structure of events shows the thoughtlessness of his act. Though so close to Jesus, his heart and spirit seem to be closer to money. John identifies him as having a habit of stealing from the communal bag (John 12:6). Probably initiating the possibility of betrayal, he is offered four months' wages by the high priests to do it and grabs the offer instantly. Annas is not above offering bribes, and Judas is out for money.

Judas kisses Jesus in the garden and is instantly convulsed by his betrayal. Immediately, accepting the bribe becomes an evil act of horror to him as he sees its consequences. He follows Jesus, the temple guards, and soldiers (John 18:3) from one location to another during the night and early morning. Within six or so hours he hunts down the chief priests in the Temple area, throws the bribery money into the inner Temple court in a gesture of recantation, and commits suicide by hanging himself, obviously in torment (Matt. 27:3–5). It is impossible to imagine what he goes through as he faces the goodness of the man he has moved toward death. Similarly, the Gospel accounts, from those who went through this extreme crisis, show weak and unaware disciples, not on top of events, but drawing back from commitment and racked by fear. This is not the story of a moral minority, but of failure by everybody.

Moreover, the structures are corrupt. The Sanhedrin resorts to dishonest legal procedure in its trial—dishonest witnesses; illegal time, place, and process; charges not related to wrongdoing; and abuse of the prisoner. It has, after all, decided on Jesus' death perhaps a month or more before he is brought to trial (John 11:53–54). This is wicked judicial procedure. Further, the relationship between the Jews and the colonial power is corrupt both ways. Pilate and the Romans govern by military power. Whether their rule is just is a sublimated question; they want to retain power with as little trouble as possible. Meanwhile, the Jewish leaders, knowing that making trouble gives them power, exploit the fact that Tiberius wants peace and quiet throughout the empire. The governor, Pilate, will probably be an appeaser if events are orchestrated in the right way. In terms of effective strategy, the Temple party is sophisticated enough to map it out. Pilate is happy to hand Jesus over to Herod Antipas, though the offense, if there is any, is in Judea, not Galilee, and not subject to Herod's jurisdiction. The kinds of corrupt calculations by which politicians get their way are figured into the system.

These political evils are similar to many that have happened in most subsequent decades. Sadly, recent events have been more horrific than those occurring in the Gospels. The Holocaust, Stalin's Gulag, the mass killings in Sudan, Indonesia, Kosovo, Chechnya, and Rwanda have all been greater evils in scale. Why should this confrontation be so significant? The reason lies not in the scope or depth of the evil, but in the goodness and love of the one who faces it.

The contrast can be seen in one small incident. We are so used to political conflict and power struggles that we can scarcely take in its absence. Judas has agreed to betray Jesus, and Jesus knows about it. Jesus, publicly before the disciples but anonymously, warns Judas of the wrong of the act and forewarns the disciples of a process that will devastate them (e.g., Matt. 26:20–25, 31–35). But then, when it is clear that Judas sets his heart on this evil, there is an extraordinary event that John records:

> "What you are about to do, do quickly," Jesus told him, but no one at the meal understood why Jesus said this to him. Since Judas had charge of the money, some thought Jesus was telling him to buy what was needed for the Feast, or to give something to the poor. As soon as Judas had taken the bread, he went out. And it was night. (John 13:27–30)

Familiarity can hide how astonishing this incident is. A traitor, a betrayer, must be exposed. One whose life is to be betrayed inevitably feels hatred and bitterness. Yet at this point, Jesus, having given Judas the opportunity of facing his deed, covers his exit from the upper room. He prevents the certain wrath of the other disciples from emerging. When everything conspires toward it and even justifies it, Jesus graciously stage-manages his exit. Even in the garden of Gethsemane, Jesus calls Judas "Friend." Jesus' goodness and freedom from self-concern are impressive. Yet it is sobering that God allows this evil, and millions since, to happen. When the choices are made, the consequences follow. The defeat of evil is not through control, for that would not be defeat. It is the victory of non-reactive goodness. The one who says, "Turn the other cheek," does so himself (cf. Matt. 5:39). Evil is faced with consistent goodness and suffering. There is no magic, but there is living open to the Spirit of God or failing so to do. Year in, year out, it is in our hands to live and suffer faithfully with the Christ or to go out into the night.

Throughout the time leading to the crucifixion, the overwhelming sense is of an innocent person being taken to judicial murder. But this is not unknowing innocence. Instead, Jesus encounters the groups in a series of awesome confrontations—parables, discourses, and events— where he insists on facing the political leaders and people with their blindness. Neither this nor other political evils have to happen, nor is the victim to blame. There is nothing fatalistic about Jesus. He inhabits the situation, walking the Temple courts, returning to teach those who need to see, addressing evil directly. Human sin, faced squarely, can lead sinners to repentance, but they will not repent. Then, it is carried in love, the supposed victim carrying through the government of God and putting mercy and grace under every failure that humanity can perpetrate.

The Confrontations

It is interesting how political stories emerge in the newspapers. Gradually bits filter out and fill in the picture. There are insiders, observers, fringe people, and outsiders. Even before Jesus' final journey to Jerusalem, the plot has been in place. Perhaps Nicodemus reports it later, as one present at the meeting. The Sanhedrin meets and voices its disquiet: "If we let him go on like this, everyone will believe in him, and then the Romans will come and take away both our place [the Temple] and the nation" (John 11:48). Then "Caiaphas . . . spoke up, 'You know nothing at all! You do not realize that it is better for you that one man die for the people than that the whole nation perish.' . . . So from that day on they plotted to take his life" (11:49, 53). It is crude, self-interested group expediency: "Let's kill our problem." Every event and bout of teaching in the final week quickens this policy.

Meanwhile, Jesus confronts each of the political parties in Jerusalem. First is the cleansing and occupation of the Temple. The exposure of the Temple party's motives was alarming. The place is a treasure trove, piled high with accumulated wealth. In the destruction of the Temple in 70, Josephus reports, "So laden with gold was every single soldier that all over Syria the value of gold was reduced by half."[1] That is quite an impact on a substantial market, caused by a vast quantity of gold. Annas's system is being attacked by Jesus, but not merely attacked. Jesus takes up residence. He heals people there. Children begin to worship and praise God, shouting, "Hosanna to the Son of David!" (Matt. 21:9). Jesus insists that all of us, with humility, repentance, and trust,

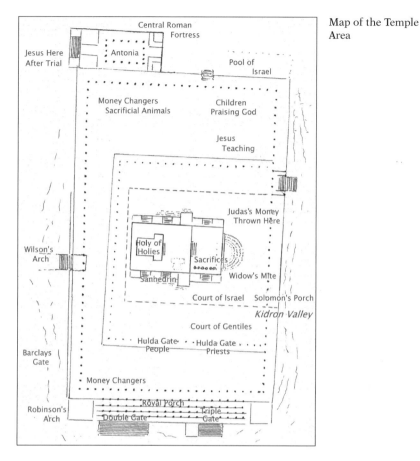

Map of the Temple Area

have access to God as our Father. Hence, this One stands against the cultic exclusivity of Temple worship, not in antithesis, but as thesis. The Emmanuel presence of God is among the people in God's house (1:23; 21:12–16).

Jesus and his disciples walk to Bethany and spend the night there. Accommodation is tight with the vast Passover crowds, and the dark is dangerous. In the early morning on the two miles back into Jerusalem, they pass a fig tree. Jesus treats it as a parable of the Temple system. It will not bear fruit, and it will wither down to its roots (Mark 11:12–14, 20–22). The acted anger of Jesus to the fig tree fixes the truth. Bearing fruit matters. Later, the Temple system does wither and die, and it has been without fruit for two thousand years. This is no game, but the shape and outcome of God's terms for history. The lesson for the disciples from the Rabbi is that their faith should be believing, pure, forgiving, and effective. So again they descend to the Kidron valley, with the temple gleaming ahead of them, and pass through Solomon's porch into the humming temple courts. The crowds converge on their Rabbi in the large paved courtyard, to hang on his words.

The Chief Priests and elders of the people are ready for Jesus. A bunch from the Sanhedrin has been mobilized. It is like going into London and being confronted by half the Cabinet as you step off the bus. The location is important. Edersheim describes it thus:

> But there were occasions on which the Temple became virtually, though not formally, a *Beth ha-Midrash*. For we read in the Talmud, that the members of the Temple-Sanhedrin, who on ordinary days sat as a Court of Appeal, from the close of the Morning-[Sacrifice] to the time of the Evening-Sacrifice, were wont on sabbaths and *feast days* to come out upon "the Terrace" of the Temple and there to teach. In such popular instruction the utmost latitude of questioning would be given.[2]

Jesus is teaching in the Temple courts, but to teach here requires rabbinic authorization; this is strict and unequivocal, and there is no evidence that Jesus has this authorization except through the sheer brilliance and rabbinic power of his teaching. Now he is a residential presence, proclaiming the good news of the Kingdom. This is the setting for critical public debates carried out in the Temple court at festival time. Everyone has a heightened awareness; there is plotting, coming, going, and a throbbing crowd. The chief priests and members of the Sanhedrin ask their first question, obviously prearranged. They are seeking to assert their right of authorization but need the reinforcement of their numbers in the face of a superior teacher. "By what authority are you doing these things [clearing the Temple and teaching here]? And who gave you this authority?" (Matt. 21:23).

The question is a trap; *they* claim authority over God's Temple. It is "their" place, and a million people have come here. They have played their trump card, but it also reveals some of their weakness.[3] The Temple really is God's house, not their place, and it is being dishonored; they know that. Jesus in turn requires a question of them. "What about John's baptism? Was it of God or his own fabrication?" (cf. 21:25). They are hung on the dilemma it contains. They do not think and dare not say that John's baptism was not of God because the people count John as a prophet. If it was of God, they have supplied the answer to their own question; Jesus' teaching is also of God. And if it was of God, why do they ignore John the Baptist and reject Jesus? They cannot answer, and Jesus will not. Round one goes to Jesus.

Then Jesus takes the initiative against the rulers of Israel. He tells a parable of two sons, whom their father asks to do something. The first one seems rebellious and yet knuckles under. The second says he will do what his father asks, but does not. "Which does what his father wants?" The rulers give the required answer, and Jesus insists on interpreting the parable for them. "Despite appearances, you who say you are dutiful are the disobedient ones. Tax collectors and prostitutes have repented and gone into the Kingdom before you" (cf. 21:28–31). Jesus returns to the Baptist: "John came to you to show you the way of righteousness, but you did not repent and believe him" (21:32). God's criterion of repentance stamps failure over the Sadducees and the Temple elite. It is a scorching condemnation, facing them with the reality of their relationship with God.

This is quickly followed by another parable given to the crowds and the leaders (Matt. 21:33–46). The Pharisees are now also here in large numbers, perhaps giving up their own poorly attended rabbinic sessions on the Temple terrace and crowding around Jesus. The story of the Tenants flows out. A landowner worked hard and planted a vineyard. Then he let it out to tenants and sent servants to collect the fruit, the due rent. The servants were beaten and even killed. Then the landowner sent his son, saying, "They will respect my son" (21:37). All round the crowd are leaders who have decided to kill Jesus, and he speaks these words in the parable at them. "But when the tenants saw the son, they said to each other, 'This is the heir. Come, let's kill him and take his inheritance.' So they took him and threw him out of the vineyard and killed him" (21:38–39). Matthew adds at the end that the chief priests and Pharisees, hearing Jesus' parables, knew he was talking about them (21:45). Of course they did. They were wriggling, exposed by their own evil.

Then Jesus throws out the great rhetorical question: "When the owner of the vineyard comes, what will he do with those tenants?" (21:40). The crowds, absorbed in the story, cry out the answer. They mouth the calamity of the tenants and hear it echoed in the warning Jesus gives. "He will bring those wretches to a wretched end, . . . and he will rent the vineyard to other tenants, who will give him his share of the crop at harvest time" (21:41). They hear the resonance: "Will you reject the one whom God has sent?"

As the implications bounce in their heads, Jesus adds more: "The stone rejected from the building of the Temple has become the aligning one in relation to which every other stone will be set; the whole Temple has to be built in line with this stone. Haven't you heard?" (cf. 21:42; Ps. 118:22–23). Their minds struggle with the idea of realignment. They know that the planning of the whole Temple area in operation for nearly fifty years involved discoveries of geometry. Is Jesus suggesting realignment of the completed buildings? The challenge becomes even more direct: "The Kingdom of God will be taken away from you and given to people who will bear fruit" (Matt. 21:43). No one can think of God being alienated from the Temple system and the Jews. The warning strikes deep. "This stone will break you. Don't underestimate what is going on here" (cf. 21:44). The chief priests and Pharisees, the rulers, feel the aimed remarks. They cannot break their mind-set and look for a way to arrest him, but he is temporarily safe in the Temple courts, protected by the adulatory crowds. The leaders do not pull back and examine their hearts; their strategy is fixed.[4]

Again, as this marathon encounter unfolds, Jesus steps up the tension with another parable of the Kingdom of God. Each time he lays God and their relationship with God before the people and leaders; unless they respond to God, their position is in tatters. In the next parable it is difficult to hear the offense because Western culture has been professionally ignoring God for decades. Media stars, moneymakers, adulterers, and the self-concerned aim to marginalize the Creator in routinized self-promotion. But the Jew worships God and has come to Jerusalem at great cost so to do. To say God is being ignored here in the Temple courts is an insult. Yet so Jesus does, and he pushes on a stage further. "You are invited to God's feast, a wedding banquet for his son, the greatest possible celebration. But you are preoccupied with your own agendas. You do not turn up, and you kill the messengers" (cf. 22:2–6). "The king was enraged. He sent his army and destroyed those murderers and burned their city" (22:7).

God's judgment is in their face, but the parable is only half finished. God extends the invitation to the Gentiles, the riffraff, "good and bad," until "the wedding hall" is "filled with guests" (22:8–10). And so it now is with several billion of us having a good time. But this is not all. One guest has not put on the proper wedding garment, probably provided by the king for these come-lately guests who have disgusting clothes. Astonishing is the severity of the treatment from the king. This casual, will-not-put-himself-out man is bound up and put out where there will be weeping and gnashing of teeth (22:11–14). In the kingdom the terms of the king operate; nobody deals with God on their own terms. How strange for the High Priests and other leaders, so carefully dressed for temple observance, to be told that they are ignoring God, that they may be excluding themselves from God's feast. They are still planning Jesus' death. The immediate dynamics show the parable to be true.

The Temple terrace is now more like a battlefield, with the intellectually bruised and injured lying about, all over the place. The words from Jesus insist on the truth. They draw back from nothing. The Pharisees regroup and bring a prepared question, taking over in the melee of groups. They try to trap him in words about taxes to Caesar that will lead to his death. The question is preceded by a mealymouthed eulogy, which recognizes that Jesus never trims his message to status or power, but always teaches with integrity. They ask their question: "Is it right to pay taxes to Caesar or not?" (22:15–17). As we earlier saw, the relentless honesty of the encounter moves on. The hidden agenda is out, and Jesus knows their evil intent. "You hypocrites, why are you trying to trap me?" (22:18). Never does Jesus let the real issue be smothered by the presenting problem. The theater of the brought coin, the dismissal of Tiberius Caesar's little image, and the central affirmation of God's claim leave the crowd gasping. The Pharisees retreat with empty hands (22:19–22). Again God is at the center of all things. They move to the back of the crowd, discomfited, and are replaced by the Sadducees, who fancy their own form of disputation.

The different style of question is evident. The Sadducees reject belief in the resurrection (22:23; Acts 23:8), and this is a long "aren't we clever people" story that aims to put down both Jesus and the Pharisees (22:23–33). They present a convoluted, hypothetical question about seven brothers dying, after each in turn marries the same woman. "At the resurrection, whose wife will she be?" (22:28). But the Sadducees are all at sea and out of their depth in relation to this man. Jesus is like Wittgenstein appearing on chat TV. He responds, "The God of Abraham, Isaac, and Jacob is not phased by sequential deaths" (cf. 22:32). "He is not the God of the dead, but of the living" (22:32). Suddenly the crowd sees that anybody who is before God is alive. Again they gasp as the Sadducees are turned on their heads (22:33).

This is not a tirade. Jesus can stop and wait for a coin. He can face a long complicated question. It is not automatic criticism, fired by a need to seem good by criticizing others. Jesus has nothing to gain, nor is he seeking to win. The focus of the whole debate is that God should be at the center, acknowledged and loved by his people. As the Sadducees back down, the Pharisees move back into the fray with one of their outstanding scholars (22:34–35). He asks a straight question about the greatest commandment in the Torah. Jesus gives the answer that is the very foundation of life, the extension of the Shema (Deut. 6:4–5). "Love the Lord your God with all your heart and with all your soul and with all your mind. . . . Love your neighbor as yourself" (Matt. 22:37–39). It is an honest question and an honest answer, perhaps the greatest answer of all.

The teacher of the law affirms all that Jesus has said and adds his own gloss about the priority of the law over temple sacrifices. There is a tenderness in Jesus' response to this man: "You are not far from the

Kingdom of God" (Mark 12:32–34). The crowd hushes, for the truth has settled on them, and no one dares to ask more questions.

But Jesus carries on and asks them the question about the Messiah as Son of David (Matt. 22:41–46). He is moving them beyond a nationalist conception, spinning their thinking one more turn, before he sets out on the great critique of those who normally occupy the terrace in the Temple courts.[5]

The Critique of the Political Establishment

Political opposition today is often massively adversarial. Thus, X criticizes Y, but merely to get into power. Ambition and self-promotion sully the critique. "They would say that, wouldn't they?" we think, hearing the self-serving attack. Biblical prophecy is something far deeper. It is not presenting what people want to hear, or saying "'Peace, peace,' . . . when there is no peace" (Jer. 6:14). It is bringing the truths, law, and justice of God incisively to the nation, the rulers, the empires, and the people. Biblical prophecy is the root meaning of all political opposition because it has a point of reference beyond opposition, examining the ruler on God's terms and exposing what needs to be faced. We have already seen how John the Baptist continues this tradition. Now this process of bringing motives, attitudes, and actions to the light, the winnowing of truth, moves up a gear as Jesus confronts the Pharisees directly.

We have to hear Jesus' great prophetic outburst carefully. He locates his critique. Then Jesus says to the crowds and to his disciples, "The teachers of the law and the Pharisees sit in Moses' seat. You must obey them and do everything they tell you. But do not do what they do, for they do not practice what they preach" (Matt. 23:1–4). Jesus teaches respect for Moses' seat, the office of teaching God's laws and political rule (cf. Exod. 18:13–16). He tells his followers to obey the Mosaic law truly taught and submit to public judgment. But the process is not mechanical obedience. Because the teachers sit in Moses' seat and administer the God-given law, they are to be obeyed beyond what they practice and even think. "Do not do what they do, for it is hypocritical." Then follows a devastating examination of their practices and human ordinances (Matt. 23:5–32). Many rulers have expected or required the blind obedience of Christians, which is clearly not warranted from this event. Respect for the God-given office, yes, but with critical awareness and exposure of injustice and hypocrisy. In the face of this founding event, it is clear that Christians have often been cowed into political passivity; rather than it being required of them by their faith.

It is important, too, to see the context. Jesus is talking partly to the crowds and also directly to the Pharisees and teachers of the law. The outer courts of the Temple are large, and everybody can gather there. Jesus has just asked the Pharisees a question, and members of the Sanhedrin and Temple party are in the area. Although Jesus first addresses the crowd, he soon moves into directly talking to the Pharisees and the Temple party. This is face-to-face political dispute (more direct than Prime Minister's Question Time), made possible by Jesus' fearlessness. We have no record of another such early confrontation, mainly because the protagonist is likely to die. This is the beginning of democratic confrontation. And what a confrontation! It is direct. "Woe to you . . ." signifies "You are wrong before God. You will reap bitterness." It is a direct attack to their hearts. "Blind" is the dominant word repeated throughout. "You are leaders, but you cannot see where you are going." Throughout the prophetic statement the awesome scale of human self-deception becomes evident.

These people purport to obey God; they should be somewhere near God's ways, but they instead are self-obsessed. Nothing can capture the great direct impact of these words delivered into the eyes of the leaders in front of him. In a sentence, Jesus deconstructs edifices, and they come tumbling down. Central precepts about equality, self-importance, service, humility, and partisanship open up. The political failure of the leaders, the Temple system, and of Jerusalem itself is exposed in a final lament (23:33–39). We can hardly handle Jesus' immediacy and power, so we will paraphrase his charges in a slightly more general political form, for the points Jesus raises with the elders and Pharisees recur throughout political history.

First, Jesus explains that the leaders do not practice what they preach. The charge devastates most of us. Half of what politicians say crumbles on this sentence. The laws they impose do not apply to themselves. They create burdens, through laws, regulations, duties, and taxes, which add up to heavy loads weighing people down. Government becomes oppressive, and the leaders do not do anything to help those suffering under them. Law should be for all of us, rulers and ruled. Putting burdens on people like this is wrong. Make sure you don't do it.

Second, the leaders do things to appear good in the public's eyes. They present themselves in the best possible light and are caught up in processes of self-importance, receiving honor, and being seen as righteous people. Status and self-approbation drive them, and that is not the right way to rule.

"Instead, you should deconstruct all status, honor, and self-importance. You are all under one Master, and you are all equal. Do not give any earthly leader the status of father, because you have only one Father,

God in heaven. And don't call yourself 'Teacher,' because you have one Teacher, the Messiah. Those of you who claim to be greatest will be so only by acting as your servant. Those who exalt themselves will be brought down low, and the humble will be raised up. I am giving you a complete reversal of present leadership relationships. No status. No honor. Only care, service, and humility."

Now Jesus switches from talking in the presence of the leaders to directly addressing them: "There is a deeper charge against you, teachers of the law and Pharisees. You actually close out God's way of living from people's lives. You yourselves don't live the right way, and you prevent ordinary people from so doing. You claim to be living righteously while you pass on false principles. Woe to you for doing this. It is a self-justifying hypocrisy, not the truth.

"You, teachers of the law and Pharisees, aim to convert people to your party. You work hard to make people support you and your views, but when that has happened, they are just trapped in the hell and futility you live in. Really, you are worshipping your way of seeing things and are trapped in the hypocrisy that involves. Woe to you.

"More than this, you find ways of reversing the relationship between the centrality of God and the peripheral. For you, the gifts to the Temple are more important in deciding people's faithfulness than their relationship with God. You blind people to God and to the meaning of their lives. You focus on petty observances, gifts, and rituals, on extracting money from people, rather on than people's relationship with almighty God. You say that covenanting with God only counts when you hand over money or go to the altar, rather than allowing them to relate directly to the God who has made them. Everything we do takes place in relation to God. If you do not see that, you are blind while trying to lead others. You are blind fools.

"You have a great ability to make trivia important, giving small amounts of the most trivial items to God, but ignoring the vast income of the Temple treasury. You ignore the important matters of law, justice, mercy, and faithfulness. You strain out a gnat and swallow a camel, and you lead others into the same blind way of thinking, so that throughout society we are concerned with trivia and ignore justice.

"Woe to you, teachers of the law and Pharisees, you hypocrites! You present yourselves to the public as squeaky clean and honest, but your motives are greed and self-indulgence. Outside you appear good; inside you are hypocrites and wicked. Government must have integrity. You can't whitewash over bones and corruption and pretend that everything is all right when leaders are really pursuing their own wickedness.

"Woe to you, leaders, you hypocrites. You pay lip service to the prophets and good politicians of the past. You erect memorials for them, but you are not really following them. You rewrite history. You pretend that you follow in the footsteps of the good and are not part of the evil of the past. But you actually follow in the ways of the wicked and do the same things as those in the past who persecuted the good and ignored injustice.

"You are like snakes and vipers, out to kill prophets who are wise and righteous. Look whom you attack. Actually, you are removing good and just people from the scene. You want to get them out of the way because they bear witness to your evil. You actually want to kill and erase those who are just and honest. You are persecutors. You are part of the evil blood-shedding tradition down through history. How will you escape being condemned to hell?"

The actual words of Jesus are far more devastating than this pallid paraphrase, presented this way to show the *structural* critique presented by Jesus. The same issues are present now—burdensome government, self-righteous leaders, putting on a front, and the persecution of good and innocent people. The words implicate us and set out the big picture of compromise and deception normal with political power. Rather than live on God's terms, these distortions dwell with us, both the governed and the rulers (Matt. 23:1–36).

Jesus' critique shows outrageous courage. Once Jesus has said this, he has to go. Given the attitudes of the rulers, this is like writing his death certificate in blood. Principled opposition always costs. Whistle-blowers lose their jobs. The critical member of Cabinet goes to the backbenches. But this is not just the sack or demotion for Jesus. Once these great reverberating words are out, Jesus will be killed. This he knows. His final words are ones of tender but incisive regret. He faces terminal danger, but his concern is for the sea of faces gathered before him who cannot see:

> O Jerusalem, Jerusalem, you who kill the prophets and stone those sent to you, how often have I longed to gather your children together, as a hen gathers her chicks under her wings, but you were not willing. Look, your house is left to you desolate. For I tell you, you will not see me again until you say, 'Blessed is he who comes in the name of the Lord.'" (Matt. 23:37–39)

This is a farewell and a warning. Often the good and truthful politicians are not voted for or are ignored, and the sycophant and the bland are elected. So often, politics travels toward desolation. Imperial conflict, apartheid, Fascism, terrorism, global warming, and the energy crisis were a long time coming and supported by the masses. "You can tell the weather when the sky is red, but you cannot discern the times [cf.

16:2–3]. You do not see, but when you do see, you will bless my coming. Instead of walking backward to regret, why not see where you are going?" (cf. 23:38–39).

The Steady Vision

From this great confrontation, through a long and turbulent day, Jesus moves out of the Temple. The leaders are too disorganized and verbally defeated to attack. He and his disciples walk over to the Mount of Olives, looking down on the buildings they have just left. The discussion begins with the Temple but moves into a discourse that the disciples are expected to absorb (Mark 13). It suggests political confrontation. "On account of me you will stand before governors and kings as witnesses to them" (13:9). Again, political witness is integral to the gospel. Often this discourse is described as apocalyptic, discussing the great climactic events of the future. Yet much of it is better described as anti-apocalyptic in the contemporary Jewish sense. Rather than looking for the immediate act of God, Jesus teaches his disciples to handle a series of events through history with equanimity.

First is the Temple. It will be razed. Unthinkable, but he says it. "Messiahs will come. Wars, conflicts, and natural disasters will happen. You will endure persecution nationally and internationally. Face your trials as they come, with the Holy Spirit as your guide. The gospel will spread worldwide. Jerusalem and the Temple will face terrible ordeals, but you are to avoid them. Especially beware false Messiahs claiming to lead you to victory. Your job is to be faithful, awake, and aware." Thus Jesus gives his disciples a route through world events so that they will not be thrown off balance. Especially, they will not be caught up in the great cataclysmic sack of Jerusalem, where a million, believing God would vindicate them, die at the hands of the Romans (in 70). Christians will follow Jesus' instructions to flee (13:14–18), finding refuge at Pella in Perea (Eusebius, *Ecclesiastical History* 3.5). As a result, that abhorrent event does not appear in the later annals of the church. The emphasis of this teaching is against apocalyptic or looking for the acts and signs of God. Rather, Christians are to have an even tenor to their way.

Jesus insists, "Nobody knows when the final vindication of God will be. Even I do not know, so do not get caught up in portents and omens. The coming of the Son of Man will rather be when everybody is living life on their own self-indulgent terms, not giving a thought for anything beyond themselves. So what is required of you is that you be ready, geared up to do God's work, remaining faithful and wise, serving as I have asked you to serve. Know that my words to you will not pass away. Watch!" (cf. 13:32–37). Thus, Jesus gives a weak, pathetic bunch of disciples some of the tools they need to cope with their, and our, subsequent history (cf. Matt. 24; Mark 13; Luke 21:5–36).

Stewards of God's Time

Then occurs an emphasis that is difficult to understand. It grows out of Jesus' words to his disciples, perhaps continued in Bethany, after they wend their way back home in the dark. But it takes off into a universal series of parables recorded in Matthew 25, which perhaps are delivered in the Temple on Wednesday.[6] They focus on the theme of being awake, ready, and accountable to God. It seems a strange theme to be so insistent about at this stage. Perhaps that is because in a secularized form it has become part of our culture. We watch time, assess work, plan ahead, and are not caught slacking. We use resources and try not to bury them. In that sense, Western culture is an heir to the Protestant ethic, which in part grows from these parables of watchfulness and accountability.

We can forget the fifteen hundred years of relative sleep, when people were prey to their circumstances and confined life to the "traditional" or "natural." But in all ages, these words go beyond us. We need to activate our consciousness in relation to God, to undertake work, events, and use of resources so that they will face the ultimate test of God's assessment and the coming again of the Son of Man. All this involves different frames of thinking.

For most of us, actively being awake to God does not happen. In Western culture, criteria of effectiveness, efficiency, profit, rewards, speed, output, sales, market share, popularity, richness, and success abound. They are like little arrows, pointing in all kinds of directions, requiring furious local effort. But they lack the concerted evaluation of these last great parables focused on God. What, in the end, will they add up to? The rule of God, the priorities of the King, are paramount and should ingrain our lives and be registered in each year's growth. Already Jesus has recounted the story of the servant who does not expect his master's return and lives indulgently. Suddenly he will face a nasty shock (Matt. 24:45–51; Mark 13:32–37; Luke 12:42–46).

The first of the great Wake Up! parables concerns ten bridesmaids who have to be ready for the wedding. Five are ready, and five do not get around to what they have to do, forgetting oil for their lamps. They flap around and are too late. "Therefore keep watch, because you do not know the day or the hour" when the Son of Man comes (Matt. 25:13, 31; cf. 24:42, 44).

Then Jesus reworks the parable of the Minas, which the crowds in Jericho have already heard (25:14–30; cf. Luke 19:12–27). Now there is no danger of triumphalism, and the focus of the parable changes. In contrast to the earlier version, this one is full of the generosity of God. Each person is given sixty times as much, great slabs of wealth. The servants who work with and for the master are congratulated on their faithfulness and invited to "come and share your Master's happiness." This is the generosity of God, not a vicious overlord. Yet here, the man who resists God and what God gives him is locked inside his own meanness. He is judged for it and put where there will be weeping and gnashing of teeth. The principle of God's abundance rules. When we are given from God, we are given to overflowing. "For everyone who has will be given more, and he will have an abundance" (Matt. 25:29). Stewardship with God opens up into abundance. We heed what we are doing as stewards of God or end up selfishly resentful.

Then, finally, Jesus gives his last public teaching. He proclaims, "The Son of Man comes in his glory and gathers the nations before him, and they are separated as the sheep are from the goats" (cf. 25:31–46). This is no parable because Jesus says, "*When* the Son of Man comes in his glory, all the nations will be gathered before him" (25:31). For one who has just signed his own death warrant, it is odd so to talk. It is clear that these are the terms of the Kingdom, beyond negotiation—neighbor love or no neighbor love. The characteristic marks of this Kingdom's politics are almost traditional womanly action: providing care, food, drink, hospitality—real caring action. All the male pomposity of politics is pared down to the King's question: "What have you done?" Words, position, power, and importance are gone. The Son of Man (= king, 25:31, 34, 40) identifies with those who are hungry, thirsty, unclothed, and imprisoned. "He will reply, 'I tell you the truth, whatever you did not do for one of the least of these, you did not do for me.' Then they will go away to eternal punishment, but the righteous to eternal life" (25:45–46).

Why does Jesus require this response? Clearly, we are held to account—for our treatment of the poor, our use of resources, and our response to Jesus. Jesus teaches that we are accountable to God for all our actions, political and nonpolitical. But more than this, our actions are focused on the Son of Man (= the King, the Son of God). What we do with this man is, at root, our central political response, and by it we are judged. This is reflected in a final pivotal saying of Jesus to the gathered crowds who are heaving with the issue of Jesus' messiahship.[7] Jesus is saying things the crowd can hardly understand, identifying the character of his coming death. Then he suddenly says, like two bullets,

"Now is the judgment of this world; now the ruler of this world will be driven out" (John 12:31 NRSV).

The first bullet lays it out clearly. In these events, the world is judged. He is not on trial; we are. True, we are not Pharisees or Romans, but we cannot extricate ourselves from all the attitudes that extrude this death. They may also be ours. When God is with us, banishing our autonomy, we too might react by wanting God dead; the horror of this possibility should bring us up short. This evil murder is not just of "a good man" (John 7:12); humanity sets out to murder God, futile though that turns out to be. Now is God's judging of the world, the place where human guilt is evident. This is the event where we are incontrovertibly revealed as evil.

The second bullet travels to another place. Now the ruler/prince of the world will be overthrown. Jesus' next statement shows that he is expecting the cross, so this great conquest will take place there. But over whom? Who is the ruler/prince of this world, the enemy? He is the Satan. But who is the Satan, the evil one? We know little about him, and many would deny his existence. Is Jesus speaking literally or figuratively? Can evil be so personified apart from the Creator? Are we dumping our evil on a dark figure? These questions gather, but it is a fool who does not see that evildoers are not actually in control; they suffer as slaves of "the evil one" (John 17:15; Matt. 6:13). The thing we know from Jesus' temptations is that Satan, the great Liar, is also political. He shows Jesus all the kingdoms of this world, to be ruled in subjection to evil, and so they have been ruled through the centuries. The evil one is deeply implicated in politics, sometimes providing direct potentates, at other times more distant ministers and advisers. It is not difficult to draw back and see the ruler of this world, the ruler who runs the show and draws his power from something within the world—slavery, killing, hate, control. Satan's students rule in many states. "*Now!*" Jesus' word is emphatic. "*Now* he is overthrown." Now is when the world political rule of the evil one is scuppered. This is some event!

Jesus: The Personal and the Political

This great political drama twists our consciousness, and yet the narrative of Jesus' last days refuses a centrally political interpretation. Although the events are full of intrigue, power, violence, and statecraft, Jesus seems to have something else on his mind. He cares about his people in their relationship with God their Father and with him, ordinary people who cannot dwell with God on their own initiative. Throughout the last days both Jesus and the Gospel writers lay out the fulfillment of the great messianic prophecies. The crowds have to face the fact that this is not "Messiah" as they expect him. Jesus' concern is not to *have* followers, the preoccupation of political "leaders" throughout history, but *for* his followers. He turns to them, converses at meals with them, loves them, and makes sure they know that they above all are his *friends*. Jesus teaches them of the intimacy of their relationship with God.

There is the beautiful tenderness of a woman pouring glorious perfume over Jesus' head and drenching his body in an act of grateful love and preparation for his burial (John 12:3, 7). He washes the disciples' feet (13:4–17). He takes them through the traumas they will shortly face (13:18–21). They do not understand, but they will understand. He prepares Peter and the other disciples for their failure, so that when it occurs, there will be a deeper truth than that failure (13:31–38). He longs to be with them (14:1–4). He prays for them and shows them the living power of abiding in their relationship with God (14:5–14). He gives them knowledge of the coming indwelling of God the Holy Spirit in their lives (e.g., 14:15–17). He moves the disciples from the position where they ask, "Show us the Father," to one where they know they have seen, touched, handled, and listened to God (14:8–14; 20:28; 1 John 1:1).

Here, as hundreds of millions of Christians know, the greatest drama of human history is being played out. The centuries have shown that the great human quest for God is often self-important, dominated by priests or philosophers coming to their own conclusions and trying to convince others, repeatedly on spurious grounds. But here in the Son, God has come to us, surprising, overturning our preconceptions (cf. John 14:11). This God is friendly, a God of love, one who understands us better than we understand ourselves (of course, but we are still surprised). God comes to us without the need for status, giving power *to* us to live good lives, not holding power over us or pushing an agenda except that he is *for* us. This is what shapes the last days before the crucifixion. Others do the political scheming. The self-importance of politics is absent in these relationships. Caiaphas, the soldiers, Judas, Pilate, and Herod will be caught up in political murder, but the focus here is far deeper. Other rulers might need subjects or servants, but the great God of creation is actually quite relaxed with us, wanting us ordinary people as friends. The invitation is to come to Jesus as friend. It is as simple and profound as that.

This personal focus reflects life. Our basic problems are not just or mainly political, but human. Through greed, power, injustice, and pride, human sin plays into politics, but the problem is bigger and deeper than politics in itself. The ideal leader, the people, a party, or a set of political ideas cannot solve the matter. All the utopian politics of the ages falls before the fact that this good man—coughing up pearls, straightening the chins of the poor, and mending the sick—has to be done away with. The problem, then as now, goes that deep. The attempt to isolate the political from the rest of life and from our relationship with our Creator will not work. Politics remains part of life, and the evils of life inhabit politics. Rightly, therefore, the church down the ages has dwelled on the fuller personal and human focus of these last days before the crucifixion.

Like us, the disciples are ordinary people who are being given a relationship with God, a relationship that they cannot comprehend and do not deserve, but which is real beyond knowing. God's relationship with humankind, still one of freedom and without coercion, is shown to us. Judas, the betrayer, makes up his own mind, before it explodes under the error he has perpetrated. Throughout every circumstance Jesus shows us God the Father coming out to meet us and welcome us back home to the feast, the feast lived in tranquillity with God. The central reality of human existence is not a political drama but ordinary people having their lives with God restored through the Savior. Jesus' concern is friends and people, not primarily matters of state.

Centrally true though this is, it is not quite all the picture, for politics intrudes even in the Last Supper.[8] After the Passover meal, Jesus raises the question about who would betray him. Defensively, the disciples move on to assert their loyalty as his followers, and then Peter also vows his superior dedication (Mark 14:29; John 13:37). Jesus responds by repeating the theme of the servant ruler, but with additions (Luke 22:24–30). He points out that the lording kings like to think of themselves as benefactors, as they give taxed and extorted things back to the people. Conversely, "the great serve as I serve." Jesus uses himself as an example: "For who is greater, the one who is at table or the one who serves? . . . But I am among you as one who serves" (22:27). Though Luke does not record it, Jesus is referring to his earlier act of foot washing, his house service to the disciples. Then follows a further statement, generous almost to the point of inaccuracy:

> You are those who have stood by me in my trials. And I confer on you a kingdom, just as my Father conferred one on me, so that you may eat and drink at my table in my kingdom and sit on thrones, judging the twelve tribes of Israel. (Luke 22:28–30)

Immediately afterward, they will hardly stand by Jesus, but in the longer term they will. And Jesus overtly discusses political succession in terms of kingdom, thrones, judges of the twelve tribes. There is no doubt that Jesus is conveying to these disciples their own subsequent political rule, different from worldly rule. Again, we know how it turned out: death for several and persecution from Agrippa. This is not a promise that can be cashed in for rewards and power. Instead, what is conferred carries on the acknowledged rule of God in an overt political outcome.

And so there are the great pastoral talks around the Last Supper, and the prayer where we listen in on Christ's relationship with the true God, our Father. The structure of that prayer is revealing (John 17). Five verses concern Jesus' relationship with the Father. Twelve verses are for the disciples, and a further six verses for those who will follow on as disciples. This great prayer, which shows the intimacy basic to all human existence, occurs a few hours before the vicious action begins.

Jesus, the Sanhedrin, and Pilate

The Last Supper, convened within the city of Jerusalem, is followed by the time of prayer and testing in Gethsemane. Involved in Jesus' arrest are officials from the Chief Priests (especially Annas and Caiaphas, who have dealt with Judas), some elders of the Sanhedrin, Scribes, Pharisees, Temple guards, and some soldiers (Matt. 26:47; Mark 14:43; John 18:3). Apart from the participation of Judas, a number of other points are significant about the arrest.

First, weapons are involved. This seems to compromise Jesus' peaceful ways, but the details are interesting. At the end of the Last Supper, Jesus warns the disciples that now times are different (Luke 22:35–38). "Now take purse, bag, and sword," he says. The disciples take him literally, a repeated failing, and produce two swords, for this is a violent culture. Jesus closes down the issue, perhaps almost embarrassed at their literalistic lack of real awareness: "Enough!" Later Peter actually cuts off the high priest's servant's ear. Jesus heals it and produces the proverb "All who draw the sword will die by the sword" (Matt. 26:52), which bites repeatedly into military history. We probably know the servant's name, Malchus, because he later becomes a Christian (John 18:10).

Second, Jesus steps forward to be arrested and insists on the disciples being let go, refusing to allow Peter's action to upset that outcome (18:8–11). The soldiers who come are probably the Temple guard not Roman soldiers. They take Jesus, bound, three-quarters of a mile down the Kidron Valley, in through the southern, Tekoa gate, and up the streets of the Tyropoean Valley to the Palace of Annas, on the slope of the Upper City. Annas is probably the chief initiator of the process and the powerful center of the Temple plot (John 18:13). Now he has Jesus, and he orchestrates the following events. Peter, probably John, and perhaps Nicodemus and/or Joseph of Arimathea also go to Annas's house, and Peter's first denial of Jesus occurs there.[9] Annas questions

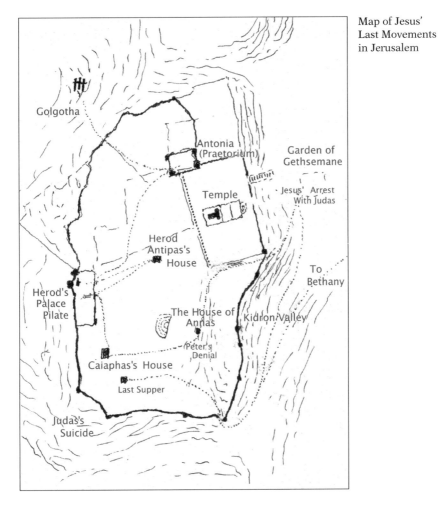

Map of Jesus'
Last Movements
in Jerusalem

Jesus and strikes him for answering forthrightly in what we now call "free speech" and openness.

Jesus is packed off to Caiaphas's palace, to go through what will amount to the official "trial" with the Sanhedrin in a hastily convened court sometime around daybreak, on Good Friday morning. The process is an ad hoc political trial, seeking to damn an enemy, not a regular criminal procedure. A proper trial would occur in the Temple, which, given the attitude of the crowds, is unthinkable. As we have already seen, Jesus' messiahship is for Caiaphas both the great blasphemy, leading him to rend his beautiful clothes, and also the clincher, proving him an enemy of Rome. The council members present assent to Caiaphas's roar of guilt, spitting and striking with naked anger at the one who has bested them and attacked their system. Joseph of Arimathea and Nicodemus retreat or are absent. Jesus is blindfolded, punched and abused, and led bound to Pilate's palace, the governor's residence in the west of the city.[10] Pilate may not expect their visit. Perhaps he does not even have time for breakfast. The members of the Sanhedrin and chief priests demand the death penalty of their prisoner.

The meeting of Jesus and Pilate is perhaps the greatest political event of all time.[11] Pilate is maybe five years into being procurator/prefect. He has the power of Rome behind him, but if he does his job badly, he can be sacked, as indeed he effectively is by Vitellius, the Syrian legate, after Samaritan protests in 35.[12] He has already had a run-in with the Jews over having Roman standards in Jerusalem. He threatens to kill the Jews if they are not prepared to have images of Caesar in the city. They say that they prefer to die rather than have the law about images disobeyed, and bare their necks en masse. Pilate gives way and already has a fair idea of how easily a revolution can emerge from this fanatical people.[13] Moreover, he is already in difficulties. Luke 13:1 mentions an incident in which Pilate has killed some Jews in or around the Temple. He is vindictive, and the Jews are resentful.

The Jewish leaders confront Pilate with their requirement. The city is already humming with Passover visitors. A crowd gathers early, and the word speeds through the tightly packed city. People decamp from the Temple area across to Pilate's (or Herod the Great's) palace. Pilate's permission is necessary for death because the Sanhedrin has no power over life and death (John 18:31). Ideally, they want Jesus condemned to death on their say-so and are embarrassed by their fabricated charges. When Pilate asks about the charges, they respond: "If he were not a criminal, . . . we would not have handed him over to you" (John 18:30). The Jewish leaders' failure to handle the case professionally gives the upper hand to Pilate. He can examine Jesus on his own terms. He goes back inside the palace, where his examination is not subject to the mob or dominated by the Pharisees. His focus is different from theirs. They fear the Son of God and have declared him blasphemous. Pilate goes straight for his concern: "Are you the king of the Jews?" (18:33). Pilate's response is built into the question. He implies, "If you say you are, you will be killed. If you say you are not, then you are no threat to the Romans, and you can go free."

Jesus insists on understanding the question. If Pilate is thinking about it, then he must be answered in his own terms. If it comes from the Jews, then that different meaning must be addressed.[14] Also at issue, of course, is the meaning that Jesus himself gives the question. Pilate's response, as of an interrogator who finds himself interrogated, is to be irritated: "It was your people and your Chief Priests who handed you over to me [and are making the fuss!] What is it you have done?" (18:35). But Jesus refuses to move off to this second question and stays focused on the first. He talks cross-culturally to Pilate: "My Kingdom is not of this world. If it were, my servants would fight to prevent my arrest by the Jews. But now my Kingdom is from another place" (18:36).

We notice the insistence of the answer—"My kingdom . . . . My kingdom . . . ." It can also be understood as "my kingship." There is no doubt that Jesus is insisting on answering the question first asked by Pilate in the affirmative: "I am King. I am King." Nor is there any doubt that Jesus is forcing a transition on Pilate, who is trying to ask if Jesus is king of the Jews on his own terms. Pilate then responds, "You are a King, then!" (18:37). He wants his own simple answer, but that does not close the issue. Jesus has required Pilate to face what kind of kingship Jesus actually represents, and he now pushes it further. This, of course, fits the situation. It doesn't really add up for Pilate. It is odd for Pilate to face a king of the Jews who is betrayed by his own leaders. Here clearly is someone who is not a normal insurrectionist. Pilate does not trust the howling crowd outside or the leaders he has to deal with. Jesus' argument that he is not mounting a rebellion with his followers and was easily arrested further validates the case. Pilate cannot easily ascertain what kind of king this person is.

Here we must stop for reflection. The short sentence "My Kingdom/ kingship is not of this world" has become for many a kind of abstract statement of Christian political otherworldliness. It means, for many, "My rule is only spiritual and does not engage with politics." This text, interpreted in an apolitical sense, has often been the reason for ignoring the political content of the Gospels down the ages, popular especially with secular rulers. We must reflect on whether this interpretation holds up. What does Jesus mean by telling Pilate, "My kingdom is not of this world"? "World" (*kosmos*) is used with a number of meanings in John—created order, human existence, people as a whole, or sinful world.[15] Within all of these meanings, except perhaps the third, which is more colloquial, the engagement of God with the world is paramount. This is not withdrawal language. "For God so loved the world" is typical (3:16). It is false to use the phrase "not of this world" in the sense of withdrawal from politics. Doing so undercuts the Johannine emphasis on God's relationship with the world and replaces it with a view that withdraws into asceticism. This can be seen from the words we earlier examined: "Now is the time for judgment on this world; now the prince [ruler] of this world will be driven out" (12:31). This is not withdrawal language. Nor is Jesus' petition: "My prayer is not that you take them out of the world, but that you protect them from the evil one" (17:15).

Consequently, "My kingdom is not of this world" and "My kingdom is from another place" are not spoken in withdrawal language.

Jesus is actually talking to Pilate in his pagan terms rather than Jewish or theological ones. He means something like this: "My kingdom does not belong to this world. My kingdom is not based on human power, or fighting, or the kind of intrigue that is going on here. It is not like the Roman Empire or Herodian rule. My kingdom has its roots with God rather than in this evil age. It has a different basis from the kingship that you or the Jews are discussing." It is, in fact, the kingdom that Jesus has been teaching throughout his ministry. Jesus is testifying to one, Pilate, who can barely understand the terms on which he is King and the meaning of Kingdom rule. Clearly, this verse does not run counter to all the previous political teachings and actions of the Messiah; instead, it addresses the different basis of Jesus' kingship. It is time for this wrong interpretation to be discarded.

The simplistic conclusion of Pilate, "You are a king, then!" (18:37), underlines three things. First, Jesus has taken the route that will lead to his death. In Roman Jerusalem, any king other than Caesar must die. Second, Pilate now has the initiative. He has the technical grounds for sentencing this man to die, and can show mercy or not, as he pleases. Third, it is superficial. Jesus' careful insistence on saying what he means by kingship is ignored in Pilate's crude assertion. Jesus' response is unequivocal and again takes Pilate beyond where he wants to go: "[It is as you say.] You are right in saying I am a king" (18:37). For the third time before Pilate, Jesus reiterates his kingship. Neither to Caiaphas nor Pilate does Jesus equivocate about his kingship or messiahship when there is every incentive to dodge it, to stay alive.

Then comes the pivotal claim: "In fact, for this reason I was born, and for this I came into the world" (18:37). Again this affirms the incarnate direction of Jesus' kingship. A king coming into the world cannot be otherworldly. The focus is on coming and the purpose for coming "*into the world*." But then comes the great culmination: "For this I came into the world, to testify to the truth. Everyone on the side of truth listens to me" (18:37). This is the denouement. Suddenly, the whole weight of what Jesus is saying is out in the open. Politics is not just about power and domination, but about truth. Moreover, Jesus is the judge, the adjudicator, and the standard of true and false. Pilate faces a different ball game and has trouble picking up the rules. He knows the charges are false and that this man is innocent and beyond him. But he has not extracted Jesus' denial of kingship, and this will be difficult with the Chief Priests.

The dynamics take over. Pilate probably moves from a semiprivate audience to follow normal procedure. He goes outside to the ceremonially clean Chief Priests, who lay their charges against Jesus and accuse him of many things. These are likely not to be much better organized than their initial charges. Pilate sees a group of vindictive leaders out to get this man, who responds in silence. He goes back inside, the Gospels record, and prompts Jesus to answer the charges: "Don't you hear how many things they are charging you of?" (Matt. 27:13). "Aren't you going to answer?" (Mark 15:4). This is insistent. Why does this man not defend himself? By this stage Pilate is aware that the charges do not amount to anything truly culpable: envy is running the accusers' agenda (Matt. 27:18). They are using Pilate against Jesus. Then, as Pilate sits on the judgment seat, he receives a message from his wife, obviously also in the palace: "Don't have anything to do with this innocent [just, KJV] man, for I have suffered a great deal today in a dream because of him" (Matt. 27:19). She is insistent, acting from conscience and direct conviction of Jesus' innocence. Dreams are not reliable, but she, like her husband, is deeply troubled by the injustice that is going on.

We do not know exactly what happens, but it is likely then that the drama moves outside again, for Pilate to give his verdict. He announces to the chief priests and the crowd, "I find no basis for a charge against this man" (Luke 23:4; cf. John 18:38; 19:4, 6). Pilate no longer dwells on the superficial judgment "You are a king then!" but faces the truth. This man is innocent and should be released. But the chief priests and the crowd respond along lines already drawn. They are nationalists, even Zealots, and once the Roman system can be seen as the object of hate, any friend of Rome is an enemy of the people, and so the crowds roar.

Pilate hears, probably from one of the Chief Priests near him, that Jesus has "come from Galilee, stirring up the people all over Judea" (Luke 23:5), and he grasps at a straw. In passing, we note that Pilate must know, as we know, the enormity of this charge. Jesus precisely is *not* allowing the crowd to be stirred up and has shown in his dialogue with Pilate that he is no rabble-rouser. His accusers are lying to Pilate, and Pilate knows it. When Pilate learns that Jesus is a Galilean and therefore under Herod's jurisdiction, he sends Jesus to Herod Antipas, weakly trying to opt out. The implication is that maybe the Herodian rulers can handle the Jews more effectively than Roman procurators, a line Agrippa pumps later in his climb to power. Jesus is taken through the now crowded streets, probably by Roman soldiers, to Antipas's palace. The chief priests also go along to argue their case to Antipas. By now the Roman guard will be working hard to isolate this group from the Passover crowds.

It is tense. The crowds do not disperse, and the Temple party and Zealots have time to work on the crowds while Jesus is being taken to Herod. And so Herod Antipas—"that fox" (Luke 13:31–33) and killer of John the Baptist (Mark 6:27)—finally has his desired meeting with Jesus (cf. Luke 9:9). Luke records, "When Herod saw Jesus, he was greatly pleased, because for a long time he had been wanting to see him. From what he had heard about him, he hoped to see him perform some miracle. He plied him with many questions, but Jesus gave him no answer" (23:8–9). This understates the full dynamics of the meeting. At times after the death of John the Baptist, Herod has wanted to kill Jesus as a possible threat (13:31). He will have heard of the feeding of the five thousand as an attempted uprising. Herod knows that, in some strange sense, Jesus is not a threat, and here he meets the one who is greater than John the Baptist and fuels his fascination with the Baptist's God (Mark 6:20).

Nevertheless, the confrontation is totally disappointing. Antipas throws questions at his prisoner. The chief priests and teachers of the law do the same (Luke 23:10). But Jesus gives no answer. He will not perform for Herod. He is not under judgment. They are. Herod and his soldiers ridicule and mock Jesus, because he has not performed as they would have him do. They undress and re-dress him in an elegant robe. Then back a quarter mile to Pilate's palace goes the whole group—the soldiers, Jesus, Chief Priests, members of the Sanhedrin, and hosts of following crowds (23:11).

First Herod Antipas delivers his verdict on Jesus possibly in person. It runs against the Priestly party. Pilate has done a good deed to Antipas in presenting him with a possible Galilean threat, but both concur in finding no fault in him. Two men enmeshed in evil, but with well-tuned political judgment, agree on the goodness and innocence of this man and become friends sharing their superiority to the rabble (23:12). Together they at least have that response to the truth. They believe, as powerful men, that they can carry the day against his accusers. Pilate makes the formal pronouncement: "Neither I nor Herod have found a basis for your charges." It is quite clear they are firm and resolute in their conclusion, and for the second time it has been given (cf. Luke 23:4, 13–16). But they are shaken.

The crowd, worked on by chief priests and elders, is insistent that they want Barabbas released and Jesus crucified (23:18–21). Mark (15:6–8) suggests that the crowd, perhaps prompted by the chief priests, takes the initiative in bringing up the release of the prisoner and changing the fulcrum of the trial from the justice of Jesus' case to their preferences. This is powerful pressure. "Barabbas was in prison with the insurrectionists who had committed murder in the uprising" (15:7). Again, this shows the weight of Zealot and nationalist fervor in Jerusalem, and the dangerous game the Temple party is pursuing in appealing to it. This is the same alliance that will lead to the devastation of Jerusalem in 70.

The crowd, now solid in opposition to Pilate, senses his weakness, and the drama becomes a direct confrontation.

Pilate has Jesus flogged. Perhaps he hopes he can be released, since a flogging is standard "behave yourself" treatment for the innocent (cf. Luke 23:17). If they see this man beaten and humiliated, perhaps that would be enough. In a crude parody of kingship, the soldiers crush thorns on his head as a crown, put him in a purple robe, and mockingly bow to him as "King of the Jews," striking him in the face.[16] The psychology of this move backfires. Pilate probably hopes that seeing Jesus' suffering will evoke some pity, but the crowd cannot own this parody as their king. To mock their king is to mock them. They reject the implication and resent even more the Roman insult. Pilate tries to say definitively, "Look, I am bringing him out to you, to let you know that I can find no basis for a charge against him. Here is the man." It is another judgment of innocence (cf. John 19:4–5). But by now, the crowd is implacable. They bay, "Crucify! Crucify!" The soldiers have their weapons ready and are fully prepared for savage crowd control, many with the memory of bloody deaths in their minds.

It is probably at this stage that Pilate breaks and gives in. Even in the face of the uproar, he still has enough conviction to wash his hands in front of them, saying, "I am innocent of this man's blood. . . . It is your responsibility" (Matt. 27:24). This reflects both his weakness and his insistence on staying with the truth of the situation. Perhaps it is an attempt to get the crowd to take responsibility for what it is doing. They respond by saying, "His blood be on us and on our children" (27:25). Now Pilate has effectively handed over his power to them. But still he does not give up. John records, and this seems to be the final dynamic, the Jewish leaders claiming, "We have a law, and according to that law he must die, because he claimed to be the Son of God" (John 19:7). The Jews are arguing vehemently for the priority of their law in Jerusalem, but Pilate is again stopped dead by the man. Who is this bleeding, lacerated person?

Once more Pilate goes with Jesus into the palace, away from the crowd. John describes Pilate as being afraid (19:8). He seems to be afraid of who Jesus is, rather than of the baying crowd outside. His question, "Where do you come from?" refers back to Jesus' "My kingdom is from another place" (19:9; 18:36). Now Pilate wants to find out more, but Jesus does not answer. The situation is beyond control. It is a pregnant silence, and we shortly learn that it does not reflect Jesus' antipathy toward Pilate, but rather the opposite. Pilate further loses his composure and bullies, "Do you refuse to speak to me? . . . Don't you realize I have power either to free you or to crucify you?" (19:10). By this stage, Pilate probably does not have this power because they are speaking against a background of implacable, chanting crowds. But Jesus' response finally puts everything in perspective. He acknowledges and even excuses Pilate's difficulty in doing justice. Jesus sympathizes with Pilate's dilemma. In the middle of his own utter weakness, he serenely acknowledges the power and sovereignty of God and recognizes the directing actors in this evil drama. Pilate is now the pawn in the proceedings.

Jesus says: "You would have no power over me if it were not given you from above. Therefore the one who handed me over to you is guilty of a greater sin" (19:11). Thus, Pilate faces the enormity of this man who is utterly in control under the sovereign power of God, even as he is being fed to the death lust of the crowd. Again in spiritual panic, Pilate rushes out and tries to set Jesus free, but he is shouted down. "Anyone who is a king opposes Caesar." The people intone loyalty to the hated Caesar in order to get their own way. "He claims to be a king. You cannot free him without being an enemy of Caesar" (19:12). If that report reaches Rome, Pilate is lost. So, finally, he concurs. "Here is your king!" "Take him away! Take him away! Crucify him!" "Shall I crucify your king?" (19:14–15). "We have no king but Caesar," the chief priests answer (19:15). Through this assertion of their loyalty, they checkmate and defeat Pilate, who hands Jesus over to be crucified.

Pilate's guard marches Jesus condemned into the Antonia fortress, the Praetorium, where the main Roman guard is (Mark 15:16). There Jesus is stripped, mocked, hit repeatedly over the head, and spat at. The full company then leads him away to crucify him. They will make sure that a pretender to the throne is humiliated, crucified, and is an example to every other potential rebel. After celebrating their victory, the crowd eventually disperses. The enormity and injustice of the act have psychologically shredded Pilate. The Roman process of crucifixion takes over. This time there is no rebellion because the crowd has been bought off.

The Cross

The petulance continues. The sign JESUS OF NAZARETH, THE KING OF THE JEWS is hoisted by Pilate, affirming something about the man, but at the same time stating Pilate's loyalty to Caesar (John 19:19). The chief priests scuttle back to Pilate's palace, complaining against this gesture because it ridicules Jews in general and opposes their view of Jesus, but Pilate, strong and obstinate in defeat, dismisses them (19:21–22).

Our political reflection on the cross takes account of several things. Jesus' kingship and rule stand against all kinds of things like empires, controlling people, state violence, and power politics. But in terms of popular support, it did not work. All of these conspired to kill Jesus on the cross. We can have faith in this man and his way and stand against these empty ways of doing politics, for such they are. But it is a position of weakness. In this sense the question posed by the cross is whether Jesus' way of politics can ever work. It will be opposed and seemingly defeated by the evils of control, nationalism, and self-serving power. Those who live politically for peace, gentleness, law-abiding, and justice invite suffering and attack. Thoroughgoing good politics is not recognized as strong in a sinful world. What we see at the trial of Jesus is more normal than we like to pretend.

It also brings into doubt the principle that government is good. Paul iterates it as a Christian principle in Romans 13, but much government is not, as the Roman Empire was not. God's purposes can use it for good, but often it actually does evil in tension with God's purposes. We know that from raw experience, history, and daily news. In many countries, evil and corrupt regimes try to suppress those who are more just. This is sobering. We, when we are evil, oppose what is good and try to destroy it. This man Jesus was killed by such as walk our streets, sick unto death. That Jesus should be killed by due political process should bring optimists up short. Evil government is our problem, and it is so serious that we cannot skate over it. Western liberalism tends to believe we are all good guys, really. But much of the time Western governments are not. Wars, corruption, the abuse of power, economic exploitation, political murder, providing weapons to corrupt regimes, and state-sponsored terrorism feature in recent Western history. Often good people are eliminated. Good politicians go to the backbenches because they will not toe the party line. Any fair reading of history will conclude that governments do and are evil in politics.

Our self-assessment has to be deeper and more realistic. We *and* our governments are corrupt and compromised. For decades, we manufactured millions of murderous land mines, though we now say they are evil. The people chose Barabbas rather than Jesus; modern and democratic people are substantially no different in many of their political choices. In many elections the worse candidate may be chosen, not the better. We are also trapped in various kinds of political evil, even to the extent that we will kill the innocent and good. Romans 13 is not a flaccid acceptance of the status quo, but a manifesto of God's purposes beyond the Empire's politics.

At another level far more is happening here than an exemplary leader being killed. Humanly speaking, we cannot follow this man's example. We are just not good enough. The failures of our leaders are written in corruption, war, indifference, and broken promises, but they are patterns that we all share. Like the disciples, we desert Jesus and his ways when the pressures come. No resolution to do better is enough. We share the same patterns of evil and compromise. Any other assessment is untrue and delusive, cutting us off from the realities in which we live. We are essentially in the same realpolitik as the first-century Jews. We might have ideas of justice and be against xenophobia, but we are separated from God and fundamentally out of touch with what is good. On our own we are helpless, floundering like Pilate, the chief priests, the Sadducees, or the rabble, trying but usually failing to work out our own local visions of what might be better. The events we have traced, or political history down the ages, or our personal histories—these cannot but make us aware of our helplessness, of human impotence to live remotely good lives. Occasionally there are pockets of self-congratulation, but usually they come from people who have managed to get others to do their work, or their dirty work. Apart from God, we are lost.

But here is a gentle man who has come to be our ruler, God with us. That is what he has been saying all along. We need God's help, as did the people of Jerusalem and Galilee. We need the one who understands the depth of the problem and is prepared to enter into it and carry it. We need a Savior. Also in politics, the depth of our dependence on this man is unqualified. We need God with us, for us, sucking the boil of our depravity. Here is the one who understands. In Jesus, God comes among us and faces the evils of intent and twisted thinking in human politics as in the rest of life. Jesus teaches God's ways of justice, mercy, and peace so that they are forever revealed to us. Yet there is this further stage: Jesus is prepared to carry human failure, including human political failure, in the love of God. Humanity is like a child in a tantrum and beyond sorting things out. Jesus carries this child into the place of God's calm and blessing. This child, however, is not small and helpless, but an adult monster that turns and knifes the carrier. Yet the porter will see the job through.

As the persistent and naked evils gather and power Jesus to the cross, he faces and carries them. Our evil is undergirded by the love of Christ, even unto death. In his beatings, we are healed. In the strangest reversal of all, the Old Testament insistence on wrong being by an atoning sacrifice to God is completely turned around. Here the wrongs are ours, and *God* provides the sacrifice. The Son of God is barbarically sacrificed, steady in grace and undeserved love to us. That is all we need to know. While we were enemies of God, for this is the human condition, we are made right with God through the atoning death of Jesus. He carries in his body the horrific punishment that rightly dwells with us.

> You cannot make the journey, nor can I;
> but come along the track a little way.

Say, you were good, and gave and gave and gave,
fed, healed and cared for crowds who followed,
but, when it counted, chose a murderer.
Say, you withstood all evil when it grew
and carefully exposed its origins,
until the predators all turned on you,
saliva venom, hating all you did.
Say, you as teacher shared the greatest thoughts
with those you'd nurtured through to understand.
They, vacuous, threw the pearls away.
Does not self-pity work within your soul,
resentment that this good should be so spurned,
and anger that such truth is trampled on?
The more you know and love, the lonelier,
the deeper good, the greater gulf between.
And then to know they want to crucify
God's love expressed in you.
Now love them more, nasty and fickle,
blind after wickedness and fools,
yearn for their lostness, care less
for death, know and forgive.
Then lose yourself, the Father in your heart,
and freely sacrifice your very self,
for this dear scum.[17]

This journey to the cross we cannot comprehend; we are fools to pretend we can. Jesus goes beyond us. This study only touches the theology of the cross, which has been the focus of the church down the centuries.[18] Here we see love that comprehends our failure. There is no one righteous, not even one. Here is the undergirding love beyond all our evil. "Father forgive them; they know not what they do" (Luke 23:34). Here is a sacrifice, not given to God, but given by God to humankind, meeting human evil by the undeserved and unconditional love of Jesus for us. The steady love that holds at the cross will never condemn us. Always stronger than evil is God's love for us. Suddenly the egomania of politics—the people, the leader, and the nation can do no wrong—is sobered into the accuracy of humility about human evil. Also in politics we see our dependence on God's steadfast love, justice, and mercy. Our response to God and his gentle government is at issue, not our self-initiating conceptions. And we must first be healed of sin and evil. Our politics is not to act rightly, or self-righteously, but to receive forgiving and healing love from God. Here at the cross, seemingly the biggest defeat of good that has ever occurred, we find God is with us and for us in this man. It is, as Paul described it, the disarming place for all powers. It is the place of rest for all politics.

Bibliography

Aulén, Gustaf. *Christus Victor.* Translated by A. G. Hebert. London: SPCK, 1931.

Blinzler, Josef. *The Trial of Jesus.* Cork, Ireland: Mercier, 1959.

Bond, Helen K. *Pontius Pilate in History and Interpretation.* Society for New Testament Studies Monograph Series 100. Cambridge: Cambridge University Press, 1998.

Brandon, S. G. F. *The Trial of Jesus of Nazareth.* London: Batsford, 1968.

Brown, Raymond E. *The Death of the Messiah.* 2 vols. New York: Doubleday, 1994.

Edersheim, Alfred. *The Life and Times of Jesus the Messiah.* 3d ed. 2 vols. in 1. London: Longmans, Green & Co., 1906.

Hooker, Morna D. *Not Ashamed of the Gospel.* Carlisle, UK: Paternoster, 1994.

Morris, Leon. *The Cross in the New Testament.* Grand Rapids: Eerdmans, 1965.

Peterson, David, ed. *Where Wrath and Mercy Meet.* Carlisle, UK: Paternoster, 2001.

Stott, John. *The Cross of Christ.* Leicester: Inter-Varsity, 1986.

Wallace, Ronald. *The Atoning Death of Christ.* London: Marshall, Morgan & Scott, 1981.

Wenham, David. *The Rediscovery of Jesus' Eschatological Discourse.* Sheffield: JSOT Press, 1984.

Woodbridge, Paul. "'The World' in the Fourth Gospel." Pages 1–31 in *Witness to the World.* Edited by David Peterson. Carlisle, UK: Paternoster, 1999.

Resurrection Politics

Shock

Jesus' resurrection is a shock, as unthinkable then as it is now. The accounts show the disciples acutely suffering Jesus' death. Partly, they face their own failure. They are a frightened bunch, hiding, fearing for their own lives, leaderless, looking back with confusion. The women at least attend to their mourning. They gather for comfort. At this stage much of what Jesus has said about the Temple, the Kingdom, and himself is incomprehensible. The disciples' automatic response is to melt back into the Galilean hills, as many hoping for national liberation had done before. Into this scenario comes the resurrection of Jesus and all its implications. Even with empathy, we cannot come close to feeling the shock and disorientation of this to the disciples, and then the sense of transformation, trying to take in the reality they cannot believe. Clearly, this is God's doing. The loss of Christ is replaced by awesome presence: "Surely I am with you always, even to the end of the age" (cf. Matt. 28:20). For the first time ever, God is known as bigger than death.

The disciples struggle to cope with the required change in their Weltanschauung. Jesus undertakes pastoral care of Peter, Mary, Thomas, and others who cannot cope with the fact, addressing his responses carefully to each. It is interesting how these cases of pastoral care and restoration straddle the crucifixion and resurrection almost like succeeding therapy sessions. Jesus picks up where he has left off, so to speak. The disciples' immediate responses are crude: "We want proof! Women aren't to be trusted. We can't take it in." They wait on God, with blind elation about the risen Messiah, an overweening confidence. Then the disciples receive the Holy Spirit as the directing presence of their lives and begin to settle in to all that they have experienced and now know.

The cross has been total defeat, but now it is transformed into a talisman of the completion of God's work, the expression of the love of God for humanity, and the victory of God over human evil. The Son of God has carried human evil with the steadfast love and power of God. Even though the disciples are failures and the Jewish and Roman leaders have perpetrated this great evil, the love and mercy of God is deeper. It runs stronger. Jesus has been put to death on the cross, forgiving all who have come his way, and has carried human evil with the disposing power of God's grace. The disciples are on their way to seeing the cross as the victory of God over the political authorities and powers: "If this is the worst you can do, you are washed up."

They are soon exultant with power, not their own power, but the forgiving power of God. They now know the power of Christ, which is aeons beyond a messianic Deliverer. Jesus states carefully, "All authority in heaven and on earth has been given to me. Therefore go and make disciples . . ." (Matt. 28:18). Later, Paul's talk of Christ reverberates with every form of political authority. He sees what the rule of God is like and glories in it:

> That power is the working of his mighty strength, which he exerted in [Messiah] when he raised him from the dead and seated him at his right hand in the heavenly realms, far above all rule and authority, power and dominion, and every title that can be given, not only in the present age, but also in the one to come. (Eph. 1:19–21)

This is no exaggeration. Now the great reversal is complete: the gentle rule of God begins its slow diffusion worldwide, overspreading mankind. This is no triumphalism. It is voluntary. It has to be lived and requires the unlearning of other cultures. Jesus tells the disciples: "Wait for my Spirit to come and rest on you" (cf. Luke 24:49; Acts 1:4–5, 8). Now they have to depend on the meek power of the Holy Spirit and learn the terms of the government of God.

It is also a shock for the political leaders. The political machinations of years have entrenched the power of the high-priestly establishment and the Pharisees. Behind them sits the power of Rome with its soldiers, taxation, control, aggression, and slavery. The one who has lifted the lid on all of this, decreed the freedom of God, and exposed the establishment—this one is supposed to be out of the way. It was messy, but it had been done. Suddenly, he is unassailably present. They cannot produce the body or refute the evidence of scared soldiers. Those who set themselves the task of keeping this agenda of God off the political map, and have seemingly had clear success, are now facing defeat. But this is not defeat as they know it. By worldly standards, they are still in control, but control is no longer the name of the game.

The disciples—after living in the shadow of Jesus' coming death for a year, intensely so for the past few weeks, and coping with their own fear—are now fearless. "Do not fear those who can kill you," the Master said, and they assented theoretically (cf. Matt. 10:28; Luke 12:4). Now it is obvious that they have learned this lesson. They have lashes at the order of the Sanhedrin and exult in it. They dwell in his teaching, seeing all the things they have missed, avidly gathering and sorting what he has said, and realizing that they are disciples for life and beyond. They bump up against the authorities and see through them and the way they play politics. More significantly, they see the Christ's way of governing and begin the slow dissemination of service, freedom, fearlessness, and peace, though compromised by their own inadequacies.

Change by Knowledge of the Rule of God

It is important not to make the change more complex than it was. The new way is simply to know the government of Christ. As opposed to the dominance of empires and rulers, some people now know the rule of God, to whom even the greatest is subject. The change is signaled in the prayer of the early Christians after Peter and John have been threatened with imprisonment:

Sovereign Lord, . . . you made the heaven and the earth and the sea and everything in them. You spoke by the Holy Spirit through the mouth of your servant, our father David:

> Why do the nations rage
> and the peoples plot in vain?
> The kings of the earth take their stand
> and the rulers gather together
> against the Lord
> and against his Anointed One.

Indeed Herod and Pontius Pilate met together with the Gentiles and the people of Israel in this city to conspire against your holy servant Jesus, whom you anointed. They did what your power and will had decided beforehand should happen. Now, Lord, consider their threats and enable your servants to speak your word with great boldness. Stretch out your hand to heal and perform miraculous signs and wonders through the name of your holy servant Jesus. (Acts 4:24–30)

They have seen the point. God rules, and all human rulers have derivative status. The Son of God rules as the servant King. This is God's way, and any can participate in God's Kingdom on God's terms. The threats of self-made power can be opposed, and the gentle rule of Christ stands against the kings of the earth. This is the political fulcrum of all of history, and the disciples learn it in a rough and ready way. Gradually, the old models are shown up for what they are. The Jews, and others, have looked for the sign, the charismatic leader, who will produce the political liberation, but it has not come. The Greeks have constructed the state around gods of the polis (city-state) and human thought, but they have proved inadequate. The Romans build empire, relying on militarism, slavery, conquest, and taxation, but it declines and falls.[1] The apostle Paul audaciously sees the Roman state as under God's authority, and so eventually it comes to pass. Not surprisingly, knowledge of the rule of God puts human rulers in their place. The politics of submitting to God's ways and acknowledging the rule of neighbor love grows amid the ebbs and flows of history.

But there is more to it than that. The disciples started to learn, but knowledge of the rule of God means far more than this central insight. It would systematically change every area of politics. It means submission to God's law, seeking justice, meekness rather than assertiveness, addressing disputes we have caused, keeping rulers humble, redistributing wealth, reconciling nations and classes. It requires leaders to be put in their place, with no ruler worship. The humble are to be lifted up and the arrogant cut down to size. In its scope, this is the greatest political revolution ever, as the gentle rule of Christ voluntarily settles on humanity, with its structural principles and insights. Because it is so radical in obedience to God, it does not allow compromise. It is a long-term, patient Kingdom, dethroning other kingdoms and powers. It has to cope with the multiple and serious failures of Christians who hold up its growth for decades or more. It spreads in people's hearts, through conscience with God's Spirit, and allows them to see politics in a new way.

It is also a matter of power and confrontation. The early Christians saw this. When a time of persecution comes, Stephen is charged in front of the Sanhedrin with blaspheming against Moses and God. His response is to detail Moses' emergence as political leader and focus on the disobedience of the people. He is about to be killed, but his focus is on their accountability before God. Stephen confronts them with their murder of Jesus, and his furious accusers stone him (Acts 6–7). In his understanding, they are under judgment, even though they have the power of death. Paul, in prison in Rome and writing to Colosse and Laodicea, makes the point even more markedly. The shape of his thought is breathtaking: "Having disarmed the powers and authorities, Jesus made a public spectacle of them, triumphing over them by the cross" (Col. 2:15). The cross is a victory for the one who is on it and exposes those who use it. "Yes!" (2 Cor. 1:20). The meaning of power has been completely changed by the resurrection. There is nothing stronger than the gentle power of God. The government of the risen Christ settles on those who so wish it and witnesses the ways of God to those who do not. This is the underlying issue of all politics.

Change of Hearts

Nor was this magic. The resurrection was a simple act of God's power. For the God who has created the universe, and whose "Let there be . . ." words of power have kept millions of scientists in work, the resurrection was small beer. It was the verdict that the Creator did not and does not accept the dominion of evil. As Peter put it: "But God raised him from the dead, freeing him from the agony of death, because it was impossible for death to keep its hold on him" (Acts 2:24). It was a miracle, victory, and verdict, but it was not magic. In no way did the resurrection take over human history or did God assume the control of a dictator. Wars, empires, viciousness, using the work of others, and all the other despicable human actions continue, because this is not God's domination of history. Even the history of Israel continued on its self-chosen, Christ-ignoring path.

The change is in the hearts and lives of those who willingly submit to God's gentle way. Only slowly does the yeast leaven the lump. Only slowly, and if we wish, has God's rule come. The kingdom of peace can be accepted or rejected, but it is not imposed. Often it has been rejected. Political movements go their own way. The agents of change are traditionally seen as conquest, technology, class dynamics, leadership, or political vision. Never otherwise in human history has a pattern of change been established that relies so fully on the response of the human heart to God.

The reality of this long-term agenda is clear at the beginning of Acts. Because Jesus has risen from the dead, the disciples feel the surge of victory and triumphalism. Right at the end of Jesus' earthly time with them, with all the questions they can ask, their focus is still on the messianic hope of the deliverance of the nation from the Romans. They ask: "Lord, are you at this time going to restore the kingdom to Israel?"

(Acts 1:6). Jesus declines to engage with its terms and responds with his own final words:

> It is not for you to know the times or dates the Father has set by his own authority. But you will receive power when the Holy Spirit comes upon you; and you will be my witnesses in Jerusalem, and in all Judea and Samaria, and to the ends of the earth. (Acts 1:7–8)

The old messianic hope of a victory over the Romans is dismissed as irrelevant. The only power the disciples will receive is the power of the Holy Spirit, the Counselor, God's Spirit of truth, subduing the lying ego. Their task is to be witnesses, also political witnesses, to the gentle good news of Jesus. They are to lift their heads above their national focus and witness to the Jews and to the ends of the earth. This word *witness* is simple but important. Both their words and lives are to speak of the truths of Jesus. These truths of an open relationship with the Father, of love, grace, and service as the condition of lives and relationships, are to spread through changes in people's hearts and lives. And that is how it has, in part, happened. Through generations and across the world, through missionaries and other witnesses, the good news has spread to pagan Britain and beyond.

Yet the witness can be lost through arrogance and Christian failure. Like a clean-lapping spring tide, it needs to return, to wash us again. But always, despite the fact that some Christians still look for the shortcut of control, the changes come through people's hearts as their thinking, convictions, principles, and living open up to God's way and close to their own selfish way. So deep is God's patience with us. The God who has created human history dwells with our lives and does not run us. The sun shines on good and evil alike, but there is good news of abundant life for whoever will open their hearts to God by faith, and this is also good news for politics.

Jesus, God's Gentle World Ruler

For this is also political. Jesus is the Christ, not just of the Jews, but of all peoples. Here is God's ruler, God's Prime Minister, who has changed the meaning of rule. Politics carried out in God's terms is completely different. It does not build up enemies and is not self-glorifying. Jesus insists on this way, not overwhelming human volition, but inviting us into obedience with God. On these terms empires crumble. Here is the ruler who is with his people, the one you do not notice in the High Street, the one who wipes every tear from our eyes.

Here is the one who requires that the poor be raised and the hungry fed, who trashes weapons and heals the sick. Here is the one who is without rhetoric, unlike this paragraph. He makes peace. Only the meek are blessed.

Here the law, infused with love, is for my neighbor and always makes sense. With Christ, hostilities are reconciled and the truth is told, saving mountains of false conflict and futility. Here the servant leaders will serve so that the people are blessed. There are casualties of this rule, like the end of empire and nationalism, the closure of slavery and ethnocentrism, the deconstruction of militarism. There are also offspring, like the rule of law in people's hearts, loving justice, deep accountability to God, and searching justice. Democracy is, in part, a child of this way.

But this is no utopia. The wheat and the weeds grow together. The Old Testament is full of the inadequacies of the children of Israel from the time of Moses onward. It is a chronicle, a warning, of inadequate political responses. It shows the people wanting a tall leader, trusting in the ark, growing proud, going for affluence, accumulating wealth, being tribal, having feuds, twisting the law, plundering, warring, and compromising on the rule of God. When the people are corrupt and do not hunger and thirst after righteousness, then the polity goes astray. World politics today has a similar intermingling of problems. Contenders for power appeal to people's greed; the electorate ignores injustices; people respond to warlike and nationalist appeals; the electorate sees a politician's looks more than their principles and lives. They cannot see through dishonesty. All too often, the people of the West look like sheep, darting one way and then the other, following the bark of the latest electronic dog.

Christ requires us to go deeper. Our policies are weighed by whether we hunger and thirst for justice and righteousness, for, as Jesus taught, out of the hearts of ordinary people come evil and good. So Christianity stays with the deepest issue of whether women and men submit their hearts and lives to God. Conversion to be a follower of Jesus is the deepest political act.

The politics cannot be marginalized. For the teaching, actions, and person of Jesus are also political. He is Messiah in the terms he gradually unfolded. He is king of the Jews, but not ethnocentrically. He is the revealer and focus of the worldwide government of God, also in politics. He is the Prince of Peace and disarms those who would control. All too easily Christians have been persuaded of the apolitical Christ, often by those with vested interests. Rather, we see the transformer of politics, the ruler who can bear evil and shine light on our ideological darkness. We glimpse in him the wisdom that runs like gold in the clay of our politics. Here we see the deconstruction of nationalism, self-rightness, and the drive to power and control. Here we see God's view of politics, albeit dimly. We recognize God's gentle world ruler.

And so, in some ways, it has turned out, as hundreds of millions of people to some extent perceive the Nazarene's politics and follow his ways. But the political witness of Christians has lacked coherence. The Christian failures are mortifying. Christians have espoused empire, autocracy, and nationalism. They have been more governed by local political ideologies than the teaching of Christ. Often they have relegated the truths here examined to a subsidiary position and have let other loyalties of party or class dominate their reactions and understanding. "Christians" have made compromises with militarism, the arms trade, aggression, and murder. They have promulgated hatred or self-interest. Western Christians have often retreated into ecclesiastical matters, withdrawing their faith from issues of justice and mercy, and changing Christ into merely a surname. They become caught in subcultures and make ineffectiveness an art. The extent of these failures leaves a muddy reflection of Christ's way for politics.

Nevertheless, the good news (gospel) for politics is filtering out. Lessons are littered through history; we can face and study them and learn from them. We can become a community of Christian political wisdom, avoiding some of the errors and allowing the characteristics of the rule of Christ to flourish among us.

Christian Politics

Yes, the lack of basic education and thought in this area is often overwhelming, even in so-called advanced countries. There is little sense of Christian political understanding in the body politic. Even in the United States, a supposedly Christian country, most of the political thought is presented in secular terms, with many theorists ignoring or disavowing Christian contributions. Worse still, the new Christian Right bottles a political faith in the carbon dioxide of American capitalism and nationalism. When we recognize the poor quality of many so-called Christian contributions, it may be best for us to ignore them.

Yet there are a crowd of witnesses from whom we can learn, who represent two thousand years of Christian political theory. Thanks to the work of the Composer and Conductor, here are parts of an orchestra that substantially plays in tune. The instruments are the political principles of Augustine, Aquinas, Luther, Calvin, Grotius, William the Silent, Milton, Cromwell, Lilburne, Fox, Penn, Wilberforce, Shaftesbury, Lincoln, Acton, Kuyper, Gladstone, Pope Leo XIII, Tolstoy, Keir Hardie, Haile Selassie, Tawney, Maritain, Barth, Luther King, Romero, Carter,

Solzhenitsyn, Tutu, and many others. This formidable list of people owe their central insights to Jesus. Often Christian political education has not drawn on these people or known where it stands in such a tradition of thought and political principle.

Most people do not know of or understand important traditions of political reflection: Reformed thought, Anabaptist politics, Mennonite and Quaker pacifism, evangelical reform, Catholic social thought, Christian socialism, black Christian politics, Kuyperian politics, European Christian democracy, liberation theology. They all make contributions to Christian awareness that we can both affirm and critique. Many of us are not even conscious of the music of Christian politics that groups and parties are playing on every continent—peacemaking, providing aid, mending families, healing, empowering, and freeing slaves. Christian politics under the rule of Christ can be an explicit part of public discourse, not privatized and unspoken, not marginal to other commitments, but centrally focused on Jesus.

All too often this response has been implicit, pushed into the background by those who want to control. The surprise is that what we have looked at in this book is not a normal understanding of Christ. Given the weaknesses of the book, it is hardly a contentious understanding. A thoroughgoing Christian political response could be part of the normal Christian life for hundreds of millions of people. Political organizations can explore and embody Christ's great principles. Christ's politics can be made explicit in parties and groups for whom this is their central motive. Indeed, such a commitment cannot easily be subordinate to any other political motive. The title "Christian" in politics claims priority over any other perspective. We cannot marginalize God. The scale of political transformation that comes as part of the good news of Jesus is vast. It is possible to learn good Christian politics and transform public life and culture in country after country.

Nor is this true just for Christians. We are coming to the end of the great Western modernist political tradition, in which major ideologies have played themselves out. State socialism or democratic socialism, with faith in the directing state and the working class, has many locally good points but has partly foundered on its own paternalism and stiffness. The capitalist West, so self-confident and dominant, must be dimly aware that it is eating people in the name of the great corporations. This is true both within their own organizations through stress, by the demands of unconditional loyalty, and in worldwide domination of the poor. Liberal individualism, validating the autonomous individual and letting loose the magical hope of consumerism, is fragmenting and destroying the lives of millions. The ideological conflicts of two hundred years have lost their sense. Words like *democracy, constitution, the rule of law, freedom, toleration*, *justice*, and *peace* have lost their moorings. The deeper verdict may well be that this is the result of retreat from real obedience to the gentle rule of Christ into the froth of Western culture. We may all find that with Jesus lie the real treasures of political wisdom. All this adds up to a debate needing to happen in the empty public square.[2]

There are also dangers. For centuries secular leaders, parties, and ideologies have deluded Christians with empty minds, untuned to their Lord's incisiveness. Others have mixed their ego or secular ideologies with the way of Christ, taking Christ's name in vain and confusing Christian witness. Many Christians, at first following the one who abjured control, have begun to love power and crave control. Christians, both personally and politically, can claim the name even while having none of the content, tainting Christian parties with corruption and dishonesty.[3] There are Christian divisions among those who have absorbed secular culture and have prior party allegiances. Others do not see their own subcultural construction of Christianity[4] or are unjustifiably opinionated. Empty vessels often do make the most sound. There are national and denominational distortions of Christianity and Christian politics. English Anglicanism, for example, has scarcely escaped from automatic support for the political establishment. In the United States many Christians unthinkingly cozy up to nationalism, blessing American militarism, tax cuts that hurt the needy, and establishment lies. Nor can witness come from those of us who do not walk the talk. Self-promotion is not part of this kingdom, or manipulation, or making enemies, or self-righteousness. Some people who want to lead are not fit for it, do not understand service, and are a danger to those around them.

Membership in this kingdom is not secondary to the United States of America, my party, or my career. It requires top priority. We seem to think that God can wait until we get things right. But we can do Christian politics only on the terms of Christ, and we have scarcely opened to them. We can fully trust Christ, but Christians are worthy only of conditional trust. The emergence of Christian self-righteousness, though a fundamental contradiction, is an existential danger.

Yet, if the account in this book roughly reflects what the Gospels present of Jesus, Christians are called to respond to Jesus with a consistent political response. This response is not merely concerned with ethics, nor is it secondary to other political commitments or ideologies. Rather, it is fully political in its inner patterns of obedience and vision, shaped in Christian faith and principles. It involves reflection and reforming action on global trade, business, consumerism, family breakdown, and militarism. It requires rigorous thought about all areas of God's creation and how we should live in them. The politics of race, childhood, ecology, and transport are Christian concerns. Prophetically, we should see issues before they arise. Christian political groups should be deeply self-critical. However unpopular the issue, we need to face it honestly and with a burning desire for justice and rightness. We dare not limit Christian politics to a single issue or a small agenda. Christ has always brought us the big picture and the relation of all of politics to God. We follow the one of whom the Word of God declares, "The government is on his shoulder," not a single-issue politician (cf. Isa. 9:6). Above all, Christian politics is about presenting and sharing Jesus as God's ruler, and always with a sense of weakness and need.

This is not a matter of activism and anxiety. These are faith responses to Jesus. We are dependent on him. He has gone to the center of political rule and plumbed the depths of the human condition before God. He addresses human evil, including political evil, without myth and the distortions of self-justification. He goes further, carrying this evil in the power and forgiveness of God's love, redeeming this area of our lives, beyond our own achieving and even our own imagining. At its deepest level, political activity is a matter of grace, where the joyful love of God rules, not us. Jesus is the ruler who has carried our sin and evil into the redeeming love of God. Gross political evils can be black-holed into oblivion. A Christian political party is first a place for rejoicing in God's justice, and not a self-important organization.[5] Through Jesus, we have clear intimations of the lovely government of God and the deepest truths that define our politics. The need for God's gentle ruler is the greatest political issue of our time, worldwide, and of all times.

Bibliography

Hauerwas, Stanley, et al., eds. *The Wisdom of the Cross*. Grand Rapids: Eerdmans, 1999.

Head, Peter, ed. *Proclaiming the Resurrection*. Carlisle, UK: Paternoster, 1999.

Moltmann, Jürgen. "The Resurrection of Christ: Hope for the World." Pages 73–86 in *Resurrection Reconsidered*. Edited by Gavin D'Costa. Oxford: Oneworld, 1996.

O'Donovan, Oliver. *Resurrection and Moral Order: An Outline for Evangelical Ethics*. Leicester: Apollos, 1994.

Williams, Rowan. *Resurrection: Interpreting the Easter Gospel*. London: Darton, Longman & Todd, 1982.

Wright, N. T. *The Challenge of Jesus: Rediscovering Who Jesus Was and Is*. Downers Grove, IL: InterVarsity, 1999.

———. *Jesus and the Victory of God*. London: SPCK, 1996.

Reporting and Hermeneutics

This book uses slightly different ways of interpreting the New Testament texts than those that have often been used in modernist hermeneutics. This appendix sets out in note form some of the differences for discussion and debate.

Some Questions in Modernist Hermeneutics

1. Modernism has been marked in part by an emphasis on epistemology and the hope that if the right *grounds* for forming knowledge can be established, then the resultant knowledge will be well formed and reliable. Hermeneutics has largely followed the same agenda. If the right way of interpreting the text can be found, then the correct meaning of the text will emerge. We will call this the foundational stance in both epistemology and hermeneutics. Foundational epistemologies require certain kinds of method for establishing knowledge. A variety of epistemic foundations—historicism, positivism, logic, consistency, formalism, and phenomenology—have been developed philosophically and espoused in certain disciplines. This in itself raises the question of whether any of them has the epistemic certainty claimed for them. Generally, they cannot provide an indubitable foundation for knowledge. The endeavor has failed, and postmodern epistemology has moved

on from this foundational faith to a more plural and fragmented view of knowledge.

2. Hermeneutics has largely followed the same path. Historiography, linguististic study, or textual methods have operated as possible foundations for interpretation. Though useful, they have often required the text to be considered in their foundational terms, often at odds with other methods. The text has to be treated in a certain way—redactively or whatever. The result is often that the Bible has been bent to the foundational method.

3. This work marks a retreat from redaction study. Broadly, the reasons are as follows. When the inner dynamics of the person and events being described dominate the text and hold together, it seems wrong to locate the prime meaning of the text's construction in the redaction process at a later time. The dominance of Christ's teaching and actions in the construction of these texts is evident. The authors are reporting these as they best can. Their authorial contribution is more subsidiary than primary, more akin to the conductor in relation to the composer. Moreover, the redaction idiom, that of constructing a text from other documents as a later historian would do it, may not fit the ways in which these texts were built up. Idioms such as reporting, interviews, teaching, and apostolic witness may give a more powerful and accurate model of textual construction as a more immediate process. For example, rather than Luke's use of Q, we consider Luke's use of Mary as a character, or John's experience of Jerusalem. Obviously, this involves some shift in the locus of interpretation.

4. The frame of interpretation used here is post- (or pre-) foundational and also plural. There is no one foundational method. Nor should method dominate content. Often substantive knowledge allows us to refine method as well as the other way round. We also approach the subject matter with a plurality of disciplinary criteria and judgments—theological, social, psychological, economic, political, geographical, historical, and so on. Because the subject is bigger than any foundational frame, no one frame, like the historical, dominates. Each of the disciplines provides a way of interpreting that may contribute to the whole. Social, political, and geographical interpretations reflect some of the subject matter and provide methods. When the whole matters as much as the New Testament does, such aids and disciplines are best seen as contributory, partial, and occurring within a bigger purview.

5. When Thomas after the resurrection set out his grounds for epistemic certainty, within a few minutes he had dropped it in the face of the risen Christ (John 20:24–29). Jesus both offered to

meet Thomas's criteria and commended those who would not be so bound. Biblical revelation is bigger than *our* need for epistemic certainty.

6. The same Christ also expected and proclaimed that people would not properly hear what was said, that the word would fall on stony ground, and that the hypocrisy of word and deed would judge us. In other words, though proper interpretation and good knowledge are important, and we pursue them here, they are caught up in the bigger issue of how we live. The words of the Nazarene have the character of interpreting *us*. This reverse hermeneutic is powerful and an important part of the picture. Our Western presentiments are dominant, but they often close our eyes. The Bible interprets us as well as we the Bible. It has penetrative power—or we can opt out for fear of exposure.

From the Idiom of Textual Criticism to Reporting

1. Redaction studies reflect concern about the way *texts* have been formed. Implicitly, they focus on direct and derivative authorship, literary dependence, textual construction, literary sources, style, and language. Sometimes the preoccupation is with what the *scholar* can be sure of; that is, its dominant concern is with the current review of knowledge. It fits the modernist concern for epistemic certainty within the scholarly community *now*, actually rather an odd preoccupation. Studying texts is fine, but the way they are studied may not be. Most writing points beyond itself to information, history, sharing, planning, or events. The New Testament writing is about Jesus, his life, teaching, and stories; about God, faith, the events and perceptions of New Testament; and about God's revelation. The question is whether our way of studying the texts inhibits seeing what these texts are about. One answer, of course, is that studying the texts is the only way we can discover what the texts are about. That is *an* answer, but it is not *the* answer. Studying a printed text in a typeface may be the only way of reading it, but studying typefaces does not even establish whether the text is in German or French. The question remains to what extent redaction criticism uncovers what a New Testament text is about. My feeling is that redaction critics may wrongly presume to uncover what a later writer sought to import or show about the subject, not what the subject was. In the case of Edward Gibbon, we know that he wrote *The History of the Decline and Fall of the Roman Empire* (6 vols.; 1776–88) more than a mil-

lennium after the (Western) Roman Empire fell (476). His text of the empire is interesting, but the question remains as to whether his view represents what the Roman Empire was actually like. Reflection on Gibbon is part of postclassical classical studies, but a small part, and it should not dominate classical studies. Many New Testament studies seem to focus on (mutatis mutandis) Gibbon, or Gibbon's sources, or even a hypothetical Gibbon, and not even get close to their subject matter.

2. Perhaps it is more fruitful to consider New Testament documents as *reporting,* on a par with the idioms of newspapers and the spoken media, like *Yesterday in Parliament.* That is Luke's stated idiom and implicitly is what the other Gospels largely follow (Luke 1:1–4). Reporting is committed to conveying important events and what people have said truthfully, with a sense of priority and relevance. Of course, New Testament reporting is culturally different from the many reporting idioms of today. We see its subject matter as more important than horse racing or celebrity relationships. But it is similarly direct. Reporting removes the focus from the text itself to what the reporting is about. Usually, too, it demotes authorial significance. Many newspaper reporters are not named. Style, construction, and language become instrumental rather than focal.

3. Reporting conveys how much distance there is from events. Daily reporting is close. Weekly more distant, and historical reporting both more removed and more dependent on other sources. Clearly, reporting in the Gospels was intrinsic to the Christian community, basically because what Christ said and did was so important. *My judgment is that many of the reports in all Gospels are so detailed—conveying full conversation, nuance, group psychology, misunderstanding, false interpretation, and debate—that they defy distance.* They are immediate. Much of the text is closer to reporting in quality daily papers (but with higher levels of participant observation) than more distant historical genres. John especially has this character, reporting conversations, audience reactions, plot, and contemporary interpretation. John 21:20–23, for example, identifies the spatial position of two disciples, the *interpretation* that should be ascribed to a particular statement of the risen Christ, and how it has been misunderstood. It reflects both the immediacy and the later distance of nonparticipants. The *closeness* of New Testament texts to events is a fruitful mode of hermeneutical reflection.

4. The dominant purpose for the construction of the Gospel texts was to faithfully teach Christian disciples (students, learners) what

Christ taught. The evangelists gathered what Jesus did and taught (both were significant) in order to faithfully pass on his teaching. The rabbinic schools already cultivated similar remembering, but the commitment to Christ far outran that to a rabbi. This concern for faithfulness, existing from the earliest times of the church, shapes the texts. Oral tradition was still fairly strong when the Gospels were written, and apostles would be furious if a pericope misrepresented (the substance of) what Jesus said and did. Thus, the system of establishing veracity seems likely to have been much stronger and more immediate than redaction and source analysis implies.

5. Redaction criticism tends to underplay the importance of "interviews" in the construction of the Gospels. Reporting sees them as part of normal information gathering. The writers of the Gospels must have gathered information, even with some degree of formality (cf. Luke 1:1–2). Informants would be Mary, Nicodemus, those in contact with Herod Antipas, John the Baptist's disciples, the woman with an issue of blood, Martha, the Samaritan woman, Mary Magdalene, and all the other disciples. Often emotions are recorded: "The women hurried away from the tomb, afraid yet filled with joy" (Matt. 28:8). It would be odd to posit these feelings unless the subjects had reported them. Normally, interviews are conducted with some view of going to press or reporting to others or gathering an accurate composite picture. Abstract redaction does not allow interviews much scope. Again, reporting is a better idiom for viewing the text. Comparing reports allows consistent pictures to be built.

6. Much New Testament work focuses on the authors, their presumed authorial intentions, and their theological construction of texts. This has produced much fruitful work, but it seems to miss another point, really of greater significance. The disciples taught by Jesus were in one sense mere note-takers and scribes compared with the teaching of their Rabbi. Even after years of study, there is much that they and we cannot understand properly of the Master. As the students of Einstein or Wittgenstein concentrated first on recording and reproducing the teaching of the master, not on *their own* interpretation, more so with the students of Jesus. The disciples were educated on the teaching of Jesus; he clearly decisively affects their later understanding. They build his thinking into their lives. The primary focus of New Testament studies should therefore not be authorial, but focus on the subject and teacher (Jesus), just because this person and teaching are so decisive in the formation of the reported texts.

7. The disciples report so many of their own failings that there is an extraordinary honesty in the texts and a commitment to reporting selflessly.

8. As a textual activity, reporting does not require the omniscience that has often been required in modernist history. The latter aims at being definitive as history. The former aims to bear true witness to its subject. Often biblical criticism and historiography have criticized the Gospels for not being definitive history. Sensible historians now see the hubris of this position. Definitive history is beyond historians.

9. The reporting idiom allows us to nuance the Gospel writers' contributions more immediately. Luke arrived after the events and collected interviews, evidence, pericopes, context, and so on. John, surprisingly Jerusalem focused, linked with different people—Nicodemus, the woman at the well, the Sanhedrin—in ways that intimate a different and intriguing social life. Matthew and Mark seem Galilean. They give us four normally different yet deeply inspired faithful reports.

10. The modernist Synoptic Problem becomes the postmodern Synoptic Bonus when the value of plural texts is recognized and a contributional hermeneutic supplants an oppositional one. Similarly, the *Guardian* and *Independent* newspapers mainly add to our understanding of an event. There are a few odd people who turn to the errors section in *The Guardian* first. New Testament studies seem to be full of such people. A good newspaper will send four or more reporters to an important event or to research a story. That is the synoptic bonus.

11. Reporting, which can be both oral and written, is not literary in its focus. Its meaning does not dwell in the *text* like novel or poem, but drives to its subject. Self-referencing textual study can actually miss the subject of the text by closing in on the linguistic aspect and ignoring the real referent. It studies lost coins, or even the Aramaic word for "lost," as its focal activity, when the point then and now is to understand the parable. The New Testament is written to be read as faithful reporting of Jesus and the acts of God.

12. The New Testament documents report the life, teaching, death, and resurrection of Jesus, the revelation and salvation of God in Christ, and the later growth of the church through the acts of God. That is their formative intention, and we cannot honestly erase that from our study.

Revelation, Worldviews, and Cultural Transposition

1. The New Testament requires reading in cultural terms, because the coverage of Jesus' life and teaching will not allow any other interpretation. "You cannot serve God and mammon" and "It has been told you . . ." require a cultural perspective (cf. Matt. 6:24; 5:21; et al.). Moreover, this is not a matter of local or subcultural interpretation. Both the Old Testament and Jesus' teaching offer a worldview, a global perspective in terms of God-given revelation. One may disagree with these perspectives, but one cannot treat them as merely subcultural, for they are not, as hundreds of millions of people worldwide affirm. If one does not see the full cultural implications of a parable, one has missed the point. Behaviorally, individualistically, and ecclesiastically confined interpretations frequently do miss the point by being subcultural.

2. Much cultural analysis and work in the history of ideas look for and gather cultural sources and antecedents, and it is no different with religious leaders. Muḥammad's dependence on Arabian Judeo-Christian culture is an obvious case in point. Jesus' dependence on the law of Moses and the prophets is similar, as Jesus acknowledges in his teaching. But it is equally important to identify difference. Here Jesus presents us with a range of major cultural themes radically different from his immediate background. They include the following: total dependence on God, intimacy with God the Father, the grace of God, a theory of peacemaking, the deconstruction of status, noncultic faith, a theory of redemptive suffering, reinterpretation of messiahship, denial of the holy place, attack on legalism, the centrality of the rule of God, the care of God in creation, stewardship, a revelation of the emptiness of domination, and the deconstruction of human deserving. These great countercultural themes and actions, punished by the dominant groups of the day, cannot be presented accurately as merely the product of antecedents. When these differences are so radical and so many, it is perverse to assume that antecedents explain the teaching and the man. Consider the following statement on parables, hardly important in itself, but symptomatic:

> Not only do these parables come from sources two to four centuries after the time of Jesus, very few can be traced to the early Tannaitic period. Why this is so is puzzling. But at the same time we should not suppose that Jesus was the originator of the popular parable, which was later taken up and developed in rabbinic circles. It is

better to conclude that Jesus' habitual use of parables is itself evidence that parables were in use in his time, but that our sources, outside of Jesus himself, fail to document this. In all probability Jesus made use of a known form and of popular images.[1]

The word *conclude* is extraordinary. There is no evidence of antecedents, and yet there is the conclusion of cultural dependence. Historical priority, albeit on limited evidence, normally suggests the *possibility* of originality and later dependence, not the *conclusion* that it be ruled out.

3. The deconstruction of first-century Jewish culture by Jesus was far-reaching and complete. Christ was in principle not ethnocentric and attacked such cultural constructions as Jewish ethnicity, nationalistic messiahship, and the temple cult. Jesus and the Christian faith are in principle transcultural and universal, focusing on the universal rule of God, and should be recognized as such. Later church experience in Acts and Pauline theology follow this teaching with some initial tension, avoiding subcultural expressions of Christianity. Scholarship is not honest in pushing Christianity back into subcultural expression.

4. At the same time, Jesus' interpretation of the Old Testament Scriptures claims orthodoxy in terms similar to those of the rabbinic and Pharisaic tradition. That is, we are confronted by different interpretations of the Hebrew Scriptures, the Law, and the Prophets; rabbinic interpretations are largely ethnic, and Christ's are far wider. In the Gospels we see not one Judaism but a range of different "Judaisms," represented by various groups, alongside emerging Christianity. The cultural construction of rabbinic Judaism consolidated after 70, growing largely from Pharisaism. Thus, there are two faiths, growing from a parent stem, not Christianity growing from rabbinic Judaism. The debate between these two interpretations, both respecting the Hebrew Scriptures, could be opened up much more fully.

5. New Testament scholarship can push into subcultural analysis of, for example, the Essenes. They were, however, largely a withdrawn group, and the fact that they are not mentioned in the New Testament could signify that their broader cultural significance outside Jerusalem and southeast Judea was not so significant, especially in Galilee and elsewhere. Some scholars may overstate the significance of these subcultures, especially when Galilean village people are likely to have cultures formed around work, family, sickness, synagogue, taxes, food, and clothing—issues accessible to most of us and reflected in Jesus' teaching.

6. New Testament cultural study requires a sensitive response to the text, capable of operating at the level of worldviews, history of ideas, gender culture, cross-cultural studies, ethnic cultures, ethno-methodology, cultural objects, myths, sacred texts, religious cultures, and many others. What is important is that none of these is imported to dominate what the text presents. John 4, for example, reflects cross-culture, worldview, gender culture, and so on, and the text reveals how it does so.

Historicism in Interpretation

1. The philosophical frame that requires us to see the New Testament primarily as history gives a false historicist slant to its interpretation. In contrast, the historical study of the New Testament is an entirely valid disciplinary mode of biblical study alongside others. The latter can raise any historical question of the texts, such as whether Luke is accurate on Quirinius and the census at the birth of Jesus. The historicist frame of study ignores a number of key issues and therefore becomes dogmatic.

    a. The Old Testament and New Testament give us one of the most important understandings of what history is, and they require a consideration of the relationship of history to God.

    b. Historicist approaches assume they know what history is— progress, evolution, one damn thing after another, class struggle, sociocultural formation. They tend to be humanist in presuming no Creator and no God of history. They cannot do so without being dogmatically closed. Historicists can argue for their own view of history but cannot presume it. The text requires some view or another on the God of history.

    c. Historiography often transposes the issue from the past to the present of history students—to journal issues, evidential disputes, modes of historical inference. Our quest for historiographic certainty closes down the issue of what we do not know and replaces necessary humility of knowledge and acknowledgment of what we do not know. We know very little certainly, when we could know far more with a degree of uncertainty.

    d. Much of the New Testament does not have history as its prime or only frame of reference. "Love your enemies" is normative, not historical (Matt. 5:44). A parable is an art form, not history. Either eternal life transcends history or it is a false promise, but it cannot be addressed only in historical terms.

2. The locus of New Testament history is important. It is focused not on Rome and the Herodian powers, nor on the progression of events, nor on technology, literature, and culture, but on the life and teaching of Jesus and the acts of God. The New Testament should not be blamed for not doing what historians may want it to do, any more than we should blame Harold for not leaving us his account of what the weather was like in Norfolk in 1066; he had other things on his mind.

3. The modernist hubris of historicism is that we know better. My study of the teachings of Jesus convinces me that we are exposed and understood to a degree that is still beyond us. We have the task of transposing Jesus' teaching, of seeing its significance in relation to our own lives and culture. In many cases this is easy, and in other cases it involves perspectival awareness.

4. It is important to involve sociological understanding and observe the location of institutions, other social structures, and networks in the New Testament world. The text usually gives a sense of its own social dimension, but it is important not to import Western, modernist, prescriptive, and anachronistic assumptions that close down our understanding.

Political Hermeneutics

1. Has there been a partial failure of New Testament scholarship to recognize the political content of the New Testament? Yes, I think there has, and it may have two sources. First, biblical scholars and teachers have largely been employed by the institutional church and academy and have addressed the concerns of these subcultures formed *after* substantial Christian retreat and exclusion from politics. Second, secular powers want to exclude Christianity from politics. This is not true just of Fascism, Communism, and Islam, but also of liberalism and laissez-faire capitalism. My worry is that these sociological factors may have (largely) subverted the ordinary meaning of the text, even among "conservative" scholars committed to it.

2. Many secular scholars will not acknowledge the cultural impact of Christianity on politics and the dependence of many meaning frameworks on it. They presume secular hegemony and marginalize this Christian influence. Yet Christianity is a revelation covering all areas of human life and will not be marginalized. In the West, dependence on Christianity extends into many areas of principle and practice. The rule of law, separation of powers, political ser-

vice and office, accountability, a law-abiding society, human rights, and many other perspectives have Christian formation built into them. This has been wrongly ignored in some political studies and neglected in recent Christian study, whether of the Scriptures or of Christian faith. Better scholars see the influence clearly.

3. Political perspectives that claim to be self-referencing—such as state absolutism, Fascism, state socialism, and Jeffersonian democracy—face in Christianity a political perspective that sees politics as partial and dependent on prior truths and understanding given by God. This basic difference of understanding and principle cannot be gainsaid. Self-referencing political perspectives will always tend to distort the political interpretation of the New Testament.

4. This study sees politics as an aspect of Christ's life and teaching, not as the whole or the center. The gospel is also political. This seems to me entirely uncontroversial in terms of the content of the texts studied here, or in the Old Testament. It also reflects the worldview that the Scriptures convey and the institutional pluralism before God formalized by Kuyper and others. The Social Gospel controversy of the early twentieth century shows fundamentalists resisting modernist moves toward an ethical-only interpretation of the gospel by moving into an apolitical, asocial one. Two wrongs don't make a right.

Modern/Postmodern Interpretation

1. The modernist belief that there is a single interpretative model is reductionist and flawed in principle. Models that have been linguistic, literary, historical, sociocultural, and theological have tended to overstate their own perspective and withdraw from the richness of texts or events. The time has arrived for plural or contributory models.

2. Modernist preoccupations—including authorship and originality, sources and footnoting, textual analysis, definition, and linguistic analysis—are often just that: preoccupations. Perhaps scholarship should honor the richness of biblical meanings and not force them into positivist or historiographic frameworks.

3. The Christian metanarrative cannot be reduced to the form of Enlightenment ones, because it presumes human dependence, fallibility, and need of revelation. In other words, there is a lot we don't know; as creatures needing guidance, we depend on God. The failure of "infallible" Enlightenment metanarratives is what Christians would expect, rather than simply being a postmodern

discovery. Indeed, many Christian scholars have been flagging this failure decades before postmodernism arrived. This is not a failure of revelation or of faith-based human knowledge as the only possible kind of knowledge. After all, we are necessarily responsive, and all knowledge embodies faith of one kind or another.

4. Postmodern reading is often happy with fragmented meaning. Thus X, Y, and Z's perceptions of what X said, and why, will be different. That is part of the picture. But staying with fragmented meanings is not adequate. Shared meaning and more universal statements are both valued and sought, in science, story, music, philosophy, proverbs, and other areas of life. Indeed, all communication is premised on this possibility. Coherent statements must be examined as such, at least without being dismissed a priori. Because the Bible gives revelation and coherent meaning, it stands against this kind of postmodern fragmentation, as it did in the culture of ancient Rome.

Sociological Hermeneutics

1. Analyzing social dynamics is a powerful way of entering the biblical texts and getting closer to their subject. This is partly because the relations between people cohere and carry much of the meaning of texts. Such social analysis is tentative and provisional and should not dominate, but it is useful. Often the social dynamics engage with the meaning of the text because relationships matter to God and fill the Gospels and Letters.

2. On the grounds of disciplinary or scientific supposition, scholars have claimed privileged knowledge that can no longer be privileged. Scholarship matters no less, but it cannot claim a priori privileged status over its New Testament subject matter. Thus, we may better understand the healing of the Gerasene demoniac from the text than through those who just see it as unscientific.

3. We cannot import sociologies, like structural-functionalism, phenomenology, conflict theory, or whatever into the biblical texts, because this is anachronistic and these sociologies have worldview weaknesses and more detailed sociological flaws. Again, modernist hubris can frame such theoretical structures.

4. The sociology of the New Testament is a partial contribution to our understanding of the New Testament. We construct such sociology with due awareness of the limits of our understanding. Yet more important is the truth that the New Testament gives us a sociology presenting people, relationships, and institutions in dynamic

relationship with God. This Christian sociology examines us and contends with our views. We need to understand it, recognize its influence, and use it to critically examine our own views.

5. The social dynamics of the New Testament give us some grasp of what detailed plausible understanding might be. They show to whom Jesus is reacting, or why the woman at the well is alone. But they do not dominate the words or acts of Jesus because he is not locked into these dynamics. He blows open status systems, self-righteousness, quarrels, self-justification, the abuse of power, presumed impotence, ruling elites, ethnocentrism, and notions of what people deserve. Thus, social understanding is contributory, not dominating. All we can do is agree or disagree with this man.

Chronologies

Herod the Great's Chronology

Roman	World	Herodian	Jewish	Christ
		73 BC Birth of Herod the Great.		
			66 Hyrcanus II, king and High Priest of the Jews, deposed by Aristobulus.	
63 Pompey captures Jerusalem and defeats Aristobulus II, who is exiled.				
			63 Hyrcanus appointed High Priest and ethnarch by Pompey (63–40).	
		63 Antipater (Herod's father) gains administrative responsibility.		
59 Julius Caesar in triumvirate with Pompey and Crassus.				
57–55 Aristobulus II and sons revolt against Rome.				
			54 Crassus, governor of Syria, pillages Temple.	
49–48 Roman Civil War.				
49 Julius Caesar crosses Rubicon.				
48 Julius Caesar dictator; death of Pompey.				
	47 Julius Caesar reinstates Cleopatra as ruler of Egypt (until 30).			
		47 Pharsael, Herod's brother, appointed governor of Jerusalem. Herod, governor in Galilee, puts down Zealot-type revolt of Hezekiah.		

Roman	World	Herodian	Jewish	Christ
			47 Pharisees' attempt to arraign Herod before Sanhedrin fails.	
		47 Herod marries Doris (daughter of Nabataean king, Aretas IV).		
			Rebuilding of walls of Jerusalem authorized.	
		45 Antipater born to Herod and Doris.		
44 Death of **Julius Caesar** at hands of Brutus et al.				
	44 Cassius, proconsul of Syria (44–42), terrorizes Judea.			
43–42 Civil War between Caesarians and Liberators.				
42 Death of Brutus and Cassius at Philippi.				
		43 Antipater, Herod's father, poisoned.		
		42 Herod appointed governor of Coele-Syria.		
		42 Herod betrothed to Mariamme and banishes Doris.		
		41 Herod and Pharsael appointed joint tetrarchs by Anthony.		
	40 Parthian invasion of Syria, Palestine, and Jerusalem.			
	40 Antigonus, son of Aristobulus II, named king by Parthians.			
		40 Death of Pharsael at hands of Antigonus.		
		40 Hyrcanus disfigured to prevent him being High Priest.		
		40 Herod flees south with family to Masada, Alexandria, and thence to Rome. Named king of Judea, Galilee, and Perea by Anthony, Octavius, and Senate.		
39–38 Roman campaigns against Parthia under Mark Anthony. Herod helps.				
	39–38 Cleopatra dominates Anthony.			
		39–37 Herod fights through Galilee with Sossius, faces Arbela caves' massacre, and eventually besieges Jerusalem, taking control in July.		
	38–37 Ventidus Bassus governor of Syria.			
		37 **Herod the Great** becomes effective king of Jews.		
		37 Herod marries Mariamme in Samaria.		
			37 Herod purges Sanhedrin of many Pharisees.	
			36 Murder of High Priest, Aristobulus III.	
	35 Anthony gives coastal cities and Joppa and Jericho balsam plantations to Cleopatra.			
	34 Cleopatra visits Jerusalem to have tea with Herod and look at her new possessions.			

Roman	World	Herodian	Jewish	Christ
		32–31 War between Herod and Malchus of Nabataea.		
31 Battle of Actium: Octavius defeats Anthony and Cleopatra.				
30 Suicides of Anthony and Cleopatra.				
		29 Herod's execution of his wife Mariamme.		
27 Octavius becomes **Augustus Caesar** (to AD 14).				
		27 Herod marries Malthace.		
		25 Herod marries Cleopatra of Jerusalem.		
23 Alexander and Aristobulus (sons of Mariamme I) to Rome for education.				
			23 Rebuilding of **Temple** starts.	
		23 Birth of Archelaus to Herod and Malthace.		
		21 Birth of Antipas to Herod and Malthace.		
		20 Augustus visits Herod. Gives him territory east of Galilee.		
		20 Birth of Philip to Herod and Cleopatra.		
17 Herod's visit to Rome to fetch sons Alexander and Aristobulus.				
		16 Sons marry—Alexander to Glaphyra and Aristobulus to Berenice.		
		14 Herod quarrels with sons, names Antipater in his second will.		
12 Herod's second visit to Rome; trial of Alexander and Aristobulus before Augustus.				
		12 Herod president of Olympic Games.		
		10 Herod imprisons Alexander and Aristobulus.		
		12–9 Nabataean tension.		
		9 Herod invades Nabataea. Trouble with Augustus, who disciplines Herod.		
		8 Nicholas of Damascus reconciles Herod and Augustus.		
				6/5 John the Baptist born.
				5 Jesus born in Bethlehem.
		5 Wise men visit Jerusalem and confer with Herod.		
				Early 4 Jesus' flight into Egypt. Slaughter of Bethlehem innocents
		Early 4 Herod's son Antipater also killed.		
		Spring 4 Death of Herod the Great.		

Roman	World	Herodian	Jewish	Christ
		4 Herod's will confirmed in Rome by Augustus. Caesar says Archelaus in control of Judea and Samaria, **Herod Antipas** of Galilee and Perea, and Herod Philip of Iturea and Trachonitis.		
		4 Uprising after Archelaus comes to power and promises too much. 3,000 Jews killed in Jerusalem.		
		4 Zealot-type revolt in Galilee led by Judas, son of Hezekiah. Sepphoris and its arsenal seized. Revolt put down by Roman forces.		
				3–1 Joseph and Mary return from Egypt with the infant Jesus and relocate in Nazareth.

Jesus' Political Context

Note: This table is an attempt to define the Gospel chronology more closely. Many of the Roman dates are firm, others can be located quite well, and others are guesstimates. Jews had a weaker sense of politico-historical chronology than we tend to have, and so this is, in part, our imposition.

Roman	World	Herodian	Jewish	Christian
31 BC–AD 14 Augustus Caesar Emperor.				
			6/5 BC John the Baptist born.	
				5 Jesus born in Bethlehem.
		4 Death of Herod the Great.		
				3–1 Joseph and Mary return from Egypt with the infant Jesus and relocate in Nazareth away from Antipater in Judea.
			1 BC Joshua, son of See, appointed High Priest (until AD 6).	
		AD 1 Herod Antipas begins rebuilding Sepphoris (Autocratoris) just north of Nazareth as his capital.		
			6 Census of Judea by Quirinius.	
		6 Deposition of Archelaus in Judea and Samaria. Direct Roman rule.		
		6–9 Coponius governor of Judea.		

Roman	World	Herodian	Jewish	Christian
	6/7 Varus legate of Syria.			
			6 Annas (or Ananos) son of Seth appointed High Priest by Quirinius until 15.	
				Passover 7 Jesus at age 12 visits Temple and stays behind with teachers of the law.
9 Roman defeat in Germany, losing three legions in battle of Teutoburg Forest. Rhine becomes border of Empire.				
	9 Aretas IV King of Nabatea.			
		10 Salome, Herod the Great's sister, dies.		
		13 Founding of Livia in Perea by Herod Antipas honoring Augustus and Livia's fiftieth wedding anniversary and her seventieth birthday.		
14 Tiberius Caesar begins rule (until 37).				
		15 Valerius Gratus, governor of Judea (until 26/27).		
			15 Annas deposed as High Priest. Three High Priests in three years.	
			18 Joseph Caiaphas, Annas's son-in-law, High Priest until 37. With Annas controls the Temple system and leads Sadducees.	
19 Death of Germanicus, adopted nephew of Tiberius. Agrippina angry at Tiberius.				
19 4000 Jews deported from Rome to Sardinia by Tiberius because of fraud against Fulvia and proselytes.				
19 Egyptians deported to Sardinia because of wicked goings on in the Temple of Isis. Statue of Isis thrown in the Tiber.				
		20 Fourteen-year periodic census.		
		22 Herod Antipas founds Tiberius as his new capital beside Lake Galilee.		
23 Death of Drusus, Tiberius's favored successor.				
26 Tiberius retires to Capri. Wants Empire without disturbances.				
26 Pontius Pilate becomes procurator of Judea and Samaria (until 36). Initially tries to suppress religious Judaism with cruelty.				
		December 26 Pilate upsets Jews in Jerusalem by bringing standards bearing image into Antonia Fortress in Jerusalem when soldiers go to their winter quarters. They go to Caesarea and face him down when he threatens their lives.		
		28? Pilate clubs down Jews who protest at his using Temple treasury funds to build aqueduct for Jerusalem. An Annas/Caiaphas inspired protest?		
29 Death of Empress Livia.				
29 Sejanus, praetorian prefect and effective ruler of Rome, at height of his power. Official celebration of his birthday.				

Roman	World	Herodian	Jewish	Christian
		29 Herod Antipas visits Rome, meets Herodias on the way and begins affair, plans marriage, and asks Sejanus if the marriage to Herodias is acceptableand for the right to strike his own coins. Antipas close to Sejanus. Aretas's daughter flees back to her father fearing for her life.		
		29 Herodias leaves her husband Philip Herod for Herod Antipas. Takes daughter Salome.		
			29 John the Baptist starts preaching and baptizing in the Judean wilderness.	
Early 30 Aretas IV moves up from Petra and occupies Machaerus, threatening Perea. Marriage of Antipas and Herodias becomes public issue.				
				30 Jesus baptized by John. Teaching, calling disciples.
				Summer 30 Temptations in Wilderness.
			Summer/Autumn 30 John criticizes Herod Antipas and Herodias for adultery and other evils.	
				Autumn 30 Jesus calls some disciples, Cana miracle.
				Late 30 Jesus moves to Capernaum.
				Passover 31 Jesus cleanses the Temple. Talks with Nicodemus.
				Spring 31 Jesus goes back through Samaria to Cana and Nazareth.
Spring 31 Herod Antipas moves south into Perea with forces to combat Aretas IV. Picks up John the Baptist in South Perea and takes him on to Machaerus, which he retakes.				
				Summer 31 Jesus in Capernaum, preaching in synagogues, through Galilee, healing and preaching.
				Summer 31 Sermon on the Mount summarizes the summertime's teaching.
				Autumn 31 Jesus prepares twelve disciples and sends them out in Galilee.

Roman	World	Herodian	Jewish	Christian
				Autumn 31 John communicates with Jesus from Machaerus.
				Autumn 31 Jesus heals the Centurion's servant, Lord of Sabbath.
				Autumn 31 early Kingdom parables.

October 31 Sejanus's plot to exterminate all successors to Tiberius and establish himself as Caesar is exposed by Antonia. He is executed by Tiberius, and many others die of treason. Serious internal weakness in Roman government. Antipas's position weaker in Rome?

Roman	World	Herodian	Jewish	Christian
		31 John the Baptist beheaded on the orders of Herod Antipas at Machaerus.		
				Early Spring 32 Jesus Feeds the five thousand. Turns down mass support for Kingship and insurrection.
		Passover 32 Jesus avoids Passover. Pilate's massacre of Galileans whose blood mingled with their sacrifices.		
				Spring/Summer 32 Jesus in Tyre, Sidon, Trachonitis and the Decapolis to quell messianic movement.
		Spring 32 Herod Antipas travels back to Tiberias and Sepphoris.		
			Spring 32 Pilate faces opposition over the votive shields bearing Tiberius's name in Herod the Great's palace, Pilate's residence.	
		Spring 32 Four Herodian kings oppose Pilate to Tiberius. Beginning of Herodian attempts to oust Pilate and replace him with a Herod. Sign of Pilate's weakness.		
		Summer 32 Agrippa, Herodias's brother, sponges on Antipas and is given post of commissioner of markets in Tiberias. Falls out with Antipas after year or so.		
				Late Summer 32 Jesus reveals himself as **Messiah** at Caesarea Philippi.
			32? Barabbas captured in insurrection.	
				October 32 Jesus at the Feast of Tabernacles. Long teaching and disputation with Scribes and elders (John 7–10:21). Lazarus raised to life.

Roman	World	Herodian	Jewish	Christian

December 32 Jesus at the Feast of Dedication. "Are you Messiah?" (John 10:22)

32–34/35 L. Pomponius Flaccus Legate of Syria.

32–33 Agrippa stays with Flaccus after row with Herod Antipas. There rows with Aristobulus and drifts off to Italy.

March/April 33 Jesus' final journey to Jerusalem.

Passover 33 Pilate and Herod Antipas in Jerusalem.

April 33 Jesus' crucifixion and resurrection.

33 Pentecost, explosion of Christians.

33 Rome financial crisis.

34 Death of Philip Herod, Tetrarch.

34 L. Vitellius, governor of Syria, incorporates tetrarchy of Philip (Gaulanitis, Trachonitis, Batanea) into Syria.

34 Fourteen-year periodic census.

Summer 35 Martyrdom of Stephen. Caiaphas High Priest. Church scattered with persecution.

Late 35 Conversion of Saul.

35 Tiberius moves from Capri to Tusculum near Rome.

36 Pontius Pilate sent to Rome by Vitellius after row with Samaritans attacked after messianic uprising on Mount Gerazim.

36 Marcellus appointed by Vitellius to be acting procurator of Galilee.

37 Tiberius Caesar dies. Caligula made Emperor.

Passover 37 Vitellius in Jerusalem, well received, remits agricultural taxes. Gives High Priests custody of the Temple vestments.

37 Birth of Flavius Josephus.

40 Deposition of Antipas. Galilee and Perea added to Agrippa I's kingdom.

41 Claudius Emperor in Rome

44 Death of Agrippa I

54 Nero Emperor in Rome.

64 Fire of Rome.

68 Dethronement of Nero.

Roman	World	Herodian	Jewish	Christian
			66 Outbreak of Jewish War.	
69 Vespasian proclaimed Emperor.				
			70 Seige of Jerusalem.	
			73 Masada captured. Jewish War ends.	

Notes

Abbreviations in Notes

Ant.   Josephus, *Jewish Antiquities*

EH   Eusebius, *Ecclesiastical History*

JW   Josephus, *Jewish War*

MCD   Movement for Christian Democracy
           (http://www.cpjustice.org/stories/storyReader$1034)

NT   New Testament

OT   Old Testament

Schürer   Emil Schürer, *A History of the Jewish People in the Age of Jesus (175 B.C.–A.D. 135)*. 1885–1924. Revised and edited by Geza Vermes and Fergus Millar. Translated by T. A. Burkill et al. 3 vols. in 4. Edinburgh: T&T Clark, 1973–87.

Introduction: Jesus' Politics?

1. Alexander Solzhenitsyn, *The Oak and the Calf* (London: Harvill; New York: Harper & Row, 1980) and *Invisible Allies* (London: Harvill, 1997) tell the story.

2. In Britain in 1660 the Restoration leaders' requirements of conformity set out to tame the pursuit of Christian politics; they mostly succeeded.

3. In an Edinburgh sermon Mrs. Thatcher famously commandeered the parable of the Good Samaritan to the need to make money. Better was the sermon preached in St. Lawrence Jewry Church in the City of London on March 4, 1981, and printed in *Third Way* May 1981, where the presentation of how some "Christian assumptions" influence her statecraft is spelled out more fully.

4. Alfred Edersheim, *The Life and Times of Jesus the Messiah* (1883; 3d ed.; 2 vols. in 1; London: Longmans, Green & Co., 1906).

5. John Howard Yoder, *The Politics of Jesus: Vicit Agnus Noster* (Grand Rapids: Eerdmans, 1972; 2d, rev. ed., 1994).

6. N. T. Wright, *Jesus and the Victory of God* (London: SPCK, 1996).

7. Seán P. Kealy, *Jesus and Politics* (Collegeville, MN: Liturgical Press, 1990).

Chapter 1: King Herod the Great

1. Josephus, *JW* 1.10; *Ant.* 14.8.
2. I accept the understanding that Josephus tries to marginalize these groups in his histories.
3. Josephus, *JW* 1.10; *Ant.* 14.9.
4. Schürer, 1:267–73.
5. Or by cutting off his ears; Josephus, *Ant.* 14.13.10.
6. Josephus, *JW* 1.13.10; *Ant.* 14.13.10.
7. Josephus, *JW* 1.16.4.
8. Josephus, *Ant.* 15.4.2–4.
9. Ibid., 15.10.5.
10. Josephus, *JW* 1.33.1–4; *Ant.* 17.6.2–4.
11. R. T. France, *The Gospel according to Matthew: An Introduction and Commentary* (Leicester: Inter-Varsity; Grand Rapids: Eerdmans, 1985), 83.
12. Yet the understanding of Messiah's birthplace is equivocal. Popular discussion in John 7 identifies Bethlehem (v. 42) and also says Messiah comes from an unknown location (v. 27).
13. Josephus, *JW* 1.33.6–8.
14. Stern sees this story as legend, but it seems too idiosyncratic to be such. See Shemuel Safrai and Moritz Stern, eds., *The Jewish People in the First Century: Geography, Political History, Social, Cultural and Religious Life and Institutions* (2 vols.; Philadelphia: Fortress, 1974–76), 1:278.
15. Schürer, 2:330–32; Josephus, *JW* 2.1.3.

Chapter 2: Jesus' Political Arena

1. See www.urantiabook.org/graphics/gifmap1.htm or a Bible atlas.
2. Josephus, *Ant.* 18.2.1.
3. Harold W. Hoehner, *Herod Antipas* (Society for New Testament Studies, Monograph Series 17; Cambridge: Cambridge University Press, 1972; repr., Grand Rapids: Zondervan, 1980), 93–102.
4. Josephus, *Ant.* 18.2.3.
5. Schürer, 1:361–65.
6. See Aaron Wildavsky, *The Nursing Father: Moses as Political Leader* (Tuscaloosa, AL: University of Alabama Press, 1984).
7. S. A. Cook et al., eds., *The Augustan Empire, 44 B.C.–A.D. 70* (vol. 10 of *The Cambridge Ancient History;* Cambridge: Cambridge University Press, 1934), 329.
8. This changed after the war of AD 66–74, when the procurator became a legate of senatorial rank, and a full legion of some six thousand Romans was quartered at Jerusalem; Schürer, 1:367.
9. Mendels notes this as the policy stated in the correspondence between Pliny the Younger and the Emperor Trajan; Doran Mendels, *The Rise and Fall of Jewish Nationalism* (New York: Doubleday, 1992), 192.
10. Eusebius, *EH* 2.7.
11. Schürer, 1:377.
12. Josephus, *Ant.* 18.251–52.
13. Hoehner, *Herod Antipas*, 331–42.
14. Philo, *Legatio ad Gaium* 299–304.
15. Hoehner, *Herod Antipas*, 350, assigns this incident to the Feast of Tabernacles half a year before Jesus' trial and death.

16. E. P. Sanders, *Judaism: Practice and Belief* (London: SCM, 1992), 173–82.

17. Cook, *Augustan Empire*, 332.

18. It is not clear whether the Pharisees did this within the Temple system or separate from it. We guess the latter. They would seek donations for synagogues and for Torah work from the rich Herodian and Roman establishment—hence, the centurion's donation (Luke 7:5).

19. Horsley's statement, "Thus there is no basis for imagining that the Pharisees had already expanded their activities from Judea to Galilee in the middle of the first century," seems to fly in the face of biblical and archaeological evidence; Richard A. Horsley, *Hearing the Whole Story: The Politics of Plot in Mark's Gospel* (Louisville: Westminster John Knox, 2001), 154. Donald Binder details one or possibly two synagogues at Gamala, far off near the Golan Heights, which predated its sacking by the Romans in AD 67. This suggests an earlier spread in Galilee proper. See Donald D. Binder, *Into the Temple Courts: The Place of Synagogues in the Second Temple Period* (Atlanta: Society of Biblical Literature, 1999).

20. Some commentators see them as centers of worship. See, e.g., Eric Werner, *The Sacred Bridge* (2 vols.; London: D. Dobson; New York: Columbia University Press, 1959–84); G. F. Moore, *Judaism* (Cambridge: Harvard University Press, 1962), 1:281–307.

21. Binder, *Temple Courts*, sees the priests and Temple as quite integral to the synagogue movement. Though the priests have participated locally, I suspect that the synagogue movement was strongly Pharisaic. The Roman centurion's cooperation with a Pharisaic movement shows another form of accommodation in Luke 7:5. Synagogues were locally generated and supported, not part of a national financial system, and were the object of local civic pride.

22. Here I use some of Weber's characterizations, which are useful for cultural location; Max Weber, *Ancient Judaism* (New York: Free Press, 1953), 396–400.

23. Here I accept Irving Hexham's insight about the formation of Judaism after Christianity began, though that later Judaism was prefigured in the Pharisees.

24. Jacob Neusner, *An Introduction to Judaism* (Louisville: Westminster/John Knox, 1991).

25. See William Horbury et al., eds., *The Early Roman Period* (vol. 3 of *The Cambridge History of Judaism;* Cambridge: Cambridge University Press, 1999), 428–43.

26. Josephus, *Ant.* 18.2.4; *JW* 2.8.14.

27. Louis H. Feldman in notes to *Ant.* 18.26; in *Josephus* (trans. Feldman; Loeb Classical Library; London: Heinemann, 1965), 9:23 (references omitted).

28. See Joachim Gnilka, *Jesus of Nazareth: Message and History* (trans. Siegfried Schatzman; Peabody, MA: Hendrickson, 1997), 37–41.

29. Martin Hengel's study is decisive: *The Zealots: Investigations into the Jewish Freedom Movement in the Period from Herod I until 70 A.D.* (trans. David Smith; Edinburgh: T&T Clark, 1989).

30. Josephus, *JW* 2.21.1–10; 4.2.1–5.

31. Ibid., 2.21.1.

32. Ibid., 7.8.1.

33. Ibid., 1.16.4–5.

34. From www.spartacus.schoolnet.co.uk/FWWshellshock.htm.

35. Hengel, *Zealots*, 340–41.

36. Horbury, *Early Roman Period*, 817.

37. Josephus, *JW* 2.8.2–143.

Chapter 3: Jesus and John the Baptist

1. See below, note 6.

2. Josephus, *Ant.* 18.5.1–2.

3. See Elaine Storkey, *Mary's Story, Mary's Song* (London: Harper Collins, 1993), ch. 2; Wendy Virgo, *Mary: The Mother of Jesus* (Eastborne: Kingsway, 1998), ch. 3.

4. As such, the OT prophets lie behind much Western critical political thought from the Levellers to Tutu, more than is usually recognized. Marx, though atheist, began with a prophetic style.

5. My reasons are as follows: The Philip who became tetrarch was in alliance with Herod the Great's sister Salome, who after the death of her ruler brother was against Archelaus (Josephus, *JW* 2.2.1–7). She was influential and with the death of Aristobulus, Herodias's father, would have a say in her marriage if it occurred before her death in AD 10, when Herodias was about 20–22 (conceived before the imprisonment of Aristobulus), which is likely. The rest pans out as suggested here. The argument against this is Josephus's statement that the Salome who danced in the beheading scene "was married to Philip, Herod's son and tetrarch of Trachonitis. When he died childless, Aristobulus, the son of Agrippa's brother Herod, married her. Three sons were born to them" (*Ant.* 18.5.4). This requires Salome to marry her granduncle Philip the tetrarch across two generations and within one to four years of her dancing before Antipas, for Philip died in AD 34. He would be an old or dying man, marrying two generations down. Much simpler is the idea that he earlier married his niece, Herodias, which would leave him father of Salome. But against this, it is unlikely that Rome would have accepted Herod Antipas cuckolding his neighboring tetrarch. Intriguing issue.

6. Herod Antipas is about 52 and Herodias perhaps 40 or so, with Salome likely in her late teens.

7. Josephus, *Ant.* 18.5.1.

8. Ibid., 18.7.

9. Ibid., 18.5.2.

Chapter 4: Jesus and Herod Antipas

1. A. H. M. Jones, *The Herods of Judaea* (Oxford: Clarendon, 1938), 105–10.

2. Friedrich von Logau, *Sinngedichten* (3 vols.; Breslau, 1654), 3.2.24 (trans. Longfellow).

3. Lord Acton's letter to Bishop Mandell Creighton (April 5, 1887).

4. Josephus (*JW* 2.8.4) later records the Essenes undertaking similar peaceful missions, though with greater asceticism and a stronger sectarianism. It would be interesting to know if there was Christian influence on the Essenes as Josephus reports them, or vice versa.

5. Josephus records that at the beginning of the Jewish War, John of Gischala aroused a crowd of one hundred thousand against Josephus. They gathered at Tachichaeae/Magdala, on the lake between Capernaum and Tiberias. Then Josephus boasts about how he defused the situation. Even if there is exaggeration in Josephus's report, it shows a similar, larger crowd mobilizing some forty years later than Jesus (*JW* 2.20.6–2.21.10).

6. There seems a possibility of the following sequence of events: Herod Antipas's affair and adultery. His wife flees back to her father, Aretas, king of Nabataea. Antipas takes Herodias as his wife. John the Baptist publicly rebukes him. Antipas captures John and imprisons him in Machaerus for some time (while Jesus begins his public ministry in Galilee). John is beheaded. Antipas's wife's father, Aretas, attacks Antipas and defeats his forces while he is in Machaerus, thus weakening him. The crowd of five thousand men gather in Galilee, and Jesus repudiates an uprising. This reconstruction is surmise. It seems unlikely that the Jews would see defeat as judgment unless it occurs soon after John's death. Hoehner (*Herod Antipas*, 111–12, 125–26, 142–44, 152–53) dates the conflict later (AD 35–36), though discussing many possibilities.

7. Josephus, *Ant.* 18.5.1. Yet Josephus, in speaking of John's imprisonment and execution (*Ant.* 18.5.2), notes Herod Antipas being in control of the fortress at Machaerus, referring back to the previous reference. If we conclude that this was not an error, it sets up the following possible scenario: Machaerus is remote. Aretus's forces initially have control of Machaerus. When his daughter returns, the Nabataean king declares war on Antipas, who musters forces and travels down to Perea. Because John the Baptist is criticizing him over Herodias, he becomes more dangerous in this situation and is rounded up east of Jordan. When Antipas wins an initial victory and regains Machaerus, he takes John along with him in perhaps spring 31, then beheads him there in early 32 in a celebration of his victory. Shortly, as Josephus records, Aretas defeats Antipas in what is seen as judgment for the death of John, helped by some treachery of refugees from Philip's territory. At this time the feeding of the five thousand takes place amid speculation about Herod's weakness. These detailed dynamics are hypothetical and do not matter much to the Gospel writers, but they show what some of the Herodian fears might have been.

8. Josephus, *Ant.* 18.5.1.

9. Ibid., 18.5.2.

10. Josephus, *JW* 3.10.9.

11. Gerard Kelly's point in personal communication.

12. Delbert Burkett, *The Son of Man Debate* (Cambridge: Cambridge University Press, 1999), 121–24 and passim.

13. "Peter," built on a pun in both Greek (*petros*) and Aramaic (*petra*). How can this be?

Chapter 5: Jesus the Messiah?

1. R. T. France, "Messiah in the New Testament," *The Illustrated Bible Dictionary* (ed. J. D. Douglas; Leicester: Inter-Varsity, 1980), 995.

2. Many Christians have adopted this paradigm: Bible > Ethics > Engagement; they produce much good Christian thought within it. Yet it also has weaknesses in not addressing the central structural issues of politics or the rule of Christ fully. Even John Howard Yoder's great study partly adopts this perspective. In chapter 1 he sets up a "Messianic Ethic" (*The Politics of Jesus: Vicit Agnus Noster* [Grand Rapids: Eerdmans, 1972], 11–25) to bridge the NT and social ethics. Ethics, as often understood, is only part of politics and tends not to engage with the philosophical issues of state, law, power, and institutions. Perhaps "Christian *ethics*" is not as good a paradigm as is sometimes assumed by those who use it, involving as it does a dualism between supposed neutral social scientific empirical study and normative evaluation.

3. Elaine Storkey, *Mary's Story, Mary's Song* (London: Harper Collins, 1993), meditates on its full content.

4. James H. Charlesworth, ed. *The Old Testament Pseudepigrapha* (2 vols.; Garden City, NY: Doubleday, 1983–85), 1:34.

5. See Jacob Neusner, "The Messianic Idea in the Apocryphal Literature," in *Society and Religion in the Second Temple Period* (ed. Michael Avi-Yonah and Zvi Baras; London: Jewish History Publications/W. H. Allen, 1977), 153–86.

6. Peter Head, *Christology and the Synoptic Problem* (Cambridge: Cambridge University Press, 1997), 174–75.

7. Florentino García Martínez, *The Dead Sea Scrolls Translated* (Leiden: Brill, 1994), 106.

8. Neusner, "Messianic Idea," 185.

9. Josephus, *JW* 2.13.4.

10. Josephus's account is a little less euphoric (*Ant.* 12.9.5–7).

11. Alec Motyer, *The Prophecy of Isaiah* (Leicester: Inter-Varsity, 1997), 13.

12. As N. T. Wright's *Jesus and the Victory of God* (London: SPCK, 1996) much more fully develops.

13. "This is the one I esteem: he who is humble and contrite in spirit, and trembles at my word" (Isa. 66:2).

14. This is Jimmy Dunn's conclusion; "The Messianic Secret in Mark," in *The Messianic Secret* (ed. Christopher Tuckett; Philadelphia: Fortress; London: SPCK, 1983), 116–31, esp. 128.

Chapter 6: The Government of God

1. The secular dualism of natural/supernatural, worldly/otherworldly has often pushed Christian thinking into otherworldly conceptions of the kingdom. Christ's teaching is of the present kingdom, because clearly God cannot be other than present throughout the whole of existence and time. "In him we live and move and have our being" (Acts 17:28). Not surprisingly, the somewhat otherworldly Essenes do not feature in the Gospels.

2. Studies like Herman Ridderbos, *The Coming of the Kingdom* (ed. Raymond A. Zorn; trans. H. de Jongste; Philadelphia: Presbyterian & Reformed, 1962; St. Catharines, ON: Paideia, 1978).

3. Kingdom theology is a big study in itself. Reformed theology, perhaps especially in the work of Abraham Kuyper and Karl Barth, reopened the significant scope of God's rule, which has since developed in a wide-ranging literature. Within political theology are further emphases, including liberation theology, Anabaptist teaching, Reformed kingdom theology, and a Christian socialist perspective. These can be seen as contributions to a bigger perspective growing out of the teaching of Christ.

4. The Barmen Declaration of 1934: "We reject the false doctrine that there could be areas of our life in which we would not belong to Jesus Christ, but to other lords."

5. As in Bob Hawke's confidence upon his election victory: "The people of Australia had got it right once again"; in *Memoirs* (London: Heinemann, 1994), 485 (don't bother to read the book).

6. Herbert Butterfield and a string of other historians have debunked the grand narrative.

7. Halevy's thesis on the circumvention of revolution in Britain, Merton's on Protestantism and science, Weber's on Protestantism and economic development—these are examples of a whole series of sociological arguments that can be made about Christian influences on political and public culture. The big political one is that Protestantism has been the ground for the emergence of democracy.

8. There are a variety of Islamic positions on this, but they all have to deal with both Muḥammad's patterns of conquest and the hegemonic control conceived in Medina and Mecca.

9. Max Weber, *Economy and Society* (ed. G. Roth and C. Wittig; 2 vols.; Berkeley: University of California Press, 1978), 2:901.

10. There are good Christian critiques of the Constantinian settlement, especially from the Anabaptist tradition. The Carolingian, Holy Roman Empire, and Norman Christianity reflect in part similar compromises, as do pre- and Counter-Reformational Catholicism.

11. My understanding is that the OT "theocracy" also follows the same pattern. The covenant was that to which subjects, families, tribes agreed to submit. The rather simple view that sees Moses and the period of the judges as a theocracy era, followed by monarchy, ignores the continual interplay between God's faithfulness and law and wayward human responses. In the era of judges, people were further away from the rule of God,

and David was closer; so this polarization scarcely works. The continuous rule of God, theocracy, sits much looser to particular forms of government and can be seen as voluntaristic throughout, involving the response of rulers and people, sometimes given, often not. The pattern is continuous through the OT and the NT.

12. Understanding "Your kingdom come" as the subject opening her or his life to God's government.

13. Kuyper's understanding of the way God's sovereignty dethrones all human political pretensions to sovereign authority reflects this truth.

14. The use of religion to control and dominate, either through its internal direction or by political manipulation, is a vast and understudied subject. The Egyptian dynasties and the priesthood, emperor worship in the Far East and Roman empires, the caste system, the use of churches to control, the conquest idiom in Islam, and the enforcement of Shariah in the Middle East—these all now show widespread patterns of enforcement. The United States' disestablishment of religion, by contrast, is a Christian political principle growing out of dissent and nonconformism.

15. Demonstrating this requires an analysis of the transmutation of Christian political freedom and toleration into liberalism.

16. Indebted to Leo Tolstoy, *Walk in the Light While There Is Light* (Grand Rapids: Baker, 2001), 24–26.

17. Secular persecution under Lenin, Mussolini, Hitler, Stalin, Mao, and the determined marginalization of Christianity have scarcely been recognized or analyzed by secular political historians. It is a dominant motif of the century.

18. This is inscribed on her statue outside the National Portrait Gallery, London. Worth a visit.

19. H. G. Wells, *History of the World* (Middlesex: Pelican, 1960), 157; quoted in Tony Benn, *Arguments for Socialism* (London: Jonathan Cape, 1979), 25.

20. Much U.S. Christian politics is without the awareness to recognize that what Christians are supporting is often subcultural American nationalism and not really Christian.

21. The Anglican Church has long been used to support the establishment. In the United States churches and preachers across the country have repeatedly and cravenly blessed war efforts. Ray H. Abrams has recorded this for World War I in *Preachers Present Arms* (New York: Round Table, 1933); cf. Mark Twain, "The War Prayer," written to protest the Spanish-American War of 1899–1902, rejected by his publisher and then printed thirteen years after his death, in his anthology *Europe and Elsewhere* (New York: Gabriel Wells, 1923).

22. Ernest Barker, *Greek Political Theory* (London: Methuen, 1960), 9.

23. Ibid., 315.

24. Karl Popper, *The Open Society and Its Enemies* (London: Routledge, 1945); Aristotle, *Politics* 1.2: "Man is by nature a political animal."

25. See A. D. Nock on ruler worship in Rome, in *The Augustan Empire, 44 B.C.–A.D. 70* (vol. 10 of *The Cambridge Ancient History*; ed. S. A. Cook et al.; Cambridge: Cambridge University Press, 1934), 489–502.

26. Ibid., 496–97.

27. Josephus, *Ant.* 18.8.1–9.

28. Transmitted by oral tradition.

29. Groen van Prinsterer identified this problem in the French Revolutionary conception and founded the Dutch Anti-Revolutionary Party in response. The insight was deep. Founding a party on an anti-label was not.

30. This is developed especially in the Kuyperian idea of sphere sovereignty and Catholic social teaching since *Rerum Novarum* (papal encyclical of 1891).

31. They showing how the sovereignty of God issues in human institutional pluralism. Opening up the perspective are Abraham Kuyper, *Lectures on Calvinism* (Grand Rapids: Eerdmans, 1931); Peter S. Heslam, *Creating a Christian Worldview: Abraham Kuyper's Lectures on Calvinism* (Grand Rapids: Eerdmans, 1998); and James D. Bratt, ed., *Abraham Kuyper: A Centennial Reader* (Grand Rapids: Eerdmans, 1998).

32. There are four totalitarian failures: (1) The ruler claims the sovereignty of God. (2) The ruler claims the ultimate meaning of the person. (3) Political control of other institutions interferes where there is no competence. (4) Interfering in other institutions obscures the proper functioning of the state. See Alan Storkey, *A Christian Social Perspective* (Leicester: Inter-Varsity, 1979), 140–46.

33. The emergence of constitutional thought in Reformational and Counter-Reformational thought is an exciting topic in itself. For some material, see Quentin Skinner, *The Foundations of Modern Political Thought* (vol. 2 of *The Age of Reformation*; Cambridge: Cambridge University Press, 1978), 113–34; and J. H. Burns et al., eds., *The Cambridge History of Political Thought, 1450–1700* (Cambridge: Cambridge University Press, 1991), 254–97, 374–411.

34. The Catholic doctrine of subsidiarity emphasizes that responsibility better belongs with other institutions before God than being centralized in the state. Kuyper's horizontal pluralism, recognizing the range of God-given institutions within which we live, opens up a similar truth. These two sources have had a strong impact on European thinking, though this may be waning.

35. Weber's *Protestant Ethic* thesis in part charts the emergence of work and economic activity into its relationship with God and away from control by the state in Protestant Europe; *The Protestant Ethic and the Spirit of Capitalism* (trans. T. Parsons; New York: Scribner, 1930).

36. The dialectic between liberal individualism and statism, which has characterized much of modern Western history, is often seen as the failure of one or the other. Especially since 1990 it is seen as the failure of state socialism and Fascism. The failure of both, and the way each generates the other as reaction, needs to be recognized. See the Movement for Christian Democracy's (MCD) *Westminster Declaration* (http://www.cpjustice.org/stories/storyReader$1034; February 1991).

37. For this discussion see Alan Storkey and Jonathan Bartley, *Europe: Community of Nations* (London: Movement for Christian Democracy, 1999).

38. Often debate about church and state has been bedeviled by a weakness that arises from the way the (institutional) church has often claimed the authority of God for its own institutional dominance over the state. As I understand it, the Christian truth of God's gentle rule does not give the institutional church that position. Christians exercise their faith coherently within politics, but not with a view to institutional dominance. The Anabaptist tradition has reflected this better. Much Reformed politics from Calvin onward has not fully grasped this point and has stayed with a possessive view of power.

39. The point here is Evan Runner's. See his brilliant exposition in *Scriptural Religion and Political Task* (1961; repr., Toronto: Wedge, 1974), showing that contrary to the usual Christian response, often reactive and antithetical, God's way for us is the thesis, the original truth growing out of our creation.

Chapter 7: Jesus' Political Principles

1. Sometimes political philosophy casts itself within a self-contained conception of politics and ignores the way in which political principles more generally adhere to life. My approach recognizes this link, as do most other approaches to political philosophy. Liberalism is usually based on some more general understanding of human freedom.

2. George Orwell, *Animal Farm* (New York: Harcourt, Brace, 1946), ch. 10.

3. Tony Campolo, *The Kingdom of Heaven Is a Party* (Dallas: Word, 1990), hits the note.

4. John Ruskin's great book *Unto This Last* (London: George Allen, 1900) weighs this parable against classical economics.

5. Jürgen Moltmann, *The Way of Jesus Christ: Christology in Messianic Dimensions* (London: SCM, 1990), 99–102.

6. One of MCD's six central principles, vastly important in human affairs and fundamental, is stated in the Sixth Commandment, covered by much Christian and Jewish thought and not elaborated here: "You shall not murder" (Exod. 20:13).

7. Jacques Maritain, *True Humanism* (trans. M. R. Adamson; London: G. Bles, 1938); *The Twilight of Civilization* (trans. L. Landry; New York: Sheed & Ward, 1943); *Christianity and Democracy* (trans. D. C. Anson; London: G. Bles, 1946); and *The Person and the Common Good* (trans. J. J. Fitzgerald; South Bend, IN: University of Notre Dame Press; New York: C. Scribner's Sons, 1947).

8. The views of the Levellers, Diggers, and others were a bit diffuse, but the main sense of their egalitarianism they gathered from the Bible and their understanding of people's status before God.

9. The argument is that democracy has flourished the most in strongly Protestant countries, because of the impact of Protestant faith on political culture, similar to Weber's Protestant ethic thesis (*The Protestant Ethic and the Spirit of Capitalism* [trans. T. Parsons; New York: Scribner, 1930]). Norway, Sweden, Denmark, Germany, the Netherlands, the United States, Canada, New Zealand, and Australia have been associated with stronger democratic forms and have also been identifiably Protestant. More recently, Catholic countries have been similar. The question is whether cultural differences help to explain this ethos. Candidates for the cultural direction are created personhood, equality before the law, God is no respecter of persons, universality of sin, the openness of salvation, human response-ability before God as the basis for freedom, respecting the integrity of individual faith. These kinds of precepts must have some impact on the public culture.

10. Reference to God was in the end excluded from article 1 of the Universal Declaration of Human Rights. See Asbjørn Eide et al., eds., *The Universal Declaration of Human Rights* (Oxford: Oxford University Press; Oslo: Scandinavian University Press, 1992).

11. See, for example, Zbigniew Brzezinski, *Out of Control: Global Turmoil on the Eve of the Twenty-First Century* (New York: Charles Scribner's Sons, 1993); and Matthew White, *Historical Atlas of the Twentieth Century* (http://users.erols.com/mwhite28/20centry.htm, 1998).

12. Again, mainly Matthew White's work in *Historical Atlas*.

13. The urgency of addressing Saddam Hussein's weapons of mass destruction was matched by the fact that they had not existed for much of a decade.

14. Lloyd George could have done differently at Versailles as Keynes, as others have noted. He probably pushed for reparations partly to maintain electoral popularity, though he was never elected again.

15. A phrase used by an English civil servant.

16. An interesting postmodern focus on intersubjective meaning when his life is in danger!

17. The inadequacy of various modernist philosophical ideas of truth such as positivism, logical truth, or analytical truth has emerged over the last half century. This is something far deeper.

18. Sean Boyne, "Uncovering the Irish Republican Army," *Jane's Intelligence Review*, August 1, 1996.

19. As I edit, the Hutton Inquiry is under way in London.

20. This paragraph is important even though it hopelessly truncates a long argument about the locus of truth in various political philosophies. The deepest division is whether truth lies with God and depends on revelation, with our human response as fallible and faith dependent, or whether it is in some sense a human possession. The paragraph tries to identify some main themes within the latter tradition.

21. Plato's *Republic* is the archetypal philosophical construction of the state and vests in the philosopher kings the wisdom to run the system. For more thorough treatments, see Ernest Barker, *Greek Political Theory* (London: Methuen, 1960); and G. Klosko, *The Development of Plato's Political Theory* (London: Methuen, 1986).

22. Enlightenment belief in rational possession of truth by certain elites produces forms of absolutism reflected in seventeenth- and eighteenth-century European rulers and their philosophical advisers. See Geoffrey Bruun, *The Enlightened Despots* (2d ed.; New York: Holt, Rinhart & Winston, 1967).

23. Hegel's weaving of dialectical truth into the fabric of the state is the most dangerous form of modern truth possession. Marx's later materialist essentialism has the same form, bringing everything into subjection to the proletariat and revolutionary politics. This is a common theme running through Karl Marx and Friedrich Engels, *The Communist Manifesto* (Centenary ed.; London: Socialist Party of Great Britain, 1948); Karl Marx, *The Grundrisse* (trans. D. McLellan; New York: Harper & Row, 1971); and idem, *Capital* (Chicago: Encyclopaedia Britannica, 1963).

24. The political position of the Brahmans and their relation to Vedic religion, the Harappa and Indus Valley civilizations, and the "Aryan invasion" are not clear, but they seem to have imposed a religious-political system that validated their dominance. See Koenraad Elst, *Update on the Aryan Invasion Debate* (New Delhi: Aditya Prakashan, 1999); and Shankar Nadar, *Brahmin Gold: The Plunder of Paradise (1500 BC–1000 AD)* (3 vols.; Jabalpur: Sudrastan Books, 1999; reissued, http://www.dalistan.org/books/b_gold/).

25. The same appears in much classical and neoclassical economics, where greed and the social construction of profit and ownership are more or less ignored.

26. This is well exposed by Michael Oakeshott, *Rationalism in Politics and Other Essays* (Indianapolis: Liberty Fund, 1991).

27. Jacques Ellul's *Propaganda* (New York: Random House, 1965) is the key Christian text. Cf. Helmut Michels, *Ideologie und Propaganda: Die Rolle von Joseph Goebbels in der nationalsozialistischen Aussenpolitik bis 1939* (Frankfurt: P. Lang, 1992).

28. Joseph R. and William L. Blaney, *The Clinton Scandals and the Politics of Image Restoration* (Westport, CT: Praeger, 2001), present an example of the genre.

29. This appears in group, game, rational choice, and systems theory. This approach assumes some kind of neutrality, but it actually takes as its ultimate framework of reference what voters, parties, and other entities decide is in their rational interest, often adapting economic choice theory. Within this perspective the (consistent) voter cannot be gainsaid.

30. Theresa M. L. Lee, *Politics and Truth: Political Theory and the Postmodern Challenge* (New York: State University of New York Press, 1997); Richard Rorty, *Truth, Politics and "Post-modernism"* (Assen: Van Gorcum, 1997); Michèle Barrett, *The Politics of Truth: From Marx to Foucault* (Cambridge, UK: Polity, 1991).

31. The Watergate tapes were recorded in the White House basement on a system that Nixon secretly ordered to be set up. These tapes led to his resignation to avoid impeachment.

32. This is Edmond Burke's (1729–97) justification of conservatism.

33. Responding to Jean-Jacques Rousseau, *Du contract* [*sic*] *social* [About the Social Contract] (Amsterdam: M. M. Rey, 1762). This originates an important tradition in Christian political philosophy. Groen van Prinsterer has discerned the idolatry of the French

Revolution residing in its unqualified belief in the people. Robespierre (1758–94), the Terror, the plans for a General Assembly building like a football stadium—all grew out of the idea that the people must be right. The Anti-Revolutionary Party of the Netherlands, led first by Abraham Kuyper (1837–1920), obviously stood against this both in its left- and right-wing expressions. It was a prophetic recognition of the false stances of both Communism and Fascism. J. L. Talmon's *The Origins of Totalitarian Democracy* (London: Secker & Warburg, 1952) shows the links between populism and dictatorship, the ruler who offers to give the people what they want, but who, of course, embodies them in his own image.

34. The false faith in the demos opened up by Groen van Prinsterer, Abraham Kuyper, and others requires long-term analysis. We critique the collective forms but are more indulgent to the dominant American and British liberal forms. With great prescience Kuyper sees the liberal form as leading to the breakdown of institutional links, relationships, and the meaning of justice, as we assert that we are not our neighbors' neighbor in a range of areas of life.

35. Herbert Marcuse's study of *One-Dimensional Man* (1964; new ed.; London: Routledge, 2002) may be one of the great prescient books. The theorists who talk of the end of ideology may be speaking of consumerism globalized. This culture cannot see outside itself even to the third world or Islam. Nor can it see its own internal conflicts with nationalism, individualism, communitarianism, and subjectivism as it vies for ideological dominance. But the deepest tragedy of all is the way the conflict between Christianity and neoliberal consumerism has been buried in North American nonthought.

36. See Alan Storkey's *The Conduct of Elections* (London: Movement for Christian Democracy, 2001), built around the commandment, "You shall not bear false witness" (Exod. 20:16 NRSV).

37. The reader should know that I have had relatively low votes in two General Elections; yet I hope this point is more substantial than being generated by pique.

38. This point is shown in the failure of the 2002 Johannesburg Earth Summit.

39. Niccolò Machiavelli's *The Prince* (written c. 1505; published 1515) is probably the first objectification of power in modern European political theory. During the Renaissance power begins to be seen as self-referencing, really an odd idea. The literature on power is rich and interesting, and Shakespeare is not a bad place to start. Macbeth and a number of others got it wrong.

40. Maurice Duverger, *Modern Democracies: Economic Power versus Political Power* (trans. C. L. Markmann; Hinsdale, IL: Dryden, 1974), 12–18.

41. Thomas Hobbes, working in a way that moved away from Christian thinking into Renaissance mechanistic thought, solves it by vesting power in Leviathan and thereby eliminating conflict. Lord Acton works in more Christian terms and is an important Christian political theorist.

42. Frederick Nietzsche, *Twilight of the Idols/The Anti-Christ* (trans. R. J. Hollingdale; Middlesex: Penguin, 1990), 127.

43. Ibid., 140–41.

44. The antithesis between the West and Fascism is often stressed, but the links and continuation less so. These are not just the personal links of Wernher von Braun (1912–77) and others, but far deeper. Perhaps the United States' participation in the idea of *superpower* is far more Nietzschean and anti-Christian than has been recognized.

45. The emphasis of the Dutch CDA (Christian Democratic Appeal political party) and the European People's Party on response-ability has long reflected this theme.

46. This is shown, for example, in the Kairos Document: Kairos Theologians (Group), *Challenge to the Church: A Theological Comment on the Political Crisis in South Africa: The*

Kairos Document (Geneva: World Council of Churches, 1985; Grand Rapids: Eerdmans, 1986).

47. South American and African Christians opened up this important Christian theme fully and beautifully by emphasizing God's liberation from economic and political slavery as part of God's purposes, as grounded in the exodus from Egypt. Christians have stood powerfully against power and with the weak. See, for example, Gustavo Guttiérrez, *A Theology of Liberation* (trans. and ed. Sister C. Inda and J. Eagleson; rev. ed.; London: SCM, 1974); idem, *The Power of the Poor in History* (trans. R. R. Barr; London: SCM; Maryknoll, NY: Orbis Books, 1983); Andrew Kirk, *Liberation Theology* (London: Marshall, Morgan & Scott, 1979); J. M. Bonino, *Towards a Christian Political Ethics* (London: SCM, 1983). One of the great secrets of liberating history is teaching the poor and weak to see that power comes from God, and that they should not accept the imposed power cultures of elites and the economically dominant. The great revolution is of God-given empowerment.

48. William B. Quant, *Camp David: Peacemaking and Politics* (Washington: Brookings Institution, 1986); Rod Troester, *Jimmy Carter as Peacemaker: A Post-presidential Biography* (Westport, CT: Praeger, 1996); Jimmy Carter, *The Blood of Abraham* (Boston: Houghton Mifflin, 1985).

49. See Truth and Reconciliation Commission website: http://www.doj.gov.za/trc/.

50. See, for example, Bob Goudzwaard's work on stewardship as the basis of economics, *A Christian Political Option* (Toronto: Wedge, 1972); also the bibliography in Hermann Noordegraaf and Sander Griffioen, eds., *Bewogen realisme* (Kampen: Uitgeverij Kok, 1999).

51. Goudzwaard looks at the place of free God-given goods in economic life. Sometimes they are abundant and sometimes scarce. Normally we add value (or devalue) what God has given us.

52. This is an argument that cannot be pursued here. But constructing the study of economic life on the calculus and idea of marginal variations is surely an abstruse approach.

53. In an interesting economic debate in the mid-nineteenth century, several economists tried to establish economics as the science of wealth, which they called "plutology." They drew on John Stuart Mill and pushed further into a classical understanding of self-subsistent wealth. There is a good discussion in Bonamy Price, *Chapters on Practical Political Economy* (2d ed.; London: Kegan Paul & Co., 1882), 1–31. Ruskin's *Unto This Last* demolishes it magnificently (see n. 4, above).

54. A Christian review of this is in Stanley Carlson-Thies and Jim Skillen, eds., *Welfare in America: Christian Perspectives on a Policy in Crisis* (Grand Rapids: Eerdmans, 1996).

55. R. H. Tawney, "Christianity and the Social Order" (notes for speeches on various occasions; London School of Economics). See Ross Terrill, *R. H. Tawney and His Times* (London: André Deutsch, 1974).

56. For a seminal work, see Thomas Chalmers, *The Christian and Civic Economy of Large Towns* (3 vols.; Glasgow: Chalmers & Collins, 1821–26; repr., London: Routledge/ Thoemmes, 1995).

57. The underground church is a worldwide phenomenon. See the writings of Richard Wurmbrand, Watchman Nee, and others.

58. A. G. Dickens, *The English Reformation* (2d ed.; London: Batsford, 1989), 293–30. Also, obviously, John Foxe's *Book of Martyrs* (1583 [last ed. for which Foxe personally responsible]; available in many editions/expansions).

59. Edwin S. Gaustad, *Liberty of Conscience: Roger Williams in America* (Grand Rapids: Eerdmans, 1991).

60. See Elisha Williams, "The Essential Rights and Liberties of Protestants: A Seasonable Plea for the Liberty of Conscience and the Right of Private Judgement in Matters

of Religion without Any Control from Human Authority," in *Political Sermons of the American Founding Era, 1730–1805* (ed. Ellis Sandoz; 2d ed.; Indianapolis: Liberty Fund, 1998), 51–118.

61. John Milton, *Areopagitica, and Other Political Writings* (1644; Indianapolis: Liberty Fund, 1999), 46.

62. Christopher Hill, *The Century of Revolution* (London: Sphere, 1969), 154.

63. Nigel G. Wright, *Disavowing Constantine: Mission, Church and the Social Order in the Theologies of John Howard Yoder and Jürgen Moltmann* (Carlisle, UK: Paternoster, 2000).

64. Technically, Kuyperian understanding identifies two kinds of pluralism: *Vertical* pluralism exists within institutional areas like politics, religion, education, and business; it reflects the differences of belief and worldview that occur in these areas—religious toleration or a plurality of parties in a democracy. This recognizes that faith shapes institutional life. *Horizontal* pluralism is the understanding that the main institutional areas of life—economics, family, marriage, politics, religion, the arts and media, community—have their own integrity before God, because they are God-instituted parts of life. This requires a view of society that is neither state-focused nor individualist, but recognizes the rich institutional pattern of life before God and refuses to try to establish some totalitarian philosophy covering these plural institutions. See Abraham Kuyper's Stone Lectures on Calvinism, in *Religion, Pluralism, and Public Life: Abraham Kuyper's Legacy for the Twenty-First Century* (ed. Luis E. Lugo; Grand Rapids: Eerdmans, 2000).

65. Paul Marshall, ed., *Religious Freedom in the World* (Nashville: Broadman & Holman, 2000), gives an assessment.

66. Companies have claimed ordinary words like *sun, Monday,* and *orange* and sought to be parasitic on their normal meanings.

Chapter 8: Jesus' Statecraft

1. Thomas Carlyle, ed., *Oliver Cromwell's Letters and Speeches,* in *Collected Works of Thomas Carlyle* (3d ed.; vols. 14–18; London: Chapman & Hall, 1849), esp. vols. 14–15.

2. Tony Blair so announced on becoming prime minister in 1997.

3. Being without norms, reflected in Emile Durkheim's study on *Suicide* (London: Routledge & Kegan Paul, 1970).

4. This analysis goes behind the normal modernist understandings of law as positive, liberal, sociological, and so on, which do not go deeply enough into the origin of law in our lives.

5. There is an incident in Lilburne's trial when the point is made. Philip Jermin presents what Burgess describes as the "classic" common lawyer's view: "You must know that the law of England is the law of God. . . . And this is our laws, that have been maintained by our ancestors, and is subordinate to the law and will of God." But Lilburne pushes it further "upon your own grant, which is, That the laws of God are the laws of England, I desire to have the privilege of the law of God, which you yourself said is the law of England; and I am sure the law of God is, That you should 'do as you would be done to.'" As Burgess notes, Milton sums it up: "'Tis not the common law nor the civil, but piety and justice that are our foundresses." Glenn Burgess, *The Politics of the Ancient Constitution: An Introduction to English Political Thought, 1603–1642* (London: Macmillan, 1962), 227–31.

6. Many philosophers of law do ignore Christian legal reform. The conceptual attempts to construct law out of contract theory, a utilitarian calculus, Kelsen's legal essentialism, the legal process, social mores, statutory interpretation, or rights theory are actually quite weak. This is so because law must express our understanding of what is wrong and unjust, and because the Bible (and experience) show God has a better grasp on this than we do.

See Herman Dooyeweerd, *Encyclopedia of Legal Science* (5 vols.; Lewiston, NY: Edwin Mellen, 1998–2004); J. W. Harris, *Legal Philosophies* (London: Butterworths, 1980).

7. This alludes to a much longer argument that needs to be made for the failure of these different moralities to grasp comprehensively what human normativity involves. If God is Creator, only a God-given and focused normativity can comprehensively map our lives. These other moral philosophies prove lococentric. See Dennis P. Hollinger, *Choosing the Good* (Grand Rapids: Baker, 2002) for a fine study.

8. The rich and full biblical doctrine of law is often dumped into a single debate about law and grace—a sad declension.

9. This is a point only weakly acknowledged in much modern political history in Britain and the United States.

10. Quoted from a Shaftesbury Project Study Paper on Sir Edward Coke, by Philip Turl, 1969.

11. There is a vast literature associated with this area. Some good texts are Christopher J. H. Wright, *Living as the People of God: The Relevance of Old Testament Ethics* (Leicester: Inter-Varsity, 1983); and idem, *Walking in the Ways of the Lord: The Ethical Authority of the Old Testament* (Leicester: Apollos, 1995). It is interesting to see Emil Brunner, *Justice and the Social Order* (trans. M. Hottinger; London: Lutterworth, 1945), fighting the disintegration of the European idea of justice in Christian terms during the war. Jan Dengerink, *The Idea of Justice in Christian Perspective* (Toronto: Wedge, 1978), has a range of insights.

12. Mosaic law emphasizes recompense in Exodus 22 and elsewhere.

13. See Christopher Marshall, *Beyond Retribution: A New Testament Vision of Justice, Crime, and Punishment* (Grand Rapids: Eerdmans, 2001), for a thorough treatment of this theme.

Chapter 9: Jesus as World Ruler

1. Count of military regimes: 61 in Africa, 50 in Central and South America, 18 in Asia, 8 in Europe, and 6 in the Middle East; J. Denis Derbyshire and Ian Derbyshire, *Political Systems of the World* (2d ed.; Oxford: Helicon, 1996).

2. See Oliver O'Donovan's fine treatment of Christendom in *The Desire of the Nations: Rediscovering the Roots of Political Theology* (Cambridge: Cambridge University Press, 1996), 193–242.

3. Alfred Edersheim's perception of this passage still shines: *The Life and Times of Jesus the Messiah* (3d ed.; London: Longmans, Green & Co., 1906), 1:364–76.

4. Desmond Tutu's phrase embodies the theology: *The Rainbow People of God* (London: Bantam, 1995).

Chapter 10: Jesus and Taxation

1. Cf. Warren Carter, "Paying the Tax to Rome as Subversive Praxis: Matthew 17:24–27," *Journal for the Study of the New Testament*, no. 76 (December 1999): 3–31.

2. Martin Goodman, *The Ruling Class of Judaea* (Cambridge: Cambridge University Press, 1987), 115–16.

3. See Josephus, *The Jewish War* (trans. and ed. G. A. Williamson and E. Mary Smallwood; New York: Dorset Press, 1959), 464.

4. A reasonable assumption from the Gospel narrative.

5. Luke 3:12–14 shows the problem addressed by John the Baptist.

6. There were furious attacks on the Samaritans some twenty years later; Josephus, *JW* 2.12.3–5.

7. Josephus describes an emergency collection a decade or so later under Agrippa I, where "magistrates and councillors went to various villages and collected the tribute, quickly getting together the forty talents due." Agrippa in a speech to the crowds points out specifically that Florus, the procurator, "will not receive your money." See *JW* 2.16.4.

8. Judas the Galilean, rising against the census of Quirinius around the birth of Christ (Luke 2:1–2), aimed at streamlining Roman taxation around the world; Gamaliel mentions this Judas in his speech in Acts 5:37.

9. F. C. Grant, *The Economic Background of the Gospels* (London: Oxford University Press, 1926), 104; Richard A. Horsley, *Archaeology, History, and Society in Galilee: The Social Context of Jesus and the Rabbis* (Valley Forge, PA: Trinity, 1996), 73–76, 80.

10. Harold W. Hoehner, *Herod Antipas* (Grand Rapids: Zondervan, 1980), 77.

11. Based on Mark 7:11, which is Galilee-based. The term "gift devoted to God" was also used of Temple gifts. We do not know whether there was priestly-Pharisaic rivalry in collecting such gifts or how the Pharisees raised income through gifts. Perhaps there was a synagogue collection.

12. David Fiensy, "Leaders of Mass Movements and the Leader of the Jesus Movement," *Journal for the Study of the New Testament*, no. 74 (June 1999): 3–27.

13. Shemuel Safrai and Moritz Stern, *The Jewish People in the First Century: Geography, Political History, Social, Cultural and Religious Life and Institutions* (2 vols.; Philadelphia: Fortress, 1974–76), 1:331.

14. Josephus, *Ant.* 18.3.2; *JW* 2.9.4.

15. This is based on a native Jewish population estimate of 2.75 million, assuming it was an adult male levy, and assuming that a million expatriate Jews also pay the tax—a rough guesstimate (see Safrai and Stern, *Jewish People in the First Century*, 108–10).

16. About 5–6 million drachmas of the 11 million or so would be going into the Herodian-Roman system.

17. Grant, *Economic Background*, 105.

18. G. M. Trevelyan, *English Social History* (Middlesex: Penguin, 1967), 360.

19. The sociological point is that often we try to define nationhood in ethnic, geographical, linguistic, or statist terms. On the other hand, it might be better identified by the criterion of effective neighbor love, making it a much more flexible unit than we often allow. Historically, what a nation is has varied quite radically.

20. My perception is that those who emphasize the voluntary and individual nature of such giving protest too much. Jesus obviously presented this kind of care as a societal norm growing out of the command of neighbor love. It does not need to be restrictively individualized.

21. See Donald A. Hagner, *Matthew* (2 vols.; Word Biblical Commentary; Dallas: Word, 1993–95), 2:538.

22. Josephus, *Ant.* 12.4.4.

23. Alfred Edersheim, *The Life and Times of Jesus the Messiah* (3d ed.; 2 vols. in 1; London: Longmans, Green & Co., 1906), 488–92.

24. *Social Trends* (London: Her Majesty's Stationery Office, 1991–2002) shows the redistribution of income through taxes and benefits table for various years, comparing gross income and post-tax income.

Chapter 11: The Journey to Jerusalem

1. John's Jerusalem-linked commentary opens up the tension Jesus has generated in the capital throughout a number of visits.

2. But the Pharisees warn Jesus about Herod wanting to kill him, in Luke 13:31.

3. Lord Acton, *Essays in Religion, Politics, and Morality* (vol. 3; Indianapolis: Liberty Fund, 1988), 519. This is, of course Acton's Christian insight reflecting on Jesus' third temptation and the construction of human-centered possessive power.

4. Shakespeare, *Richard II* 5.5.38–41.

5. Shakespeare, *Hamlet* 5.1.76–78.

6. Alfred Edersheim, *The Life and Times of Jesus the Messiah* (3d ed.; 2 vols. in 1; London: Longmans, Green & Co., 1906), 350.

7. Josephus, *Ant.* 17.11; *JW* 2.1–2.

8. Schürer, 1:355.

9. Martin Goodman, *The Ruling Class of Judaea* (Cambridge: Cambridge University Press, 1987), 40.

10. Josephus, *JW* 6.8.5.

11. In C. F. Andrews, *Mahatma Gandhi's Ideas* (London: George Allen & Unwin, 1929), 186.

Chapter 12: Jerusalem and the Cross

1. Josephus, *JW* 6.6.1.

2. Alfred Edersheim, *The Life and Times of Jesus the Messiah* (3d ed.; 2 vols. in 1; London: Longmans, Green & Co., 1906), 247.

3. "The real issue in the passage concerns not information about the authority of Jesus but the unbelief and unreceptivity of the Jewish leadership"; Donald A. Hagner, *Matthew* (2 vols.; Word Biblical Commentary; Dallas: Word, 1993–95), 2:610.

4. For an account of this parable, which is a pearl, see Leo Tolstoy, *Walk in the Light While There Is Light* (Grand Rapids: Baker, 2001), 24–26.

5. From the patina of these texts, my guess is that for some time the Pharisees have gradually asserted their teaching role, dominating the schools and crowding the Sadducees' dominance of the Sanhedrin, though not dominating Annas and his family. In Acts 5:27–42 Gamaliel, a Pharisee, swings the decision against the high priesthood.

6. In Matthew 26:1–2 the text says, "When Jesus had finished saying all these things, he said to his disciples, 'As you know, the Passover is two days away.'" Jewish counting included the current day; hence, Jesus rose the third day (counting Friday, Saturday, Sunday), when our usual counting would say the second day. This suggests that he finishes saying "these things" on Wednesday, perhaps as a final peroration in the Temple. But he may be addressing just the disciples.

7. Though it is difficult to locate this Johannine passage (John 12:20–36) among the sequence of other events, it seems close to the Passover.

8. Only Luke records the dispute at the Last Supper and the theme of servant-ruler. It may be a pattern of Jesus' repetition of teaching with quite significant differences, rather than different redaction (Luke 22:20–31).

9. What John's links were in Jerusalem is an interesting issue. The Jerusalem focus of his Gospel needs more understanding. Surely only someone in the Sanhedrin like Nicodemus could gain entrance at this unusual hour. John 18:15 suggests that John is there, seeing the dynamics of Peter's entry. John also is aware of the two locations of the denial—in Annas's house and Caiaphas's house—which the other Gospels conflate. Perhaps Mark has fled (Mark 14:51–52); Matthew and Luke treat the incident topically.

10. Fairly clearly not the Antonia (Praetorium) at this stage (Mark 15:16).

11. See Helen K. Bond, *Pontius Pilate in History and Interpretation* (Cambridge: Cambridge University Press, 1998), for valuable extra reflection. Raymond E. Brown opens up the complexity of the trial into seven scenes in *The Death of the Messiah* (2 vols.; New York: Doubleday, 1994).

12. Schürer, 1:387.

13. Josephus, *JW* 2.9.3.

14. A potent warning against sloppy Christian understanding.

15. See Paul Woodbridge, "'The World' in the Fourth Gospel," in *Witness to the World* (ed. David Peterson; Carlisle, UK: Paternoster, 1999), 1–31.

16. John (19:1–5) locates this scene at this point, while Matthew (27:27–31) and Mark (15:16–20), who treat the end of the trial, briefly describe the crown of thorns as being jammed on Jesus in the Praetorium, or Antonia fortress, at the end of the trial. John has the most detailed awareness of the dynamics and was probably there.

17. Alan Storkey, "Postmodern Easter." Unpublished poem.

18. For a fuller treatment, see John Stott, *The Cross of Christ* (Leicester: Inter-Varsity, 1986).

Chapter 13: Resurrection Politics

1. The thought-form that sees the Roman Empire as success and its decline as failure contains its own false assumptions. If empire means slavery, militarism, taxation, and cruelty, then the deconstruction of empire is in part progress, as the dismantling of the British Empire is progress.

2. It has been happening for several decades in the States, but those who have raised it, such as Richard John Neuhaus and others, would probably agree that its terms and depth have scarcely matched what they would hope.

3. Examples are the Italian and German Christian Democrat parties for a while.

4. The example of the Afrikaaner construction of apartheid is enough.

5. This I learned from my son, Amos, in the 1974 British General Election in Bassetlaw. Fred Jones and I went out with a loudspeaker to announce a Christian Party meeting in the evening, and the three-and-a-half-year-old Amos also came along in the Mini. We came back, and Elaine asked him what we had been doing. His wide-eyed, happy summary was, "We are going to have a party!" And so we are sooner or later.

Appendix A: Reporting and Hermeneutics

1. Craig A. Evans, "Jesus and Rabbinic Parables, Proverbs, and Prayers," in *Jesus and His Contemporaries* (Leiden: Brill, 1995), 266.

A Short Annotated Bibliography
on Christian Politics

Acton, Lord. *Selected Essays in Religion, Politics and Morality.* Indianapolis: Liberty Fund, 1988. Good late-nineteenth-century Christian reflection.

Althusius, Johannes. *Politica methodice digesta.* 3d ed. 1614. *Politica: An Abridged Translation.* Translated by Frederick S. Carney. Indianapolis: Liberty Fund, 1995. Great Calvinist reflection on civil society.

Alton, David. *Faith in Britain.* London: Hodder & Stoughton, 1991. A Christian Democrat perspective.

Augustine. *Concerning the City of God against the Pagans.* AD 413–26. Middlesex: Penguin, 1972. Classic Christian political reflection on Christianity, the Roman Empire, and paganism.

Barth, Karl. *The Church and the Political Problem of Our Day.* New York: Scribner's, 1939. The thought behind the great Barmen Declaration.

Bartholomew, Craig G., et al. *A Royal Priesthood? The Use of the Bible Ethically and Politically.* Edited by C. G. Bartholomew. Scripture and Hermeneutics Series 3. Grand Rapids: Zondervan; Carlisle, UK: Paternoster, 2002. Opens up the hermeneutics.

Bonino, José Míguez. *Towards a Christian Political Ethics.* London: SCM, 1983. Formative liberation perspective.

Brunner, Emil. *Justice and the Social Order.* Translated by Mary Hottinger. London: Lutterworth, 1945. Classic emerging from World War II.

Dooyeweerd, Herman. *New Critique of Theoretical Thought.* 4 vols. Translated by David H. Freedman, William S. Young, and H. de Jongste. Amsterdam:

H. J. Paris; Philadelphia: Presbyterian & Reformed, 1953–58. Great Christian understanding of the theoretical structure of the state.

———. *Roots of Western Culture*. Toronto: Wedge, 1979. Looks at the worldview background to great political movements like the Roman Imperium, Hobbesian thought, and so on.

Figgis, J. N. *Political Thought from Gerson to Grotius, 1414–1625*. New York: Harper, 1960. Christian political reflection of a key period.

Fogarty, Michael. *Christian Democracy in Western Europe, 1820–1953*. London: Routledge & Kegan Paul, 1957. Classic study of the shape and strengths of this influential movement.

Goudzwaard, Bob. *A Christian Political Option*. Toronto: Wedge, 1972. Christian insights on the challenge of Christian party politics.

Gutiérrez, Gustavo. *The Power of the Poor in History: Selected Writings*. Translated by Robert R. Barr. London: SCM; Maryknoll, NY: Orbis, 1983. Deconstructs elitist politics.

———. *A Theology of Liberation: History, Politics and Salvation*. Translated by Sister Caridad Inda and John Eagleson. Maryknoll, NY: Orbis, 1973. Important formative text in liberation theology.

Harper, William A., and Theodore R. Malloch, eds. *Where Are We Now? The State of Christian Political Reflection*. Washington, DC: University Press of America, 1981. A summary of responses from the 1980s.

Hodder, Edwin. *The Life and Work of the Seventh Earl of Shaftesbury*. London: Cassel, 1887. Biography of a great Christian politician.

Holman, Bob. *Towards Equality: A Christian Manifesto*. London: SPCK, 1997. An honest, clear presentation of a Christian understanding of poverty.

Koyzis, David T. *Political Visions and Illusions: A Survey and Christian Critique of Contemporary Ideologies*. Downers Grove, IL: InterVarsity, 2003. Does as its title suggests.

Kuyper, Abraham. *The Stone Lectures on Calvinism*. Grand Rapids: Eerdmans, 1931. Shows how the sovereignty of God over all of life provides a Christian view of the state.

———. *The Problem of Poverty*. Edited by James Skillen. Grand Rapids: Eerdmans, 1991. Shows poverty as a structural problem of the rich in relation to God.

Maritain, Jacques. *Christianity and Democracy*. Translated by D. C. Anson. London: G. Bles, 1946. Great Christian critique of Fascism and formulation of Christian democracy.

Moltmann, Jürgen. *A Theology of Hope*. Translated by James W. Leitch. London: SCM, 1967. Opens up a public understanding of the resurrection power of Christ.

Mouw, Richard J. *The God Who Commands: A Study in Divine Command Ethics*. Notre Dame, IN: University of Notre Dame Press, 1990. A wise relocation of Christian public ethics.

O'Donovan, Oliver. *The Desire of the Nations: Rediscovering the Roots of Political Theology*. Cambridge: Cambridge University Press, 1996. Fine historical theology of Christ and politics.

Papal Encyclicals, The. Compiled by Claudia Carlen. 5 vols. Wilmington, NC: McGrath Pub. Co., 1981. Crucially important encyclicals such as *Rerum Novarum* and *Pacem in Terris*.

Preston, Ronald. *Church and Society in the Late Twentieth Century: The Economic and Political Task*. London: SCM, 1983. Good hundred-year survey of Christian responses.

Rauschenbusch, Walter. *The Righteousness of the Kingdom*. Nashville: Abingdon, 1968. Interesting American kingdom theology from early twentieth century, described as the "Social Gospel."

Runner, Evan. *Scriptural Religion and Political Task*. Toronto: Wedge, 1974. Deep, formative political vision.

Storkey, Alan. *Towards Christian Democracy*. London: Christian Studies Press, Movement for Christian Democracy, 1990. Short perspective.

Storrar, William. *Scottish Identity*. Edinburgh: Handsel, 1990. Study of Christian understanding of national identity.

Temple, William. *Christianity and the Social Order*. London: SCM, 1942. An archbishop's response to the wider social challenge from within World War II.

Wolterstorff, Nicholas. *Until Peace and Justice Embrace*. Grand Rapids: Eerdmans, 1983. Reflection on world justice issues.

Wright, Nigel Goring. *Disavowing Constantine: Mission, Church and Social Order in the Theologies of John Howard Yoder and Jürgen Moltmann*. Carlisle, UK: Paternoster, 2000. Yoder, Moltmann, Mennonite, and Anabaptist themes considered from a radical Baptist perspective on church, society, and state.

Wright, N. T. *Jesus and the Victory of God*. London: SPCK, 1996. Extended study of the kingdom of God and the messiahship of Jesus.

———. *The Resurrection of the Son of God*. London: SPCK, 2003. Theological reflection on the scope of Christ's resurrection.

Yoder, John Howard. *The Christian Witness to the State*. Newton, KS: Faith & Life Press, 1964. Repr., Scottdale, PA: Herald Press, 2002. Reflection on Anabaptist and other views of the state.

———. *The Politics of Jesus: Vicit Agnus Noster*. Grand Rapids: Eerdmans, 1972. 2d, rev. ed. 1994. Path-breaking text on Jesus and politics.

Index